JAHRBUCH JUNGE RECHTSGESCHICHTE 6
YEARBOOK OF YOUNG LEGAL HISTORY 6

Viktoria Draganova, Stefan Kroll,
Helmut Landerer, Ulrike Meyer (Hg.)

Inszenierung des Rechts

Law on Stage

Martin Meidenbauer »

Bibliografische Information der Deutschen
Nationalbibliothek
Die Deutsche Bibliothek verzeichnet diese
Publikation in der Deutschen Nationalbiblio-
grafie; detaillierte bibliografische Daten sind
im Internet über http://dnb.d-nb.de abrufbar.

© 2011 Martin Meidenbauer
Verlagsbuchhandlung, München

Umschlagabbildung: © Bundesverfassungsgericht

Printed in Germany

Gedruckt auf
chlorfrei gebleichtem, säurefreiem und
alterungsbeständigem Papier (ISO 9706)

ISBN 978-3-89975-242-7

Verlagsverzeichnis schickt gern:
Martin Meidenbauer Verlagsbuchhandlung
Schwanthalerstr. 81
D-80336 München

www.m-verlag.net

Inhaltsverzeichnis

Kapitel III „Medien des Rechts"

Kapitel IV „Legitimation und Verfahren"

Kapitel V „Recht und Macht"

Autorenverzeichnis   340

Vorwort

Das *Europäische Forum Junger RechtshistorikerInnen* bietet Nachwuchs-wissenschaftlerinnen und Nachwuchswissenschaftlern aus Europa und darüber hinaus seit 1995 im Jahresturnus die Gelegenheit, aktuelle Forschungsprojekte zu präsentieren. Das vorliegende Jahrbuch der *Vereinigung Junger RechtshistorikerInnen* dokumentiert die XVI. Auflage dieser interdisziplinären Nachwuchskonferenz, die vom 24. bis 27. März 2010 in Frankfurt am Main stattfand.[1]

Das Forum in Frankfurt stand unter dem Motto: „Die Inszenierung des Rechts/ La mise en scène du droit/ Law on Stage", womit die Organisatoren ein interdisziplinäres Themenfeld eröffneten, in dem rechtsgeschichtliche Forschungen in einer kulturtheoretischen Perspektive behandelt werden konnten. Die Verbindung von Recht und Kultur greift einen aktuellen Trend auf, dem gegenwärtig diverse Forschungsprojekte und Veranstaltungen gewidmet sind. Unter den Schlagworten „Recht als Kultur" (Käte Hamburger Kolleg, Bonn), „Recht im Kontext" (Wissenschaftskolleg zu Berlin), „Kulturtechniken des Rechts" (Sommerakademie 2010 an der Bauhausuniversität Weimar) und „Convergences. Law, Language und Culture" (internationale Sommerschule der Universität Osnabrück) – um nur einige herauszugreifen – wird versucht, das Recht von „der genuin juristischen Perspektive zu befreien, [und] mit den Geistes-, Sozial- und Kulturwissenschaften ins Gespräch zu bringen"[2].

Für die *Junge Rechtsgeschichte* ist eine solche Perspektive nicht neu. Obgleich die Dogmatik und die Institutionen des Rechts nach wie vor die Kerngebiete rechtshistorischer Forschung darstellen, warfen insbesondere die zurückliegenden Foren Junger RechtshistorikerInnen neue Perspektiven auf, die die Kontextualisierungen des Rechts verstärkt in den Blick nehmen und damit über dogmatische Fragestellungen

---

[1] Das XVI. Forum Junger RechtshistorikerInnen wurde von folgenden DoktorandInnen des Max-Planck-Instituts für europäische Rechtsgeschichte gemeinsam organisiert: Sabine Arheidt, Maximilian Becker, Viktoria Draganova, Lena Foljanty, Piotr Gotowko, Lea Heimbeck, Chung-Hun Kim, Stefan Kroll, Helmut Landerer, Christian Lange, Kristina Lovrić-Pernak und Ulrike Meyer.

[2] http://www.wiko-berlin.de/index.php?id=425 (28.03.2011).

hinausgehen. So haben sich die Foren nicht nur als Plattform für rechtsvergleichende Untersuchungen etabliert, sondern erweitern die klassischen Forschungsfelder um transnationale Perspektiven, akzentuieren die Kulturbezogenheit des Rechts, lösen die Rechtsgeschichte aus dem engen Korsett der Staatsbezogenheit und richten ihren Blick auf „Europa" und die globale Weltordnung. In der Folge zählen etwa Rechtspluralismus, Weltrecht und Weltkultur zu den Phänomenen mit denen sich die Junge Rechtsgeschichtsforschung intensiv beschäftigt.

Das Forum 2010 richtete den Blick dezidiert auf die Inszenierung des Rechts. Die Metapher der Inszenierung adressiert Techniken des Sichtbarwerdens, der Repräsentation, der Legitimation. Für das Recht bedeutet dies eine Schwerpunktverlagerung weg von einer rechtsdogmatischen Diskussion hin zu einer Debatte, die von rechtsfremden Rationalitäten dominiert wird; etwa der Politik, der Religion oder der Kunst. Zudem wird nach dem Medium des Rechts gefragt, das zwar vom Recht konstituiert wird, im Gegenzug aber selbst wiederum Recht definiert und normiert. Der Fragestellung nach der Inszenierung liegt die elementare Unterscheidung zwischen Inhalt und Form des Rechts zugrunde. Diese sollte – so explizites Ziel des Forums – nicht rechtsphilosophisch bzw. rechtstheoretisch begründet, sondern möglichst anhand konkreter Beispiele plastisch werden. Es galt, die exemplarischen und bildhaften Spuren, die die Unterscheidung zwischen Form und Inhalt im Laufe der Geschichte hinterlassen hat, aufzuzeigen und ihnen nachzugehen.

Die Inhalte des Rechts variieren zeitlich und räumlich. Diese Kontingenz in ihrem Facettenreichtum aufzublättern und differenziert auszuweisen, zählt zu den elementaren Kernkompetenzen rechtshistorischer Forschung. Dies spiegelte sich auch in den diesjährigen Forumsbeiträgen wider. Die TeilnehmerInnen folgten der Einladung, nicht nur historische oder dogmatische Selbstbeschreibungen des Rechts aufzunehmen, sondern auch Fremdbeschreibungen einzubeziehen und zu reflektieren. Daneben fand – gleichsam als zweiter Schwerpunkt – das ehern-ambivalente Verhältnis von Rechtsform und Rechtsinhalt eine breite Rezeption. Die Definition der Form, die erst in der Abgrenzung zum Inhalt erkennbar wird, kam dabei ebenso zur

Sprache wie das Amalgamieren der beiden Ebenen, das in Verfahren, Rechtsakten und Kompetenzen als den Form-Festlegungen, die das Recht parallel zu und trotzdem losgelöst von den Inhalten im Laufe dogmatischer Debatten vorgegeben hat, zum Ausdruck kommt. Im *Call for Papers* war zudem ein weiteres (postmodernes) Verständnis der Form angedeutet: die Form als der *andere* Inhalt des Rechts, welcher vom Recht gesetzt wird, aber zugleich auf das Recht zurückwirkt und es modelliert. Mit beiden Schwerpunkten: der Frage der Fremdbeschreibung und - bestimmung des Rechts einerseits und jener nach dem Unterschied zwischen Form und Inhalt andererseits waren zwei neuralgische Punkte berührt, die die stete Verschiebung der „Definitionshoheit" und ihre Bedeutung für das Recht haben sichtbar werden lassen.

Die Frage der Inszenierung, die die verbindende Klammer des Forums bildete, war insofern ambitioniert, als sich mit ihr der Anspruch verband, Impulse für neue rechtshistorische Themenfelder zu setzen und eine Reflexion über die klassischen Methoden und Ansätze des Genres anzustoßen. Entsprechend zeichnen die in diesem Band versammelten Beiträge nicht nur ein repräsentatives Bild gegenwärtiger junger rechtshistorischer Forschung, sondern setzen mit der Behandlung der spezifisch rechtlichen Bedeutung von Symbolen, Medien oder Legitimationsstrategien – teils mit klassischen, teils mit neueren Ansätzen – konstruktive und innovative Impulse für die rechtshistorische Disziplin.

Der Band gliedert die Beiträge in fünf Kapitel, die zugleich die Themen- und Diskussionsschwerpunkte des Forums widerspiegeln. Den Auftakt bildet Kapitel I zur „Inszenierung des Rechts". Hier wird der Bogen von literarischen Aufbereitungen des Rechts über theatralische Inszenierungen auf der Bühne und vor Gericht bis hin zu Schauprozessen gespannt. WIM DECOCK eröffnet dieses Feld mit einer Expertise zur juristischen Gewichtung der Liebe und der literarischen Bearbeitung des Rechts in Étienne Forcadels *Cupido Jurisperitus*. Ihm folgt – ebenfalls zur Beziehung von Recht und Literatur – der Beitrag von JOHANNA BERGANN, der am Beispiel der (Ver-)Mittlerrolle unterschiedliche Konfliktinszenierungen literarischer Dramen analysiert. Mit den Parallelen zwischen Rechts- und Theaterinszenierungen warten TAMÁS NÓTÁRI und JUKKA SIRO auf. Anhand der *Caeliana*, einer

Gerichtsrede Ciceros aus dem Jahr 56 v. Chr., und von Schauprozessen, die im Rahmen des finnischen Bürgerkrieges von 1918 abgehalten wurden, heben die beiden Autoren den (gezielten) Gebrauch theatralischer Elemente vor Gericht und die Bedeutung des Unterhaltungsmoments hervor. Eine weitere – „Law on Stage" wörtlich verstehende – Facette zeigt der Beitrag von EGBERT KOOPS auf, indem er die Eigenheiten des antiken Theaters als Raum rechtlicher Beziehungen behandelt und die soziale Bedeutung rechtlicher Konstellationen beleuchtet.

Kapitel II widmet sich den „Symbolen im Recht" und arbeitet anhand unterschiedlichster Beispiele die Bedeutung, Omnipräsenz und Varianz von Sinn-Bildern des Rechts heraus. Am Beispiel der Roben der deutschen Bundesverfassungsrichter diskutiert SEBASTIAN FELZ den unmittelbaren Zusammenhang zwischen Rechtsautorität und Präsentation, während ADAM MONIUSZKO anhand einer Fallstudie zu Polen im 17. Jahrhundert die essentielle Symbolkraft des Eides illustriert. HELMUT LANDERER lenkt in seinem Beitrag das Augenmerk auf die rechtliche „Alltagsebene", indem er den „Sinn" des Führerscheins und dessen Auswirkungen auf den Lebenslauf der Normalbiografie aufrollt.

Kapitel III rückt die „Medien des Rechts" ins Zentrum. BART COPPEIN exemplifiziert am Beispiel des *Journal des Tribunaux* und seiner Geschichte, Gestalt und Bedeutung die potentielle und faktische gesamtgesellschaftliche Funktion rechtswissenschaftlicher Organe, die über die Fachöffentlichkeit hinaus Einfluss auf die Sozialisierung rechtlicher Diskurse nehmen. Eine detaillierte Auseinandersetzung mit den verschiedenen Formen der Rechtskodifizierung liefert u. a. der Beitrag von SARAH BACHMANN, der die Einführung des Notariatswesens in Deutschland und die daraus hervorgehende Neuschöpfung und Handhabung der Notariatsurkunde behandelt. Auch ALEXANDER KREY und REGINA SCHÄFER wenden sich in ihrem gemeinsamen Aufsatz der schriftlichen Fixierung von Recht und deren Auswirkungen – insbesondere auf die Konfliktbewältigung – zu, und legen am Beispiel der Ingelheimer Haderbücher die umfassende Präsenz rechtlicher Konfliktlösungsstrategien dar. IVAN MILOTIĆ unterstreicht schließlich anhand der römischen Grenzsteine in Kroatien, und der Aussagekraft ihrer Inschriften, sowohl die Vielfalt rechtlicher Medien als auch ihre Unverzichtbarkeit für das Recht.

Kapitel IV versammelt Beiträge, die den Zusammenhang zwischen Legitimation und Verfahren rechtlicher Normgebung und/ oder deren Durchsetzung diskutieren. Gerade bei diesem für den praktischen Ordnungserfolg des Rechts essentiellen Bereich erweisen sich die zeitliche und räumliche Bandbreite der Beispiele als besondere Bereicherung. Der erste von BIRGIT NÄTHER verfasste Beitrag beschreibt kurfürstliche Visitationen des 17. Jahrhunderts, die als „legitimationsverstärkendes" Instrument zur Kontrolle, aber auch zur Befriedung genutzt wurden. LEA HEIMBECK verbreitert die Perspektive und nimmt die internationale Ebene – genauer gesagt: die Genese völkerrechtlicher Regulierungsregime in den Blick und spürt der Verrechtlichung internationaler Finanzbeziehungen und Staatsbankrotte im 19. Jahrhundert nach. Den Faden der Verrechtlichung nimmt auch NINFA CONTIGIANI auf und rekonstruiert anhand der rechtlichen Behandlung des Vatermordes im 19. Jahrhundert den parallel verlaufenden Prozess der rechtlichen Verstetigung in verschiedenen europäischen Staaten. Der vierte Beitrag des Kapitels verweist auf das Problem der Rechts- und Verfahrenspluralität und offenbart damit die Grenzen der auf Einheit abzielenden Verfahren. Die Autorin, DORÁ FREY, arbeitet für die ungarischen „Zigeuner" die Kollisionen zwischen tradierten und „neuen" justiziellen Verfahren heraus und hinterfragt Ursachen, Folgen und Perspektiven der Pluralisierung und Wandlung des Rechts.

Kapitel V, das den Band beschließt, fokussiert das Verhältnis von Recht und Macht. FREDERIK DHONDT betrachtet hier am Beispiel der Verträge von Ripperda aus dem Jahr 1725 das Prinzip des Mächtegleichgewichts und unterzieht selbiges insofern einer Neubewer-tung, als er – entgegen der gängigen Einordnung des Mächtegleich-gewichts als politischem Prinzip – die rechtliche Qualität herausstellt und eine Deutung als genuin rechtliches Prinzip vorschlägt.

Zu guter Letzt möchten wir das Erscheinen des vorliegenden Bandes zum Anlass nehmen, um dem Max-Planck-Institut für europäische Rechtsgeschichte in Frankfurt am Main – insbesondere dem geschäftsführenden Direktor Herrn Prof. Dr. Thomas Duve und der Verwaltungsleiterin Frau Carola Schurzmann – zu danken. Auch an die "Freunde des Frankfurter Max-Planck-Instituts für europäische Rechtsgeschichte e.V." sei an dieser Stelle ein herzlicher Dank gerichtet; ohne ihre großzügige Unterstützung wäre die Veröffentlichung des Jahrbuches in dieser Form nicht möglich gewesen. Der Sozietät Hengeler Mueller sind wir ebenfalls für die finanzielle Förderung des Forums zu großem Dank verpflichtet; Gleiches gilt auch für das Exzellenzcluster „Die Herausbildung Normativer Ordnungen" an der Goethe-Universität Frankurt am Main, welches das Forum kooperativ unterstützte.

Frankfurt am Main, im März 2011
Viktoria Draganova, Stefan Kroll, Helmut Landerer und Ulrike Meyer

Kapitel I
„Inszenierung des Rechts"

Law on Love's Stage:
Étienne Forcadel's (1519-1578) *Cupido Jurisperitus*

Wim Decock[*]

The Imaginative Power of a Renaissance Jurist

When I was about to start writing on both law and love, there was reason to fear, I believe, that I had blindly engaged myself into a job twice as hard as usual, which, on top of it, was going to give the impression that I confessed something about my own way of life.[1]

The opening sentence of the preface to the treatise on *Cupid the Jurist* (*Cupido Jurisperitus*), published in 1553, leaves no doubt about the self-conscious audacity of its author, the French humanist Étienne Forcadel (ca. 1519-1578) from Béziers.[2] Given the controversial subject of his latest undertaking, Forcadel had obvious reasons, indeed, to suspect that the common opinion would take offence at it. Moreover, his project to put law on the stage of love could not be considered a sin of his youth anymore. By the time his *Cupid the Jurist* appeared, Forcadel had reached the age of 34 and churned out a series of books in which he had continuously explored the boundaries between magic, satire and legal argument.

In his *Oracle of a Jurist or Dialogues on Occult Jurisprudence* (*Necyomantia iurisperiti sive de occulta jurisprudentia dialogi*) of 1544, for example, Forcadel had staged a fictitious encounter between classical Roman jurists, famous representatives of the Medieval *ius commune*, and lawyers of his own time.

[*] The author wishes to thank Drs. Ken Andries and the participants to the Fifteenth European Forum of Young Legal Historians for their comments on this paper during and after the session.

[1] Forcadel, Étienne (Latinized form: Forcatulus, Stephanus), *Cupido iurisperitus*, Lyon, apud Ioannem Tornaesium, 1553, preface: "Scripturo me de iure et amoribus, verendum, opinor, fuit ne vel onus duplex temere susciperem, vel de moribus meis quicquam viderer confiteri."

[2] Scant bio-bibliographical details on Forcadel are contained in Géraldine Cazals's contribution in: Arabeyre, Patrick - Halpérin, Jean-Louis - Krynen, Jacques (eds.), *Dictionnaire historique des juristes français, XIIe-XXe siècle*. Paris: Presses Universitaires de France, 2007, pp. 337-338.

They discussed perennial legal issues against a magical background highly reminiscent of the fantastic setting of the witty dialogues written in Greek by the satirist Lucian of Samosata (ca. 125-180). Five years later, in 1549, he had produced another series of surrealistic dialogues describing the history of law in magical terms, the *Legal Globe* (*Sphaera legalis*), putting on stage different mythological figures and planets representing different stages in the development of Roman law. For example, whereas the harsh Law of the Twelve Tables was connected with the grim planet of Saturn, Jupiter was considered as the astrological proxy to the more mitigated law under the praetorians. The birth of Mars was seen as the origin of an epoch of endless disputes, which was not restored into peace until Justinian's *Digest* came into being as a child of the Sun. In the meantime, Forcadel had also published a collection of poems in the vernacular, *Le Chant des Seraines* (1548). They often alluded to juridical themes, and were, allegedly, well-appreciated by Pierre de Ronsard (1524-1585).[3] An updated version of his poetic experiments appeared in 1551 under the title *Poésie*.

Perhaps no one who had witnessed the early stages of Forcadel's scholarly career would have expected these provocative eruptions of literary genius to occur one day, although his excellency in both classical and legal studies was clear from the beginning. Initially, Forcadel seemed to follow quite faithfully into the footsteps of the grave father of French humanism, Guillaume Budé (1468-1540). Although a man of letters himself, Budé was not really known for his taste of extravagant magical satire. Budé had foremostly promoted the study of law in its historical context by investigating the monetary and financial context of Roman case law in his *De Asse*.[4] In the same vein, Forcadel's first publication was a safely historical treatise, the *Penus juris civilis* (1542). It explored an important aspect of the material context in which Roman law had emerged. Taking title *De penu legata* (Dig. 33, 9) as a starting point, Forcadel discussed the food supply and the alimentation in Roman Antiquity on the basis of quotes from classical authors.

---

[3] Cf. Joukovsky, Françoise (ed.), Étienne Forcadel: Œuvres poétiques, opuscules, chants divers, encomies et élégies, Genève: Librairie Droz, 1977, p. 7.
[4] On the connection between Renaissance humanism and the historical study of law, see the classical article by Kelley, Donald R.: The Rise of Legal History in the Renaissance. In: *History and Theory* (1970) 9.2, pp. 174-194.

A turning point in Forcadel's life was 1557, when he became a professor of law at the then absolutely top university of Toulouse, leaving behind Jacques Cujas in the concours.[5] The famous French historian of political thought, Pierre Mesnard, thinks that it is this happy and at the same time unhappy coincidence which might have contributed to the fact that Forcadel has largely fallen into oblivion. Although there are no traces of some kind of poisonous feud between Forcadel and Cujas themselves, the latter's biographer, Jean Papire Masson (1544-1611) was particulary scathing over Forcadel's intellectual capacities to the greater glory of the genius of his demi-god.[6] So, eventually, Forcadel paid a high price for having eclipsed the star of French humanism in this interminable concours which had started in 1554. History would now eclipse him in its turn.

Once he had landed his job in academia, Forcadel became more circumspect in choosing the themes of his writing. Altough he may have continued to write virtuoso prose and poetry, prudence undoubtedly summoned him to find an outlet for his literary genius in secret notes. After all, the folly of love poetry would have been difficult for the public to square with their image of a distinguished member of the Toulouse law faculty. Hence, Forcadel increasingly dedicated himself to the more ordinary albeit no less demanding business of writing purely historical or legal treatises, some of which were published by his son posthumously: a historical account of the institutions of Poland and France (*Polonia foelix*, 1574; *De Gallorum imperio et philosophia*, 1579), studies on feudal law (*De feudis*, 1579), and on servitudes (*De servitutibus*, 1579). By the end of his life, he had even grasped the meaning of networking, at least if his eulogy of Henri de Montmorency-Damville (*Montmorency gaulois*, 1571) is anything to go by.

As he grew older, Forcadel obviously departed from the turbulent times in which he used to fuse the dizzy worlds of jurisprudence and literary magic into a foolish game of satire and play. Still, even if he ended up being a dim shadow of his literary self, he will undoubtedly

---

[5] The exciting intellectual climate at Toulouse throughout the 16th century is highlighted in several contributions assembled in Dauvois, Nathalie (ed.), *L'humanisme à Toulouse (1480-1596), Actes du colloque international de Toulouse, mai 2004*, Colloques, congrès et conférences sur la Renaissance européenne 54, Paris: Honoré Champion Éditeur, 2006.

[6] See Mesnard, Pierre: Jean Bodin à Toulouse. In: *Bibliothèque d'humanisme et renaissance* (1950) 12, pp. 44-51; Mesnard, Pierre: Un rival heureux de Cujas et de Jean Bodin: Étienne Forcadel. In: *ZRG Rom. Abt.* (1950) 67, pp. 440-441.

remain one of the most eminent prototypes of the Renaissance man. In a letter added as a "postface" to his *Cupid the Jurist*, Forcadel defended the idea of the *giurista universale* against specialist lawyers with a lack of culture and general interests:[7]

It is entirely wrong to think that it is sufficient for a man with a truly human spirit to focus on just one trade. The Muses would consider that to be absolutely ridiculous. While playing the lyre with their fingers, their mind is performing arithmetic, their voices are singing and their feet dancing softly in the rhythm.

Discordant Concordance

As pointed out above, Forcadel's *Cupid the Jurist* (*Cupido Jurisperitus*) was the summit in the form of a novel of a couple of satirical dialogues in which he had already dealt with some of the most persistent problems of law since ancient times against a magical and mythological background. This time, his Lucian-like way of staging reality led him to embark upon an initiatic journey through the secret realm of the young boy of love, Cupid (also known as Amor), and his mother Venus. As regards the form of his novel, Forcadel seems to have drawn inspiration not only from Lucian of Samosata, but also from the highly influential, yet anonymous *Hypnerotomachia Poliphili* (1499), an allegoric love story in which the hero, Poliphilus, dreams about a quest for his beloved Polia. This adventure leads him along secret forests, beautiful valleys, fairylike gardens, curious inscriptions, architectural masterpieces and fantastic landscapes, much as is the case with the hero in Forcadel's *Cupid the Jurist*.[8]

Forcadel's alleged aim in *Cupid the Jurist* is to demonstrate to Hephaestion, a friend of his, that looking at law from the perspective of

---

[7] Forcadel (as in 1), p. 131: "Ne quis imposterum arbitretur hominis ingenui animum uni negotio obeundo duntaxat sufficere: quod quidem materiam ridendi praeberet musicis, qui dum testudinem digitis pulsant, mente numeros concipiunt, canunt interim, ac leniter terram pede certa lege quatiunt."

[8] The hero of Cupid the Jurist is said to be a certain Callidemus; cf. Dauvois, Nathalie, *Jura sanctissima fabulis et carminibus miscere. La concorde de la poésie et du droit dans quelques traités d'Étienne Forcadel: Necyomantia (1544), Sphaera legalis (1549), Cupido jurisperitus (1553)*. In Dauvois (ed.) (as in 5), p. 101. The identification of the addressee with Hephaestos seems to be rather unlikely (cf. below).

love and considering love from the perspective of law is a mutually beneficial experience. In the preface to *Cupid the Jurist*, Forcadel insists that love and law form a harmonious couple, since both of them promote concord and peace:[9]

Until I will have revealed the essence of my advice, there is hope that love and law will be seen to be contained within the same frontiers, to the extent that both love and law lead mankind to concord.

This central message is also driven home through a somewhat surprising, yet remarkable formal procedure. In order to illustrate or to underscore interpretations of legal matters, Forcadel quotes poets and philosophers, while references to Roman and Canon law abound as testimonies to the events which occur in the love story. Through the very texture of his novel, then, Forcadel makes a wonderful attempt at illustrating the alleged compatibility of the logic of love and the logic of jurisprudence.

Yet the ultimate message Forcadel keeps in store for his reader turns out to be quite different. The end-effect of the hybrid texture of quotes taken from both literary and legal sources is to perplex and to amuse the reader.[10] For example, it is rather uncommon in a novel to find a 4-page systematic list of references to all the passages taken from the Roman and the Canon law which are going to be interpreted in the course of the adventure story. The juxtaposition of a grave reference, say to Justinian's Digest, in the middle of a narrative description of, say, desperate lovers, leaves the reader surprised and smiling.

Actually, instead of reading the initial statement about "concord" (*concordia*) as a uniform tribute to the exalted neo-Platonic philosophy of harmony and concord - as it is usually understood - it seems equally probable to think of Forcadel's *Cupid the Jurist* as an incredibly intelligent *satire* on the *disharmonious* co-existence of love and law.

Should not the very fact that he provocatively conceives of Hephaestion as the addressee of his adventure story lead us to suspect

---

[9] Forcadel (as in 1), preface: "Donec ego consilii mei rationem detexero, spes est visum iri, amorem et ius, quo perducuntur homines ad concordiam, iisdem finibus contineri."
[10] In order to convey a minimal sense of this technique, we have maintained the references to legal text from the Roman and the Canon law in their original form in this paper (cf. below).

right from the outset that the Realm of love is governed by a child-God who loves upsetting the good morals and legal foundations of society?[11] As is well-known, Hephaestion was the lover-boy of perhaps one of the most powerful homosexuals and adventurers the world has ever seen, Alexander the Great (356-323 B.C.). Along this line of interpretation, we might even wonder if the implied hero who narrates his journey through the realm of love in the first person singular could not be Alexander the Great, one of the greatest adventurers of all times?[12]

As it turns out, what Forcadel really shows in the course of *Cupid the Jurist*, is that the state of chaos usually associated with love is actually the common state of the law, while love turns out to be much more regular and rule-bound than the life of the law itself. A wonderful connection between love and law exists, then, precisely because the chaos of love is only apparent, whereas the apparent order of law rests on the contradiction and chaos usually associated with love.

Lovely Playboy, Sweet Despot

The story of Forcadel's adventure in the land of Cupid and Venus opens with an idyllic scene that reveals a paradise of harmony and concord. As he enters the gardens of the Realm of Love, Forcadel is enchanted by the variety of fine colored flowers, mellow fruit trees, and sweet-smelling perfumes that arouse his senses as the breeze blown by Favonius, God of winds, plays with his hair. But as a land of plenty similar to the mythical land of the Cyclopes rises in front of our hero, his blissful tranquillity is disturbed by a deadly serious reflection. Here comes the first paradox which crosses and troubles our jurist's mind: For this prosperity in the mythic land of the Cyclopes to exist, what apparently mattered was to keep councils, assemblies, and lawmakers at bay – the very institutional mechanisms which humans employ all the time in an effort to attain precisely the state of plenty the Cyclopes

---

[11] See the apostrophe directed to Hephaestion in the opening sentence; cf. Forcadel (as in 1), chapter 1, nr. 1, p. 9.

[12] To leave this interpretation open (since the ambiguous identity of the hero of his novel is undoubtedly part of the intellectual game Forcadel is typically playing with his reader), in what follows we will identify the first person recounting his journey through the realm of love with Forcadel. This is the safer option, since it can be deduced from "mihi iuris civilis studioso" in *Cupido iurisperitus*, chapter 1, nr. 1, p. 10 that the narrator is a legal scholar. We also learn that the narrator's (fictitious) mistress is Clytia; see chapter 14, p. 74.

possessed. Mankind is on the wrong track. It is the absence of those institutions which is a sign of prosperity.[13]

Forcadel wonders, therefore, why he still finds that there are laws in the prosperous Realm of Love in the first place. In fact, it is precisely in the Realm of Love where you can find people most truly obedient to laws and rules – even if, at first sight, there seems to be no trace of a single law in the usual sense of the word, that is a law issued by a legislative assembly and which needs to be enforced through power. With a sense of irony, Forcadel quips that normally there should be no need of laws in a country with so harmless citizens, and, since the land is so rich, it must even be very fruitful for him as a legal scholar.

As Forcadel subsequently learns, the spontaneous observance of the law in the Realm of Love is actually a by-product of the tyrannical rule from which it suffers. Its terrific ruler is none other than Cupid himself, Amor, that mighty God of Heaven, Sea, and Underworld, that mighty conqueror of the entire pantheon and mankind, who from high in the sky rules the crowd of lovers and with a voice as clear as a bell orders those madmen each year on the last day of April to renew their loyalty to him on pain of grave punishment.[14]

Cupid's despotically ruled empire, Forcadel muses, is simply unlimited in time and space. He quotes evidence from Hesiod (the first Greek epic poet), Parmenides (the philosopher who believed that nothing really changes), and, last but not least, the Roman law (the ultimate source of wisdom for lawyers). Even the famous Paragraph *Ius naturale* of Title *De iustitia et iure* (= Dig. 1, 1, 1)[15] is adduced by Forcadel, indeed, to argue

---

[13] Forcadel (as in 1), chapter 1, num. 1, p. 10: "Nam ora ipsa coelo soloque iuxta felix Cyclopum agros mihi referebat, in quibus fructus, fruges etiam, sponte naturae ac sine cultura uberrime proveniunt. Unum illud interest, quod his ut Homerus ait, out' agorai boulèphoroi oute themises, id est, neque conciones consiliariae sunt, neque leges. Atqui leges ipsae et legum disceptationes nusquam libentius audiuntur quam in hac regione, quae cum incolis admodum fructuosa sit, mihi quoque iuris civilis studioso non parum fructus et emolumenti attulit. Caeterum fuit quod mirarer leges ibi constitutas inveniri, ubi minimûm mali homines, legum severitate non egeant."

[14] Forcadel, (as in 1), chapter 1, num. 1, p. 10: "Iubet Cupido, aethereus, marinus, plutonicus, deum atque hominum victor et triumphator semper Augustus, turbae populoque amantium uti adsint pridie Calendas Maias, et sacramento se quotquot sunt denuo adigant, foedusque recens feriant dominum salutari, ni male multari quisque maluerit."

[15] As mentioned before, we have put the references to Roman and Canon legal texts in the main text so that the reader has the opportunity to experience the surprising and witty

that from times eternal, from the very beginnings of mankind, people have known how to make love and how to make sure that the species survives as a matter of natural law.[16] In conclusion, the most absolute power in the world belongs to Cupid, as is further attested by Paragraph *Illud*, Title *Quibus modis naturales filii efficiuntur legitimi* (= Coll. 6, 1, 4 = Nov. 74, 4).[17]

Another illustration of Cupid's extraordinarily extensive powers concerns his reign over the deceased. Contrary to ordinary rulers and governments, whose power is limited to living human beings, Cupid extends his jurisdiction far beyond death. Forcadel demonstrates this by quoting the following passages from Justinian's Code and *Novellae*. The soul of a dead husband is said to be painfully afflicted and depressed by the second marriage of his wife in Paragraph *Quae vero*, Title *De nuptiis* (= Coll. 4, 1, 43 = Nov. 22, 43). Moreover, when a husband makes a legacy to his spouse on condition that the spouse does not enter into a new marriage, this condition is to be observed by the spouse on pain of nullity of the legacy, as is attested in Title *De indicta viduitate* (= C. 6, 40, 2).

From the canon law, however, Forcadel infers that this clause is to be deemed invalid in legacies and last wills made to virgins. Stipulating such a harsh condition at the expense of a young lady who is not yet your lawful wife would be a great testimony to your angst and selfishness. It would also be highly disadvantageous to that girl, as Forcadel playfully suggests with an ironical reference to ecclesiastical authority, namely

---

effect brought about by the mere formal structure of Forcadel's narrative. In addition, we give the modern version of these references, for which the following citations are used:

Dig. 1, 1, 1, 1: *Digesta Justiniani*, Book 1, Title 1, Law 1, Paragraph 1

C. 1, 1, 1: *Codex Justiniani*, Book 1, Title 1, Law 1

Inst. 1, 1, 1: *Institutiones Justiniani*, Book 1, Title 1, Law 1

Coll. 1, 2, 3: *Novellae Justiniani*, Collection 1, Title 1, Fragment 1 (I have added the modern equivalent to these Medieval citations from the Novellae)

C. 1, q. 1, c. 1: *Decretum Gratiani*, Causa 1, Quaestio 1, Canon 1

X. 1, 1, 1: *Decretales Gregorii IX*, Book 1, Title 1, Canon 1.

[16] Forcadel (as in 1), chapter 1, num. 2, pp. 10-11: "Amoris igitur imperium ubique latissimum est, et perantiquum: nam Hesiodus in Theogonia ex Chao simul cum terra genitum tradit, nec dissentit Parmenides. | Proinde ab initio ubi creati fuere homines, amare noverunt, et liberorum procreationi operam dare, l. 1, par. ius naturale, ff. de iustit. Et iure."

[17] Forcadel (as in 1), chapter 1, num. 4, p. 11: "In summa, nihil est amore ipso vehementius."

Canon *Viduas*, Paragraph *Si virgines* (= C. 27, q. 1, c. 8), since virgins esteem even higher those pleasures which they have not yet had the chance to experience [...].[18] According to Forcadel, the Gods therefore prefer virgins to widows, as is explained in Paragraph *Optimum*, Title *De non eligendo secundo* (Coll. 1, 2, 3 = Nov. 2, 3).

Forcadel also illustrates the eternal jurisdiction of Cupid over mankind, even over its heroes, by reference to Vergil's story of Dido, Sichaeus and Aeneas. Sichaeus, Dido's late husband, still welcomed her very heartily in the underworld after she had committed suicide for love of Aeneas. Again, one of the most sacred texts of law gives us a clue as to how late husbands get informed about the ongoing love stories of their former spouses. In Forcadel's view, Canon *Fatendum* (= C. 13, q. 2, c. 29) indicates that the dead are informed about second marriages by the Angels and by those who die. Every time a new dead person enters the Underworld, he makes happy the *anciens*, who continuously suffer from never-ending boredom, with breaking news about the exciting world of the living. How, then, Forcadel wonders at the end of the first chapter of his *Cupid the Jurist*, could it be that the most frequent wish expressed amongst the subjects to Cupid's jurisdiction is the desire to die for love: "Oh darling, I would die for you"? This is a pointless wish, since love cannot possibly be extinguished by death:[19]

So to come back on what I said earlier, since love cannot even cease to live when lovers die, why, then, I beg you, is it that in love there is no more frequent wish than to die?

The universal order of passion and love transcends everything, and it is small wonder that Forcadel is dying of curiosity to find out more about the secrets of this fascinating Realm of Love. In the twenty-one chapters that follow, he seeks to share with us some of the most secret

---

[18] Forcadel (as in 1), chapter 1, num. 7, pp. 12-13: "At si testator nonnihil virgini reliquerit, ita ne nubat, voluntate nimium anxia et improba | nititur, de re nondum ad suam vel alterius iustam affectionem pertinente sollicitus. Praeterea in virgine durior est huiusmodi conditio, quae pluris eam voluptatem facit, quam nescit, can. Viduas, par. si virgines, 27, q. 1. Proinde diis habetur virgo gratior quam quae vidua permanet, par. optimum de non elig. secund., col. 1."

[19] Forcadel (as in 1), chapter 1, num. 8, p. 13: "Cum ergo (ut ad superiora regrediar) ne morte quidem ipsa, amor vivere desinat, cur, quaeso, fit ut in amore nullum votum morte sit frequentius?"

answers to some of the most profound questions that rattle the nerves of mankind and of jurists, in particular, since the origins of time: What are the signs and proofs of love? Are children the highest good and source of happiness for their parents? Why are the members of the female sex so much earlier mature than men? What is the normal duration for a pregnancy? Can partners who break up bring an action for deceit against their former lovers? Is it possible for lovers to survive if they have no money? Is marriage the best type of relationship? What is the power of music in the seduction of women? Are good looks decisive for attraction? In what follows a short impression is given of the manner in which Forcadel treats of this kind of themes through the example of his story about the relationship between contracts and love.

Passionate about Contracts

From his trip to the gardens of Love in the first chapter, Forcadel moves on to the midst of a dark and sacred forest in the second chapter. There he hears lovers crying and moaning with pain and pleasure at the same time: "ô eia, eia mala ô". This, he says, is the fate of lovers, some praising the sublime beauty of their sweetheart, some decrying her inconstancy and unfaithfulness.[20] As Roman law has it, indeed, more precisely in Law *Inter*, Title *De usu fructu* (= C. 3, 33, 15) the life of man is exposed to thousands of shocks and vicissitudes. Yet lovers suffer from the most precarious condition, since the female sex is notably prone to change and inconstancy, as is attested by Canon *Forus de verborum significatione* (= X. 5, 40, 10).

Forcadel is puzzled at the pitiful sight of these broken relationships. As a committed jurist and Christian he can not believe his eyes. For did not God reveal himself as the God of Love in the Bible? Does not the law of the Church, notably in Canon *Iuramenti* (= C. 22, q. 5, c. 12), affirm that God esteems a naked promise as highly as an oath? Did not pagan philosophers in Antiquity hold that trust and fidelity are the cornerstones of society, as Roman law confirms in Title *De pactis* (= Dig. 2, 14, 1).[21] Why, then, do lovers break up and make up all the time?

---

[20] Forcadel (as in 1), chapter 2, num. 1, pp. 13-14: "Haec erat sors amantibus aptissima, quorum alii puellae praeclaram faciem, alii insignem perfidiam per tumultum decantabant et inconstantiam subinde arguentes | vociferabantur."

[21] Forcadel (as in 1), chapter 2, num. 1, p. 14: "Debuerunt saltem hae conversiones rerum

Shall not love affairs be considered as contracts, in which mutual consent is sufficient to produce a real, continous and enforceable obligation? Is not this expressed in Law *Sufficit*, Title *De sponsalibus* (= Dig. 23, 1, 4) and Law *Mulierem*, Title *De ritu nuptiarum* (= Dig. 23, 2, 5)? Alluding to an age-old debate about the possiblity of concluding contracts at a distance, Forcadel states that love can be concluded from a distance, as long as the declaration of will is transmitted to the other party or lover by means of a messenger or a letter. Apparently, the Roman poet Propertius had deplored the loss of his writing tablets – a topic among the poets in Antiquity – precisely because they were capable of transmitting messages to his mistress as persuasively as the lover himself: "from now on these tablets are able to placate girls without me; and wihout me some speak very eloquently".[22] Could this have meant, perhaps, that, tragically, some young ladies eventually even preferred the love letters to the lover himself?

What we get in the second chapter of Forcadel's *Cupid the jurist*, then, is a witty parody on one of the most crucial developments in the history of contract law, namely the development from the traditionally Roman, closed system of contracts, involving many formalities, towards a general, open category of contracts based on mutual consent.[23] As a rule, stipulations and real contracts could not be concluded unless the contracting parties were in the same place at the same time. This was a crucial evolution, already reflected in 14th century Castilian law, which was further developed on the basis in canon and natural law. It became mainstream contract theory in the scholastic tradition, but it still formed the subject of fierce debates amongst the humanist jurists of 16th century

---

in amore propter perfidiam quiescere, cum Amor Deus sit, et Dii nudam promissionem tanti faciant quanti iusiurandum (…) Deinde cum amor a iure naturae omnibus insitus sit, ut paulo ante dixi, humanae fidei nihil magis congruit quam pacta servare (…) Amor enim ut pactum in duorum consensu versatur, eumque tantum desiderat (…)."

[22] Propertius, *Elegiae*, 23, 3, v. 5-6 "Illae iam sine me norant placare puellas, et quaedam sine me verba diserta loqui".

[23] See, for instance, Barton, John (ed.): *Towards a general law of contract*, Comparative studies in continental and Anglo-American legal history, 8. Berlin: Duncker & Humblot, 1990; Birocchi, Italo: *Causa e categoria generale del contratto. Un problema dogmatico nella cultura privatistica dell'età moderna. I. Il cinquecento*, Il Diritto nella Storia, 5. Torino: Giappichelli, 1997. Duve, Thomas, "Kanonisches Recht und die Ausbildung allgemeiner Vertragslehren in der Spanischen Spätscholastik." In: Condorelli, Orazio – Roumy, Franck – Schmoeckel, Mathias (eds.): *Der Einfluss der Kanonistik auf die Europäische Rechtskultur*, Band 1: *Zivil- und Zivilprozessrecht*, Norm und Struktur, 37, 1. Köln-Weimar-Wien: Böhlau, 2009, pp. 389-408.

France, precisely because a general law of contract did not correspond to the original Roman law of contract (which the humanists sought to recover).

With an amusing sense of humor, Forcadel puts these serious and complex juridical debates on contract law into perspective by putting them against the background of his adventure story in the Realm of Love – the ultimate reality, and a reality which Forcadel does not seem to consider as wholly harmonious and peaceful. After all, the basis of life, Love, is chaos, disruption and war.

Hence we find Forcadel wondering whether the Latin word for contract or agreement (*pactum*) is etymologically derived from the Latin word for peace (*pax*), or conversely. In other words, he wonders whether agreement is a consequence of peace or rather a condition for the establishment of peace? In the canon law tradition, particularly Canon *Pactum*, Title *De verborum significatione* (= X. 5, 40, 11) a text of Isidor of Seville (ca. 560-636) was cited, to the effect that peace (*pax*) precedes agreement (*pactum, pactio*), since peace is a condition for agreement.[24] Forcadel points out that on this account it is perfectly possible to explain why love affairs fall apart so quickly.

Lovers break up as soon as the peace on which their "love agreement" was built is disturbed, but then they make up again as soon as peace is restored, only for their relationship to break up again. Quite cynically, Forcadel thinks Isidor's is a sound etymology, precisely because it helps to explain the reality of the continuous making and breaking of love affairs.[25] As the Latin poet Publilius Syrus (1st century B.C.) noted: "concord is appreciated all the more after a period of discord".[26] So there is nothing strange about the big number of shattered love affairs.

However, against this line of thought, identified with the canon legal tradition, Forcadel puts the contrary interpretation which is ascribed to Ulpian. The Roman jurist Ulpian indicated that agreement (*pactum, pactio*) is derived from peace (*pax*) in Dig. 2, 14, 1. Agreement (*pactum*) is precisely the instrument through which the transition from war to peace

---

[24] Isidor of Seville, *Etymologiae* (ed. Lindsay), book 5, chapter 24, num. 18: "Pactum dicitur inter partes ex pace conveniens scriptura, legibus ac moribus conprobata."

[25] Forcadel (as in 1), chapter 2, num. 7, p. 16: "Pactum a pace deduxit Isidorius (…) ne mirum sit pacta amantium non servari, cum pax eorum parvo duret tempore, vigent bella, et quaedam induciae, mox utcunque redeunt in gratiam (…)."

[26] Publilius Syrus, *Sententiae* (ed. Friedrich), p. 38: "Discordia fit carior concordia."

(*pax*) is brought about.[27] So the word "agreement" (*pactum*) must logically preceed the word for peace (*pax*). This realistic approach is reiterated in Law *Conventionum*, in Title *De pactis* (= Dig. 2, 14, 5). What Forcadel is doing here, of course, is poking fun at the usual, pretty much Stoic procedure jurists of his time used to try and find the right interpretation of words, while at the same time raising the fundamental question of whether law, and contracts and treaties in particular, are a precondition for order and peace, or conversely? Of course, arguments can be raised in favor of both opinions. This is simply a chicken-and-egg problem.

Forcadel brings his ironic discussion of love as a contract to a head when he integrates the whole Roman discussion about nominate versus innominate contracts into his analysis of love. In Roman law, nominate contracts were recognized as having their own name, and therefore being enforceable through actions specific to that contract, whereas innominate contracts were thought to be merely "naked" pacts and hence unenforceable in court.

By the time Forcadel wrote his treatise, this Roman distinction had been superseded by the idea, derived from canon law, that every promise is binding (X. 1, 35, 1: *pacta quantumcumque nuda sunt servanda*) and that the fidelity to the given word was the highest good. Forcadel actually cites Roman texts in order to argue that this was also the original view of the Romans (Dig. 50, 17, 84 and C. 4, 18, 1). This was a procedure often employed by the scholars of Roman law in order to save the face of Roman law in light of the dominant norms and values of an almost uniformely Christian society.[28]

As Forcadel wisely points out, the Romans soon found out that shame was not sufficiently present in most human beings in order to prevent them from becoming unfaithful to their promises.[29] That explains why,

---

[27] Forcadel (as in 1), chapter 2, num. 7, p. 16: "Sane Ulpianus maluit a pactione pacem deducere (…) Pactum, inquit, a pactione dicitur, unde et pacis nomen appellatum est. Nisi sic intelligas, pactum esse appellatum nomen pacis, id est, nomen ad pacem faciens, sive pacificum, quia pacto et foedere saepissime a bello disceditur."

[28] Cf. Dolezalek, Gero, "The Moral Theologian's Doctrine of Restitution and its Juridification in the Sixteenth and Seventeenth Centuries". In: Bennett et al. (ed.), *Acta Juridica. Essays in Honour of Wouter de Vos*. Cape Town-Wetton-Johannesburg: Juta, 1992, pp. 104-107.

[29] Forcadel (as in 1), chapter 3, num. 1, p. 19: "Sed perfidi pudor tantummodo onerabatur, quae vero remedia promissum servare cogerent, nondum ipsi legumlatores induxerant, qui tandem indignati ob multorum singularem impudentiam et perfidiam, actiones composuere, per quas promissor stare pacto adigeretur (…) quia nemini sibi ius dicere

eventually, the Roman law became different from the principles expressed in the canon law and prescribed by the law of nations. In granting actions to the victims of breach of contract, the Romans wanted to prevent people from taking the law into their own hands, Forcadel argues. This might sound a little bit anachronistic. Even if, obviously, there is evidence that the Romans disliked self-justice (Dig. 4, 2, 13; Dig. 3, 5, 5, 2), the increasing monopolization of dispute resolution by the State is a phenomenon pretty much typical of Forcadel's own time and the modern period in general.

In Forcadel's view, the Romans finally decided to attach procedural actions only to the most frequent contracts, say sale-purchase. But to this list of enforceable contracts, the French humanist from Béziers now adds... love:[30]

There is a grave and useful debate going on about whether a love affair (*amor*) must be classified among the nominate contracts or not. I certainly call it a contract, since a mutual obligation exists from the moment of its inception. It is also allowed for scholars to call it a nominate contract, since it has the most elegant name one could desire to have, as is clear from Law *Iurisgentium*, Title *De pactis* (= Dig. 2, 14, 7). Would not all people wish to distinguish love from the general concepts "agreement" or "contract"? What is more, love should with reason be considered as the most excellent of agreements. It should be given its own action for enforcement and its own name.

A love affair, then, is a nominate contract which can be enforced in court. Typical of Forcadel, however, is that he ridicules the deadly serious discussion about nominate versus innominate contracts by asking the following questions: How do we need to classify contracts for paid love? Are love affairs involving payment, namely prostitution, also worthy of a name? Is paid love enforceable before the courts?

---

licuit, aut in iudicium venire sine actione (…)."

[30] Forcadel (as in 1), chapter 3, num. 1, p. 19: "Gravis et utilis est illa contentio, cum dubitatur, utrum amoris contractus nomen suum habentibus inseri debeat an non. Contractum appello, quia ultro citroque obligat, cum vere initus est. Et doctoribus nominatum dicere licebit, cum tam elegans nomen habeat, quam quod maxime desiderari potest, l. iurisgentium, ff. de pact. Nam quotusquisque amorem a generali conventionis vel contractus nomine non separaverit? Quinetiam conventionum excellentissima merito haberi debet, et actione sua non minus quam nomine donari."

Apparently, there was a most learned dispute going on about this question. Yet, as decent French manners demand, Forcadel rejects the objectionable idea that paid love could ever be worthy of a name.[31] Paid love is simply an innominate contract. It is a contract of the type "I do something for you so that you give me something in return" (*facio ut des*) or "I give you something so that you do something for me in return" (*do ut facias*) in particular. A contract for paid love has no specific actions named after it, although the actio *praescriptis verbis* and the *actio de dolo* can be used to enforce or dissolve it.

Wickedly in love

From a discussion of the law of contract we move to a discussion of criminal law in chapter four of *Cupid the Jurist*. Finding himself in the midst of a vast forest, Forcadel suddenly notices Sylvanus, the mythic guardian of sacred woods. As it turns out, he has been employed by Cupid as Chief of Police in the forests of the Realm of Love. Forcadel listens as Sylvanus prays to the Godess of Witchcraft, Hecate. Apparently, the Chief of Police is asking her to bewitch a young girl and make her fall in love with him. Sylvanus' love-sickness leads Forcadel into a reflection on the devastatingly poisonous nature of Cupid's power:[32]

Is there anything capable of escaping from under love's coercive spell? Love orders you to break the law. Particularly, love urges you to break those laws, prescribed already in ancient times, which forbid you to use love potions, lest sorcery and black magic increase the libido of chaste souls, thereby leading them astray.

Forcadel adduces the usual amount of citations from the Roman law (e.g. C. 9, 18, 4; Dig. 48, 8, 3; Dig. 48, 19, 38, 5) to substantiate his point

---

[31] Forcadel (as in 1), chapter 3, num. 5, p. 21: "Non ero nimius in recensendis aut refellendis duarum factionum opinionibus (…) Nam altera interpretum pars multum ineptiarum, altera parum iudicii coniecit et habuit. Itaque perpetuum hoc esse volo in omnibus innominatis contractibus, ut tam praescriptis verbis actio quam de dolo dari possit, si dolus aliquis arguatur, modo de dolo agere malim (…)."

[32] Forcadel (as in 1), chapter 4, num. 1, p. 24: "Quid non cogit amor? Leges certe violari iubet, quae vetant ne pudici animi philtris vel incantationibus ad libidinem deflectantur (…)."

about the criminal nature of love potion abuse. Referring to Paragraph *Novimus*, Title *Quibus modis naturales filii efficiuntur legitimi* (= Coll. 6, 1, 4 = Nov. 74, 4) he concludes that, in fact, love is pure madness (*amor furor merus*).[33] This explains, according to Forcadel, why in Title *De successionibus sublatis* (= Inst. 3, 12) the term "bacchari" is used to denote the behavior of a women who has fallen in love with a slave. Women in love behave as insanely as the Maenads, the drunken, female followers of Bacchus, the ancient God of wine and ecstasy. Moreover, Paragraph *Apud* of Title *De aedilitio edicto* (= Dig. 21, 1, 1, 9) indicates that "bacchari" is to be derived of your senses and is to suffer from a vice as pernicious to the soul as fever is to the body.

In short, Forcadel admits:[34]

I could no longer control myself. I could no longer restrain myself from taking the audacious step to take Cupid to court, since he lies at the basis of a big number of grave crimes. It is a case which does not require long-drawn-out testimonies. The story of Myrrha is telling enough. Under Cupid's influence, Myrrha (called Smyrna by Hyginius[35]) desired to sleep with her father Cinyras, the king of the Assyrians. Against all good morals and laws, as is obvious from Law *Nuptiae* and Law *Quinetiam* in Title *De ritu nuptiarum* (= Dig. 23, 2, 53 and 55) she finally had

---

[33] Cf. Nov. 74, 4 (ed. Schoell-Kroll): "Novimus etenim et castitatis sumus amatores et haec nostris sancimus subiectis: sed nihil est furore amatoris vehementius, quem retinere philosophiae est perfectae, monentis et insilientem atque inhaerentem concupiscentiam refrenantis."

[34] Forcadel (as in 1), chapter 4, num. 5, p. 25: "Non potui tunc mihi temperare, quin Amorem audacter accusarem, velut causam multorum magnorumque scelerum. Res non eget prolixis testimoniis praesertim cum illo suadente Myrrha (quam Smyrnam vocat Hyginius) Cinyrae Assyriorum regis filia patris concubitum appetierit, et eo tandem temulento ac ignorante contra fas et leges turpissima potita sit (…)."

[35] Caius Julius Hygin(i)us (ca. 64 B.C. - 17 A.D.) wrote a book on fables (*Fabularum liber*) containing a summary of the most important myths used in Greek and Latin poetry. It was succesful among Renaissance humanists as a key to reading the classical authors. Hyginus recounts how Smyrna was punished by Venus on account of the irreverential feelings of her mother Cenchreis. She had deared to say that her daughter was more beautiful than Venus; cf. *Fabularum liber*, Basle, apud Ioannem Hervagium, 1549, Fabula 58, p. 15. To show off his erudition and antiquarian curiosities typical of most Renaissance humanists, certainly in 16th century France, Forcadel elaborates on the origins of this confusion of the names Smyrna and Myrrha in the text that followes the quote which we have translated above.

intercourse with him in an act of utter turpitude while he was drunk and ignorant.

There is absolute proof that Cupid is the cause of thousands of crimes, so he must be punished, according to Forcadel. If people burning cities are sentenced to death by burning, as is evident in Law *Capitalium*, Paragraph *Incendiarii*, Title *De poenis* (= Dig. 48, 19, 28, 12); if Phaëthon died because he mistakenly set the sky on fire when he wished to take over the reins of the Sun from his father Helios; then why does Cupid go free? He sets on fire heaven, earth and seas all the time. Worse still, he is a most unfair judge, since he strikes lovers with absolute blindness, which is contrary to the procedure prescribed in Law *Sancimus* (= C. 9, 47, 22)?[36] What is more, as Forcadel points out in chapter 17, should we not question the legitimacy of Cupid as a jurist and judge in the first place?[37] Can it be allowed for an ever-juvenile playboy to become a judge? Did he take a law degree? Does he have legal capacity, in the first place, given his juvenile age?

Forcadel's fictitious accusation of Cupid is a witty illustration of the impotency and powerlessness of the human legal system in the face of that eternal God of potency. Ironically, Cupid does not even fulfill any of the conditions required in civilized societies for occupying a powerful position within the legal system. Cupid reigns as an absolute despot. Through an entirely unwholesome joint venture with his mother Venus, he rules everything. What beats the limit is that Cupid does not even need coercion in order to enforce his power. There is a law of love which imposes itself on human beings automatically, without the slightest need for coercion. Cupid detains a power politicians and judges in the real world can only dream of. In fact, he rules over all secular rulers, and is therefore to be called the second Lord of the World.[38] His jurisdiction is parallel to that of secular empires. Worse still, Cupid constantly intrudes into those jurisdictions and upsets their patterns.

Tragically, Forcadel's journey to the Realm of Love seems to suggest that the collective potency of judges, legislators and the whole fabric of

---

[36] Forcadel (as in 1), chapter 4, num. 6, p. 26: "Quid obest quominus Amor puniatur, qui coelum terras et maria pergit accendere? Potissimum cum ipse iudex adeo iniquus sit, ut oculis delinquentibus cor affligat, adversus l. sancimus, C. de poen."

[37] Forcadel (as in 1), chapter 17, num. 6, pp. 92-93.

[38] Forcadel (as in 1), chapter 9, num. 2, p. 48: "Quod si Cupidinem ad reliquos principes referas, quos omnes ad unum superavit, mundi secundus dominus iure optimo dicendus est. Nam si potior mundi principibus est, mundum ut sibi asserat necesse est."

our legal hierarchy do not come close to half of Cupid's power, even if it got a collective boost of Viagra. During a conversation with Cupid's mother Venus, she confesses to Forcadel, not without a certain self-esteem, that even the divine power of our Holy Father, the Pope, is largely inferior to that of her playboy son.[39] Whether she was thinking of the number of love affairs in which she had seen certain Popes indulge, or rather of the sex scandals that infected the clergy every now and then, is unsure. Yet Cupid's omnipresent hold over society, and divine as well as secular jurisdictions, in particular, seems to be beyond any doubt. That is way Cupid deserves severe punishment. He is a false jurist. He is a ruthless judge. He is nothing but a silly playboy. In the name of law, Forcadel vindicates the rights of the true jurists. Yet he keeps on smiling regardless.

A Human(ist) Comedy?

Put on the stage of love, law reveals its weakness, frailty and fragility. In Forcadel's view, the legal order of society is under constant pressure of a God of Love who seems to proceed in more regular patterns than law itself. Contrary to his initial statement, which was aimed at reassuring his readership, the relationship between law and love as it is described in his novel turns out to be anything but harmonious. The dynamic of this odd couple appears to correspond to Heraclitus' restless unity of the opposites instead of Plato's blissful idea of concord.[40]

The final verses of Forcadel's *Cupid the Jurist* are telling in this respect. Incidentally, they are composed in the form of an elegiac distich, which as a matter of course recalls the priceless Latin love poetry of Catullus, Properce and Ovid. At the same time, the elegiac distich transmits these very Roman poets' sense for novelty, provocation, and controversy. In poetic terms, Forcadel mocks even at his own, prosaic enterprise.

---

[39] Forcadel (as in 1), chapter 9, num. 2, pp. 49-50: "Quid si committantur ille et hic, singulari certamine? An neuter vincet alterum? Vereor ne Cupido sit superior. Nam quo suam potestatem summam esse prae caeteris ostendat Pontifex, omnes reges Lunae confert, se unum Soli, cap. Solitae de maior. et obedi. Atqui Solem ab Amore victum, cum multis eventibus, tum a Daphne fugitiva probari et argui potest."

[40] Interestingly, one of Forcadel's poems (*Le pleur d'Héraclite et le ris de Démocrite, philosophes*) expresses both the melancholy with which Heraclitus was struck on account of his impious philosophy, and the excessive mockery displayed by Democritus for the same reason; this *opusculum* is contained in Joukovsky's edition (as in 4), pp. 127-137.

Tongue in cheek, he finishes his novel by putting his literary effort into a laughable perspective:[41]

When He saw that laws were being mixed with the tenderness of love,
He burst out laughing,
Cupid, that playboy Who is bound by no law.

Forcadel, then, seems to have been capable of smiling at the insight that his fate was no less subject to the vicissitudes of Cupid's frivolous laws than the legally ordered society. Self-conscious and humble at the same time, Forcadel indulged in the sight of both his and society's pointless struggle under the sun. True, to the extent that love and law both further concord, they seem to be partners in the same country. But, as is obvious from *Cupid the Jurist*, their interplay produces rather discordant sounds.

Contrary to what posterity and Forcadel's contemporaries believed they needed to infer from this provocative book on love and law, the French humanist teaching at Toulouse strongly denied that he had stepped out of his role as an established legal authority. For one thing, Forcadel tried to defend his cause by implicitly recognizing a right to provoke (*ius provocationis*) to all men of virtue and experience.[42] More important, however, is the apologetic letter addressed to his calumniators (*Epistola ad calumniatores*) and added to his *Cupid the Jurist*. In this letter, Forcadel found it as hard to hide his self-esteem and to denounce the envy (*invidia*) of his colleagues as in the preface to his book. This was not entirely uncommon among the humanists, who frequently displayed an innate tendency to loathe conformist academic thought.

In the preface, Forcadel had compared his fate with that of God the Creator: by his very act of Creation, God had also allowed his enemies, the atheists such as Epicurus, to come into existence.[43] By the same token, Forcadel faced the prospect of feeding his very enemies and envious hairsplitters with his publications. In the apology, Forcadel

---

[41] Forcadel (as in 1), p. 124, in fine: "Legibus ut teneros misceri vidit amores / risit, qui nulla lege tenetur Amor."

[42] Forcadel (as in 1), preface: "Verum si ad peritos et bonos viros ius provocandi fuerit, si iudicium suum tantisper sustineant, donec ego consilii mei rationem detexero, spes est visum iri, amorem et ius, quo perducuntur homines ad concordiam, iisdem finibus contineri."

[43] Forcadel (as in 1), preface.

raised himself to the same status as the honest and honourable lawyers, leaders and philosophers, ranging from Solon to Ulpian and Cicero, who had served the law and worshipped the Muses simultaneously. They, too, according to Forcadel, had faced the unjust accusation that combining the cult of the law with the cult of fiction and poetry is almost tantamount to violating the legally established order.[44]

A brilliant jurist, Forcadel must have perceived better than anyone else that every attempt at ordering society suffers from its own passions, its own frailties, and its own "non-dits". He found no better place to reveal them than on Cupid's stage. He was also aware of the costs in terms of success among posterity of expressing such sceptic convictions aloud. His narcissitic fears became real through Papire Masson's hagiography of Jacques Cujas. It included a truculent criticism of Cujas' rival from Béziers. Consequently, Forcadel had been banned almost definitively from legal historical memory.

At least with regard to its vain hope for glory, Forcadel's genius posthumously got a firm reason to believe in the tragic Greek proverb which, tellingly, preceded *Cupid the Jurist*: "hope without hope" (*elpis aneu elpidos*). Still, the most sane conclusion to be drawn from this proverb as well as from his enthralling novel, is that there is no hope that love and law will ever be seen to coexist peacefully. This is Forcadel's ultimate advice.[45]

---

[44] Forcadel (as in 1), p. 129: "Ac, ut ipsi loquuntur, iura sanctissima fabulis et carminibus permiscere, quasi violare. Et hoc est vetus accusationis caput, adversus quam aequitate atque innocentia pro disertissimo patrocinio muniemur."
[45] See footnote 9.

Der scheiternde Dritte: Inszenierungstechniken der Vermittlung in der literarischen Streitkultur

Johanna Bergann

1. Die Inszenierung von Rechtskonflikten

In der Literatur werden Rechtskonflikte und ihre Lösung inszeniert. Nicht das rechtliche Urteilen, sondern die Technik der Vermittlung steht im Mittelpunkt: der Vermittler wird zu Auseinandersetzungen als Dritter herbeigerufen und versucht die Parteien auszugleichen oder zu versöhnen. Im Unterschied zur gerichtlichen Entscheidung benötigt die konsensuale Methode im kontradiktorischen Verfahren ein anderes Personal. Der Vermittler entzieht sich im Vergleich zu Richter, Anwalt und Staatsanwalt einer eindeutigen Funktionsbeschreibung.

Das utopische Ziel des Vermittlers ist die Einigung zwischen den streitenden Parteien durch Kompromiß. Das Recht funktioniert jedoch nicht nur als ein „Konfliktlösungs[...]-"[1] oder „Ausgleichsmechanismus"[2], denn es ermöglicht und erzeugt auch Konflikte.[3] Recht führt demnach zu einer Vermehrung von Konfliktchancen,[4] die ein produktives Potential bergen, namentlich die Chance auf Auseinandersetzung und Veränderung. Konflikte zeichnen sich durch eine hohe Bindungswirkung aus. Indem der Streit ständig durch Rede und Gegenrede aufrechterhalten wird, ist die Rollenverteilung der Gegner klar aufgeteilt. Konflikte bewirken Erwartungssicherheit durch die Kenntnis von der Gegnerschaft.[5] Da es nicht ausschließlich um die Vermittlung im Sinne der Vermeidung oder Lösung von Konflikten geht, lassen sich auch die folgenden, positiven Seiten des Konfliktes herausstellen: „Konflikte restabilisieren allzu instabile Strukturen, sie ersetzen unsichere durch problematische [...]."[6] Das Ideal der

---

[1] Luhmann, Niklas: Ausdifferenzierung des Rechts. Beiträge zur Rechtssoziologie und Rechtstheorie. Frankfurt am Main, 1981, S. 104.
[2] Luhmann, Niklas: Soziale Systeme. Grundriß einer allgemeinen Theorie. Frankfurt am Main, 1987, S. 514.
[3] Luhmann, Niklas: Ausdifferenzierung des Rechts (Fn. 1), S. 104.
[4] Luhmann, Niklas: Soziale Systeme (Fn. 2), S. 511.
[5] Luhmann, Niklas: Ausdifferenzierung des Rechts, (Fn. 1), S. 99.
[6] Ebd. S. 98.

Vermittlung, also Einigung und Harmonie, ist in diesen Überlegungen nicht das Hauptinteresse. Die Frage richtet sich vielmehr an das Janusgesicht der Vermittlung, denn der Vermittler verkörpert das „Element der Einigung oder der Uneinigung."[7]

Wie werden jedoch rechtliche Konflikte inszeniert und auf welche Art und Weise ist das Recht in der Literatur Inszenierungspraktiken unterworfen? Der Begriff der Inszenierung ist der Welt des Theaters entlehnt und benennt die Strategie, die „durch eine spezifische Auswahl, Organisation und Strukturierung von Materialien/Personen etwas zur Erscheinung bringt."[8] Indem die Inszenierung durch Technik und Praxis etwas sichtbar macht, läßt die Rechts-Inszenierung das Recht selbst nicht als ein Normgefüge, sondern als eine Kulturtechnik erscheinen. Dieses Zusammenspiel zeigt sich in der interdisziplinären Verhandlung von Recht in der Literatur sowie in der Frage, wie das Recht inszeniert wird und wie mit dem Recht in der Literatur verfahren wird.

Insbesondere der Begriff des Rechtsverfahrens[9] ist bedeutsam, weniger im Hinblick auf Fragen der Legitimation als vielmehr der Differenzierung zwischen Entscheidungspraxis und Vermittlungstechnik. Luhmann weist auf die Wechselbeziehung zwischen rechtlicher Verfahrenstechnik und theatraler Rolle hin, indem die Annahme einer Rolle zur Voraussetzung für den Eintritt in das Recht wird: „Vermutlich ist dies die heimliche Theorie des Verfahrens: dass man durch Verstrickung in ein Rollenspiel die Persönlichkeit einfangen, umbilden und zur Hinnahme von Entscheidungen motivieren könne."[10] Gerichtsverhandlung und Bühne sind eins, der Prozeß wird wie eine Theaterveranstaltung inszeniert[11] und die Akteure handeln nicht als Individuen, sondern als Repräsentanten der staatlichen Rechtsinstitution. Indem die Beteiligten als rechtliche Funktionsträger auftreten, agieren sie

---

[7] Freund, Julien: Der Dritte in Simmels Soziologie. In: Ästhetik und Soziologie um die Jahrhundertwende: Georg Simmel. Hg. v. Hannes Böhringer, Karlfried Gründer. Frankfurt am Main, 1978, S. 90-104, hier S. 92.

[8] Fischer-Lichte, Erika: Theatralität und Inszenierung. In: Inszenierung von Authentizität. Hg. v. Erika Fischer-Lichte, Isabel Pflug. Tübingen, 2000, S. 11-27, hier S. 21.

[9] Luhmann, Niklas: Legitimation durch Verfahren. Frankfurt am Main, 1993.

[10] Luhmann, Niklas: Legitimation durch Verfahren. Frankfurt am Main, 1993, S. 87.

[11] Wulf, Christoph: Ritual und Recht. Performatives Handeln und mimetisches Wissen. In: Körper und Recht. Anthropologische Dimensionen der Rechtsphilosophie. Hg. v. Ludger Schwarte, Christoph Wulf. München, 2003, S. 29-45, hier S. 31.

als Rolleninhaber.[12] Der Gerichtsprozeß wird durch die rituellen Anforderungen der jeweiligen Gerichts-, Prozeßordnungen oder Verfahrensgesetze wahrhaftig zum in Szene gesetzten Rollenspiel. Das Recht erzeugt und verändert sich durch die Inszenierung und Aufführung von Verfahrensanordnungen beständig.[13] Unterschiede ergeben sich insoweit, als daß „das Schauspiel Möglichkeiten, das Gericht Wirklichkeiten zur Darstellungen bringen will."[14] Das Recht(ssystem) ist also auf Inszenierungspraktiken angewiesen, denn die Rollenfestlegung kommt einer Choreographie gleich und die Szene wird durch unterschiedliche Personengruppen strukturiert.[15]

In der Vermittlung ist die Verkörperung von Recht im Gütegedanken und dem Ziel von Einigung und Ausgleich entscheidend. Im gerichtlichen Streitverfahren fungiert die Entscheidung als Endpunkt des Konflikts. Im Verfahren wird durch das Urteil als Begründungsschrift und die Entscheidungsgründe der Normtext mit der argumentativen Geltung von Gründen synchronisiert. Der zugrunde liegende Normtext läßt sich als „Legitimationsinstanz in Szene"[16] setzen. Vermittlungsverfahren werden durch rhetorische Techniken der Überredung, Manipulation und Verführung inszeniert.

Anhand von zwei literarischen Texten soll die Inszenierung des Konflikts und die Vermittlungsbemühungen durch zwei verschiedene Figuren des Vermittlers erörtert werden. Der Vermittler mit dem Namen Mittler aus dem Roman *Die Wahlverwandtschaften* und die Richter-Mediatorin Athene aus der Tragödie der *Orestie* des Aischylos stehen für zwei verschiedene Vermittlungtechniken. Die außergerichtliche Mediation durch einen nicht studierten Vermittler drückt den Teil der Uneinigkeit sowie Verhinderung aus und die gerichtliche Mediation, die sich in der antiken griechischen Tragödie an die gerichtliche

---

[12] Ebd. S. 34.

[13] Ebd. S. 40.

[14] Schwarte, Ludger: Die Inszenierung von Recht. Der unbekannte Körper in der demokratischen Entscheidung. In: Körper und Recht. Anthropologische Dimensionen der Rechtsphilosophie. Hg. v. Ludger Schwarte, Christoph Wulf. München, 2003, S. 93-127, hier S. 123.

[15] Ebd. S. 101.

[16] Christensen, Ralph; Lerch, Kent D.: Transkriptionen. Das Umschreiben des Rechts im Verfahren. In: Paragrana. Internationale Zeitschrift für Historische Anthropologie. Hg. v. Interdisziplinären Zentrum für Historische Anthropologie. Freie Universität Berlin. Hg. v. Paula Diehl, Henning Grunwald, Thomas Scheffer, Christoph Wulf. Band 15. 2006. Heft 1. Berlin, 2006, S. 41-60, hier S. 46.

Entscheidung anschließt, verdeutlicht den auf Einigung sowie Harmonie ausgerichteten Gütegedanken.

2. Die Vermittlung

Jenseits der Urteilspraxis des Richters gewinnt ein Verfahren im Recht an Bedeutung, das sich weniger an Recht und Gesetz, sondern vielmehr an den Interessen der Konfliktparteien orientiert: die Vermittlung. Ver-Mittelt wird in vielen konfliktregelnden Praxen der Verhandlung, des Bargainings, des Vergleichs und der Güteverhandlung, die alle den Gütegedanken verfolgen. Ausgangspunkt der Vermittlung sind Überlegungen zu Streit und Konflikt, denn die Techniken der Vermittlung, namentlich die Einigung in Form von Konsens und Kompromiß, dienen der Regelung und Lösung von Konflikten. Die Vermittlung thematisiert die Grundfragen des Rechts: das (utopische) Ziel von Einigung und Ausgleich zwischen konfligierenden Parteien sowie die Technik der Streitbeilegung im Sinne eines Interessenausgleichs. Aus der rechtssoziologischen Perspektive fügt die Vermittlung dem entsprechend der Sozialdimension von Konsens/Dissens operierenden Recht eine weitere Facette hinzu, denn sie läßt sich nicht dem Code Recht/Unrecht entsprechend austarieren.[17] Die Ausgangsposition, nach der das Recht diskriminiert, indem es für die eine oder die andere Streitpartei entscheidet,[18] wird durch die Vermittlung transformiert. Ziel der Konfliktregelung oder -lösung ist nicht die Entscheidung nach dem Prinzip „alles oder nichts", sondern die von einer mittleren Position getragene Einigung zwischen den Parteien. Das binäre Schema wird durch die Vermittlung also um eine dritte Position ergänzt: den Kompromiß.

Aus rechtshistorischer Perspektive lassen sich drei verschiedene Figuren des Vermittlers unterscheiden: der Mittler (mediator), der Schiedsrichter (arbiter) sowie der Schiedsmann (arbitrator).[19] Der Mittler steht zwischen den streitenden Parteien und versucht die Streitigkeiten zu lösen. Seine Vermittlungstechnik ist durch die des „Vorschlagens, des

---

[17] Luhmann, Niklas: Das Recht der Gesellschaft. Frankfurt am Main, 1995. S. 130f.
[18] Ebd. S. 129.
[19] Wolff, Christian: Gesammelte Werke. I. Abteilung Deutsche Schriften. Band 19. Grundsätze des Natur- und Völkerrechts. Hg. v. Marcel Thomann, Hildesheim/New York, 1980, Nachdruck der Ausgabe 1754, § 768, S. 558f.

Ratens, des Mahnens, des Abwägens nach Billigkeitsgesichtspunkten, des Empfehlens und Kritisierens [...]"[20] geprägt. Der Schiedsrichter hat eine Entscheidungsposition inne und urteilt auf gesetzlicher Grundlage. Der Schlichter oder „Schiedsmann ist gleichsam eine Mittelsperson zwischen einem Mittler und Schiedsrichter"[21] ohne beratende Funktion und ohne Entscheidungskompetenz. Der Vermittler hingegen hat zwar das Recht im Auge, trifft jedoch keine Entscheidung auf der Grundlage von Gesetzen. Man könnte sagen, daß „im Zweifelsfall das Rechtsgut des Friedens dem Beharren auf dem Buchstaben des Rechts vorzugehen habe."[22] Der Schiedsrichter verkörpert ein juristisches Instrument, der Vermittler hingegen im Ideal ein diplomatisches.

Georg Simmel verfolgt aus rechtssoziologischer Perspektive drei verschiedene Konfiguration des Dritten: Zunächst gibt es den Vermittler, der sich durch Neutralität und Unparteilichkeit auszeichnet und der die Bedingungen der Einigung herstellt, ohne für eine Lösung zu sorgen, denn „[s]olange der Dritte als eigentlicher Vermittler wirkt, liegt die Beendigung des Konfliktes doch ausschließlich in den Händen der Parteien selbst."[23] Der Vermittler besitzt zwei Unterformen, den Mittelmann oder Mediator und den Schiedsrichter. Der Mediator hat entweder an den kollidierenden Interessen keinen Anteil und bleibt auf Distanz oder seine Anteilnahme an beiden Parteien führt dazu, daß er durch den Konflikt zerrieben wird.

Die Typologie Simmels läßt sich auf drei Klassifikationen des Dritten als Vermittler reduzieren. Erstens erscheint der Dritte als Veranlasser oder Förderer des Konfliktes, zweitens vertritt der Dritte das Element des Einverständnisses, des Vertrauens und der Einigkeit mit der Funktion der Gleichgewichtsherstellung, als Faktor des Friedens und Band der Gemeinschaft. Und Drittens verkörpert der Dritte ein „dialektisch mediatisierendes, oft mehrdeutiges Moment",[24] das „Eintracht sowohl wie die Zwietracht, die Freundschaft ebenso wie die

---

[20] Durchhardt, Heinz: Studien zur Friedensvermittlung in der Frühen Neuzeit. Wiesbaden, 1979. S. 109.

[21] Wolff, Christian: (Fn. 19), § 770, S. 561f.

[22] Durchhardt, Heinz: (Fn. 20), S. 110.

[23] Simmel, Georg: Gesamtausgabe. Band 11. Soziologie. Untersuchungen über die Formen der Vergesellschaftung. Hg. v. Otthein Rammstedt. Frankfurt am Main, 1992. S. 131.

[24] Freund, Julien: Der Dritte in Simmels Soziologie. In: Ästhetik und Soziologie um die Jahrhundertwende: Georg Simmel. Hg. v. Hannes Böhringer, Karlfried Gründer. Frankfurt am Main, 1978, S. 90-104, hier S. 97.

Feindschaft stiften kann."[25] Als konziliatorischer Charakter sorgt der Vermittler damit für Einigung und Ausgleich und verkörpert gleichzeitig den „Agent des Streits",[26] da er sich selbst in den Konflikt einschreibt und stört. Das Wesen des Vermittlers oszilliert um die Funktionen von Friedensstifter und Störenfried. Die Stiftung von Verbindung, Kompromiß und Übereinkunft ist ein utopisches Ideal. Der Vermittler verkörpert nicht zwangsläufig die positiv gedachte Lösung eines Konfliktes und übermittelt nicht immer die Friedensbotschaft als neutrale Figur. Als Katalysator bringt er unterschwellig bestehende Uneinigkeit und latente Schwierigkeiten in Beziehungskonstellationen zum Vorschein. Der Vermittler ist auch Verhinderer, da durch ihn nicht nur die Versöhnung verhindert wird, sondern der Streit neu entfacht wird.

a) Mittler aus *Die Wahlverwandtschaften*

Mittler aus den *Wahlverwandtschaften* ist ein Vermittler, das zeigt sein Name, der die Funktionsbeschreibung einer Vermittlungsinstanz ausdrückt. Name und Sein von Mittler sind eins, denn Mittler, der frühere Geistliche, wechselte von der sakralen Mittlerschaft zwischen Gott und den Menschen zur profanen Mittlerschaft zwischen den Menschen. Mittler hat sich auf die Mediation zwischen Ehepartnern spezialisiert und zeichnet sich dadurch aus, daß „er alle Streitigkeiten, sowohl die häuslichen als die nachbarlichen, erst der einzelnen Bewohner, sodann ganzer Gemeinden und mehrerer Gutsbesitzer, zu stillen und zu schlichten wußte."[27] Er wird zu einer Entscheidungs-situation herbeigerufen, als Eduard und Charlotte, ein frisch vermähltes Ehepaar in den besten Jahren, um die Einladung des Hauptmannes und der Nichte Ottilie auf das Schloß ringen. Seine Antwort auf die Frage nach der Einladung des Gastes lautet:

„Ist denn hier Streit? ist denn hier eine Hülfe nötig? Glaubt ihr, daß ich in der Welt bin, um Rat zu geben? Das ist das dümmste Handwerk, das einer treiben kann. Rate sich jeder selbst und tue, was er nicht lassen

---

[25] Ebd. S. 97.
[26] Ebd. S. 97.
[27] Goethe, Johann Wolfgang: Die Wahlverwandtschaften. Frankfurt am Main, 1972 [2006]. S. 23.

kann. Gerät es gut, so freue er sich seiner Weisheit und seines Glücks; läufts übel ab, dann bin ich bei der Hand. […] Tut, was ihr wollt: es ist ganz einerlei! Nehmt die Freunde zu euch, laßt sie weg: alles einerlei!"[28]

Wenn Mittler ein Vermittler ist, so ist er zumindest kein guter, denn der betitelt „Rat geben" als das „dümmste Handwerk" und lehnt die Rechtsberatung als eine Hauptaufgabe der Vermittlertätigkeit grundlegend ab. Mittler hört den Ratsuchenden nicht zu, seine Verweigerungsrede zeichnet sich durch Freude an Streit aus, wodurch er seine eigene Position stark macht. Mittlers Ablehnung einer Hilfeleistung bestärkt den Verdacht, daß er eine Figur der „Scheinjurisprudenz"[29] und einen „Antijuristen" verkörpert. Seine Verweigerung begründet er mit einer Unzuständigkeit, da zur Zeit seiner Ankunft keine lautstarken Streitigkeiten bestehen, wodurch er sich, nach Inka Mülder-Bach, erst künftige Zuständigkeiten durch Abwarten verschafft[30] und zur Entstehung von unlösbaren Beziehungkonstellationen beiträgt. Mittler hat nicht verstanden, daß seine Vermittlungsbemühungen einerseits Verhandlungshilfe als Regelung eines Sachproblems und andererseits auch Versöhnungshilfe als Hilfestellung bei der Bewältigung von Beziehungsproblemen verlangen.[31]

In einer positiven Deutung kündigt Mittler allerdings eine neue, kommunikative Mittelbarkeit an. Er durchbricht durch seinen Auftritt die Entscheidungsblockade der Eheleute, initiiert die Einladung der Gäste und wird zum „Katalysator der narrativen Dynamik".[32] Mittler bringt also die Handlung in Gang, wenn auch in Richtung Katastrophe. Als Vermittler inszeniert er den Streit.

---

[28] Ebd. S. 23f.

[29] Uwe Diederichsen: Die 'Wahlverwandtschaften' als Werk des Juristen Goethe. In: NJW 2004, S. 537-544, hier S. 539.

[30] Mülder-Bach, Inka: Symbolon-Diabolon. Figuren des Dritten in Goethes Roman 'Die Wahlverwandtschaften' und Musils Novelle 'Die Vollendung der Liebe." In: Figur und Figuration: Studien zu Wahrnehmung und Wissen. Hg. v. Gottfried Boehm, Gabriele Brandstetter, Achatz von Müller. München, 2007, S. 121-138, hier S. 127.

[31] Goebel, Joachim: Zivilprozeßdogmatik und Verfahrenssoziologie. Berlin, 1994, S. 256ff.

[32] Mülder-Bach, Inka: Symbolon-Diabolon, (Fn. 30), S. 127.

b) Athene aus *Die Orestie*

Die Richter-Mediatorin Athene tritt im dritten Teil der *Orestie* des Aischylos, den Eumeniden, in einer Entscheidungssituation auf: Orestes hat seine Mutter Klytaimnestra getötet und über seine Schuld wird Gericht gehalten. In der Gerichtsszene wird der Übergang vom stofflichen Blutprinzip zum bürgerlichen Sühnestrafrecht der Polis, vom Mutterrecht zum Vaterrecht dargestellt. Der von Athene installierte Areopag verhandelt als Blutgerichtsbarkeit den Muttermord durch Orestes, sie selbst überträgt die Entscheidungsgewalt auf das Schwurgericht. Die Figuren repräsentieren rechtliche Funktionen, die sich zum Teil doppeln oder ausschließen: die Erinnyen sind die Anklägerinnen, Orestes der Angeklagte, Apollon sein Anwalt und gleichzeitig Zeuge, Athene die vorsitzende Richterin oder Vermittlerin und der Areopag das Richtergremium oder die Geschworenen. Athene setzt den Areopag als das erste menschliche Gericht ein, das über menschliche Straftaten richtet. Dessen ungeachtet gibt sie eine Stimme für Orestes ab und begründet den Freispruch von Orestes mit ihrer Zugehörigkeit zum männlichen Geschlecht, denn sie wurde von keiner Mutter geboren. Die Gründe ihrer Entscheidung wurden als ein Meisterstück von Parteilichkeit und Ungerechtigkeit analysiert. Ob sie ihre Stimme mit den menschlichen Richtern zusammen abgegeben und damit den Gleichstand hergestellt oder bei schon bestehender, gleicher Stimmanzahl die entscheidende Stimme für Orestes abgegebenen hat, ist nicht entscheidend.

Maßgeblich für die Frage nach dem rechtlichen Verfahren ist die Überlegung, Athene als eine Richter-Mediatorin anzusehen sowie die Verbindung zwischen gerichtlich-autoritativer Entscheidungspraxis und Vermittlungstechnik der unterlegenen Partei herauszuarbeiten. Der letzte Teil der Tragödie endet nicht mit der Entscheidung zugunsten von Orestes. Nach Beendigung des offiziellen Rechtsstreits und der Niederlage der Erinnyen versucht Athene diese zu besänftigen und zu befrieden, denn sie wollen nach ihrer Niederlage die Pest über die Stadt bringen und sie verwüsten. Ihre Argumentation, daß die gleiche Stimmanzahl und der Freispruch keinen Verlust an Ehre bedeute, ist auf die Konstruktion einer win-win-Situation beider Parteien angelegt, kann die Position der besiegten Partei aber nicht aufwerten. Nach dem Willen von Athene sollen die Erinnyen nach der Verwandlung von den Rachegöttinnen in die Eumeniden, die segenspendenden Schutzgottheiten, einen wichtigen Platz in der Polis Athens einnehmen. Athenes Vermittlung repräsentiert keinen Einigungsversuch zwischen zwei Parteien in einer Dreierkonstellation, sondern es handelt sich um eine Verhandlung mit der unterlegenen Partei. Die Vermittlungstechnik von Athene basiert auf einer geschickten Argumentation, gutem Zureden und sprachlicher Überzeugungskraft: „Dir freundlich zuzureden, werd ich müde nicht." (Vs. 881) „Wie könnte zu Verständigen nicht von guter Zunge führen ein Weg?" (Vs. 988)

Interessant ist, daß sie die von ihr angewendete Kunst der Überredung als sprachliche Magie während ihres Einsatzes selbst reflektiert: „Wenn aber Peithos hohe Macht dir heilig ist, Beschwichtigung und Zauberkunde meines Munds, so bleibst du wohl."[33] (Vs. 885-887) In der Übersetzung von Peter Stein hingegen wird das erotische Moment der Peitho stärker betont: „Wenn dir die erhabene Macht der Peitho heilig ist – die Versöhnungskraft, die Zauberkraft des Wortes, die schmeichelnde Verführung durch meine Zunge –, so wirst du bleiben."[34] (Vs. 884 b) Marie Theres Fögen sieht in der Vermittlung durch Athene einen „erbärmliche[n] Mediationsversuch", „Bestechung" und schließlich eine „Gehirnwäsche".[35] Im Ergebnis richtig, übersieht diese Ansicht jedoch, daß in Athene die Kräfte von Peitho als Kunst der Überredung wirksam sind. Von den Hellenen als der allmächtige Zauber der Rede einer Göttin verehrt, ist die Überredung durch zwei Faktoren gekennzeichnet, namentlich die sprachliche und die erotische Überzeugungs- und Verführungskraft: „Denn der Mund ist ja recht eigentlich das Eigenthum der Peitho, deshalb hat sie dort ihren Sitz, den sie erst mit dem Lebensodem verlässt."[36] Mit dieser Kunst ist nur der sanfte Zauber gemeint, denn Zwang und Gewalt gehören nicht zum Wesen von Peitho.[37] Die Überredungskünste tendieren jedoch zu einem eindeutigen Bestechungsversuch, denn Athene verspricht den Erinnyen einen hohen

---

[33] Aischylos: Die Orestie. Agamemnon. Die Totenspende. Die Eumeniden. Deutsch von Emil Staiger. Stuttgart, 1958, S. 140.

[34] Stein, Peter: Die Orestie des Aischylos. 2. Auflage, München, 2007, S. 207.

[35] Fögen, Marie Theres: Die Tragödie des Entscheidens. Eine Anmerkung zu den 'Eumeniden' des Aischylos. In: ancilla juris (anci:ch) 2007: 42 – Synopsis, S. 42-47, hier S. 47.

[36] Jahn, Otto: Peitho die Göttin der Ueberredung. In: Einladungsschrift zu einem am Geburtstage Winkelmanns den IX December um XI Uhr in der kleineren akademischen Aula von Prof. G. F. Schoemann zu haltenden Vortrag. Greifswald, 1846, S. 1-28, hier S. 6.

[37] Ebd. S. 7.

Stand in der Polis, Land und große Würden. Die Kraft des Wortes verwandelt sich an dieser Stelle in einen bösen Zauber:

„[…] Athene's winning-over of the Furies is openly described as a triumph of *peitho*. But what she does goes beyond what we would call 'persuading': she uses a veiled threat, promises, argument, and so forth. If we recognize that the main sense of Πειθώ is 'I get (someone) to acquiesce', then the character of the scene is more adequately conveyed."[38]

In dem Maße, in dem Athene die Kunst der Überredung überschreitet und mit drohenden und bestechenden Elementen anreichert, erliegen die Erinnyen den verführerisch bestechlichen Worten Athenes am Ende: „Bezaubert deine Rede mich? Der Groll entweicht." (Vs. 900) Nicht durch das Recht in Form eines rechtlichen Urteils, sondern durch die nachträgliche Versöhnungsarbeit Athenes nach der Entscheidung wird Rechtsfrieden hergestellt.

Das in der Polis neu institutionalisierte Recht besteht in der Zusammensetzung aus gerichtlicher Entscheidung und Vermittlung durch Überredung und Verführung. Der Weg zu Einigung und Ausgleich basiert nicht auf guten Vorsätzen sowie Vertrauen und beabsichtigt keinen freien Interessenausgleich. Der Frieden in Athen ist mit einer die Grenzen der Kunst der Überredung überschreitenden Bestechung der Vermittlerin auf die Unterliegenden verbunden. Die Verwandlung der Erinnyen in die Eumeniden, also von den Rachegöttinnen in die Schutzgöttinnen, vollzieht sich zu schnell und zu geschönt, um eine ideale, das heißt eine von Bestechung freie Vermittlungsleistung repräsentieren zu können. So heißen die letzten Worte der Eumeniden: „Der junge Zeus, der Allessehende, und die alte Moira, haben sich versöhnt, sie wirken zusammen: Frieden für immer!" (Vs. 1047) Was die Eumeniden im Hinblick auf Athenes Vermittlung inszenieren, ist eine unglaubwürdige Friedens- und Konfliktlösungs-politik, denn sie produziert Zweifel im Hinblick auf die Rolle des Vermittlers. Vermittlung bedeutet in diesem literarischen Beispiel nicht

---

[38] Buxton, Richard G. A.: Persuasion in Greek Tragedy: A study of peitho. Cambridge, 1982, S. 49.

nur rhetorische Überredung und erotische Verführung, sondern auch Bestechung und Manipulation.

3. Inszenierung von Vermittlung und Verhinderung

In den literarischen Beispielen wird die ambivalente Rolle des Vermittlers in Szene gesetzt: die Vermittlung schafft Verbindungen und stellt gleichzeitig Distanz her, sie kann sowohl Einigung und Versöhnung fördern als auch den Konflikt verstärken. Die Vermittlungstechnik in der Literatur ist nicht durch Neutralität gekennzeichnet, sondern durch eine Verweigerungsrede von Mittler und durch Verführung und Bestechung von Athene.

Die Vermittlung scheitert in diesen Fällen, denn Manipulation, Bestechung und Verweigerung stellen keine legitimen Mittel der Vermittlung dar und entsprechen nicht dem Muster der Vermittlung als einer Technik zur Herstellung von Harmonie ohne bestechende Gewalt. Beiden Beispielen gemein ist, dass die Vermittlung auf das utopische Moment der Versöhnung sowie auf Einigung und Ausgleich abzielt, wohingegen Urteil und Entscheidung auch dadurch erreicht werden, dass Recht gesprochen wird, ohne dass es auf die Frage von Harmonie ankäme. Die alternative Form der Konfliktlösung ist zumindest im Ideal dazu geeignet, durch bestechenden Zauber zu harmonisieren oder durch (ver-) störende Reden den Konflikt für einerlei zu erklären.

Die „improvisierte" Komödie als forensische Taktik in Ciceros *Caeliana*

Tamás Nótári

Anfang April des Jahres 56[1], am ersten Tag der *Ludi Megalenses* fand der Prozess gegen den wegen *vis* angeklagten M. Caelius Rufus statt. Die Verteidigung und die Gerichtsrede boten für Cicero eine glänzende Gelegenheit, seinen sowohl für sein persönliches Schicksal als auch für die Republik folgenschweren Kampf mit Clodius und dessen Klan fortsetzen zu können. Der Konflikt zwischen Clodius und Cicero nahm 73 seinen Anfang als Clodius die Vestalin Fabia, die Halbschwester der Gattin Ciceros, eines Sexualfrevels *(incestum)* bezichtigte, was Schande über die ganze Familie und Verwandtschaft Ciceros brachte. Diesen Schritt wollte der unter anderem von seiner Gattin Terentia angestiftete Cicero rächen, indem er im Jahr 61 als Zeuge gegen Clodius im sog. Bona Dea-Prozess auftrat, der aber für Clodius mit einem Freispruch endete. Clodius trieb mit Hilfe der Konsulen des Jahres 58 Cicero ins Exil und ließ sein Haus auf dem Palatin zerstören. Für Cicero schien in 56 die Gelegenheit gekommen zu sein, Clodius und dessen Schwester Clodia mit seiner *Caeliana* einen tödlichen Hieb versetzen zu können, indem er sie im Prozess gegen Caelius mit den Mitteln der römischen Komödie anprangerte und an den *Megalensia*, die nach römischer Tradition zur Veranstaltung der *ludi scaenici* dienten, vor Gericht eine eigentümliche Komödie inszenierte.

Nach einer kurzen Skizze des als Ausgangspunkt für die Feindseligkeit zwischen Cicero und der gens Claudia/Clodia dienenden Bona Dea-Prozesses gilt es hier zuerst die historischen Hintergründe des Prozesses gegen M. Caelius Rufus aufzuzeigen (1.). Hiernach soll die durch die *Ludi Megalenses* gebotene und von Cicero meisterhaft verwendete rhetorische Situation erläutert (2.), und die in der *Caeliana* angewandte Tatbestandsbehandlung und forensische Taktik analysiert werden (3.).

---

[1] Alle im Text angeführten Jahreszahlen sind – sofern nicht anders vermerkt – v. Chr. zu verstehen.

1. Der Bona Dea-Skandal und der historische Hintergrund der *Pro Caelio*

Die Feindschaft zwischen Cicero und Clodius bzw. seiner Schwester Clodia Metelli lässt sich ohne die Beweggründe der Zeugenaussage Ciceros im Bona Dea-Prozess schwerlich verstehen. Anfang Dezember 62 begingen die Matronen und Vestalinnen unter dem Vorsitz der Gattin des *pontifex maximus* Caesar das Fest der Bona Dea.[2] (Das Fest der Bona Dea wurde in Rom alljährlich im Hause eines Magistrats *cum imperio* begangen, dem nur die Matronen der Patrizier und die Vestalinnen beiwohnen durften. Aus unserer Hinsicht ist es von maßgebender Wichtigkeit, dass die Teilnahme an der Zeremonie allen männlichen Wesen –Menschen ebenso wie Tieren – untersagt war.[3]) Was in jener Nacht passiert ist, davon sind wir aus den Quellen[4] nicht mit eindeutiger Sicherheit unterrichtet, Folgendes lässt sich aber auf jeden Fall zusammenfassen: Clodius drang irgendwie in das Haus Caesars ein; nach Plutarch soll er die Tür offen vorgefunden haben. Er soll sich als Harfenspielerin verkleidet haben,[5] wobei den Bemerkungen Plutarchs und Appians, dass es Clodius die Tarnung erleichtert habe, dass ihm zu dieser Zeit noch kein Bart wuchs, kein Glauben zu schenken ist, da Clodius zu dieser Zeit bereits neunundzwanzig oder dreißig Jahre alt gewesen sein muss.[6] Die Leitung der Zeremonie der Bona Dea hatte Caesars Mutter Aurelia inne,[7] und das gestörte Fest wurde später von den Vestalinnen im Rahmen einer *instauratio* wiederholt.[8]

---

[2] Zum Kult der Bona Dea siehe Macrobius: *Saturnalia* 1, 12, 25; Latte, Kurt: Römische Religionsgeschichte. Beck. München, 1967 S. 228.

[3] Vgl. Plutarchus: *Cicero* 19; Dio Cassius: *Historia Romana* 37, 35, 4; Cicero: *Epistulae ad Atticum* 1, 13, 3; *De haruspicum responso* 37.

[4] Velleius Paterculus: *Historia Romana* 2, 45, 1; Plutarchus: *Cicero* 28; *Caesar* 9; Suetonius: *Divus Iulius* 6, 2; Appianus: *Bella civilia* 2, 14, 52; Dio Cassius: *Historia Romana* 37, 45; Livius: *Periochae* 103.

[5] Ciceto: *De haruspicum responso* 44; Plutarchus: *Cicero* 28, 2; *Caesar* 10, 1; Iuvenalis: *Saturae* 6, 337.

[6] Nach Dio Cassius hatte Clodius vor Pompeia, die Gattin Caesars zu verführen (und nach Dios Meinung mit Erfolg), was aber auch nicht unbedingt als bare Münze gelten darf.

[7] Suetonius: *Divus Iulius* 74, 2.

[8] Zum Verlauf des Prozesses siehe Baldson, John Percy Vyvian Dacre: Fabula Clodiana. In: *Historia* (1966) No. 15. S. 65-73, 69; Tatum, W. Jeffrey: Cicero and the Bona Dea Scandal. In: *Classical Philology* (1990) No. 85. S. 202-208, 206; Spielvogel, Jörg: Clodius S. Pulcher – eine politische Ausnahmeerscheinung der späten Republik? In: *Hermes* (1997) No. 125.

Die Erhebung der Anklage gegen Clodius fand vor dem 15. März 61 statt, aber zum Prozess selbst sind unsere Informationen äußerst dürftig: Die Anklage wurde von den drei Cornelii Lentuli vorgetragen[9] und Clodius war bemüht sich ein Alibi dafür zu verschaffen, dass er sich an jenem Tag nicht in Rom, sondern in Interamna aufgehalten hatte. Um dieses Alibi zu erschüttern, traten zahlreiche Matronen, die am Fest der Bona Dea teilgenommen hatten, als Zeuginnen auf; unter ihnen auch Aurelia, die Mutter, und Iulia, die Schwester Caesars. Cicero sagte aus, dass ihn Clodius am Tage der Bona Dea-Zeremonie besucht hatte – nach dem Zeugnis einiger Quellen[10] fand dieser Besuch drei Stunden vor dem Skandal, d.h. am späten Abend, nach anderen anlässlich der am Morgen abgehaltenen *salutatio* statt.[11] Wenn wir jedoch für einen Moment dem wenig glaubwürdigen Alibi des Clodius, das von C. Causinius Schola, einem seiner Gastfreunde aus Interamna bestätigt wurde, Glauben schenken wollten, gälte es festzustellen, dass er den Weg von ungefähr hundert Meilen an einem Tag hätte zurücklegen können. Clodius wurde im Prozess freigesprochen, wobei allerdings nicht auszuschließen ist, dass die Richter von Crassus mit einer Summe von drei- bis vierhunderttausend Sestertius je Richter bestochen wurden.[12] Einigen nicht bestochenen Richtern kann es auch vorgeschwebt haben, dass Aurelia Clodius vielleicht nicht genau erkannt haben kann.[13] Da der Prozess nicht den von Cicero erwünschten Ausgang nahm und er sich mit seiner Zeugenaussage Clodius zum erbitterten Feind gemacht hatte, was für seinen weiteren Lebenslauf tragische Folgen nach sich zog, lohnt es sich, kurz dabei zu verweilen, was Cicero dazu bewegt haben kann, in diesem Prozess zu energisch gegen Clodius aufzutreten. Cicero legte das Gewicht natürlich auf die moralischen Beweggründe seines Einschreitens,[14] aber seinem ersten vom Bona Dea-Skandal an Atticus verfassten Bericht[15] haftet ein zynischer Beigeschmack an. Cicero versuchte den Anschein zu erwecken, als ob er im Auftreten gegen Clodius die Fortsetzung des Kampfes gegen die Catilianer gesehen

---

S. 56-74, 60.
[9] Baldson S. 71.
[10] Cicero: *Epistulae ad Atticum* 1, 16, 2; 2, 1, 5.
[11] Quintilianus: *Institutio oratoria* 4, 2, 88.
[12] Cicero: Epistulae ad Atticum 1, 16, 5.
[13] Baldson S. 72.
[14] Cicero: Epistulae ad Atticum 1, 18, 2.
[15] Cicero: Epistulae ad Atticum 1, 12, 3.

hätte.[16] Diese Erklärung scheint schon insofern nicht gänzlich zufriedenstellend, als Clodius Catilina zu seinen persönlichen Feinden zählte und an seiner Verschwörung gewiss nicht beteiligt war.[17]

Plutarch glaubt in den folgenden Umständen die Gründe für Ciceros Auftreten gegen Clodius im Bona Dea-Prozess finden zu können.[18] Seine Gattin Terentia soll Cicero zu diesem Schritt angestiftet haben. Sie hegte einen erbitterten Hass gegen Clodius, besonders aber gegen Clodia, weil Clodia angeblich vorhatte, den Redner Terentia zu entfremden, um eine Ehe mit ihm eingehen zu können. Terentia wollte das Verhältnis zwischen Cicero und Clodia im Keim ersticken, und Cicero, der seiner Gattin gegenüber nie ganz die Oberhand gewinnen konnte, sah sich gezwungen, sich vom Verdacht des Scheidungsvorhabens befreien zu müssen. Plutarch erwähnt diesen Grund als bloßes Gerücht und die moderne Fachliteratur stempelt diesen auch als solches ab. Dennoch scheint es nicht ganz überflüssig, einen prüfenden Blick auf diesen Erklärungsansatz zu werfen: Plutarch datiert Clodias Vorhaben bezüglich der Heirat mit Cicero auf 61 und obwohl die plutarchische Chronologie manchmal irreführend sein mag, besitzen die von ihm berichteten Tatsachen meist einen gewissen Wahrheitsgehalt.[19] Aber auch wenn wir diese Hypothese von der Hand weisen, erscheint es aufgrund eines früheren Konfliktes zwischen der Familie Ciceros und der gens Claudia/Clodia als höchst wahrscheinlich, dass Cicero von seiner Gattin zur Zeugenaussage im Bona Dea-Prozess angeregt wurde. Die Feindschaft zwischen Terentia und Clodius rührte aus dem Jahre 73 her, als Clodius die Vestalin Fabia (die Halbschwester der Terentia) des *incestum*s mit Catilina angeklagt hatte. Catilina und Fabia wurden zwar freigesprochen, aber der Skandal brachte die Familie der Terentia in Verruf und machte sie zum Gespött der römischen Elite. Von Fall erfahren wir aus den Quellen ziemlich wenig; Sallust hingegen erwähnt das *incestum* als bewiesene Tatsache, und auch bei Cicero lassen sich einige Anspielungen auf das Vorgefallene finden.[20]

---

[16] Vgl. Cicero: *Epistulae ad Atticum* 1, 14, 5.

[17] Vgl. Epstein David F.: Cicero's testimony at the Bona Dea Trial. In: *Classical Philology* (1986) No. 80. S. 229-235, 230.

[18] Vgl. Plutarchus: *Cicero* 29, 2-3.

[19] Vgl. Baldson S. 72; Dorey, T. A.: Cicero, Clodia, and the pro Caelio. In: *Greece and Rome* (1958) No. 5. S. 175-180, 179.

[20] Vgl. Epstein S. 232; Sallustius: *De coniuratione Catilinae* 15, 1; Cicero: *In toga candida* 82.

Es ist nicht auszuschließen, dass Cicero in 63 zum Auftreten gegen Catilina auch durch den Kult der Bona Dea weiter motiviert wurde, denn als die Verschwörer schon gefangengenommen wurden und Cicero noch keine Entscheidung über ihr Schicksal traf, sahen die Matronen und die Vestalinnen, die das Bona Dea-Fest unter Vorsitz der Terentia im Hause Ciceros begingen, den Altar aufflammen, worin sie ein *prodigium* sahen und seine Deutung darin fanden, dass Cicero energischer gegen die Verschwörer auftreten sollte.[21] Die weder von Cicero noch von Terentia vorausgesehenen Konsequenzen der Feindseligkeit zwischen Cicero und Clodius sind hinlänglich bekannt.[22] Im Jahre 58 wurde Clodius zum *tribunus plebis* gewählt, zuvor aber musste er von einem Plebejer adoptiert werden, wozu Caesar als *pontifex maximus*, der bei der *arrogatio* als Vorsitzender der *comitia calata* mitzuwirken hatte, gerne assistierte. Als Volkstribun ließ er am Ende des Jahres 58 rückwirkend die *lex Clodia de capite civium* in Kraft treten, die das Hinrichten römischer Bürger ohne ein Gerichtsurteil ebenso mit der Todesstrafe bedrohte wie die Möglichkeit der *provocatio ad populum*. Das Gesetz enthielt zwar nicht ausdrücklich den Namen Ciceros, nichtsdestotrotz war das Ziel dieses in Gesetzesform gehüllten Racheaktes für jeden unmissverständlich, da er im Dezember des Jahres 63 einige Catilianer im Tullianum – zwar ohne Gerichtsurteil, jedoch durch das *senatus consultum ultimum* legitimiert – hinrichten ließ. Nachdem er die düsteren Aussichten wahrnahm, zog Cicero im März 58 freiwillig ins Exil, da – wie er im Nachhinein seine Entscheidung zu begründen versuchte – sein Bleiben einen blutigen Bürgerkrieg ausgelöst hätte, was er nicht hätte verantworten können. Sein Haus wurde geplündert, die Beute teilten sich Clodius und die Konsulen.

Im April 56 erhoben L. Sempronius Atratinus als Hauptankläger und L. Herennius Balbus und P. Clodius als *subscriptores* vor der *quaestio de vi* gegen den damals fünfundzwanzigjährigen[23] Marcus Caelius Rufus

---

[21] Hierzu siehe ausführlicher Will, Wolfgang: Der römische Mob. Wiss. Buchgesellschaft. Darmstadt, 1991 S. 48; Moreau, Philippe: Clodiana religio. Un procès politique en 61 av. J.-C. Les Belles Lettres. Paris, 1982 S. 15; Spielvogel S. 59; Epstein S. 234.

[22] Materiale, Filippo: L'ideale politico di Cicerone nella pro Sestio. In: *Cicerone e la politica*. Ed. F. Salerno. Satura. Napoli, 2004 S. 145-153, 147; Cic. *Sest.* 43 ff.; 53; Fuhrmann, Manfred: Cum dignitate otium. Politisches Programm und Staatstheorie bei Cicero. In: *Gymnasium* (1960) No. 67. S. 481-500, 496.

[23] Heinze, Richard: Ciceros Rede pro Caelio. In: *Hermes* (1925) No. 60. S. 193-258, 194; Stroh, Wilfried: Taxis und Taktik. Die advokatische Dispositionskunst in Ciceros Gerichtsreden. Teubner. Stuttgart, 1975 S. 243.

Anklage. Neben dem Angeklagten[24] sprachen als Verteidiger M. Licinius Crassus Dives und – seiner Gewohnheit gemäß als Letzter[25] – Cicero. Der Anklage lag wahrscheinlich die aus dem Jahre 65/4 stammende *lex Plautia (Plotia) de vi* zugrunde,[26] die Ciceros Bericht zufolge dazu berufen war, aufständischen Bürgern, die den Senat mit Waffengewalt stürmen, gegen Magistrate mit Gewalt vorgehen und den Staat in Gefahr stürzen wollten, Einhalt zu gebieten.[27] Es ist natürlich nicht auszuschließen, dass sich die Anklage nicht auf die – auf prätorisches oder tribunizisches Betreiben – *lex Plautia*, sondern auf die *lex Lutatia de vi* gründete. Allerdings ist das Verhältnis dieser beiden Gesetze – fraglich ist überhaupt, ob es sich hierbei um zwei verschiedene Gesetze handelt – ziemlich problematisch.[28] Die *lex Lutatia* verbindet man gewöhnlich mit dem Namen des Konsuls Q. Lutatius Catulus und datiert ihre Entstehung auf das Jahr 78 oder 77.[29]

Bezüglich der *lex Plautia* scheint in der Fachliteratur ungeklärt zu sein, ob eine Verbindung zwischen der im Jahre 65 entstandenen *lex Plautia de vi* und der aus dem Jahre 89 stammenden *lex Plautia de reditu Lepidanorum*, die vom Volkstribunen Marcus Plautius Silvanus vorgeschlagenen wurden, besteht. Die Bestimmung der gesetzlichen Grundlage des gegen Caelius eingeleiteten Verfahrens wird zudem durch die Tatsache erschwert, dass Cicero zwar in der Peroratio auf die *lex Lutatia* verweist, oder zumindest das dem Verfahren zugrunde liegende Gesetz mit dem Namen des Lutatius Catulus verbindet, dieser Verweis sich aber auch so interpretieren lässt, dass Catulus als Konsul einen Vorschlag zur Schaffung dieses Gesetzes gemacht hat, der vom Volkstribunen Plautius aufgegriffen und durchgeführt worden ist.[30] Mit großer Wahrschein-

---

[24] Es war zu Ciceros Zeiten unüblich, dass sich der Angeklagte vor Gericht selber verteidigte – vgl. Quintilianus: *Institutio oratoria* 4, 1, 46.

[25] Cicero: *Brutus* 190; *Orator* 130; Quintilianus: *Institutio oratoria* 4, 2, 27.

[26] Zur *lex Plautia* s. Kunkel, Wolfgang: Untersuchungen zur Entwicklung des römischen Kriminalverfahrens in vorsullanischer Zeit. Beck. München, 1962 S. 123; Classen, Johannes: Ciceros Rede für Caelius. In: *Aufstieg und Niedergang der römischen Welt, I. 3.* Hesg. H. Temporini–W. Haase. De Gruyter. Berlin–New York, 1973 S. 60-94, 63; Stroh S. 246; Mommsen, Theodor: Römisches Strafrecht. Duncker&Humbolt. Leipzig, 1899 S. 564.

[27] Cicero: *Pro Caelio* 1.

[28] Kiselewich, Rebecca: Cicero's pro Caelio and the leges de vi of Rome in the Late Republic. Williamstown, 2004 S. 31.

[29] Hierzu s. Hough, J.: The Lex Lutatia and the Lex Plautia. In: *The Americal Journal of Philology* (1930/2) No. 51. S. 135-147.

[30] Vgl. Cicero: *Pro Caelio* 70; Kiselewich S. 33.

lichkeit ist Lintott in jenem Punkte beizupflichten, dass die *lex Plautia de vi* die Bestimmungen der *lex Lutatia de vi* bezüglich des *crimen maiestatis* und der *vis publica* wiederholte, diese aber mit der Pönalisierung der *vis privata* ergänzte.[31] Natürlich überzeugt auch diese Hypothese, der zufolge Cicero in seiner Argumentation nicht nur auf ein Gesetz verwies, das die *vis* sanktioniert hatte, und mit der Erwähnung der *lex Plautia* und der *lex Lutatia* in derselben Rede die Tatbestände der *leges de vi* zusammenfasste, und dabei auch vor gewissen Verallgemeinerungen nicht zurückschreckte, nicht abschließend.[32]

Hier gilt es zu erwähnen, dass gewissen Ansichten nach das Verfahren gegen Caelius als politischer Prozess angesehen werden sollte, der sich in erster Linie gegen Pompeius, den Gastfreund des Ptolemaios, richtete und Cicero die Aufgabe zugeteilt wurde, den Fall von seinem politischen Kontext zu lösen.[33] Hiergegen lässt sich Folgendes einwenden: Die Ankläger wurden hauptsächlich von persönlichen und nicht etwa von politischen Motiven geleitet, da Caelius im Februar des Jahres 56 Anklage gegen L. Calpurnius Bestia, den leiblichen Vater des zur Zeit des Prozesses siebzehnjährigen L. Sempronius Atratinus, wegen *ambitus* erhob. Diesen wollte er, nachdem er – dank der Hilfe seines Verteidigers Ciceros – freigesprochen wurde, wiederum wegen *ambitus* belangen.[34] Diese zweite Anklage suchte Atratinus mit der Anklage gegen Caelius wegen *vis* zu verhindern; daher gilt es Heinze beizupflichten, der der Ansicht war, dass das Politikum in diesem Prozess nicht als Zweck, sondern als Mittel gedient haben muss.[35] Die Popularität des Pompeius erreichte zu dieser Zeit einen Tiefpunkt, daher hätte es für die Ankläger von Vorteil sein müssen, Caelius als Parteigänger des Pompeius anzugreifen. Eben aus diesem Grund war Cicero wohl bemüht, dem Prozess jegliche politische Schärfe zu nehmen. Dass der Name des

---

[31] Vgl. Lintott, Andrew W.: Violence in Republican Rome. Oxford University Press. Oxford, 1968 S. 116. So auch Robinson, Olivia: The Criminal Law of Ancient Rome. Hopkins. Baltimore, 1995 S. 29.

[32] Kiselewich S. 45.

[33] Pacitti, G.: Cicerone al processo di M. Celio Rufo. In: *Atti I. Congresso internazionale di Studi Ciceroniani, II.* Roma, 1961 S. 67-79.

[34] Vgl. Cicero: *Pro Caelio* 16. 56. 78. Ausführlicher s. Münzer, F.: Aus dem Leben des M. Caelius Rufus. In: *Hermes* (1909) No. 44. S. 135-142; Heinze S. 195.

[35] Vgl. Heinze S. 197; Classen S. 67. 93.

Pompeius kein einziges Mal in der *Caeliana* zur Sprache kam, darf daher nicht überraschen.[36]

Neben den tatsächlichen Anklagepunkten berührt Cicero zahlreiche Fragen, die nicht in unmittelbarer Verbindung zur Anklage standen. So z.B. den angeblich von Caelius gegen Clodia, die Witwe des Metellus Celer, verübten Mordversuch.[37] Er behandelt den Giftmordversuch gegen Clodia zwar gesondert von den anderen Anklagepunkten, allerdings lässt sich aus zahlreichen Bemerkungen folgern, dass gerade dieser Umstand eine überaus wichtige Rolle in der Beweiskette gespielt haben muss:[38] Caelius soll sich von Clodia Geld beschafft haben, um Dions Mörder zu bezahlen.[39] Wenn er später die Absicht verfolgte, Clodia ermorden zu wollen, so muss er von jenem Motiv geleitet worden sein, die Frau, die im Nachhinein vom Attentat erfuhr, aus dem Weg zu räumen.[40]

2. Die *Ludi Megalenses* als Kulisse der Prozessbühne

Nach diesem Überblick der historisch-politischen Lage und der Feindschaft zwischen Cicero und der gens Claudia/Clodia gilt es nun, unsere Aufmerksamkeit der rhetorischen Situation und ihrer Behandlung durch Cicero zu widmen. Eugène de Saint Denis bezeichnete die *Caeliana* als die *geistreichste Rede* Ciceros,[41] wobei der Zeitpunkt der Gerichtsrede (der 4. April), d.h. der erste Tag der *Ludi Megalenses* bzw. die geniale Umwandlung dieses etwas ungewöhnlichen Umstandes in eine glänzende Komödie, daran einen erheblichen Anteil hatte.[42] Die zu Ehren der Magna Mater (Kybelē) – deren Kult während des zweiten punischen Krieges im Jahre 205 oder 204 auf die aus den *libri Sibyllini* eingeführt worden war – veranstalteten *Ludi Megalenses* fanden zwischen dem 4. und dem 10. April statt.[43] Die römischen Gesandten wandten sich an den

---

[36] Vgl. Cicero: *Pro Caelio* 78. *Epistulae ad Quintum fratrem* 2, 6, 6. So auch Stroh S. 246.

[37] Costa S. 93.

[38] Cicero: *Pro Caelio* 56.

[39] Cicero: *Pro Caelio* 52.

[40] Stroh S. 249.

[41] Saint Denis, Eugène de: Le plus sprituel des discours cicéroniens: le Pro Caelio. In: *Essais sur le rire et le sourire des Latins*. Les Belles Lettres. Paris, 1965 S. 129-144, 129.

[42] Salzman, Michele R.: Cicero, the Megalenses and the defense of Caelius. In: *American Journal of Philology* (1982) No. 103. S. 299-304, 301.

[43] Latte S. 258.

König Attalos von Pergamon, der den Römern den schwarzen Stein, der die Göttin repräsentierte, übergab und ein Schiff ausstattete, damit sie ihn nach Rom bringen könnten.[44] (Einer anderen Tradition nach wurde der Stein direkt aus Pessinus nach Rom gebracht.[45]) Die Göttin wurde in Rom mit einer glänzenden Zeremonie empfangen; dem Zeugnis einiger Quellen zufolge blieb das Schiff an der Tiberbank hängen und die Vestalin Quinta Claudia, die hiermit ihre Unschuld bewies, bewegte ganz allein das Schiff wieder fort.[46] Im Tempel der Kybelē am Palatin stand eine Statue der Claudia.[47] Dieser Tempel wurde im Jahre 191 erbaut, und in dieser Zeit wurden die *Ludi Megalenses* eingeführt, an denen auch die *ludi scaenici* veranstaltet wurden. In den Zeremonien der *Ludi Megalenses* – wie auch im römischen Kult der Magna Mater – spielte der *gallus*-Tanz, der an die Selbstkastration des Attis erinnerte, keine Rolle.[48] Archäologische Funde beweisen allerdings, dass der Attiskult ungefähr zur selben Zeit in Rom eingeführt wurde wie der Kult der Magna Mater. Dies belegt die Irrigkeit der Annahme – die schon aus philologischen Quellen als zweifelhaft erschien –, dass der Kult der Kybelē in Rom ohne jenen des Attis eingeführt worden wäre.[49]

Wie schon erwähnt, wurden an den *Ludi Megalenses* Theatervorstellungen veranstaltet. Neben der Rolle zweier Mitglieder der gens Claudia und dem Kontrast zwischen Clodia und Quinta Claudia[50] besteht zwischen den *Megalensia* und der Familiengeschichte der gens Claudia ein weiteres Bindeglied: Clodius störte mehrere Male das Fest der Magna Mater. Den zweiten Skandal verursachte er am 8., 9., bzw. 10. April 56,[51] d.h. einige Tage nach Ciceros Gerichtsrede, als er mit seiner Knüppelbande das Theater stürmte.[52] An dem ersten Angriff konnten die Hörer der Gerichtsrede sich wohl erinnern, da Clodius im Jahre 58 an einer Aktion gegen den Kybelētempel in Pessinus aktiv mitwirkte,[53]

---

[44] Livius: *Ab urbe condita* 29, 10, 4. 14, 5; Ovidius: *Fasti* 4, 255; Silanus: *Punica* 17, 1; Appianus: *Hannibalica* 233.

[45] Cicero: *De haruspicum responso* 27; Livius: *Ab urbe condita* 29, 10, 7; Strabo: *Geographica* 12, 567; Ammianus Marcellinus: *Res gestae* 22, 9, 5.

[46] Suetonius: *Tiberius* 2, 3; Lactantius: *Divinae institutiones* 2, 7, 12.

[47] Tacitus: *Annales* 4, 64.

[48] Latte S. 260.

[49] Altheim Franz: Römische Religionsgeschichte, II. Göschen. Berlin, 1932 S. 51.

[50] Cicero: *Pro Caelio* 34.

[51] Salzman S. 303.

[52] Cicero: *De haruspicum responso* 21-29.

[53] Cicero: *De haruspicum responso* 27.

als der Galatafürst Brogitarus die Bande des Clodius mit Geld unterstützte, und er als Gegenleistung mit der Hilfe des Clodius den Rang des Kybelēpriesters erhielt, zu dem eine Königswürde gehörte.[54] Somit bestand sowohl eine historische, als auch eine aktuelle Verbindung zwischen der *Ludi Megalenses* und der gens Claudia/Clodia.

3. Die „improvisierte" Komödie als forensische Strategie

Am Anfang der Rede bringt Cicero sein Mitleid für die Richter Ausdruck, denen nicht einmal an einem Festtag Ruhe und Erholung zuteil wird und denen es versagt bleibt, die Theatervorstellung anschauen zu können.[55] Deshalb beschließt er, den Richtern eine improvisierte Komödie zu präsentieren, in deren Mittelpunkt er die Drahtzieherin der Anklage, Clodia, stellt.[56] Hiermit beabsichtigt er nicht die Person des Angeklagten im günstigeren Licht darzustellen, sondern die Aufmerksamkeit der Richter auf die Motive, d.h. *opes meretriciae* der Ankläger zu lenken.[57] Für die Hörer durfte es von hieran nicht mehr fraglich gewesen zu sein, wer hinter dem Ausdruck *„meretrix"* gesteckt haben mag: Die Hauptzeugin des Attentates gegen Dion war niemand anders als die mondäne lustige Witwe der römischen Elite: Clodia Metelli. Vor einer wirklichen Antwort auf die tatsächlichen Anklagepunkte *(de vi)* erachtet es Cicero für notwendig, auf die gegen Caelius vorgebrachten Verleumdungen zu reagieren.[58] Aus den sich auf die *vita ante acta* beziehenden Paragraphen[59] lassen sich folgende Anklagepunkte herauslesen: Caelius leistete nicht die *pietas* und *fides*, die er seinem Vater schuldete[60] und auch gegenüber Calpurnius Bestia verhielt er sich auch nicht gebührend, als er ihn vor Gericht lud,[61] die

---

[54] Cicero: *De haruspicum responso* 28; Köves-Zulauf, Thomas: Bevezetés a római vallás és monda történetébe (Einführung in die römische Religions- und Sagengeschichte). Telosz. Budapest, 1995 S. 7.
[55] Cicero: *Pro Caelio* 1.
[56] Cicero: *Pro Caelio* 2.
[57] Cicero: *Pro Caelio* 1.
[58] Cicero: *Pro Caelio* 3.
[59] Cicero: *Pro Caelio* 3–22.
[60] Cicero: *Pro Caelio* 4. 18.
[61] Cicero: *Pro Caelio* 26.

luxuria,[62] die sowohl Herennius als auch Clodius Caelius vorgeworfen haben,[63] der ausschweifenden Lebenswandel,[64] die Freundschaft zu Catilina;[65] die angebliche Teilnahme an der Verschwörung,[66] die *crimina ambitus*,[67] der Angriff auf einen Senator bei den Pontifexwahlen.[68] (Die Anordnung der Anklagepunkte mag zwar zufällig sein, aber ihre Reihenfolge richtet sich nach den Lebensereignissen des Caelius.[69])

Im dritten Teil wird das Attentat gegen Dion behandelt.[70] Die Anklage, mit der versucht wurde die Aussage der Clodia zu unterstützten, dass angeblich Caelius Geld von ihr geliehen haben soll, um die Sklaven des Lucceius zu bestechen, mit dem Ziel sie später als belastende Zeugin aus dem Weg zu räumen.[71] Cicero behandelt diese Aussagen der Clodia als zwei separate Punkte[72]: die Anklage wegen *aurum*[73] und *venenum*[74] erörtert er getrennt.[75] Eines der klar ersichtlichen Ziele Ciceros ist es, die politischen Untertöne des Prozesses zu vertuschen; u.a. deswegen versucht er, das Attentat gegen Dion in den Vordergrund seiner Darstellung zu rücken. Das *crimen veneni* war in Rom hinlänglich bekannt und es müssen neben Clodias Geständnis auch andere zur Verfügung gestanden haben, die bestätigten, dass Caelius versucht hatte, Clodia den Sklaven zu übergeben. Interessanterweise erwägt Cicero während seiner ganzen Rede keine andere Version der Ereignisse, sondern begnügt sich damit, die Widersprüche der Schilderung der Gegenseite lächerlich zu machen, und zu betonen, dass kein *corpus delicti* zur Verfügung steht. Hiermit kann er zwar nicht gänzlich den Verdacht von Caelius lenken, schafft es aber, dieses Motiv aus seinem ursprünglichen Kontext zu lösen.[76]

---

[62] Cicero: *Pro Caelio* 4. 17.
[63] Cicero: *Pro Caelio* 27.
[64] Cicero: *Pro Caelio* 6-14.
[65] Cicero: *Pro Caelio* 10-14.
[66] Cicero: *Pro Caelio* 15.
[67] Cicero: *Pro Caelio* 16.
[68] Cicero: *Pro Caelio* 19.
[69] Heinze S. 214.
[70] Cicero: *Pro Caelio* 51. 69.
[71] Cicero: *Pro Caelio* 63.
[72] Cicero: *Pro Caelio* 51.
[73] Cicero: *Pro Caelio* 51.
[74] Cicero: *Pro Caelio* 56.
[75] Stroh S. 260.
[76] Stroh S. 261.

Im mittleren Teil der Rede werden zahlreiche Fragen aufgeworfen: nach den *de vita-*, bzw. *de moribus*-Paragraphen wendet sich der Redner den tatsächlichen Anklagepunkten zu.[77] Die Ermordung Dions tut er mit wenigen Sätzen ab und verweist darauf, dass der Urheber des Mordes der König Ptolemaios gewesen sein muss, den er mit Hilfe des inzwischen freigesprochenen Asicius durchgeführt hat. Daraus schlussfolgert Cicero, dass auf Caelius kein Schatten des Verdachts fallen könne.[78] Hiernach kehrt er mit einer unerwarteten Wende zu der gegen Caelius vorgebrachten *deliciarum obiurgatio* zurück:[79] Bezüglich den kleineren Freizügigkeiten nimmt er eine liberale Stellung ein und behauptet, dass die Jugend, solange sie keinen größeren Schaden damit verursacht, hierzu berechtigt wäre[80]; bezüglich den größeren Vergehen aber bittet er die Richter darum, einen Unterschied zwischen der Sache *(res)* und dem Angeklagten *(reus)* zu machen und macht sie darauf aufmerksam, dass die Vorwürfe, die gegen die Jugend vorgebracht werden, nicht persönlich Caelius zur Last gelegt werden sollten.[81] Mit einer energischen Wendung schickt er sich hiernach an, das *crimen luxuriae* zu behandeln: Das von Clodia geliehene Geld lässt auf eine intime Beziehung schließen, die wiederum ein bitteres Ende gefunden hat.[82] Anstatt einer auf den ersten Blick logischen Folgerung (einerseits hätte er die Existenz des Liebesverhältnisses leugnen können, andererseits hätte er aus dem plötzlichen Ende der Affäre die Glaubwürdigkeit der beiden *crimina* hinterfragen können,) schlägt er folgenden Weg ein: Er zieht die Zeugenaussage der Clodia mit jener Begründung in Zweifel, dass sie als verlassene und eifersüchtige Geliebte unfähig sei, Caelius objektiv zu beurteilen.[83] Hiermit antizipiert er die zur Argumentation gehörende *vis*,[84] wodurch die *vis* und die *luxuria* sich in den betreffenden Paragraphen abwechseln:[85] *vis*,[86] *luxuria*,[87] *vis*,[88] *luxuria*,[89] *vis*.[90]

---

[77] Cicero: *Pro Caelio* 23-50.
[78] Cicero: *Pro Caelio* 24.
[79] Cicero: *Pro Caelio* 27.
[80] Cicero: *Pro Caelio* 28.
[81] Cicero: *Pro Caelio* 29-30.
[82] Cicero: *Pro Caelio* 31.
[83] Cicero: *Pro Caelio* 32-36.
[84] Cicero: *Pro Caelio* 51-69.
[85] Cicero: *Pro Caelio* 23-51. Vgl. Stroh S. 266.
[86] Cicero: *Pro Caelio* 23-24.

Nach Richard Heinzes glänzender Feststellung stützte sich die Anklage gänzlich auf Clodias Zeugenaussage, so dass es den Anklägern unmöglich war, ihre Glaubwürdigkeit dadurch in Frage zu stellen, dass sie sie als die verlassene Geliebte des Clodius bloßstellten. Einzig und allein Cicero kann diese Liaison im Prozess zur Sprache gebracht haben,[91] d.h. er versucht Caelius von einem solchen Anklagepunkt reinzuwaschen – denn das Verhältnis zu Clodia bewegte sich nicht mehr auf der Ebene solcher allgemeinen Vorwürfe, wie der *amores* und der *libidines* –, die gegen ihn überhaupt nicht vorgebracht worden waren.[92] Heinzes Feststellung scheint umso zutreffender, als sich in der ganzen *Caeliana* keine einzige Stelle findet, an der Cicero nahezulegen versucht, dass die Liaison von Clodia und Caelius eine stadtbekannte Affäre gewesen wäre. Zwar verschweigt der Redner nicht jene Gerüchte, die über den freizügigen Lebenswandel der beiden kursierten, aber von einem Gerücht über ein Verhältnis zwischen ihnen ist nie die Rede. Er bringt den liederlichen Lebenswandel der Clodia und des Caelius auf einen Nenner und erdichtet zwischen ihnen eine Liaison; aus dem Umstand der Dichtung lässt sich freilich nicht schlussfolgern, dass Clodia und Caelius nie in einer intimeren Beziehung zueinander gestanden hätten, sondern bloß, dass diese nicht weit und breit bekannt gewesen war.[93]

Ein weniger genialer Redner hätte die Situation folgendermaßen zum Vorteil seines Klienten ausgeschlachtet: Zum einen hätte er versucht, die *crimina luxuriae* zu bagatellisieren und auf die allzu allgemeine Art dieses Anklagepunktes hinzuweisen bzw. die Richter davon zu überzeugen, der Jugend das Recht zu gönnen, sich auszutoben. Zum anderen hätte er sich angeschickt, die Glaubwürdigkeit der Clodia zu untergraben, was ihm unter den gegebenen Umständen nicht allzu schwer hätte fallen dürfen, weil zu dieser Zeit die Schmählieder über die inzestuöse Beziehung, die sie mit ihrem Bruder Clodius unterhielt, ziemlich verbreitet waren;[94] diese hätten ausgereicht, um bei den Richtern Zweifel

---

[87] Cicero: *Pro Caelio* 25-31.
[88] Cicero: *Pro Caelio* 32-36.
[89] Cicero: *Pro Caelio* 37-50.
[90] Cicero: *Pro Caelio* 51.
[91] Heinze S. 228.
[92] Heinze S. 245.
[93] Stroh S. 272.
[94] Cicero: Ad Quintum fratrem 2, 3, 2.

darüber zu säen, ob das Gericht der Zeugenaussage einer *meretrix* Glauben schenken dürfte.

Solch ein – wie gesagt weniger genialer – Redner wäre allerdings mit den folgenden Schwierigkeiten konfrontiert worden: Wie kann er dem Vorwurf der Doppelmoral entkommen, wo er nicht dieselben Maßstäbe für alle Beteiligten geltend zu machen scheint, d.h. einerseits Clodia wegen ihres liederlichen Lebenswandels verurteilt, andererseits bei Caelius aber bereit ist, großzügig darüber hinwegzusehen? (Zwar war Caelius nur ein junger Ritter, während Clodia die Witwe eines Konsularen war, dennoch wäre die Authentizität des Redners durch die Anwendung dieses doppelten Maßstabes ins Schwanken gebracht worden.) Selbst wenn Clodia wegen ihres Lebenswandels als keine glaubwürdige Zeugin galt, hätte das nicht nahegelegt, dass sie unbedingt eine falsche Zeugenaussage ablegte. Und warum wäre sie überhaupt dazu bereit gewesen gegen Caelius falsch auszusagen?[95]

Cicero zieht den Giftzahn der möglichen Einwände mit einer genialen Konstruktion: Wie stünde nun die Sache, wenn Clodia die Geliebte des Caelius gewesen wäre? Die Einwände gegen Caelius könnten gerade durch eine Darstellungsweise entkräftet werden, der zufolge das Verhältnis mit einer Frau wie Clodia nicht als *adulterium* gewertet werden sollte, da dies in die Kategorie der *amores meretricii* gehört. Hiermit löste sich auch die Frage nach den Motiven der Zeugenaussage der Clodia: die verlassene Geliebte dürstet nach Rache, so dass ihrer Aussage, die Lug und Trug sein muss, kein Glaube geschenkt werden kann. Auf den ersten Blick steht aber Cicero kein allzu großer Raum offen, um das Liebesverhältnis zwischen Caelius und Clodia zu erschaffen; beide wohnen auf dem Palatin und sind nicht für ihren asketischen Lebenswandel bekannt. Und doch findet der Redner einen Punkt, an den er anknüpfen kann: die Ankläger haben behauptet, dass Clodia Caelius, der sie später vergiften wollte *(aurum et venenum)*, Geld gegeben habe. Für Cicero liegt nun auf der Hand, dass es hierzu nur aufgrund einer intimen Beziehung und deren bitterem Ende gekommen sein kann. Wenngleich das Dilemma auch unter diesen Vorzeichen nur schwer auflösbar erscheint, da entweder die Behauptungen der Ankläger wahr sein müssen, was die Beteiligung des Caelius am Attentat gegen Dion beweist, oder aber erdichtet sind; dann aber kann die Erzählung von der Liaison

[95] Stroh S. 274.

zwischen Clodia und Caelius nicht untermauert werden. Cicero bemühte sich, der Aufgabe gerecht zu werden, den Freispruch des Angeklagten zu erwirken (Leitwort *luxuria*) und die Aussage der Clodia als unglaubwürdig erscheinen zu lassen (Leitwort *vis*). Wenn das Verhältnis zwischen den beiden stadtbekannt gewesen wäre, hätte Cicero die Ausführung über die *luxuria* in den Teil „*de vita ac moribus*", die Invektive gegen Clodia aber in den Teil „*crimen de vi*" einbauen müssen – unter den gegebenen Umständen hat er sich im Teil „*crimina auri et veneni*" mit der Person der Clodia zu befassen und die Liaison zwischen Caelius und Clodia aufzubauen.[96]

Es gilt nun einen prüfenden Blick darauf zu werfen, wie Cicero diese Liaison aufbaut, und zwar mit dem Ziel, den Anschein darüber zu wahren, dass diese von Anfang an bestanden hätte. Zu Beginn der Rede[97] nennt er Clodia noch nicht bei Namen, sondern erwähnt nur die Rolle der *opes meretriciae*, was sich inhaltlich gut und Interesse weckend auf die *intolerabilis libido* und das *nimis acerbum odium* reimt.[98] Als er vom Umzug des Caelius auf den Palatin spricht, drückt er sich schon deutlicher aus: Er stellt seinen Hörern das Bild der liebeskranken Medea vor Augen.[99] Cicero bedient sich des Öfteren des bekannten Medea-Motivs, das im Prozess schon mehrere Male Anwendung fand: Atratinus nannte Caelius einen *pulchellus Iason* und verwies mit Blick auf das geliehene Geld auf die Geschichte vom goldenen Fließ bzw. bezeichnete seinen Ankläger Atratinus als *Pelia cincinnatus*.[100] Der Redner führt den Gedankengang fort, indem er behauptet, dass alle Schwierigkeiten, denen der junge Caelius nun ins Auge sehen muss, auf die palatinische Medea zurückzuführen sind.[101] Die Motive des Geldes und des Giftes *(duo sunt autem crimina, auri et veneni)* verweist er in den Bereich der *luxuria* und versucht hieraus Folgerungen für die Liaison zwischen Clodia und

---

[96] Stroh S. 275.

[97] Cicero: *Pro Caelio* 1. skk.

[98] Cicero: *Pro Caelio* 2.

[99] Cicero: Pro Caelio 18. Quo loco possum dicere id quod vir clarissimus, M. Crassus, cum de adventu regis Ptolemaei quereretur, paulo aute dixit: 'utinam ne in nemore Pelio ...' ac longius mihi quidem contextere hoc carmen liceret: 'nam numquam era errans' hanc molestiam nobis exhiberet 'Medea animo aegro, amore saevo saucia'.

[100] Quintilianus: *Institutio oratoria* 1, 5, 61.

[101] Cicero: Pro Caelio 18. Hanc Palatinam Medeam migrationemque hanc adulescenti causam sive malorum omnium sive potius sermonum fuisse.

Caelius zu ziehen – spräche er dies allerdings offen aus, so müsste er den Anklagepunkten beipflichten.[102]

Die von den Anklägern vorgetragenen Punkte wiederholt Cicero mit einem *„ut dicitur"*, lässt diese aber nur unter Vorbehalt gelten – und zwar unter der Bedingung, dass sie seinen Zielen dienlich sind. Dafür hält er ihre Beantwortung in der Schwebe.[103] An diesem Punkt beschwört er mit dem rhetorischen Griff der Prosopopoiia Appius Claudius Caecus aus der Unterwelt, was in diesem Fall keineswegs ein zum *genus grande* gehörendes Mittel zu sein scheint,[104] sondern vielmehr ein Moment, das einer gewissen Komik nicht entbehrt[105], um die altrömischen Tugenden mit dem Lebenswandel der Clodia zu kontrastieren. Dies scheint auf den ersten Blick mit den Zielen der Verteidigung nicht im Einklang zu stehen, da Cicero den Urvater der gens Claudia/Clodia sich so äußern lässt, als ob dieser von der Richtigkeit der Anklage wegen des Goldes und des Giftes überzeugt sei.[106] Allerdings ist das Auftreten des alten Zensors für den Redner nur insofern von Bedeutung, als er den Zuhörern bzw. den Richtern den unsittlichen Lebenswandel der Clodia und das Liebesverhältnis zwischen Clodia und Caelius als unbestreitbare Tatsache im Gedächtnis verankert.[107]

Hiernach kommt Cicero bezüglich Clodia auf die *reprehensio testis*, in der er Clodia als eifersüchtige, verlassene Geliebte darstellt und zu beweisen versucht, dass Caelius kein Ehebrecher *(adulter)*, sondern nur ein Liebhaber *(amator)* der Clodia sei, mit der – da sie nach Dirnenart lebt – kein Ehebruch im strengeren Sinne des Wortes möglich ist. Wie zuvor Cicero einerseits selber sprach, andererseits aber Appius Claudius Caecus das Wort ergreifen ließ, lässt er nun den Bruder der Clodia, P. Clodius Pulcher, als Sprecher auftreten. Auf diese Weise wälzt er gleichsam die Beweislast auf die zwei fiktiven Sprecher ab. Hierdurch wird die Taktik Ciceros noch deutlicher: Wenn die Anklage wegen des Giftes und des Goldes wahr sein sollte, dann war Clodia gewiss die Geliebte des Caelius; wenn sie aber seine Geliebte war, dann ist sie bei ihrer Aussage nur von Rach- und Eifersucht getrieben, so dass die Vorwürfe wegen des Giftes

---

[102] Stroh S. 278.
[103] Cicero: *Pro Caelio* 30-32.
[104] Quintilianus: *Institutio oratoria* 12, 10, 61; Geffcken Kathrine A.: Comedy in the pro Caelio. Brill. Leiden, 1973 S. 18.
[105] So z.B. die Anspielung auf die Blindheit des Appius Claudius – vgl. Cicero: *Pro Caelio* 33.
[106] Cicero: *Pro Caelio* 33-34.
[107] Stroh S. 282.

und des Goldes nicht als erwiesen gelten können.[108] Die Anklage wegen des Giftes und des Goldes, die Cicero in dieser Form zusammengefasst hat, um die Liaison der Clodia und des Caelius erschaffen und seinen Hörern einprägen zu können, ist nun überflüssig geworden und muss dementsprechend nun unauffällig aus der Welt geschafft werden. Und zwar so, dass die Richter gleichsam vergessen sollten, auf welche Prämissen sie ihre Schussfolgerung gegründet haben.[109] Die *crimina auri et veneni* werden somit mit dem *crimen luxuriae* verschmolzen und tauchen in den folgenden Paragraphen der Rede nicht wieder auf. In der Rede, die Cicero Clodius in den Mund legt, wird das Liebesverhältnis zwischen Clodia und Caelius als unzweifelhafte Tatsache präsentiert, während der von Cicero als Sprecher heraufbeschworene Appius Claudius nur aus gewissen Indizien auf diese Liaison schließen konnte.[110] (Die Informationen, die den beiden fiktiven Sprechern Cicero zumutet, entsprechen dem jeweiligen Wissen der Hörer.) Cicero lässt Clodius als seinen Resoneur die Liaison ins Detail gehend ausmalen und versetzt Clodia bzw. der Glaubwürdigkeit ihrer Zeugenaussage hiermit den tödlichen Hieb.[111]

In den Paragraphen, die sich auf die *Caeliana* beziehen, lassen sich mehrere, nebeneinander laufende Fäden entdecken. Inhaltlich lassen sich folgende Schichten erfassen:[112] eine hypothetische Folgerung, die vom Gold und Gift auf das Liebesverhältnis und die Trennung schließt (Sprecher: Cicero)[113]; die tatsächliche, nunmehr nicht hypothetische Folgerung (Sprecher: Appius Claudius Caecus)[114]; die hypothetische Folgerung, die aus dem Verhältnis und der Trennung die Unglaubwürdigkeit der Zeugenaussage Clodias ableitet (Sprecher: Cicero)[115]; und die tatsächliche Folgerung hierauf (Sprecher: Clodius).[116] Aus der Sicht des wirklichen Zieles der Beweisführung, ist die ciceronianische Argumentation folgendermaßen angelegt:[117] der Beweis

---

[108] Stroh S. 282.
[109] Cicero: *Pro Caelio* 35.
[110] Cicero: *Pro Caelio* 36.
[111] Stroh S. 284.
[112] Cicero: *Pro Caelio* 30-36.
[113] Cicero: *Pro Caelio* 30-32.
[114] Cicero: *Pro Caelio* 33-34.
[115] Cicero: *Pro Caelio* 35.
[116] Cicero: *Pro Caelio* 36.
[117] Stroh S. 286.

der Liaison[118] und die Zerstörung der Glaubwürdigkeit Clodias;[119] aus der Perspektive jener Punkte, von denen Cicero seine Hörer scheinbar zu überzeugen versucht, kann folgende Gliederung aufgestellt werden: die Verteidigung des Caelius gegen die Vorwürfe der *crimina luxuriae*[120] und die Diskreditierung Clodias.[121] Nach dieser Argumentation befreit Cicero Clodius von der Appostition „*adulter*", da er bewiesen hat, dass Clodia nicht das Leben einer römischen Matrone führt und es infolge dessen unmöglich ist, mit einer Dirne Ehebruch zu begehen. (In den betreffenden Paragraphen wird zwar Clodia nicht namentlich genannt,[122] und das Werturteil ist auch mehr oder minder hypothetisch abgefasst, später aber behauptet er *expresis verbis*, dass Clodia ein Leben *meretricio more* führt.[123]) Mit dieser Behauptung reflektiert Cicero auf die Gedankengänge der zwei als Resoneure angeführten Väter. Er lässt allerdings beide Väter einig werden,[124] dass man der Jugend immer eine gewisse Freizügigkeit zugestehen müsse und dass eine Liaison mit einer Clodia-artigen Frau, die in die Reihe der *amores meretricii* eingestuft werden kann,[125] einen Teil des freizügigen Lebenswandels bilden kann.[126]

---

[118] Cicero: *Pro Caelio* 30-34.
[119] Cicero: *Pro Caelio* 35-36.
[120] Cicero: *Pro Caelio* 30-31.
[121] Cicero: *Pro Caelio* 32-36.
[122] Cicero: *Pro Caelio* 38. 49.
[123] Cicero: *Pro Caelio* 57.
[124] Cicero: *Pro Caelio* 37.
[125] Stroh S. 289.
[126] In der Darstellung des Verhältnisses zwischen Clodia und Caelius greift Cicero des Öfteren zu den Waffen des Humors und der Ironie. Segal wies auf zahlreiche wesentliche Elemente der römischen Komödie hin; darunter u. a. darauf, dass der sog. plautinische Tag, dessen Hauptmerkmale der *ludus* und die *voluptas* sind, im krassen Gegensatz zu dem vom *negotium* und der *industria* beherrschten römischen Alltag steht. (Vgl. Segal, Erich: Roman Laughter. University Press. Cambridge, 1968 S. 42.) An jenen Festtagen, an denen Theatervorstellungen stattfanden, d.h. an den *Ludi Romani*, den *Ludi Apollinares*, den *Ludi plebei* und den *Ludi Megalenses* wurde jene *gravitas*, von der das Alltagsleben der Römer durchdrungen war, aufgehoben. In den Komödien trat jeder aus der Welt des Alltages heraus: die Jugend gehorchte ihren Eltern nicht, die Ehefrauen fügten sich nicht dem Willen ihrer Ehegatten, und die Sklaven konnten ihren Herren ohne Konsequenz eine Belehrung erteilen. Das Lachen richtete sich immer gegen die Außenseiter, die, wenn sie die Kritik beherzigen, in die Gesellschaft eingestuft, wenn sie die Belehrung jedoch ablehnen, ausgegrenzt und als negative Persönlichkeiten der Komödie dargestellt werden. (Vgl. Frye, Northrop: Anatomy of Criticism. Schocken Books. New York, 1969 S. 163.) Schaden nahmen des Öfteren in den Komödien des Plautus die *miles gloriosi* und die Cato maior-artigen, konservativen Personen; bei Terenz fand sich öfters das Motiv des Gegensatzes zwischen den lebensfrohen Söhnen

Bei der Charakterisierung der Clodia zitiert Cicero einige Zeilen aus der Tragödie *Medea exul* des Ennius und erreicht gerade durch diese tragisch klingenden Verse im unangemessenen Kontext einen komischen Effekt. (Clodia wurde nicht nur mit Medea, sondern auch mit Clytaemestra, einer ebenfalls nicht gerade positiven konnotierten Frauengestalt der antiken Mythologie verglichen, wenngleich dieser Vergleich nicht in der *Caeliana* zu finden ist; die Bezeichnung *quadrantaria Clytaemnestra* stammte mit großer Wahrscheinlichkeit von Caelius selbst.[127]) Somit stilisiert Cicero Caelius zu Iason, seinen Umzug in die Nachbarschaft der Clodia-Medea zu einer mythischen Reise, und die verlassene lustige Witwe zur unheilbringenden Zauberin.[128] Die Erzählung der Übergabe der *pyxis*[129] verwendet Cicero nicht mehr die Mittel der römischen Komödie, sondern die des *mimus*, in dem meistens unter anderen – und in dieser Hinsicht ist Clodias Charakterisierung als *meretrix* maßgebend – Prostituierte auftraten.[130] Der *comedia dell' arte*-ähnliche *mimus*, der über keine feste Handlung verfügte, galt als keine wertvolle Unterhaltung, der *risus mimicus* wurde zumeist durch vulgäre Obszönitäten ausgelöst. Zur beliebten Thematik dieser Gattung gehörten der Ehebruch und die Giftmordversuche. Dementsprechend bezeichnet Cicero die Szene, die sich angeblich im Bad abspielte völlig zu Recht als *obscenissima fabula*.[131] Den Vorfall, der sich bei der Übergabe der rätselhaften *pyxis* ereignete, beschreibt Cicero als *muliebre bellum*, bei dem Clodia zur *imperatrix* wird und ihre Leute sich zur im trojanischen Pferd steckenden *provincia* wandeln.[132] Die Charakterisierung Clodias als

---

und den herben Vätern, die im Laufe des Stückes lernten den Lebenswandel ihrer Söhne zu tolerieren. (Vgl. Segal S. 70.) In den betreffenden Paragraphen der *Caeliana* (37–38.), d.h. in der *synkresis* der zwei Vatertypen zitiert Cicero aus den Komödien des Caecilius und des Terenz: der erste Vater erscheint als hart und herb, der zweite hingegen – nicht zufällig werden von Cicero hierbei die Worte des Micio aus der *Adelphoe* wiedergegeben – nachsichtig und mild. Die Worte der beiden Väter können mit den Darstellungen in Verbindung gebracht werden, mit denen Cicero einige Paragraphen zuvor Appius Claudius Caecus und P. Clodius Pulcher als Resoneure beschreibt; zugleich bilden sie eine Parallele zur Beziehung zwischen Cicero und seinem geistigen Sohn, Caelius, bzw. kontrastieren das Verhältnis zwischen Clodia und ihrem Bruder (und vielleicht auch Liebhaber) Clodius. (Vgl. Terentius: *Adelphoe* 120-121; Geffcken S. 23.)

[127] Vö. Quintilianus: *Institutio oratoria* 8, 6, 53.
[128] Geffcken S. 15.
[129] Cicero: *Pro Caelio* 61-69.
[130] Lactantius: *Divinae institutiones* 1, 20, 10
[131] Cicero: *Pro Caelio* 69.
[132] Geffcken S. 25.

meretrix[133] bildet einen vollkommenen Gegensatz zum Bild der gehorsamen und auf die Reinheit ihres Lebenswandels und ihres Hauses bedachten römischen Matrone. Clodias Erscheinung und Benehmen sind demnach einer *meretrix*, und keiner *mater familias* würdig,[134] unter anderem gerade deswegen, weil ihre Sklaven und der Bademeister zu ihren *familiares* gehören.[135] In diesem Zusammenhang verweist Cicero sogar zweimal auf ihre gängige Bezeichnung als *quadrantaria*.[136] Nach Plutarch soll dieser Name deswegen an ihr gehaftet haben, weil sie von ihren Liebhabern angeblich je einen *quadrans* als Bezahlung empfangen haben soll.[137] Caelius bestärkte dieses Gerücht gerade durch die für Clodia gebrauchte Bezeichnung „*quadrantaria Clytaemnestra*".[138] Caelius wurde nach Cicero mit *opibus meretriciis* angegriffen,[139] d.h. dass Clodia ihr Heer als eine Art *miles gloriosa* leitete.[140]

Die Anklage im Prozess gegen Marcus Caelius Rufus lautete auf *vis*, einen Sammeltatbestand, der von der gewalttätigen Störung des öffentlichen Friedens bis auf Totschlag mehrere Straftaten beinhaltete. Den historischen Hintergrund der *Caeliana* bildet die langjährige und folgenschwere Feindschaft zwischen Cicero und Clodius, der ihn 58 in die Verbannung trieb. Dank der *Pro Caelio*, der geistreichsten Gerichtsrede Ciceros, wurden die Richter, die während der *Ludi Megalenses*, des Festes der Magna Mater zu Gericht saßen, Zuschauer einer meisterhaften Komödie, deren *personae* Clodius, der Ankläger des Caelius und die (zumindest Ciceros Aussage nach) mit ihrem Bruder im Inzest lebende Clodia, die berühmt-berüchtigte lustige Witwe der römischen Oberschicht, die mit Catulls Lesbia höchstwahrscheinlich identische Geliebte des Caelius bildeten.

Ciceros rednerische Laufbahn wies zahlreiche glorreichere und geschichtsträchtigere Momente auf als die der *Caeliana*, aber es wurde ihm kaum ein anderer Moment zuteil, in dem er als Redner den Richtern ein schillernderes Schauspiel auf die Bühne stellen konnte als an den

---

[133] Cicero: *Pro Caelio* 49.
[134] Cicero: *Pro Caelio* 32. 57.
[135] Cicero: *Pro Caelio* 62.
[136] Cicero: *Pro Caelio* 62. 69.
[137] Plutarchus: *Cicero* 29.
[138] Quintilianus: *Institutio oratoria* 8, 6, 53.
[139] Cicero: *Pro Caelio* 1.
[140] Geffcken S. 38.

Megalensia des Jahres 56. Der Erfolg blieb Cicero natürlich nicht versagt, da sein Klient freigesprochen wurde; überdies bot der Prozess dem Redner eine glänzende Gelegenheit zu einer intellektuellen Rache an Clodius und Clodia und zur Vergeltung der Atrozitäten, die er erleiden und erdulden musste.

Show Trials of the Red Revolution – Political Trials and Public Opinion during the Finnish Revolution of 1918

Jukka Siro

1. Introduction

The topic of this publication is Law on Stage. In this article I will address that topic through the concept of a show trial and by examining the trials "staged" during the Finnish revolution of 1918. However, first it seems to be necessary to indentify what a show trial actually is.

The term show trial normally brings to mind, for example, the famous trials in the Soviet Union in the 1920's and 1930's, in which the so-called "enemies of the people" were executed after summary and thorough political proceedings. They were, indeed, show trials, especially with regard to the high-profile cases of former Bolshevik leaders, such as Grigory Zinovyev, Lev Kamenev and Nikolai Bukharin, which even attracted international attention.[1] In these trials legal procedure was clearly used for political ends, and this is the way Otto Kirchheimer definied the concept of a show trial.[2] Other examples can also be easily found.[3]

At worst, these and other famous show trials have been characterized by falsified evidence, discrimination against the defendant and fantastical charges. The sentences have been harsh, capital punishments as well as verdicts as in the cases mentioned above have often been decided before the proceedings had even begun. It is now clear that the accused had not usually committed the crimes they were prosecuted for. These show trials were usually deeply unfair and manifestly against the standards of due process of law. Their function was to hide the fact that the regime wanted to silence its real, imagined or potential opponents.

This has been the usual understanding of the concept of a show trial. However, although common, this is not the only way that justice and the courts have been used for political purposes. There are other

---

[1] See e. g. Conquest, Robert: The Great Terror – A Reassessment. Oxford University Press. Oxford 1990 and Radzinsky, Edvard: Stalin. Anchor Books. New York 1997.
[2] Kirchheimer, Otto: Political Justice. Princeton University Press. New Jersey 1961.
[3] See e. g. Evans, Richard J.: Rituals of Retribution. Oxford University Press. Oxford 1996, p. 822-828.

motives for staging trials than the desire to punish opponents in a quasi-judicial way.

I will highlight this with evidence from the Finnish Revolution and its courtrooms. The trials that took place during the Finnish Revolutionary Courts in 1918 were indeed sometimes show trials, but in a slightly different sense. I will show this by examining three cases that were of great public interest in revolutionary Finland and were therefore important for the public profile of the revolution.

The trials I will focus on are (1) the case of Eero Erkko, a famous liberal politician and editor-in-chief of Helsingin Sanomat, an influential liberal newspaper, (2) a trial of two arms smugglers, and eventually (3) the case concerning an alleged counterrevolutionary terrorist act that took place in a mansion just outside Helsinki. The explosion destroyed a cottage, killed four, injured thirteen and became big news in the capital.

I will try to show how differently political enemies were treated in these trials compared to those whose cases did not receive the same publicity. I will argue that these trials were used to promote the idea that the revolution did not represent a change for the worse in the field of law and judicial procedure. These trials were staged to appear humane and civilized in contrast to other cases, in which the revolutionaries did not always pay the same attention to the well-being of suspects or their procedural rights. They were, therefore, show trials, but their function was different to that of Stalin's purges. These cases were used for propaganda and to hide the fact that justice was not always administered as fairly. Through these trials I will try to show how the law was staged in Finland in 1918.

2. The Finnish Revolution of 1918

Finland had been an autonomous Grand Duchy in the Russian Empire since the Napoleonic Wars,[4] but it only became independent when the Empire started to disintegrate during the First World War. Finland

---

[4] Finland had relatively large autonomy. The Grand Duchy had its own Diet and a judicial system staffed exclusively by Finnish bureaucrats, and it was allowed to retain its old laws from the time the country was a part of Sweden. The administration and the judiciary were not under the direct control of the imperial authorities. Finland was also separated from the Russian Empire by having, for example, a customs barrier and, from 1860, its own currency.

declared independence on December 6th, 1917.[5] When the Russian authorities lost their power, there was no generally accepted police force or army, and it was not clear who ruled the country. Political turmoil and the emergence of Conservative and Socialist military organizations led to an escalation of violence. Among other issues, a food shortage, inflation, a lack of municipal democracy, the unsolved question of tenant farmers and the successful example of the Russian Bolsheviks[6] led to the spread of revolutionary ideas and radicalism. The Social Democratic Party, which represented the working class, radicalized and some of its supporters accepted violent means to correct social injustice.[7] After months of political turmoil, the party finally decided to take power at the end of January 1918. The revolution began on January 27th, 1918.

The success of the revolution was limited to southern Finland. The Conservative government maintained power in the other parts of the country.[8] The revolution led to a civil war between the revolutionaries (the 'Reds') and the governmental forces (the 'Whites'), just as in the Russian Civil War. However, unlike the Russian Revolution, the war in Finland was soon over as the Whites were militarily superior, owing mostly to German assistance.[9] Red Finland quickly collapsed and by May

---

[5] Mostly, Finland avoided the war. No battle took place in Finland, and Finland did not have to supply recruits to the Russian Army, as the Russian authorities considered the citizens of the Grand Duchy too unreliable for military service. However, the war meant, among other things, inflation, food shortage, and more draconian suppression of the political opposition.

[6] In Russia, the Bolsheviks had taken power in the October Revolution on November 7th, 1917.

[7] The Finnish Social Democratic Party was established in 1899. It was mostly supported by the growing working class both in the cities and in the countryside. Universal suffrage had been introduced in Finland in 1906, and by the 1910's the Social Democratic Party had nearly 50 per cent of the seats in the unicameral parliament. However, as the Tsar could still refuse to ratify the laws passed by the parliament, many Social Democrats begun to feel that Socialism could never be achieved by democratic, parliamentary means.

[8] The area controlled by the Whites was much larger, but Southern Finland was more densely populated and more industrialized. The four largest and most important cities of Helsinki, Viipuri, Turku, and Tampere were in the hands of the revolutionaries.

[9] The German Baltic Sea Division was sent to Finland to assist the Whites and to bring Finland under German influence. The arrival of the Division and the Whites' triumphant victory in the battle of Tampere at the beginning of April 1918 were the decisive moments of the war.

1918 the Whites controlled the whole country. The Civil War led to major casualties especially among the Reds.[10]

Between January and May 1918, southern Finland was in the hands of the revolutionaries. They were led by the Kansanvaltuuskunta, the People's Delegation. This body formed the revolutionary government and stood behind nearly all legislation and important political decisions. It did not, however, have complete control over the revolutionary army, the Red Guard. The Guard's task was to wage war and so it could not always understand the administrative demands of the revolutionary government. It was never clear who really lead the revolutionary struggle, the Guard or the civilian leaders in the People's Delegation. However, the Red Guard can be held responsible for the victims of the 'Red Terror', who numbered around 1,600.

It is not entirely clear what kind of society the Reds were striving for. The new regime was neither based on Soviets as in Russia, nor was private property nationalized, except on a very small scale. At least in public, the revolutionaries called for a highly democratic state.[11]

I will focus on the trials that took place in revolutionary Red territory during its three months of existence. The revolutionaries tried to replace the old state apparatus with a system that was loosely based on both the Soviet model and the old Finnish model. They abolished the old court system and replaced it with Revolutionary Courts, which were mostly presided over by reliable party members and local Socialist activists. These new Courts had a dual function. Their duty was both to adjudicate in normal criminal and civil matters and to punish those who had somehow opposed the Red regime. However, the Red Guard often interfered in the proceedings or did not deliver suspects to Court, preferring either

---

[10] In summary, the total number of victims of the civil war was nearly 40,000, nearly two per cent of the country's population at the time. Therefore, the Finnish Civil War can be regarded as one of the bloodiest internal conflicts of 20th century Europe.

[11] Most literature on the Finnish Civil War and its background has been written in Finnish or Swedish. References thereto can be found, for example, in the following English and German monographs: Alapuro, Risto: State and Revolution in Finland. University of California Press. Berkeley 1988; Upton, Anthony F.: The Finnish Revolution 1917–1918. University of Minnesota Press. Minneapolis 1980; Ylikangas, Heikki: Der Weg nach Tampere. Die Niederlage der Roten im finnischen Bürgerkrieg 1918. Berlin-Verlag Arno Spitz GmbH. Berlin 2002; Haase, Clemens-Peter: Die Neuformierung der finnischen Linken nach dem Bürgerkrieg. Westfälische Wilhelms-Universität Münster 1986; Jussila, Osmo, Hentilä, Seppo and Nevakivi, Jukka: From Grand Duchy to Modern State. A Political History of Finland since 1809. Hurst. London 1999.

to hold them as prisoners for an indefinite period of time or shoot them after a summary trial by court-martials that were illegal even by the revolutionaries' own standards. This rendered the relatively lenient and progressive practices of the Revolutionary Courts meaningless.[12]

3. The Trial of Eero Erkko

In the first case I will concentrate on the trial against Eero Erkko. The liberal politician was one of the most prominent opponents of the revolution and the editor-in-chief of Helsingin Sanomat at that time.[13] Helsingin Sanomat was one of the country's leading newspapers, with a circulation of over 70,000 copies, an impressive figure for Finland at that time.[14]

When the revolution began, most right-wing leaders fled Helsinki for northern Finland, where the government was still in power. Erkko did not. Foolishly, he chose to hide in Helsinki and wait for the city to be liberated. Due to the notorious incompetence of the revolutionary police, Erkko's strategy seemed, at first, successful. Although the newspaper had obviously been closed down by the Reds, he was able to live quite freely for several weeks. However, on March 1st, 1918 he was found and arrested.[15]

Erkko found himself in an extremely precarious situation following the first hearing at the headquarters of the Red Guard on March, 5th 1918. He was perhaps the most influential bourgeois leader ever to have been arrested by the revolutionaries. Helsingin Sanomat's anti-Socialist articles were well remembered. In the police report he was characterized as extremely dangerous and referred to as the leader of the Whites in the

---

[12] On the revolutionary judiciary see Siro, Jukka: Tuomiovalta kansalle. Finnish Lawyers' Association. Helsinki 2009.

[13] Eero Erkko (1860–1927) was not only the editor of the newspaper, but also its main shareholder and thus a considerably wealthy man. In addition, he was a notable politician. He was the chairman of the Young Finns Party, a liberal, centre-right party. During the 1910's the party had held 10–15 per cent of the seats in the parliament.

[14] Zetterberg, Seppo: Eero Erkko. Otava. Helsinki 2001, p. 473–501. Helsingin Sanomat was a liberal, moderately right-wing newspaper. Before independence, the publication of the paper had been suspended on numerous occasions as its strong advocacy of greater Finnish freedoms and even outright independence had irritated the Russian authorities. The paper was anti-Socialist and was thus hated by the revolutionaries.

[15] Zetterberg 2001, p. 501–507. Helsinki Revolutionary Court, Second Division, Case 58 (March 20th,1918), Finnish National Archive, VROSyA D a 2.

capital. Strict orders were given regarding his incarceration: no visitors, no correspondence and no newspapers.

If the Red Guard had had its way, Erkko would probably not have had many days to live. Another well-known politician and friend of Erkko, Antti Mikkola, had been shot immediately after his arrest a couple of weeks earlier. However, Mikkola was just an ordinary Member of Parliament, whereas Erkko had powerful friends both in Finland and abroad. In anticipation of the unfairness of the forthcoming proceedings, Erkko's friends and his wife Maissi adopted an extralegal defense strategy. By Finnish standards of the day, the Erkkos were a cosmopolitan couple, and they were able to contact their Swedish and British friends immediately.

In spite of the revolution, the Swedish embassy was still open, and it served as a secret refuge for the Whites of the city. In public, the Swedish ambassador remained neutral, but he did not hesitate to protest against the arrest of Swedish nationals or anything that he considered violating Swedish interests. The arrest of Erkko was clearly such a matter.

The strategy of contacting foreign powers proved effective. The Swedish ambassador learnt of the case and informed the revolutionary officials that he was following the proceedings. Normally, the revolutionaries paid attention to the views of foreign powers and respected their wishes, rightly seeing this as essential to their attempt to gain legitimacy for revolutionary rule, and Erkko's case was exception.

Sources do not reveal the content of the discussion between revolutionary leaders and the Swedish ambassador, but the results are known. Erkko was transferred from the crowded rooms of an old school building, where most prisoners were kept, to the relative luxury of a cell in a city prison. The restrictions were lifted. He was allowed to correspond with his wife and friends, and he could even consult a lawyer. Furthermore, Erkko was, as most men then, a dedicated smoker and suffered severely from the non-smoking regulations in the prison. In his case, an exception was made and he was allowed to receive cigars from a friend.

Erkko no longer needed to worry about the forthcoming trial. He was not tried in a kangaroo court but was given a proper trial. He was allowed to defend himself and to be assisted by a lawyer. Although he was found guilty, the trial was, in the end, a mere formality. The Revolutionary Court decided to postpone the sentence until more peaceful times, when further investigations could be made. The charges of having been in unauthorized contact with foreigners against his wife, Maissi Erkko, were also dropped. As a result, Mrs. Erkko was free for the rest of the war, while her husband was held in the safety of his cell in the city prison and released by the invading Germans a month later. In the post-war government, he served as a minister.

In this case we can see how the law was staged. From the beginning everybody knew that in the Erkko trial neither revolutionary nor pre-revolutionary laws would be followed. Due to the publicity surrounding the case, its result was known in advance, but it was important that everybody saw that the case was dealt with in a thorough manner and that the judiciary at least appeared to be independent. The verdict was a compromise between foreign pressure and the demands of the military situation. Its aim was to highlight the reasonableness and humanity of the new regime. Although both the authorities and the accused knew what the likely outcome would be, they played their parts in the trial and in doing so helped the revolutionaries to promote their rule in the eyes of the citizens. The Finnish public saw a show and learned a lesson: The enemies of the regime were punished fairly and only after a thorough investigation.

At the same time, the case was part in the revolutionaries' attempt to gain international recognition for their rule. In this case they demonstrated to the foreign powers that the rule of law was still respected and that the revolution had not led to chaos, terror or the damaging of the interests of neighboring countries. These were the lessons of this show.

4. The Trial of Johan Holmen and Nils Holst

The impact of foreign pressure was even more apparent in the case of two arms smugglers.[16] The Civil War had turned office clerk Johan Holmen and pharmacist Nils Holst into partisans of the White Army. They hid in Helsinki and attempted to collect guns and ammunition for the resistance movement and the White Army, which at that point was waging war hundreds of kilometers away.

---

[16] Helsinki Revolutionary Court, Second Division, Case 34 (March 12th, 1918) and Cases 39a and 39b (15th March 1918), Finnish National Archive, VapSA 23A.

Resistance in and around Helsinki was a major concern for the Red Guard and it paid special attention repressing it. Consequently, at the beginning of March 1918 Holmen and Holst were also arrested and put on trial at the Helsinki Revolutionary Court.

The charges were heavy. The men had been caught with machine guns, which were very rare in Finland at that time. The public prosecutor claimed that he had seldom encountered worse crime. To make matters worse, Holmen and Holst defended themselves with open defiance, admitting their guilt, but declaring the court and the Red government unfit to judge them.

It seemed like an open and shut case for the Court. However, it suddenly transpired that Holst was, in fact, a Swedish national. This cast a different light on the proceedings. The case was first postponed in order to verify if he really was a Swede. When sufficient evidence from the embassy was produced, the accused appeared to hear the verdict. Even though the court found the accused equally guilty, it sentenced Holmen to five years of penal labour and the confiscation of all his property, while Holst was only given a fine of 2,000 marks. Unlike his Finnish accomplice, he could walk away from court as free man. Even though there were no formal or legal obstacles, the Court could not take the risk of provoking the Swedes by giving Holst a fitting punishment for his crime.

5. The Case of the Tavastkulla Mansion

The third and most revealing case concerned an explosion that took place in the Tavastkulla mansion, close to Helsinki. Unlike the aforementioned cases, the audience of this show-trial was solely Finnish. The facts of the case were simple. Revolutionary soldiers had entered an annex of the mansion searching for hidden ammunition and, due to the cold, started to heat an oven.[17] However, as it turned out, the oven was filled with dynamite and the annex blew up, killing four soldiers and injuring thirteen.[18]

---

[17] It was suspected that owners of such mansions were hostile towards the Revolution and were hiding counterrevolutionary fighters and saboteurs. Although this was often the case, nothing indicates that there had been enemy soldiers or hidden ammunition in the Tavastkulla mansion.

[18] Helsinki Revolutionary Court, First Division, Cases 17, 18, 19 (February 11th, 1918) and

The Red Guard was certain that the explosion had been a terrorist trap. They claimed that the dynamite had been placed in the oven so as to detonate when the building was searched. Consequently, the owner of the mansion, Johan Pelin, his son, Onni Pelin, and the farm superintendent, Kalle Takala, were brought to the Revolutionary Court to be tried on four counts of murder. Obviously, the accused did not agree with this version of events, arguing quite reasonably that they could not be responsible for a tragically failed attempt to heat an oven.

The explosion and the trial were big news in revolutionary Finland, not only due to the size of the explosion, but also because the owner of the mansion, prime suspect Johan Pelin, was a wealthy businessman and in this capacity well-known in the city's bourgeois circles.[19] Consequently, the press and citizens alike keenly observed the ensuing trial.[20]

In this trial there were also certain unexpected events. Firstly, the trial was extraordinarily lengthy. Contrary to expectations, the alleged terrorists were not given a summary trial or shot on the spot by the Red Guard. Although the Revolutionary Courts usually reached a verdict in one session, this particular case needed five sessions and even then the Court was unable to decide on the guilt of the accused, claiming it needed more witnesses and more time for consideration.

The second peculiarity was the court's attitude to the defense attorneys. The accused were not only allowed to use a legal professional, Birger Nyman, but the Court also tolerated the attorney's unorthodox methods and disrespectful manner. For instance, in court Nyman was allowed to preach to the judges on the fact that he considered the revolutionary regime and the court in particular illegal and criminal. Moreover, in his written statement he accused court clerks of lack of professionalism and incompetence. He also annoyed the court by refusing to provide it with certain documents and by repeatedly requesting the adjournment of the trial on various pretexts. Despite these transgressions, Johan Pelin and the other accused were allowed to keep their legal counsel with Nyman continuing to defend them.

Case 41 (18th February 1918), Finnish National Archive, VROSyA D a 2; Helsinki Revolutionary Court, Second Division, Case 5 (March 2nd, 1918), Case 25 (March 9th, 1918) and Case 92 (2nd April 1918), Finnish National Archive, VROSyA D a 2.

[19] He traded in timber, Finland's number one export commodity at that time.

[20] See e. g. articles in the newspaper *Työmies* on February 4th 5th 12th and 19th, 1918.

A third point was the court's attention to detail. Despite the fact that the Revolutionary Courts were encouraged to ignore formalities, the court took a different approach in this case. The case was repeatedly adjourned, due, for example, to the lack of a few signatures with regard to the power of an attorney or because the victim's claims for damages were not specified meticulously enough.

Consequently, a verdict was never given. Such attention to detail slowed down the proceedings so much that the court had never had time to rule on whether the accused were guilty because by the sixth session, the German Baltic Sea Division had invaded Helsinki forcing court members to flee. The triumphant Whites released the accused from the city prison.

As we can see the proceedings differed markedly from other similar cases. Normally, such attention was not paid to the bureaucratic demands of pre-revolutionary law, especially not when the Red Guard could dictate the proceedings.

The court's attention to detail was not due to its reluctance to adjudicate in a case as big as this. Verdicts in other important cases were pursued to the bitter end. The difference was in the publicity of the case, which made the revolutionaries want to demonstrate the justice and decency of their new rule. This meant that they had to follow old practices more diligently and tolerate the insults of the defense attorney, making this case, in essence, a show trial.

6. Conclusions

The function of courts in a society is not only to grant justice to those who seek it. Courts also instruct the public on the law and demonstrate the power and authority of the state. In judging cases, courts set precedents for behaviour that is considered desirable and good. In doing so they also project an image of the regime to which they belong.[21] Trials are visible manifestations of state authority and citizens form their opinion of the regime partly on the basis of what happens in its court rooms. Thus court cases can be of vital importance for the state. This is particularly true when the legitimacy of the regime is under question.

---

[21] See e. g. Wood, Elizabeth A.: Performing Justice. Agitation Trials in Early Soviet Russia. Cornell University Press. Ithaca and London 2005.

Through the cases presented above, I attempted to show how law was staged during the Finnish Revolution. What was written in revolutionary or other legal documents or how the law was normally applied was not important. In these cases law and judicial procedure were used as a means to achieve certain political ends, which is Kirchheimer's definition of political justice. However, the results were unlike those traditionally attributed to show trials and political justice.[22] Although these were show trials, they were unlike those under Stalin in the Soviet Union. The point of the trials was not only to provide a legal basis for political decisions, but more importantly to spread propaganda and strengthen the legitimacy of the new rule. The accused were merely extras in these shows.

The trials I presented were deliberate attempts to influence public opinion by allowing the accused rights and benefits that others could only dream of. When there was sufficient public interest and scrutiny, as there was in these three cases, the revolutionaries had to pay attention to the correct procedure. They knew that the public would judge the Revolution, and particularly its judiciary, on the basis of these trials. Foreign opinion was particularly important. Consequently, the proceedings in high profile cases were necessarily different from the way the revolutionaries normally administered justice. Their function was to show the moral superiority of the new rule and hide the fact that justice was not always administered so fairly. Although cases like the ones I presented were few in number, due to the publicity they were more effective in spreading information about the new legal order than other cases that, however numerous, did not receive the same attention. Thus the public image of the revolutionary regime, both at home and abroad, was the ultimate reason for the outcome of these trials.

One may ask why the trials were staged in such a way. I think the answer is, firstly, because the Reds wanted to show the public that the new regime was not the tyranny it was portrayed to be in enemy propaganda. The revolutionary regime suffered from a lack of legitimacy and could not even rely on the support of the people in areas where the Red rule was the strongest, let alone in enemy-controlled parts of the country. The legitimacy of the Revolutionary Courts themselves was also extremely weak. In these circumstancesAgainst this background, it was im-

---

[22] See e. g. Kirchheimer 1961, p. 46 and Evans 1996, p. 821.

portant to show the public that moderation prevailed and that their worst fears were unfounded.

Furthermore, the fate of the revolution was ultimately dependent on the attitude of foreign powers. With the exception of then-weak Soviet Russia,[23] neighboring countries' attitudes were hostile towards the revolution and its new rulers. Indeed, Imperial Germany sided with the Whites and invaded Finland, and Sweden took advantage of the chaos in the country by attempting to annex the Åland Islands.[24] Even though the Reds could not expect the support of foreign powers, they hoped to keep them neutral.

In such a situation, the revolutionary regime needed to employ all the means at its disposal to entrench its position. The Reds knew that they were unable to achieve their aims by force of arms against a hostile population; terror tactics were not employed on a large scale until the regime began to disintegrate and the situation became desperate. Before that, judicial proceedings gave the revolutionaries a great opportunity to show the people what the Revolution meant in practice. As they had established a large number of Revolutionary Courts across the country, they could easily be used for such a purpose. This made the staging of trials an important and welcome option.

Through these cases, I attempted to highlight another way in which judicial proceedings were used for political purposes in history. In the trials presented above, law was indeed staged, to promote the idea of a regime that took a reasonable approach to even the most reprehensible and harmful crimes, examined cases thoroughly and gave the accused the chance of a fair trial. Although the reality differed from the revolutionaries' propaganda, their motives were clear. This was how law was staged during the Finnish Revolution of 1918.

---

[23] At the time, the Russian Civil War had only begun and the Bolsheviks were far from undisputed rulers of the country. Under these circumstances, the Finnish revolutionaries could not expect substantial help from their Russian comrades.

[24] The Åland Islands are situated in the Baltic Sea between Finland and Sweden. There was a bitter dispute about the status of the islands and their Swedish-speaking population between the two Nordic countries until the matter was solved by the League of Nations in 1921.

Recasting the role of slaves in the Roman economic theatre

Egbert Koops

1. Introduction

Any Roman living in the first century A.D. would have frequented one of Rome's three great theatres, or one of the many ramshackle temporary theatres.[1] Pantomimes in particular were wildly popular and the actors in such plays could excite great emotional attachment in their fanbase, only rivalled in our time by the *res gestae* of Hollywood's finest. Even if the actors themselves stood in a certain opprobrium and were occasionally banished by the senate for their baneful influence on public virtue, many emperors and senators attended the plays and sought the company of actors, or had their own private troupe to entertain house guests.[2] 'Had' is a descriptive term here, since the majority of actors were either slaves or former slaves who had been freed by their masters.[3] Therefore a Roman attending the theatre would have had his ticket collected by a slave, would have seen slaves perform on stage and cheered them afterwards, and would, indeed, have watched a play in which over half the cast portrayed slaves.[4] The social stratification of imperial Rome was mirrored on stage.

These slave-actors had great value. A well-trained troupe of comedians could easily fetch a good price: the law responded to this social reality by stipulating that if one of the slaves was damaged, or returned because of a defective sale, the value of the entire troupe had to be taken into

---

[1] Spruit, JE: De juridische en sociale positie van de Romeinse acteurs. Van Gorkum. Assen 1966, p. 58 nt. 7.

[2] Spruit (nt. 1) p. 88-89; Griffith, M: 'Telling the tale: a performing tradition from Homer to pantomime'. In: *The Cambridge companion to Greek and Roman theatre*, Cambridge University Press. Cambridge 2007, p. 32.

[3] Spruit (nt. 1) p. 160-164.

[4] Many examples can be found in the plays of Plautus (c.254-184 B.C.). Cf. Stace, C: 'The slaves of Plautus'. In: *Greece and Rome* (1968), Series II No. 15, p. 64-77; Beacham, RC: *The roman theatre and its audience*. Harvard University Press. Harvard 1991, p. 29-37; Goldberg, S: 'Comedy and society from Menander to Terence'. In: *The Cambridge companion to Greek and Roman theatre* (nt. 2), p. 134-135.

consideration.[5] Likewise, the value of a slave could increase dramatically by training him as an actor, which could be of importance with respect to calculating damages.[6] Plinius mentions the famous comic actor Roscius,[7] who earned 500,000 sesterces per year for his labours, or half the amount needed to enter the senatorial order. Actors were prized above all other professionals. Grammarians could be worth up to 700,000 sesterces, and one was hired to teach for 400,000 sesterces a year.[8] But Plinius immediately adds that these amounts were surpassed in his own time, and not by a little, by the actors who – and this is telling, since slaves could not formally own property[9] – *bought* their own freedom.[10] This implies that actors could amass tremendous fortunes and buy their liberty *although* they were slaves.

Precisely such a case is reported in both literary and legal sources.[11] Nero encouraged rioting between rival groups of pantomime fans, taking a secret pleasure in the strife. Matters got so much out of hand that the senate had to banish all actors from Italy in 56 A.D. for order to be restored. In the same year, the senate discussed the possibility of giving patrons the power to re-enslave their freedmen if these did not show due deference. It was contended that the legal position of ex-slaves was nearly equal to that of their former masters, whom they would taunt and provoke, and so the powers of patrons over their former slaves ought to be increased. This was countered with the practical consideration that such a rule would only widen the gap between masters and their (former) slaves,

---

[5] *Actio ex lege Aquilia*: Gai. 3,212; Dig. 9,2,22,1 (Paul.); *Actio redhibitoria*: Dig. 21,1,38,14 (Ulp.); Dig. 21,1,34,1 (Afric.).

[6] Dig. 19,1,43 (Paul.).

[7] Plin., *Nat. hist.* 7,39,128. This Q. Roscius Gallus (c.126-62 B.C.) befriended such eminent Romans as the general Catulus (Cic., *De nat. deor.* 1,28,79) and the dictator Sulla (Plut., *Sulla* 36,1). Cicero defended him in court in a well-known speech (*Pro Roscio comoedus*).

[8] Suet., *Gramm.* 3; Plin., *Nat. hist.* 7,39,128. A reasonable price for unqualified slaves seems to have been 800 to 2,400 sesterces: Buckland, WW: *The Roman law of slavery*. Cambridge University Press. Cambridge 1908 (repr. 1970), p. 8.

[9] Though slaves are recognized as human beings, what separates them from the free segment of society is the fact that they have no true legal standing. As a mere thing, a slave cannot sue or defend in a court of law, he has no patrimony and he can neither acquire rights nor obligations for himself. Cf. Buckland (nt. 8) p. 2-4.

[10] Plin., Nat. hist. 7,39,128: excessere hoc in nostro aevo, nec modice, histriones, sed hi libertatem suam mercati.

[11] Tac., *Ann.* 13,26-27; Cass. Dio, *Hist. rom.* 61,8; Dig. 12,4,3,5 (Ulp.). Cf. Spruit (nt. 1) p. 129-131; Beacham (nt. 4) p. 147.

who might then realize just how numerous they were.[12] Besides, masters had two ways of releasing a slave: either into full liberty or into bonded freedom[13], so that they only had themselves to blame if their rights as patrons were infringed. Nero was persuaded by the latter opinion and convinced the senate to keep things as they were. However, later that year his aunt Domitia was sued by the pantomime Paris, who had bought his freedom for 10,000 sesterces. Dig. 12,4,3,5 (Ulp.):

"What if a free man, serving me in good faith as a slave, has given me money to set him free and I have done so: it is asked whether he can sue me if it is later proven that he was free. And Julianus writes in the 11th book of his Digests that the freedman can reclaim. Neratius too mentions in his Notes that the pantomime Paris had reclaimed from Domitia, Nero's daughter,[14] the 10,000 sesterces which he had paid her to set him free, and that the judge had not investigated whether Domitia had accepted this money knowing he was free."[15]

Tacitus mentions that Paris who was one of Nero's most trusted advisors until he was put to death in 67 A.D.[16] used his influence with the emperor to obtain the verdict that he had been freeborn – much to the emperor's discredit, Tacitus adds. In consequence, Paris had always been free and the money paid for his release could be reclaimed since no adequate consideration had been provided. What is interesting about this case in the present context is not how political favour was used to influence the judge's decision, nor how it was later used by lawyers to construct a certain type of *condictio*;[17] but how it is assumed as a matter of course that slaves

---

[12] Tac., *Ann.* 13,27; Sen., *De clem.* 1,24,1.

[13] This corresponds to the difference between freedmen with Roman citizenship and freedmen without that quality, the Junian Latins: Gai. 1,16-22.

[14] In fact she was his aunt: Tac., *Ann.* 13,27. Cf. *PIR*² D 171.

[15] Si liber homo, qui bona fide serviebat, mihi pecuniam dederit, ut eum manumittam, et fecero: postea liber probatus an mihi condicere possit, quaeritur. Et Iulianus libro undecimo digestorum scribit competere manumisso repetitionem. Neratius etiam libro membranarum refert Paridem pantomimum a Domitia Neronis filia decem, quae ei pro libertate dederat, repetisse per iudicem nec fuisse quaesitum, an Domitia sciens liberum accepisset. All translations are by the author.

[16] Suet., *Nero* 54; Cass. Dio, *Hist. rom.* 63,18.

[17] See, on the condictio causa data causa non secuta, Kaser, M: Das römische Privatrecht I. CH Beck. München 1971, p. 597; Zimmermann, R: The law of obligations: Roman foundations of the civilian tradition. Juta. Cape Town 1992, p. 843-844 and p. 857-860.

can, in fact, buy their freedom from their masters with their own money. The question, then, is how. Not merely how lawyers, and the law, constructed the capacity of slaves to enter into contracts with their masters and pay for their liberty; but also how the existence of such a construction permeated economic life.

In this regard, the metaphor of 'law on stage' is particularly apt. Following the constructivist legal positivism of Hart[18], law is often seen as a 'social construction'[19], that is to say a social phenomenon rooted in the historical development of a particular society. The content of the law has an historical explanation: it was conceived thus, and not otherwise, by jurists bound within the social context of their time.[20] This means that legal rules are 'staged': the law is the stage on which actors conduct their daily business, a necessary backdrop to economic activity. Thus, reasoning backwards, one might presumably arrive at social forms by analyzing the historical content of the law. But there is another sense in which the law is 'on stage'. Once a legal rule has been established and clothed with authority, it becomes an actor itself, performing before a captive audience. *Lex imperat* – the law dictates reasonable behaviour. In this sense, legal history (understood here as the study of the content of historical rules by use of legal source materials) can illustrate not just how legal rules reflect social concerns, but also how they help to shape them.[21]

This paper deals with the role of slaves in the Roman economic theatre. As its starting point, it is submitted that cases of wealthy slaves buying their freedom were neither few nor exceptional, like Paris, but many. The reason is found in a particular legal institution, the *peculium*, which allowed slaves a limited mastery over earmarked funds (sometimes received as gifts, sometimes as venture capital) that technically belonged to the master, but

---

[18] Hart, HLA: *The concept of law*. Clarendon Press. Oxford 1961; Hart, HLA: *Law, liberty and morality*. Stanford University Press. Stanford 1963.

[19] As far as I can tell, Hart never employed this undistinguishing and now worn-out phrase. Over the last decade, books have appeared on the social construction of gender, trust, reality, therapy, climate change, Europe, the past, management, illness, Swedish neutrality, marketing, the ocean, literacy and serial homicide, to name but a few. Cf. Hacking, I: *The social construction of what?*. Harvard University Press. Harvard 1999. On Hart's social construction, see Green, L: 'The concept of law revisited'. In: *Michigan Law Review* (1996), No. 94, p. 1687-1717.

[20] I am not concerned here with the relationship between ideal law and positive law, or with the autonomy of law, but merely assert that the content of a legal system, historically speaking, is *by necessity* 'in causa positum'.

[21] Cf. Johnston, D: *Roman law in context*. Cambridge University Press. Cambridge 1999, p. 27-28.

which a slave might properly consider his own. The prevalence of this institution, so it is argued, has not been taken into account fully enough in economic histories of the Roman Empire. Legal historians, on the other hand, have often restricted themselves to analysis of the content of the rules surrounding the *peculium*, and have seldom tried to place it in its proper social and economic context. An attempt to do so, however, faces several methodological difficulties. Three problems are identified here: first, in how far the sources are textually accurate; second, to what extent legal materials represent actual practice; and third, to what extent these materials influenced everyday practice. As this paper's main concern is to explore the methodological problems offered by 'law on stage', with reference to the *peculium* of slaves, it would be too soon to draw conclusions on the importance of this institution for the Roman economy. But the examples offered may whet the appetite, and also show that the methodological problems identified here can be overcome.

2. The ancient economy

Contemporary perspectives on classical slave-owning societies tend to be skewed, due to historical experiences with the (predominantly African) chattel slavery of modern times. It is difficult to imagine millionaire slaves in control of their own funds, sometimes richer than the free senatorial elite, if one has the cotton plantations of the American South in mind. But in antiquity, slavery spanned an entire spectrum of positions. Slaves laboured in the silver mines and on the great estates, to be sure, but they were also employed as craftsmen, domestics and shopkeepers, not to mention as managers, moneylenders – and actors.[22] As Finley put it, though slaves "all fell within a single juridical category, the legal status masked the economic and social differentiations among them."[23]

To quote Finley here may seem a bit of a gambit. In his influential book, he argued that the ancient economies of Rome and Greece were distinctly different from the European economies of the 19th and 20th century. Neither society developed a functioning theory of economics. Many occupations, including those in manufacture and salaried employment, were deemed unfit for the aristocratic classes. A Roman senator was only

---

[22] Buckland (nt. 8) p. 6-7 and 73.
[23] Finley, MI: *The ancient economy.* University of California Press. Berkeley 1973 (repr. 1999), p. 64.

interested in the "trinity"[24] of land, cash and interest-bearing short-term loans. Though the acquisition of wealth was lauded, no member of the upper classes turned an eye towards profitability. Nor was there any need: excess funds were left to starve for lack of investment opportunities, or turned towards conspicuous consumption for political purposes. Absentee landlords had no reason to improve on traditional agricultural practices. Furthermore, the cost of transportation over land made market-driven production nearly impossible. Rome was never a workshop of the world, but funded its negative balance of trade by levees, taxes and rents – it was, in short, "parasitical"[25]. The reason for this, so Finley argued, was that economic activity was not so much governed by Adam Smith's 'invisible hand', but was in fact "embedded"[26] – staged, one could say – in a social and cultural context. The Roman elite were not motivated to maximize profit because "they were inhibited, as a group, by over-riding values"[27]. According to Finley, a wealthy Roman belonging to the senatorial order would not consider it befitting of his dignity to borrow money in order to invest it in a more profitable enterprise.

Though many of Finley's finer points have come under scrutiny over the last four decades, e.g. the relevance of transportation costs, the scale of market-driven trade, the notion of consumer cities and the role of professional bankers,[28] the embedded nature of the Roman economy seems to be the new orthodoxy.[29] But did the Roman elite have no interest in investment for profit because of over-riding values? They may have been inhibited in their own commercial activities, but they could very well invest their fortunes in trade or manufacture *indirectly*, that is to say: through their slaves. It is conceivable that senators and knights could afford a status-conscious attitude precisely because they quite literally *had* people earning

---

[24] Finley (nt. 23) p. 118.
[25] Finley (nt. 23) p. 125.
[26] Finley (nt. 23) p. 176.
[27] Finley (nt. 23) p. 60.
[28] See, for instance, Duncan-Jones, R: *Structure and scale in the Roman economy*. Cambridge University Press. Cambridge 1990, p. 7-29; Woolf, G: 'Regional productions in Early Roman Gaul'. In: *Economies beyond agriculture in the ancient world*. Routledge. London 2001, p. 49-64; Cerami, P; A Petrucci: *Diritto commerciale romano: profilo storico*. G Giappichelli. Turin 2010, p. 109-217.
[29] See Andreau, J: 'Twenty years after Moses I. Finley's The Ancient Economy'. In: *The ancient economy*. Edinburgh University Press. Edinburg 2002, p. 33-49.

their money for them. Here, the legal institution of the *peculium* comes to the fore.

The *peculium*, at law, is a fund which a master has earmarked for use by his slave. In doing so, the master's liability is limited to the amount conceded. Though the fund technically belongs to the master's estate, the slave is often (though not always) free to employ the *peculium* as he sees fit. If, by careful investment, he manages to turn a profit on the fund, he is entitled to purchase his freedom out of the *peculium*; unless it has been withdrawn previously, the remainder is paid out to the slave after his release. A wealthy Roman could appoint one of his slaves as a moneylender and bankroll him by conceding a *peculium*.[30] He could then step back, safe in the knowledge that his liability for the banking operation extended no further than the amount he had advanced and the profit he had made. He could do so, and this is an important point, *at arm's length*, without sullying his reputation by the pursuit of profit. Furthermore, perhaps unlike his master, the slave-banker had a real stake in turning a profit, since the *peculium* offered a road to freedom, and he had no reputation to lose. Let us say the banker's business flourished. Out of his *peculium*, that is to say his capital and earnings, he could afford to expand – even by buying other slaves and setting them up in franchise, each with his own *peculium*. The existence of slaves owning their own underslaves (*vicarii*) is well attested in legal sources. As Finley says, "a substantial part of the urban commercial, financial and industrial activity in Rome, in Italy, and wherever else in the empire Romans were active, was being carried on in this way … those who had a peculium were working independently, not only for their owners but also for themselves"[31].

Several important notions surface here. The first (economic) function, no doubt familiar to modern company lawyers, is that of limited liability for capital investment. The second (legal) function, more technical than the first, is the chance to participate in economic activity through agents, something which was made difficult by the law of contract if free citizens were employed. A third (social) function is the opportunity which the *peculium* offered slaves to better their position.[32] In this context, it is worth

---

[30] This is precisely what Titianus Primus had failed to do in the case reported in Dig. 14,5,8 (Paul.).
[31] Finley (nt. 21) p. 64.
[32] I refrain from using the imprecise term 'agency' here, which seems current among historians as an alternative to 'empowerment', since the term has a (different) legal meaning as well.

noting that one of the earliest references to the *peculium* is in a play by Plautus. The slave Stichus has fallen in love and realizes the costs he will have to incur. "The *peculium* is squandered, it is done!", he exclaims, to which his fellow slave answers "liberty has fled this slave!".[33] The examples of Paris and Roscius, mentioned at the beginning of this paper, show that things need not be so bleak. Plinius mentions the *dispensator* for the Armenian war, who was freed by Nero after paying the stupendous amount of 13 million sesterces.[34] There was no more equality among slaves than among the rest of society.

3. Economic history and legal history

Considering the useful part which the *peculium* could play in social, economic and legal life, one would expect to encounter it at every turn. And indeed, this expectation is borne out in the legal sources. In the Digests alone, the references to slaves with a *peculium*, to slaves owned by slaves (*vicarii*) and slaves owning slaves (*ordinarii*), to stewards (*dispensatores*), slaves operating as bankers or merchants, and slaves owned in joint venture (*societas*)[35] number well over a thousand. However, when an economic historian of Finley's stature remarks that business practices were "fixed" from the beginning of the third century B.C., referring to "the absence not only of the corporation, but even of the long-term partnership"[36], it has to be assumed that he is not properly 'staging the law'. It is of course well known that the juristic person as an economic entity was never developed under Roman law. But such a remark rests on a dogmatic assumption, namely that since the Romans had no companies, they had no company law either. The question is not whether the Romans ever developed company law, but which of their many legal institutions was functionally

---

[33] Plaut., *Stich.* 748: *Vapulat peculium, actum est. Fugit hoc libertas caput.* Also see Plaut., *Asin.* 540-541. Cf. Slater, NW: 'Slavery, authority and loyalty: the case of Syncerastus'. In: *Studien zu Plautus' Poenulus.* Günter Narr. Tübingen 2004, p. 295-297.

[34] Plin., *Nat. hist.* 7,39,129. He adds that the man himself was not worth that much, but that this was the total cost of the war. I take that to mean that the *dispensator* had some very lucrative dealings with the army.

[35] See, in particular, Di Porto, A: Impresa collettiva e schiavo 'manager' in Roma antica (II. sec. a.C. – II. sec. d.C.). A Giuffrè. Milan 1984.

[36] Finley (nt. 23) p. 144. This is surprising, since Finley worked as a research assistant in Roman law at Colombia during the 1930s.

comparable in Roman society.[37] The *peculium*, at least, warrants further investigation.

Of course, the intricacies of the *peculium* have often drawn the interest of legal historians. The seminal works are by Mandry,[38] closely followed by Buckland's important book. The subject was also studied by Micolier in France, Brinkhof in the Netherlands and Zeber in Poland.[39] In a very accessible book, Kirschenbaum analyzed it with regard to principal-agent relationships.[40] Comprehensive as some of these studies are, they often treat their topic mostly from a conceptual perspective: that is to say, they concern themselves with the faithful reconstruction and analysis of internally consistent legal rules. And truth be told, the complexities of the legal source materials lend themselves best to this type of analysis. However, if legal historians were to stop there, they would do historians in general a disservice.[41] The legal source materials are neglected in economic histories of the Roman Empire, precisely because their intricacies can be difficult to understand for historians without legal training.

It seems, however, that in the past ten years, more and more legal historians have turned to 'Roman law in context', to quote the title of a book by David Johnston.[42] Such explorations will undoubtedly continue, as historians are warming to the insights legal sources can provide, and jurists are gaining a better appreciation of materials outside the realm of 'law on the books', such as the tablets of moneylenders from Pompeii, and military

---

[37] This is akin to the 'functionalist' method typified by Zweigert, K; H. Kötz: *Introduction to comparative law*. Oxford University Press. Oxford 1998.

[38] Mandry, G: *Ueber Begriff und Wesen des Peculium*. H Laupp. Tübingen 1869; Mandry G: *Das Gemeine Familiengüterrecht I-II*. H. Laupp. Tübingen 1871-1876.

[39] Micolier, G: Pécule et capacité patrimoniale. Bosc. Lyon 1932; Brinkhof, JJ: Een studie over het peculium in het klassieke Romeinse recht. Krips Repro. Meppel 1978; I. Zeber, A study of the peculium of a slave in pre-classical and classical Roman law. Acta Universitatis Wratislaviensis. Wroclaw 1981.

[40] Kirschenbaum, A: Sons, slaves and freedmen in Roman commerce. Magnes Press. Jerusalem 1987. For an excellent treatment of institores, also see Aubert, JJ: Business managers in ancient Rome. A social and economic study of institores, 200 B.C. – A.D. 250. EJ Brill. Leiden 1994.

[41] They should, of course, go no further than sound reasoning allows. Aubert rightly cautions: "The temptation to write economic history on the basis of the hypothetical reconstruction of legal history can be very strong." Aubert, JJ: 'Conclusion: a historian's point of view'. In: *Speculum iuris. Roman law as a reflection of social and economic life in antiquity*. University of Michigan Press. Ann Arbor 2002, p. 189.

[42] Johnston (nt. 21). Also see Bürge, A: *Römisches Privatrecht. Rechtsdenken und gesellschaftliche Verankerung*. Wissenschaftliche Buchgesellschaft. Darmstadt 1999.

diplomas. Both disciplines have something to learn from each other and collaboration can be fruitful, as modern research on Roman banking practices shows.[43] With regard to the *peculium*, many questions remain to be asked.[44] To what extent were masters free to withdraw the *peculium*, both at law and in practice? If obligations between master and slave were not enforceable, what hope had a slave to persuade his unwilling master to sell? If the *peculium* was in fact paid out to a slave upon release, did that lead to the rise of a large middle class of freedmen and their descendants? And if not, does that say something about the prevalence of slaves with a *peculium*, or did the legal system develop other methods of protecting the interest of patrons?

4. Setting the scene: three methodological problems

Before any attempt can be made to answer such questions – and this paper is not the place to do so – some methodological problems have to be reckoned with that are peculiar to legal sources, as noted in the introduction to this paper. To stretch the metaphor of 'law on stage' a little further, it must be established that the actor is speaking the proper lines, that he is, in fact, performing in front of an audience, and that the audience is responding to his art. These may seem slight problems to many lawyers, who often take the social function of rules for granted, but for the historian they may present some difficulty.

A. Textual accuracy

The larger part of extant Roman legal writing, by far, was only codified between 529 and 533 A.D. under emperor Justinian. It is no secret that the law commissions made many modifications while drafting the codes. Some fragments were shortened, others changed to bring them into accord with Justinian's reform laws. The emperor himself had expressly authorized his

---

[43] Bürge, A: 'Fiktion und Wirklichkeit: Soziale und rechtliche Strukturen des römischen Bankwesens'. In: *ZSS* (1987), No. 104, p. 465-558; Andreau, J: *Banking and business in the Roman world*. Cambridge University Press. Cambridge 1999; Cerami, P and A Petrucci (nt. 28).
[44] Good starts are provided by Zwalve, WJ: 'Callistus's case: some legal aspects of Roman business activities'. In: *The transformation of economic life under the Roman empire*. JC Gieben. Amsterdam 2002, p. 116-127; and by Abatino, B; G Dari-Mattiacci; E Perotti: 'Early elements of the corporate form: depersonalization of business in ancient Rome'. In: *Amsterdam Center for Law and Economics Working Papers* (2009), No. 14, p. 1-36.

commissioners to make these changes.[45] There has been a time, at the beginning of the 20th century and well into the 1950s, when nearly every single word in the Digests and Codex came under suspicion, and legal historians had to wend their way through a minefield of interpolations, which were sometimes presumed to exist on spurious grounds; because the text did not fit the theory, or because the style of a fragment was thought unclassical.[46] Modern scholarship is far more generous to the surviving texts. The larger part is considered authentic and in fact, the burden of proof now rests with the scholar alleging text corruption. Certain criteria have become accepted to judge the likelihood of interpolation: reformatory laws, parallel texts and internal consistency are only part of the arsenal.[47]

An example may be of use here. In Dig. 17,2,63,9[48], Ulpian discusses a case in which two persons own one slave and one of them leaves the slave a bequest *without setting him free*. In this case, the other owner acquires the entire bequest. Should he share with the heir of his partner because of the joint venture? Several older jurists answered that he need not share, since he has not acquired the bequest on behalf of the joint venture, but through his own share in the slave. That reasoning is hardly convincing, since the heir to the testator could then also claim the bequest through his own share in the slave, who – it needs reminding – has not been freed; why would he resort to the action on joint venture? Besides, there are other places which show that Justinian fundamentally changed the law on this count.[49] As he describes it, the old rule was that if a co-owner released a slave, the other owner acquired full property so that the slave was still not free. This was changed to uphold the *favor libertatis*: the slave was free and the co-owner who had not freed the slave, but still lost his share, could sue for the damage. Now we can make sense of Ulpian's text. Under the old law, the slave would have been (implicitly) freed in the bequest, only to become full

---

[45] Const. *Deo auctore* 7.
[46] Wieacker, F: *Römische rechtsgeschichte I*. CH Beck. München 1988, p. 154-182; Johnston (nt. 21), p. 17-21.
[47] Ibid.
[48] Dig. 17,2,63,9 (Ulp.): Si servo communi legatum [sine libertate] unus ex dominis reliquit, hoc ad solum socium pertinet: an tamen pro socio iudicio communicari debeat cum herede socii, quaeritur. Et ait Iulianus Sextum Pomponium referre Sabinum respondentem non communicari, et posse hanc sententiam defendi Iulianus ait: non enim propter communionem hoc adquisitum est, sed ob suam partem, nec oportet id communicari, quod quis non propter societatem, sed propter suam partem adquisierit.
[49] Inst. 2,7,4; Cod. 7,7,1 (a. 530).

property of the co-owner who then acquired the entire bequest 'because of his share'. For this reason, the heir could not sue for the bequest on his own share (which had perished) and had to resort to the action on joint venture. But that made no sense under Justinian law, where the slave would have been freed in any case, so that the co-owner could never claim the bequest. Thus, the words *sine libertate* (and no more than that) had to be added,[50] which destroyed the meaning of the original text.

If Justinian's law commissioners, on the whole, showed a marked respect for the texts delivered to them, the question remains whether this was true for postclassical copyists. Again, the original 'Textstufenlehre' has largely given way to the assumption that all texts should be considered classical unless proven otherwise. For instance, there is a marked absence of rules surrounding the *peculium* in the Theodosian Code, whereas the Justinian Code has a large number of constitutions on this subject. Apparently, this legal institution was not in need of reform during the intervening centuries,[51] which makes it more likely that the pertinent fragments in the Digests were not altered either. To conclude: though texts may have been altered or corrupted in various cases, which need to be judged on their own merit, the assumption is warranted that the opinions of Rome's great jurists, as copied in the Digests, give a largely accurate portrayal of the state of the law in their own time.

B. Fact or fiction

A common problem with legal texts is that the jurists who produce these texts are often not interested in the particularities of a case. The law speaks generally. For this reason, lawyers often seek to extract a general rule from the facts of a case, which will serve in further instances. Though the Digests[52] are filled with case law, it is rare to find identifiable litigants or concrete circumstances: Maevius, Titius and the slave Stichus abound.[53] This opens up the argument, when citing legal sources, that these cases

---

[50] In this sense already Rotondi, G: *Scritti giuridici III.* U Hoepli. Milan 1922, p. 81 nt. 2.

[51] Aubert, JJ: 'An historian's point of view' (nt. 41), p. 190.

[52] This, of course, is different for the Codex. Many imperial rescripts are quite particular in the details. But the problem there is that by far the largest part of the material dates from Diocletian and beyond, that is to say, from a period when the empire had already gone into severe decline.

[53] Though it has to be noted that in some instances, Justinian's commissioners abbreviated the texts by removing personal details and inserting generic names instead. See Johnston (nt. 21), p. 25. The implication is that generic names don't necessarily correspond to fabricated cases.

never really happened but were dreamt up by the jurists to make a point. In a sense, this is true. Legal sources of this type cannot offer quantifiable proof: they are either too particular or, more often, too general. But in a far more important sense, the allegation is false. Law as a 'staged' social construct can only fulfil its purpose if it is not too far removed from reality. The highly practical Roman jurists, who never were very interested in theoretical notions, constantly had the practical needs of practical people before their eyes.[54] This is borne out by the research Schulz, Kunkel and Liebs have done into the sociology of Roman jurists.[55]

Furthermore, certain types of legal literature remain close to the actual cases which they cover. *Responsa* and *Digesta* often cover the facts of a case. Paul's *Decreta* deserve special mention since they offer a rare insight into the inner workings of the consilium of the emperor (Severus) and his praetorian prefect (Papinian): due to the abundance of detail, many of the litigants can be matched to figures known from other sources.[56] But even a technical book such as Ulpian's commentary on the Edict can yield information not available elsewhere; the case of Paris, covered in the introduction, was taken out of that commentary. It should also be noted that many of the greatest jurists, particularly Papinian, Paul and Ulpian, who between them cover most of the Digests, rose to great prominence in the imperial administration. As such, they had access to the collection of letters and rescripts stored in the imperial archives.[57]

If Ulpian quotes a letter by Marcus Aurelius and Lucius Verus to an Urbius Maximus,[58] to the effect that a slave who had bought himself with his own money was brought into such a state that he became free, he most likely had this letter right in front of him. The addition that a slave could not, of course, properly speaking own money; but that he is understood to have been bought with his own money, as long as he is not bought with the

---

[54] Johnston (nt. 21), p. 24.

[55] Schulz, F: Geschichte der römischen Rechtswissenschaft. H Böhlau. Weimar 1961; Kunkel, W; D Liebs: Die römischen Juristen. Herkunft und soziale Stellung. Böhlau. Cologne 2001.

[56] See, for example, Peachin, M: 'The case of the heiress Camilia Pia'. In: *Harvard studies in classical philology* (1994), No. 96, p. 301-341; Zwalve, WJ: 'Valerius Patruinus' case. Contracting in the name of the emperor'. In: *The representation and perception of Roman imperial power*. JC Gieben. Amsterdam 2003, p. 157-169.

[57] Even the public at large could consult (copies of) imperial sentences and the edicts of former praetors: Aul. Gell., *Noct. att.* 3,16,12 and 11,17,1.

[58] Dig. 40,1,4,pr. (Ulp.): Is qui suis nummis emitur epistula divorum fratrum ad Urbium Maximum in eam condicionem redigitur, ut libertatem adipiscatur.

money of the formal purchaser, is Ulpian's own.[59] One may quibble about the precise meaning of 'purchaser's money' in this context – for instance whether it would be enough to reimburse the purchaser out of the *peculium* afterwards – but it seems foolish to deny that Ulpian presented the state of the law in his time: that is to say, that slaves could purchase their freedom out of their 'own' money.

C. Influence and command

It is quite impossible to say, *a priori*, whether legal rules have any effect on human behaviour. They probably do, but probably not to the extent lawmakers would like. People still run traffic lights and speed on the highway – to assume Romans were any different would be absurd. That said, the law does, in fact, command people to certain rational behaviour. This is obvious in public law (including criminal law), but also in private law it does no good to have different expectations of the legal content of a contract of sale, for instance. What these truisms mean, in practice, is that legal sources will never suffice to construct economic histories on their own, for the simple reason that people may not have followed the law as it stood during their time. One cannot point to the many *leges*, senatusconsults, and constitutions covering the different classes of freedmen and their obligations towards their patrons[60] – clearly a social concern of the greatest order, as the passage from Tacitus discussed in the introduction shows – and say that the emperors continuously influenced the social stratification. Perhaps the actors were shouting all the louder because the theatre was empty, to employ that metaphor one more time.

But it is also possible to exaggerate. A rescript had an immediate effect, in the sense that it decided a legal dispute for the parties involved. The same is true for an imperial *decretum*. And even if we cannot establish the precise relation between cause and effect, between 'law on stage' and 'staged law', it is safe to say that Rome was full of amateur lawyers who loved to litigate. This implies some knowledge of the law – a fact confirmed by the many legal tangles discussed in non-legal, for instance literary documents – and also some access to the courts. Of course people in such a society would regulate their economic activity by their expec-

---

[59] Dig. 40,1,4,1 (Ulp.): Et primo quidem nummis suis non proprie videtur emptus dici, cum suos nummos servus habere non possit: verum coniventibus oculis credendum est suis nummis eum redemptum, cum non nummis eius, qui eum redemit, comparatur.
[60] Gai. 1,23-34.

tations of legal forms. It is sufficient to show that the legal framework offered an opportunity for relatively safe, clean, capital investment through the *peculium*. Since the law mirrors societal values, it is at least possible that this particular form was used in practice. Considering the abundance of references to the *peculium*, this becomes highly probable. Quantifiable or even qualitative proof, however, will have to come from different fields: from epigraphical, archaeological, and literary sources.

Julian notes, in his commentary on Minicius Natalis, that a freedman pantomime should offer his services to his former master free of charge.[61] Not only that, but he should also entertain his patron's friends, much like a freed physician ought to treat his patron's friends at his request. The reasoning is instructive: a patron should not need to organize parties, or be ill all the time, to avail himself of the services of his freedman. Likewise, a Roman citizen, freedman, freeborn or slave need not turn to theatricals to fulfil his role on law's stage: the law was there as needed.

---

[61] Dig. 38,1,27 (Iul.).

Kapitel II
„Symbole im Recht"

Die Historizität der Autorität oder: Des Verfassungsrichters neue Robe*

Sebastian Felz

1. Einleitung

Das Bundesverfassungsgericht (BVerfG) ist das einzige „Verfassungsorgan", dessen Mitglieder eine Amtstracht tragen. In den Schlussvorschriften der Geschäftsordnung des BVerfG heißt es lapidar zu den Roben der Karlsruher Verfassungsrichter: „Die Richter tragen in der mündlichen Verhandlung eine Robe mit Barett" (§ 64 BVerfG-GO). Hinter dieser knappen Vorschrift verbirgt sich aber – so die These – ein Teil der Erfolgsgeschichte des höchsten deutschen Gerichts, welche in der Nachkriegszeit in dieser Gestalt keiner anderen Verfassungsinstitution beschieden war und – so beklagt es der ehemalige Verfassungsrichter Dieter Grimm – auch noch nicht seinen Historiographen gefunden hat.[1]

Nach Carlo Schmid sollte das BVerfG „ein mächtiger Pfeiler im Bau der Bundesrepublik" sein.[2] Das Fundament dafür wurde in den Autoritätskämpfen der 1950er Jahre gelegt, deren für das Karlsruher Gericht siegreicher Verlauf sich in den duchesse-schwerroten[3] Roben[4] symbolisiert.

---

* Für wertvolle Hinweise bedanke ich mich bei Frau RiBVerfG a. D. Dr. Christine Hohmann-Dennhardt und Herrn Professor Dr. Fabian Wittreck (Münster).

[1] Zilcke, Andreas: Karlsruher Black Box. Zum Jubiläum der C. F. von Siemens Stiftung: Dieter Grimm wirft den Zeithistorikern vor, das Verfassungsgericht zu ignorieren. In: Süddeutsche Zeitung (12./13. Mai 2010) Nr. 108, S. 21; allgemeiner: Grimm, Dieter: Die Bedeutung des Rechts in der Gesellschaftsgeschichte. Eine Anfrage. In: Nolte, Paul u. a. (Hrsg.): Perspektiven der Gesellschaftsgeschichte, München 2000, S. 47-57; vgl. aber zur „deutschen Frage": Grigoleit, Klaus Joachim: Bundesverfassungsgericht und deutsche Frage, Tübingen 2004 (Jus Publicum. Beiträge zum Öffentlichen Recht, Band 108) und jetzt: Wehler, Hans-Ulrich: Deutsche Gesellschaftsgeschichte. Fünfter Band. Bundesrepublik und DDR 1949-1990, München 2008, S. 6 und 236-239.

[2] Schiffers, Reinhard: „Ein mächtiger Pfeiler im Bau der Bundesrepublik". Das Gesetz über das Bundesverfassungsgericht vom 12. März 1951. In: Vierteljahrshefte für Zeitgeschichte (1984) 32, S. 66-102.

[3] Laut Brockhaus (2006) bedeutet „duchesse", daß der dichte, glänzende, atlasbindiger Kleider- oder Futterstoff aus Seide besteht und stranggefärbt wird (Band 7, S. 335).

[4] Vgl. dazu: Malorny, Michael: Warum sind die Roben rot? In: Berliner Anwaltsblatt (1993),

Weil die legislative Arbeit am Bundesverfassungsgerichtsgesetz fast zwei Jahre in Anspruch nahm, hat sich das Verfassungsgericht erst im September 1951 als letztes Verfassungsorgan der Bundesrepublik konstituiert. Das Karlsruher Gericht sollte dann in mancher Hinsicht das bedeutendste und für die Bonner Republik wohl signifikanteste Verfassungsorgan werden.[5] Es entwickelte sich eine Verfassungsgerichtsbarkeit, die zu einem Vorbild für die höchsten Gerichte anderer Nationen wurde und in ihrer Kompetenzfülle und ihren Gerichtsbefugnissen einzigartig ist:

„1949, beim Inkrafttreten des Grundgesetzes, bestand das deutsche Verfassungsrecht aus 146 Artikeln; heute, 40 Jahre danach, besteht es aus beiläufig 15-16000 Druckseiten verfassungsrichterlicher Judikate" (Roman Herzog).[6]

Die bundesrepublikanische Verfassungsgerichtsbarkeit wurde konzipiert als Gegenentwurf zu seinem Vorgänger, dem Weimarer Staatsgerichtshof.[7] Diesem Gericht und seiner Rolle im Verfahren des so genannten „Preußenschlages"[8] wurde eine Mitschuld am Scheitern der ersten deutschen Republik gegeben. Die neue Institution sollte sowohl den Staat vor einer ungezügelten Massendemokratie schützen als auch den Bürger vor dem totalitären Zugriff des Staates.[9]

Unter der Adresse „Schlossbezirk 3, 76131 Karlsruhe" können Maßnahmen der öffentlichen Gewalt mit der Verfassungsbeschwerde gerügt, Regierungen und Parlament im Organstreitverfahren oder Normenkon-

---

S. 350-352.

[5] Kielmannsegg, Peter Graf: Nach der Katastrophe. Eine Geschichte des geteilten Deutschland, Berlin 2000 (Siedler Deutsche Geschichte), S. 274ff.; Kommers, Donald P.: Judical Politics in West Germany. A Study of the Federal Constitutional Court, Beverly Hills 1976, S. 69-113; Ders.; Miller, Russell A.: Das Bundesverfassungsgericht. Procedure, Practice and Policy of the German Federal Constitutional Court. In: The Journal of Comparative Law 3 (2008), S. 194-211.

[6] Zit. nach Schlaich, Klaus; Korioth, Stefan: Das Bundesverfassungsgericht. Stellung, Verfahren, Entscheidungen, München [8]2010. (Juristische Kurz-Lehrbücher), Rn. 550.

[7] Schiffers (wie in 2), S. 79.

[8] Vgl. zum „Preußenschlag": Fricke, Carsten: Zur Kritik an der Staats- und Verfassungsgerichtsbarkeit im verfassungsstaatlichen Deutschland. Geschichte und Gegenwart, Frankfurt/M. 1995, S. 126ff.

[9] Vgl. auch die Spiegelserie: „Det ham wir uns so nich vorjestellt". In: Der Spiegel 44 (1978), S. 39-57; Der Spiegel 45 (1978), S. 71-89; Der Spiegel 46 (1978), S. 84-98; Der Spiegel 47 (1978), S. 78-98.

trollverfahren von berechtigten Verfassungsorganen kontrolliert, Parteien verboten, Bundespräsidenten oder Richter angeklagt und einstweiliger Rechtsschutz gesucht werden.[10]

Etwa 5.000 Verfassungsbeschwerden gehen jährlich ein, von denen über 90 Prozent bereits in der Vorprüfung der Kammern, welche mit drei Richtern besetzt sind, scheitern. In den ersten 50 Jahren waren es fast 130.000 Verfassungsbeschwerden.[11] Nur 3.000 hatten Erfolg, was nicht einmal zweieinhalb Prozent entspricht. Auch wenn die Verfassungsrichter notorisch über die Überlastung klagen, zeugt die Klagenflut von der Akzeptanz der Institution.[12]

Das BVerfG erkämpfte sich gegenüber den anderen Verfassungssubjekten sowie dem Bundesgerichtshof und der deutschen Staatslehre[13] seinen Rang „nicht nur als Spitze der rechtsprechenden Gewalt und in dieser Eigenschaft als Hüter und Garant der Verfassung, sondern zugleich auch als ein mit höchster Autorität ausgestattetes Verfassungsorgan", welches „politisch wie verfassungsrechtlich dem Bundestag, dem Bundesrat, der Bundesregierung und dem Bundespräsidenten an die Seite gestellt werden muss".[14]

In den ersten zehn Jahren kamen viele der wichtigsten Richtersprüche aus Karlsruhe, welche die Bundesrepublik wie auch das „Verfassungsorgan" BVerfG prägen und festigen sollten. Die junge Demokratie zeigte sich wehrhaft in den Parteiverbotsverfahren gegen die Sozialistische Reichspartei (SRP)[15] sowie gegen die Kommunistische Partei Deutschlands

---

[10] Klein, Hans Hugo: Das Bundesverfassungsgericht, In: Schwarz, Hans-Peter (Hrsg.): Die Bundesrepublik Deutschland. Eine Bilanz nach 60 Jahren, Köln u. a. 2008, S. 319-332.

[11] Säcker, Horst: Das Bundesverfassungsgericht, Bonn 2003, S. 80.

[12] Roellecke, Gerd: Roma locuta – Zum 50-jährigen Bestehen des BVerfG, in: Neue Juristische Wochenschrift 2001, S. 2924-2931, hier: S. 2924; Kneip, Sascha: Verfassungsgerichte als demokratische Akteure. Der Beitrag des Bundesverfassungsgerichts zur Qualität der bundesdeutschen Demokratie, Baden-Baden 2009.

[13] Schlink, Bernhard: Die Entthronung der Staatsrechtswissenschaft durch die Verfassungsgerichtsbarkeit. In: Der Staat 28 (1990), S. 161-172; Baldus, Manfred: Frühe Machtkämpfe. Ein Versuch über die historischen Gründe der Autorität des Bundesverfassungsgerichts. In: Henne, Thomas; Riedlinger, Thomas: Das Lüth-Urteil aus (rechts-) historischer Perspektive. Die Konflikte um Veit Harlan und die Grundrechtsjudikatur des Bundesverfassungsgerichts, Berlin 2005, S. 237-248.

[14] Leibholz, Gerhard: Bericht des Berichterstatters an das Plenum des BVerfG zur Statusfrage. In: Jahrbuch des öffentlichen Rechts (1957) 6, S. 109-221, hier: S. 127f.; vgl. zur Wirkung auch: Detjen, Marion; Detjen, Stephan; Steinbeis, Maximilian: Die Deutschen und das Grundgesetz – Geschichte und Grenzen unserer Verfassung, München 2009.

[15] BVerfGE 2, 1 (SRP).

(KPD)[16]; das Gericht selbst zeigte sich standhaft gegen die „Hohe Politik" in den Entscheidungen, welche die Europäische Verteidigungsgemeinschaft (EVG) und die Wiederbewaffnung betrafen[17]; es half mit bei der Vergangenheitsbewältigung, als es sich für das Erlöschen der Beamtenverhältnisse aussprach und setzte sich damit von Bundesgerichtshof und der Vereinigung der deutschen Staatsrechtslehrer ab[18]; es formte die allgemeine Handlungsfreiheit[19] sowie die Drittwirkung der Grundrechte[20] aus. Die Beschränkung der Berufsfreiheit wurde durch die „Drei-Stufen-Theorie" ausgeformt[21] und Bundeskanzler Konrad Adenauer (CDU) wurde schließlich durch das 1. Rundfunk-Urteil untersagt, Einfluss auf die Programmgestaltung der öffentlich-rechtlichen Rundfunkanstalten zu nehmen und die Rundfunkfreiheit zu beschränken[22].

So konnte dann der Göttinger Staatsrechtslehrer Rudolf Smend mit Fug und Recht zum zehnjährigen Jubiläum des Gerichts 1961 konstatieren, daß „das Grundgesetz nunmehr praktisch so [gelte], wie es das Bundesverfassungsgericht auslegt".[23]

Die Ausdeutung dieser Judikatur entspricht der klassischen Verfassungsgeschichtsschreibung. Daß jeder Verfassungspraxis eine symbolische Dimension eigen ist, hat Barbara Stollberg-Rilinger für das Alte Reich in einem „große[n] Wurf und Meilenstein der frühneuzeitlichen Verfassungshistoriografie"[24] gezeigt.[25] Der Gerichtsort Karlsruhe, die Architektur des Gerichtsgebäudes[26] sowie die hier zu behandelnden

---

[16] BVerfGE 5, 85 (KPD).

[17] BVerfGE 2, 79 (Wiederbewaffnung).

[18] BVerfGE 3, 58 (Beamtenurteil); dagegen: BGHZ 13, 265 sowie Naumann, Richard: Die Berufsbeamten und die Staatskrisen. In: Veröffentlichungen der Vereinigung der deutschen Staatsrechtslehrer (1954) 13, S. 88-118. Über die „Grenzen der Verfassungsgerichtsbarkeit" debattierte die Vereinigung (Berichterstatter Erich Kaufmann und Martin Drath) schon 1950 (Veröffentlichungen der Vereinigung der deutschen Staatsrechtslehrer 9 (1952), S. 1-133).

[19] BVerfGE 6, 32 (Elfes).

[20] BVerfGE 7, 198 (Lüth).

[21] BVerfGE 7, 377 (Apothekenurteil).

[22] BVerfGE 12, 205 (Deutschland-Fernsehen).

[23] Smend, Rudolf: Das Bundesverfassungsgericht. In: Ders.: Staatsrechtliche Abhandlungen und andere Aufsätze, Berlin ³1994, S. 581-593, hier: S. 582.

[24] Zimmermann, Reinhard: Juristische Bücher des Jahres – Eine Leseempfehlung. In: Neue Juristische Wochenschrift, Heft 50, 2009, S. 3626-3632, hier: S. 3627f.

[25] Vgl. Stollberg-Rilinger, Barbara: Des Kaisers alte Kleider. Verfassungsgeschichte und Symbolsprache des Alten Reiches, München 2008.

[26] Bürklin, Thomas: Bauen als (demokratische) Sinnstiftung – Das Gebäude des Bundesverfassungsgericht als ,Staatsbau'. In: Ooyen, Robert Chr. van; Möllers, Martin H. W. (Hrsg.): Das

Richterroben[27] sind mögliche Themen einer solchen neuen Perspektive auf die Verfassungsgeschichte, auch in der Moderne. Die „Inszenierung des Rechts" zu untersuchen, bedeutet „Mythos", „Ritual" und „Symbol" als Dimensionen des Rechts, das sich nur auf den ersten Blick in seiner rationalen, formal gesatzten, schriftlichen Autonomie erschöpft, anzuerkennen. Jede institutionelle Ordnung bedarf der Verstetigung durch symbolisch-rituelle Verkörperungen, welche auf kollektiven Sinnzuschreibungen und sozialen Konstruktionen beruhen.[28]

„Die Verfassung", so schrieb Murray Edelman, der die Symbolforschung für die politische Wissenschaft operationalisiert hat, „wird zum treffenden und gefeierten Ausdruck der komplexen und zweideutigen Einstellung des Menschen zu seinen Mitmenschen: des Wunsches, Besitz und Macht auf Kosten anderer auszuweiten; der Angst, der mächtigen Position anderer und der Ausbeutung durch sie anheimzufallen; und des Bedürfnisses nach einem umfassenden Prinzip, das in diesen explosiven Interessenkonflikt Stabilität und Berechenbarkeit bringt".[29]

Zum „Hüter" dieses Prinzips ist das BVerfG historisch geworden.[30] Die Schiedsrichterfunktion in diesem explosiven Interessenkonflikt war im Grundgesetz angedeutet, mußte aber in der Praxis ausgedeutet werden. Die Institutionalisierung der Entscheidungspraxis zwischen Verfassungsorganen wurde in den „Autoritätskämpfen" zwischen den „Kombattanten" nach den Regeln der Verfassung ausgetragen. Dieses in-Szene-Setzen der Verfassung ermöglichte dem Verfassungsgericht, eigenmächtig seinen Status zu erklären und durch die anderen Verfassungsorgane seine „Autorität" anerkennen zu lassen. Diese Anerkennung der Autorität und der Autonomie des BVerfG wird durch die selbst gewählten Richterroben symbolisiert, deren Geschichte im Folgenden nachgezeichnet werden soll.

Bundesverfassungsgericht im politischen System, Wiesbaden 2006, S. 17-34.

[27] Vgl. zur symbolischen Dimension der Richterrobe auch die Beiträge von Thomas Glyn Watkin und Antoine Garapon in Schulze, Reiner (Hrsg.): Rechtssymbolik und Wertevermittlung, Berlin 2004 (Schriften zur Europäischen Rechts- und Verfassungsgeschichte, Band 47).

[28] Stollberg-Rilinger (wie in 25), S. 9.

[29] Edelman, Murray: Politik als Ritual. Die symbolische Funktion staatlicher Institutionen und politischen Handelns, Frankfurt am Main/New York ³2005 [Englisch zuerst: 1964], S. 15f.

[30] „Die Allzuständigkeit des BVerfG hat sich das Gericht selbst gegen den Text des Grundgesetzes geschaffen", so Roellecke, Gerd: Konstruktionsfehler der Weimarer Verfassung. In: Der Staat 1996 (35), S. 599-611, hier: S. 611.

2. Die Autoritätskämpfe des Bundesverfassungsgerichts

Am 25. Juni 1950 überschritten die Truppen des kommunistisch regierten Nordkorea den 36. Breitengrad und eröffneten damit ihren Angriff auf das von amerikanischen Truppen eben erst geräumte Südkorea.[31] Ein heißer Konflikt im Kalten Krieg. Bundeskanzler Adenauer nutzte die Situation, um die Westbindung voranzutreiben, und die junge Bundesrepublik trat einer Vielzahl von supranationalen Organisationen bei. Ein sehr wichtiger Schritt war am 26./27. Mai 1952 die Unterzeichnung der Verträge für eine Europäische Verteidigungsgemeinschaft[32] (EVG) und des Deutschlandvertrages, welche den zukünftigen Weg ebnen sollten, der Bundesrepublik die staatliche Souveränität wieder einzuräumen.[33]

Schon im Januar 1952 hatte die SPD als Oppositionspartei, welche die Politik der Demilitarisierung und Pazifizierung befürwortete, in einem vorbeugenden Normenkontrollantrag Karlsruhe aufgefordert, die Zustimmungsgesetze zur Wiederbewaffnung Deutschlands als verfassungswidrig zu beurteilen. Eine einstweilige Anordnung lehnte das Gericht aber ab.[34]

Am 10. Juni 1952 beantragte Bundespräsident Theodor Heuss auf Veranlassung der Bundesregierung die Erstattung eines Gutachtens durch das Plenum des BVerfG gemäß § 97 BVerfGG alte Fassung. Das vordergründige Motiv für diesen Schritt war seitens der Adenauer-Regierung die Sorge um einen negativen Ausgang des durch die Opposition angestrengten Normenkontrollverfahrens vor dem ersten Senat, der mehrheitlich mit vermeintlich sozialdemokratisch-orientierten Richtern

---

[31] Görtemaker, Manfred: Geschichte der Bundesrepublik Deutschland. Von der Gründung bis zur Gegenwart, München 1999, S. 294 und Schubert, Klaus von: Wiederbewaffnung und Westintegration. Die innere Auseinandersetzung um die militärische und außenpolitische Orientierung der Bundesrepublik 1950-1952, Stuttgart 1970 (Schriftenreihe der Vierteljahrshefte für Zeitgeschichte, Band 20).

[32] Heydte, Friedrich August Freiherr von der; Wanke, Walter (Hrsg.): Das Vertragswerk zur europäischen Verteidigungsgemeinschaft. Einführung, Erläuterung, Kritik, München 1952 (Schriftenreihe der Gesellschaft für Wehrkunde, München) sowie die Dokumentation: Veröffentlichungen des Instituts für Staatslehre und Politik e. V.: Der Kampf um den Wehrbeitrag. 1. Halbband. Die Feststellungsklage, München 1952; 2. Halbband. Das Gutachtenverfahren (30.7.-15.12.1952), München 1953; Ergänzungsband, München 1958.

[33] Ipsen, Jörn: Der Staat der Mitte. Verfassungsgeschichte der Bundesrepublik Deutschland, München 2009, S. 74.

[34] BVerfGE 1, 281.

besetzt war. Das Gutachten des parteipolitisch in etwa gleichgewichteten Plenums sollte der Entscheidung des ersten Senats zuvorkommen.[35]

Am 27. Juni 1952 veröffentlichte das BVerfG die „Status-Denkschrift",[36] in der das BVerfG sein Selbstverständnis als unabhängiges Verfassungsorgan zum Ausdruck brachte. Am 30. Juni 1952 wies der erste Senat den Normenkontrollantrag der Opposition als unzulässig ab: Ein solcher Antrag könne erst gestellt werden, wenn das Zustimmungsgesetz vom Bundestag beschlossen sei. Eine vorbeugende Normenkontrolle kenne das Grundgesetz nicht.[37] Daraufhin beriet der Bundestag die Verträge.[38]

Im November 1952 drohte man aus Regierungskreisen dem BVerfG mit der Beschneidung seiner Macht; im Dezember 1952 passierten die Verträge bei aufgeheizter Atmosphäre mit den Stimmen der Koalition den Bundestag. Im selben Monat stellte die Bundesregierung in einem Organstreitverfahren den wohl kuriosesten Antrag der Gerichtsgeschichte: nämlich auf Feststellung eines Grundgesetzverstoßes durch die Opposition, indem diese der Mehrheit des Bundestages verbiete, den EVG-Vertrag mit einfacher Mehrheit gemäß Artikel 42 II 1 GG zu verabschieden und auf einer Verfassungsänderung beharre.[39] Es handelte sich hierbei um einen Trick, um die Entscheidung über die Verträge dem mehrheitlich mit eher konservativen Richtern besetzten zweiten Senat zu übertragen.

Am 9. Dezember 1952 verkündete der Präsident des Gerichts, Hermann Höpker-Aschoff, daß das Gutachtenverfahren des Bundespräsidenten vor dem Organstreit der Regierungsfraktionen entschieden werden sollte und die Entscheidung, die das Plenum hinsichtlich der Verfassungsmäßigkeit der Verträge treffe, auch die einzelnen Senate binden werde. Damit war das taktische Manöver der Adenauer-Regierung gescheitert; der Bundeskanzler

---

[35] Hoffmann, Dierk: Das Bundesverfassungsgericht im politischen Kräftefeld der frühen Bundesrepublik, in: Historisches Jahrbuch (2000) 120, S. 227-273.

[36] Leibholz (wie in 14).

[37] BVerfGE 1, 396.

[38] Ipsen (wie in 33), S. 77.

[39] Wild, Michael: BVerfGE 2, 79 – Wiederbewaffnung III. BVerfG und „Hohe Politik" – Streit um das „letzte Wort" im politischen System der Bundesrepublik, in: Menzel, Jörg: Verfassungsrechtsprechung. Hundert Entscheidungen des Bundesverfassungsgerichts in Retrospektive, Tübingen 2000, S. 65-69, hier: S. 66.

und sein Justizminister kritisierten offiziell und inoffiziell die Karlsruher Richterschaft aufs Schärfste.[40]

Am 10. Dezember 1952 nahm Bundespräsident Heuss sein Gutachtenersuchen zurück; am 19. Dezember 1952 erklärte Bundeskanzler Adenauer nach einem Gespräch mit Höpker-Aschoff, daß die Bundesregierung „das Bundesverfassungsgericht als einen integralen Bestandteil des demokratischen Rechtsstaates" achten werde.[41] Am 07. März 1953 wies der Zweite Senat die Klage der Regierungsfraktionen mit der Begründung zurück, dass die Bundestagsmehrheit keine Antragsbefugnis besitze.[42]

Schließlich stellte die SPD-Opposition einen neuen – diesmal zulässigen – Normenkontrollantrag, auf , nachdem das Parlament die Verträge in dritter Lesung beschlossen hatte. Zu einer Entscheidung kam es allerdings nicht mehr, da die Adenauer-Regierung im September 1953 die absolute Mehrheit gewann und das Grundgesetz änderte. Diese Änderung erweiterte die alte Fassung des Artikel 73 Nr. 1 GG um eine Gesetzgebungskompetenz des Bundes für „die Verteidigung einschließlich des Schutzes der Zivilbevölkerung". Da eine solche Verfassungsänderung jedoch keine Rückwirkung entfaltete, wurde auch Artikel 79 Absatz 1 GG um die sogenannte „Klarstellungsklausel" ergänzt.[43]

Der Deutschlandvertrag wurde schließlich am 28. März 1954 vom Bundespräsidenten ratifiziert, während der EVG-Vertrag im August 1954 in der Französischen Nationalversammlung nicht angenommen wurde. Diese strategisch-juristischen Winkelzüge zwischen Bundesregierung und Bundestagsopposition blieben politisch nicht ohne Konsequenzen und hatte vor allem zur Folge, dass das Ansehen des BVerfG erheblich stieg, was zugleich den Grundstein für die Autoritätsgenese des Gerichts im Verfassungsleben legte. Deren Natur soll nun im folgenden Abschnitt untersucht werden.

---

[40] Wesel, Uwe: Der Gang nach Karlsruhe. Das BVerfG in der Geschichte der Bundesrepublik, München 2004, S. 69ff.
[41] Wild (wie in 39), S. 68.
[42] BVerfGE 2, 143.
[43] Ipsen (wie in 33), S. 80.

3. Die Autorität des Bundesverfassungsgerichts

Wo immer sich Menschen über einen längeren Zeitraum zu einer sozialen Organisation zusammenschließen, entstehen Beziehungen, die durch Macht- bzw. Autoritätsstrukturen geprägt sind.[44] Menschen erkennen sich nicht nur als Gleiche, sondern auch als Ungleiche an. Im sozialen Vergleich geht es nicht darum, zwischen Machtinhabern und Machtlosen zu differenzieren. Vielmehr steht die Auszeichnung von Autoritäten im Vordergrund, die sowohl die Autoritätszuschreibenden als auch die anderen Mitmenschen überragen. Wo es Macht gibt, findet sich auch Autorität – Autorität verstanden als anerkannte, geachtete Macht, die zugleich bewundert und gefürchtet wird.[45]

Autorität ist dabei eine Zuschreibung. Eine reine Selbstermächtigung zur Autorität funktioniert nicht. Entscheidend ist das Fremdbild der Anderen. Natürlich fällt es leichter, sich als Autorität zu etablieren, wenn man sich auch selbst als Autorität versteht und von seinem Rang überzeugt ist: Ohne entsprechendes Selbstbewusstsein und Ambitioniertheit wird kaum jemand Autorität erlangen.[46]

Blickt man auf die Autoritätskämpfe des Bundesverfassungsgerichts in seiner Anfangszeit im Streit um den EVG-Vertrag, so erfüllt auch das BVerfG diese Voraussetzungen. In der Status-Denkschrift wird eindeutig herausgestrichen, dass das Selbstverständnis der Karlsruher Richter davon getragen war, eine Autorität zu sein. Genauer gesagt: eine Autorität, die den Status eines Verfassungsorgans zu besitzt und dadurch zum „Hüter der Verfassung" bestellt ist. Es handelt sich hierbei aber auch nicht um eine alleinige „Selbstermächtigung", denn die Grundlagen für dieses Selbstverständnis des Verfassungsgerichts sind im Grundgesetz ebenso wie im Gesetz über das Bundesverfassungsgericht verankert.[47] Die Vorrangstellung kommt der Verfassungsgerichtsbarkeit nur aufgrund der herausgehobenen Stellung des Grundgesetzes im Normengefüge zu. Es ist eine von der Verfassung verliehene Stellung, die sich aber weder von selbst versteht

---

[44] Popitz, Heinrich: Phänomene der Macht, Tübingen ²1999, S. 104.
[45] Sofsky, Wolfgang; Paris, Rainer: Figurationen sozialer Macht. Autorität – Stellvertretung – Koalition, Frankfurt/M. 1994, S. 21.
[46] Brodocz, André: Die Macht der Judikative, Wiesbaden 2009, S. 142-177.
[47] Anders: Roellecke (wie in 30).

noch in ihren – politischen wie rechtlichen – Konsequenzen nicht unumkämpft war und ist.[48]

Hannah Arendt hat herausgearbeitet, dass in der Unterscheidung von Macht und Autorität, also *potestas* und *auctoritas*, ein wichtiger Geltungsfaktor für das Bestehen des Staatsganzen liegt. Am Beispiel der politischen Kultur des alten Roms verdeutlicht die Philosophin, dass unter *auctoritas*, welche sich vom Verb *augere*, also „vermehren" ableitet, die Verstetigung des Gründungsaktes und seiner Prinzipien zu verstehen sei.[49]

Damit wird auch eine symbolisch-kommunikative Perspektive auf die Autorität der Verfassungsgerichtsbarkeit freigelegt. Der Legitimitätsglauben moderner, demokratischer Gemeinwesen stützt sich nicht allein auf die rational gesatzten Gesetze, Institutionen und Verfahren. So wie die Verfassungsurkunde und die Verfassungsgerichtsbarkeit die Fundamente der politischen Ordnung aufbewahren, so finden sich in ihnen auch die Restbestände jener Deutungsmuster von Sakralität wieder, die politischen Gemeinwesen und ihren Verkörperungen in vormodernen Zeiten zugeschrieben wurden. Im Prozess der Sakralisierung hat sich der transzendente Charakter des Politischen vom Herrscher auf das Recht und seine Interpreten verschoben.[50]

Des Weiteren überragen Autoritäten stets mehrere untergeordnete Ebenen. Wenn dem BVerfG die Autorität des „Hüters der Verfassung"[51] zugesprochen wird, so folgt daraus, dass es kein oberstes Bundesgericht wie etwa der Bundesgerichtshof sein kann. Vielmehr folgt aus dem Status des Verfassungshüters, dass es über den anderen Gerichten angesiedelt sein muss. Hier wird auch deutlich, welcher Mechanismus sich hinter der Status-Denkschrift verbirgt. Die damaligen Verfassungsrichter schrieben der Institution der Verfassungsgerichtsbarkeit eine autoritäre Qualität zu, die gerade keine reine Selbstermächtigung von autoritäts- bzw. machtsüchtigen Richtern dokumentierte. Eine solche Anmaßung wäre am Widerstand der anderen Bundesrichter gescheitert.

---

[48] Vorländer, Hans: Deutungsmacht – Die Macht der Verfassungsgerichtsbarkeit. In: Ders. (Hrsg.): Die Deutungsmacht der Verfassungsgerichtsbarkeit, Wiesbaden 2006, S. 9-36, hier: S. 13.

[49] Arendt, Hannah: Was ist Autorität? In: Dies.: Zwischen Vergangenheit und Zukunft. Übungen im politischen Denken I, München 1994, S. 188.

[50] Vorländer (wie in 47), S. 21.

[51] Vgl. zu diesem Topos von Carl Schmitt und seiner Wirkungsgeschichte: Müller, Jan-Werner: Ein gefährlicher Geist, Darmstadt 2007, S. 75f.

Insofern explizierten die Verfassungsrichter lediglich den bestehenden Wortlaut der Verfassung; ihre Autorität zur Verfassungsinterpretation wiederum erwarben sie sich durch ihre unbelastete Vergangenheit. Ein moralisch und nicht unbedingt fachlich begründeter Autoritätsvorsprung war den Verfassungsrichtern gegenüber ihren Kollegen der Staatsrechtslehre oder auch der obersten Bundesgerichte, die zum Teil mit einer nationalsozialistischen Vergangenheit belastet waren, eigen.

Bei der ersten Wahl der damals noch 24 Richter sollte natürlich, neben der parteipolitischen Parität zwischen CDU und SPD, darauf geachtet werden, daß Gleichheit auch hinsichtlich der religiösen Zugehörigkeit sowie der „zentralistischen" bzw. „föderalistischen" Ansichten der Richter bestand. Darüber sollten die zu wählenden Persönlichkeiten ohne „braune Flecken" sein, einen reichen Erfahrungsschatz im öffentlichen Leben besitzen, so daß vor allem Männer und Frauen aus Verwaltung, Ministerien und höheren Gerichtshöfen in Frage kamen.[52]

Der erste Vize-Präsident des Gerichts, Rudolf Katz, praktizierte als einziger seinen jüdischen Glauben; daneben hatte auch Gerhard Leibholz – obwohl strenger Protestant – einen jüdischen Hintergrund, und die Richter Georg Fröhlich[53] und Bernhard Wolff besaßen jüdische Vorfahren. Aufgrund dessen teilten diese vier Richter das Schicksal, Nazi-Deutschland verlassen haben zu müssen. Zusätzlich zu diesen vier „Flüchtlingen" kamen neun Richter, die aus ihren Ämtern von den nationalsozialistischen Machthabern vertrieben worden waren. Die verbleibenden Richter bekleideten während des Hitler-Regimes meistens kleinere Ämter bzw. waren zur Wehrmacht eingezogen worden.[54] Alle hatten sich beim Aufbau der Bundesrepublik in den Jahren 1945-1951 profiliert und bekleideten oft hohe Staats- oder Richterämter.[55]

---

[52] Ley, Richard: Die Erstbesetzung des Bundesverfassungsgerichts, Zeitschrift für Parlamentsfragen (1982) 13, S. 521-541, hier: S. 535.

[53] Schröder, Peter: Georg Fröhlich – Landgerichtspräsident in Münster, In: Großfeld, Bernhard u. a. (Hrsg.): Westfälische Jurisprudenz. Beiträge zur deutschen und europäischen Rechtskultur. Festschrift aus Anlaß des 50jährigen Bestehens der Juristischen Studiengesellschaft Münster, Münster 2000, S. 349-392.

[54] Vgl. zu Höpker-Aschoff und seiner Tätigkeit in der Haupttreuhandstelle Ost: Loose, Ingo: Kredite für NS-Verbrechen. Die deutschen Kreditinstitute in Polen und die Ausraubung der polnischen und jüdischen Bevölkerung 1939-1945, München 2007 (Studien zur Zeitgeschichte Band 75) sowie zu Willi Geigers Tätigkeit als Staatsanwalt in Bamberg: Müller, Ingo: Furchtbare Juristen. Die unbewältigte Vergangenheit unserer Justiz, München 1987, S. 220f.

[55] Kommers (wie in 5), S. 121.

Ein weiteres Strukturmerkmal der Autorität ist die Anerkennung der Autorität als Anerkennung der Werte, welche sie repräsentiert.[56] Das BVerfG muss als Organisation zur Durchsetzung der Institution „Verfassung" –, sprich: des Grundgesetzes verstanden werden. Die Bindung aller Gewalten an Recht und Gesetz, Sozial-, Rechtsstaats- und Bundesstaatsprinzip sowie an die Funktion der Grundrechte als Abwehr-, Teilhabe- und Leistungsrechte gegenüber dem Staat werden erst durch die Einklagbarkeit vor dem Karlsruher Gericht effektuiert. Die Dialektik des Autoritätsgewinns im Autoritätskampf zwischen EVG-Vertrag und Status-Denkschrift wurde an der Haltung der Bundesregierung Adenauer deutlich: Auf der einen Seite sprach Bundesjustizminister Dehler davon, das Gericht in die Luft zu sprengen[57] und machte damit deutlich, dass Adenauer die „Kampfansage" aus Karlsruhe aufnehmen und ihr mit einer Gesetzesänderung begegnen wollte[58]. Auf der anderen Seite versuchte die Regierung das BVerfG für seine Politik zu vereinnahmen, ließ sich also auf die Autorität des Gerichts ein und ermöglichte damit den Bundesverfassungsrichtern durch deren geschlossenes Verhalten, ihre Autorität auf- und auszubauen.

Außerdem setzt Autorität auch voraus, innerhalb der Erwartungshaltungen der Autoritätsgläubigen zu bleiben. Die anerkannte Autorität kann nicht nach Belieben verfahren, sondern muss verantwortungsbewußt mit der Anerkennung umgehen. Sie muss sich im Erwartungshorizont des Anerkennenden bewegen. Dazu gehört vor allem, den überlegenden Umgang mit der Sache in den Dienst der Allgemeinheit zu stellen.[59]

Das Gericht verfügt über keine eigene Polizei oder Gerichtsvollstrecker. Es ist darauf angewiesen, daß sich alle Staatsorgane an seine Urteilssprüche halten. Es handelt sich bei der Durchsetzungsfähigkeit des Verfassungsgerichts also weder um eine legislative Gestaltungsmacht noch um eine exekutive Verfügungsmacht. Dieses Dilemma beschrieben schon die amerikanischen Verfassungs(-gerichts)väter vor über 200 Jahren:

---

[56] Lembcke, Oliver: Hüter der Verfassung. Eine institutionentheoretische Studie zur Autorität des BVerfG. Tübingen 2007 (Neue Staatswissenschaften 7), S. 69ff.

[57] Lenz, Otto: Im Zentrum der Macht. Das Tagebuch von Staatssekretär Lenz 1951-1953 (bearbeitet von Gotto, Klaus; Kleinmann, Hans-Otto; Schreiner, Reinhard), Düsseldorf 1989 (Forschungen und Quellen zur Zeitgeschichte, Band 11), Tagebucheintrag vom 3. März 1952, S. 268.

[58] Lenz (wie in 55) S. 493-495.

[59] Sofsky; Paris (wie in 45), S. 35ff.

„The judiciary... has no influence over either the sword or the purse; no direction either of strength or of the wealth of the society, and can take no active resolution whatever. It may be said to have neither FORCE nor WILL but nearly judgement".[60]

Aber die Folgerungen sind noch weitreichender:

„Die Verfassung bedarf der wirksamen Durchsetzung durch das BVerfG freilich nicht nur, um ihr gegenüber den anderen staatlichen Gewalten zur Wirksamkeit zu verhelfen. Die Verfassung ist hierauf existentiell angewiesen, um auf Dauer Bestand zu haben. Sie kann nur fortleben, wenn sie zumindest von einem wesentlichen Teil der Bürger innerlich angenommen wird. Kann dies letztlich auch nicht erzwungen werden, so kann die notwendige Annahme nur gelingen, wenn ihr Inhalt nicht dem ewigen Diskurs überantwortet wird, sondern im Konfliktfall der maßgebliche Gehalt für alle verbindlich bestimmt wird."[61]

Hier wird der symbolische Mehrwert der Karlsruher Verfassungsgerichtsbarkeit deutlich: In einem freiheitlichen Verfassungsstaat werden die Verfassung und ihre Leitideen durch eine Autorität ohne Macht repräsentiert.

Dieser Integrationsprozess[62] durch Verfassung und Verfassungsgerichtsbarkeit ist als ein Vorgang zu begreifen, an welchem die staatlichen Institutionen nur indirekt teilhaben. Eine direkte Form der politischen Integration durch staatliche Organe liefe auf ein in hohem Maße unfreiheitliches Regime hinaus. Institutionen können nur vermittelnd integrativ wirken – sie können ermöglichen, nicht aber zwingen. Wenn das BVerfG ein Urteil spricht, so wird damit instrumentell bezweckt, daß durch Verfassungsauslegung ein Rechtsstreit geschlichtet wird. Ob von der Sprache des Urteils, der Rationalität des Verfahrens, den Roben der

---

[60] Federalist Paper Nr. 78, in: Hamilton, Alexander; Madison, James; Jay, John: The Federalist Papers, hrsg. von Rossiter, Clinton, New York 1961, S. 465.
[61] Heusch, Andreas: Kommentierung § 31 BverfGG. In: Umbach, Dieter C. u. a. (Hrsg.): Bundesverfassungsgerichtsgesetz. Mitarbeiterkommentar und Handbuch, Heidelberg ²2005, Rn. 14.
[62] Zum Problem der „Integration": Dreier, Horst: Integration durch Verfassung? Rudolf Smend und die Grundrechtsdemokratie. In: Hufen, Friedhelm u. a. (Hrsg.): Verfassungen - Zwischen Recht und Politik. Festschrift zum 70. Geburtstag für Hans-Peter Schneider, Baden-Baden 2008, S. 70-96.

Richter, der Rezeption in den Medien oder der möglichen Akzeptanz der Parteien eine Integrationsleistung ausgeht, kann nur angestrebt, aber nicht garantiert bzw. unmittelbar initiiert werden.[63]

Da das Institutionenvertrauen in das BVerfG sehr hoch und seit Jahren konstant ist[64], scheint der Intention zur Integration ein gewisser Erfolg beschieden. Dem Gericht ist damit in seiner über 50-jährigen Rechtsprechung gelungen, was der Berichterstatter Gerhard Leibholz bereits in der Statusdenkschrift postuliert hatte:

„Erst wenn es gelingt, dem Volk die repräsentative Stellung des Bundesverfassungsgerichts auch bildhaft einzuprägen, wird das Bundesverfassungsgericht seine zugleich politisch integrierende Funktion innerhalb des Staats- und Volksganzen voll erfüllen können".[65]

4. Des Hüters neue Roben

Eine wichtige Forderung der Status-Schrift war die Unabhängigkeit des Bundesverfassungsgerichts vom Bundesjustizministerium. Als selbständigem Verfassungsorgan – so die Forderung des Gerichts – sollte ihm keine Ressortierung bei einem Ministerium vorgegeben sein; stattdessen verlangten die Verfassungsrichter einen eigenen Etat im Haushaltsgesetz, direkten Zugang zu den anderen Verfassungsorganen sowie die Ernennung der übrigen Beamten und Angestellten durch den Präsidenten des Bundesverfassungsgerichts und gerade nicht durch den Justizminister. Nach dem siegreichen Autoritätskampf mit der Adenauer-Regierung erhielt das Gericht im Juli 1953 im Haushaltsgesetz für 1953/54 zum ersten Mal einen eigenen Etat.[66]

Das Bundesverfassungsgericht konnte sich jetzt auch eine eigene Geschäftsordnung geben. Gemäß § 46 Deutsches Richtergesetz (in Verbindung mit § 76 Bundesbeamtengesetz) gelten für die anderen

---

[63] Dazu sehr kritisch: Haltern, Ulrich R.: Integration als Mythos – Zur Überforderung des BVerfG. In: Jahrbuch des öffentlichen Rechts 45 (1997), S. 31-88; modifiziert: Ders.: Mythos als Integration – Zur symbolischen Bedeutung des Bundesverfassungsgericht. In: van Ooyen; Möllers (wie in 26), S. 47-64.

[64] Vorländer, Hans; Schaal, Gary S.: Integration durch Institutionenvertrauen? Das BVerfG und die Akzeptanz seiner Rechtsprechung. In: Vorländer, Hans (Hrsg.): Integration durch Verfassung, Wiesbaden 2002, S. 343-375.

[65] Leibholz (wie in 14), hier: S. 146.

[66] Wesel (wie in 40), hier: S. 79.

Bundesrichter, daß der Bundespräsident die Amtstracht per Anordnung regelt. Für den Bundesgerichtshof gilt immer noch der „Allerhöchste Erlass zur Amtstracht der Richter des Reichsgerichts" von 29.10.1879.[67]

Nicht so für das Bundesverfassungsgericht, welches seine Amtstracht in § 64 BVerfG-GO autonom regelt, was Uwe Wesel zu dem Kommentar des „Verfassungsrecht[s] à la mode" veranlasste. Für den Staatsakt der Einsetzung des Bundesverfassungsgerichts bestimmte der damalige Präsident Hermann Höpker-Aschoff, daß die Richter eine Amtstracht tragen sollten, „wie sie auch von den Richtern am Bundesgerichtshof getragen wird".[68] Nach den bereits beschriebenen Autoritätskämpfen beschloß das Plenum des Gerichts in einer Sitzung vom 9. Juli 1957 nach einer Diskussion, ob die Richter eine Amtstracht tragen sollten, daß das Gericht den Schnitt der Robe selbst festlegen werde, und die Roben keinerlei Rangabzeichen haben sollten.

Im Folgenden wurden die Bundesverfassungsrichter Erwin Stein, Gerhard Heiland und Julius Federer damit beauftragt, die Frage nach einer neuen Robe weiter zu behandeln. So berichtete der Bundesverfassungs-richter Stein in der Plenarsitzung vom 21. November 1960 u. a. davon, daß „über die Amtstrachtenentwürfe [...] die Abstimmung erfolgt" sei. Eine geeignete Gelegenheit zur Einführung einer neuen Amtstracht könne das 10. Jahresjubiläum des Gerichts sein.[69] Bei dieser Abstimmung handelt es sich wohl um das Ergebnis einer bereits Ende 1958, Anfang 1959 unter den Richtern des Bundesverfassungsgerichts durchgeführten Umfrage, von der Erwin Stein dem damaligen Präsidenten bereits mit Datum vom 28. Januar 1959 berichtet hatte. Dieser Umfrage haben offensichtlich fünf Entwürfe einer neuen Robe zugrunde gelegen. Ausweislich einer Rechnungsanweisung vom 20. März 1958 dürften drei dieser zwei Entwürfe von der damaligen Kostümbildnerin des hessischen Staatstheaters in Wiesbaden angefertigt worden sein. Von wem die beiden anderen Entwürfe stammten, lässt sich aus den Akten der Verwaltung des Bundesverfassungsgerichts nicht mehr mit Sicherheit rekonstruieren. Möglicherweise stammten sie von der Kostümabteilung des Badischen

---

[67] Wittreck, Fabian: Die Verwaltung der Dritten Gewalt, Tübingen 2006, S. 318.
[68] Zitiert nach einem mehrseitigen Bericht von Frau Dr. Christine Hohmann-Dennhardt (Richterin des Bundesverfassungsgerichts) in einem Brief an den Verfasser.
[69] Hohmann-Dennhardt (wie in 66).

Staatstheaters in Karlsruhe, deren Beteiligung allerdings erst aus dem Jahre 1961 aktenkundig ist.[70]

In dieser Plenarsitzung wurden dann die vorgenannten Mitglieder des Gerichts beauftragt, einen endgültigen Entwurf vorzulegen. In der entscheidenden Plenarsitzung vom 18. Juli 1961 präsentierte dann Erwin Stein ein Modell der neuen Amtstracht (kardinalrote Seide mit Jabot). Dieses Modell wurde vom Plenum mit 18 gegen zwei Stimmen, vorbehaltlich Änderungen, gebilligt; zugleich wurde mit großer Mehrheit eine Amtskette abgelehnt.[71] Mit Schreiben vom 25. Juli 1961 an die Mitglieder des Bundesverfassungsgerichts teilte Bundesverfassungsrichter Stein mit, daß er sich gemäß dem ihm vom Plenum erteilten Auftrag um Schneider bemüht habe, die die genehmigte Robe anfertigen sollten. Hierzu hätten sich die Mitglieder der Kostümabteilung des Badischen Staatstheaters in Karlsruhe bereit erklärt, die ihrerseits bereits bei der Anfertigung des Modells mitgewirkt hatten. Dieser Mitteilung Steins ist zu entnehmen, dass sowohl das letztendlich genehmigte Modell als auch die endgültigen Roben von der Kostümabteilung des Badischen Staatstheaters in Karlsruhe gefertigt wurden.[72]

Umstritten ist in der Literatur, ob es sich – wie etwa Uwe Wesel[73] vermutet – bei den roten Roben um die der obersten Richter von Florenz im 15. Jahrhundert handelt.[74] Gerd Roellecke[75] geht hingegen davon aus, daß die Roben französischen Zuschnitts sind, wie sich aus einem Vergleich mit Rouaults Bild „Die drei Richter" (1936) ergebe. Wobei allerdings auch Roellecke mit Verweis auf die einheitliche europäische Rechtskultur einräumt, dass auch eine Ähnlichkeit mit den Florentiner Roben nicht ausgeschlossen sei.[76]

Unbestritten ist nur, daß sich die Verfassungsrichter die duchesseschwerroten Roben mit weißen Beffchen und roter Kappe nicht allein anziehen können. Hierbei muss ihnen ein Justizbeamter helfen.[77] Ohne

---

[70] Hohmann-Dennhardt (wie in 66).
[71] Hohmann-Dennhardt (wie in 66).
[72] Hohmann-Dennhardt (wie in 66).
[73] Wesel (wie in 33), S. 80.
[74] Freundliche Mitteilung von Herrn Professor Dr. Uwe Wesel (Berlin) an den Verfasser, in der der ehemalige Bundesverfassungsrichter Martin Hirsch als Quelle benannt ist.
[75] So die Vermutung von Herrn Professor Dr. Gerd Roellecke (Mannheim) in einem Brief an den Verfasser.
[76] Roellecke (wie Anm. 73).
[77] Wesel (wie in 40), S. 80.

Zweifel aber symbolisieren die Roben der Bundesverfassungsrichter die Unabhängigkeit dieser Institution als Verfassungsorgan und verdeutlichen damit den herausgehobenen Wert der Verfassung und ihrer Hüter für die politische Kultur der Bundesrepublik Deutschland.

The Oath as Evidence in Old-Polish Land Law Litigation in Early-Modern Period

Adam Moniuszko

1. Introduction

Law on stage may take various forms, from the literal meaning of using legal institutions in drama and prose to the situation when law itself becomes a spectacle. There is no doubt that the medieval era, with its symbolism and belief in divine intervention, furthered the staging of legal acts. Supernatural elements in medieval court litigation, especially present in the law of evidence, have been a subject of scientific consideration for many years. During recent decades, different approaches have been taken to explain this phenomenon.[1] However, it is worth mentioning that scholars and researchers have mainly focused on the undoubtedly spectacular legal custom of ordeals, whereas oaths have not drawn as much attention.[2] Moreover, in most cases medieval British Isles and Western Europe has been their point of interest. This article deals with the function of the oath in old-Polish procedural law during the early modern period. On account of the vastness of this field of research, this paper is limited to law of the nobility, i.e. land law (*ius terrestre*) mainly in the 16th-17th centuries. It is based on a variety of historical and legal sources: legal acts and literature, diaries and record books. It is worth mentioning, that hitherto existing Polish literature is also mainly focused on the oath in medieval law,[3] with an exception of academic handbooks on history of procedural law.[4]

---

[1] Bartlett, Robert: *Trial by fire and water. The medieval judicial ordeal*, Oxford 1999 (reprint); Brown Peter: Society and the Supernatural. A Medieval Change. In: *Daedelus* (1975), vol. 104, No. 2, pp. 133–151; Radding Charles M.: Superstition to Science: Nature, Fortune, and the Passing of the Medieval Ordeal. In: *American Historical Review*, (1979), vol. 84, No. 4, pp. 945-969; Colman, Rebecca V.: Reason and Unreason in Early Medieval Law. In: *Journal of Interdisciplinary History* (1974), vol. 4, No. 4, pp. 571-591.

[2] A positive exception is a recent book from Meyer, Tim: *Gefahr vor Gericht. Die Formstrenge im sächsisch-magdeburgischen Recht*, Köln et al., 2009, pp. 97-137.

[3] Borowski, Stanisław: *Przysięga dowodowa w procesie polskim późniejszego średniowiecza*, Warszawa 1926; Zaremska, Hanna: Iuramentum Iudaeorum − żydowska przysięga w średniowiecznej Polsce. In: Drzewiecki, Marcin (ed.): *E Scientia et amicitia. Studia poświęcone Profesorowi Edwardowi*

The Polish-Lithuanian Commonwealth, created by the Union of Lublin in 1569, did not develop a unitary land law legal system. Lithuanian law was codified in three statutes from 1529, 1566 and 1588, whereas Polish law remained mainly uncodified, with the exception of the *Formula processus* from 1523, a partial codification of land law litigation. Contrary to the evolution of litigation in continental Western Europe, separate criminal trial, based on the inquisitorial procedure, did not develop in old-Polish land law. Therefore, it was generally the accusatorial procedure in both civil and criminal cases that was used. Its main principles were: private accusation, formalism, formal truth, oral procedure, contradictory and public trial. The principles of formal truth and the contradictory trial implied a passive position for the judge. He was an impartial umpire, who made decisions based on the arguments and proofs presented by the contradicting parties during the trial. A crucial point in the law of evidence was the rule of proximity to the proof (*proximitas probandi*). The judge decided, although his decisions were limited by formal acts, which party would have the burden of proof. The proof was carried only once and the proximity was a privilege – a winning party could renounce it, leaving its opponent with an obligation to carry the proof. A counter-proof was inadmissible, thus if the party carried the proof successfully, they won the trial and if not, lost it.[5]

2. Construction of the Proof of Oath (*iuramentum corporale*)

The oath and the ordeals were elements of a belief in *judicium Dei*. The trial was a reflection of the Last Judgment, therefore the divine presence

---

Potkowskiemu w sześćdziesięciolecie urodzin i czterdziestolecie pracy naukowej. Warszawa 1999, pp. 229-243; Lesiński, Bogdan: Przysięga na duszę jako dowód w średniowiecznym prawie polskim. In: *Czasopismo Prawno–Historyczne* (1972), vol. XXIV, No. 2, pp. 19–36; Semkowicz Władysław: *Przysięga na słońce: studyum porównawcze prawno–etnologiczne*, Lwów 1916.

[4] Balzer, Oswald: *Przewód sądowy polski w zarysie*, Lwów 1935, pp. 152–168; Kutrzeba, Stanisław: *Dawne polskie prawo sądowe w zarysie*, Lwów–Warszawa–Kraków 1927 (2nd ed.), pp. 95–98; Rafacz, Józef: *Dawny proces polski*, Warszawa 1925, p. 160–169, 172–174; Bardach, Juliusz (ed.): *Historia państwa i prawa Polski,* vol. I, Warszawa 1965, pp. 350-353, 550-551, vol. II, Warszawa 1966, pp. 390-391.

[5] Balzer, p. 132-145; Kutrzeba, pp. 100-102; Rafacz, pp. 155-157; Matuszewski, Józef: Bliższość do dowodu w Statutach Kazimierza Wielkiego. In: *Studia z dziejów państwa i prawa polskiego*, vol. V, Łódź 2002, pp. 47-59. The same situation can be observed in other legal systems, see: Meyer (as in 2), pp. 98-99.

was obvious part of it. During the ordeals divine intervention showed guilt or innocence. The oath did not have such an immediate effect. The party, while swearing it, called on God as a witness to confirm the truth of their statement. The consequences of perjury were more of an eschatological nature – it was one of the most grievous sins. However, it was only a sort of punishment as perjury was not penalized by the legal system. Batłomiej Groicki, a lawyer and legal writer from the end of the 16th century, stated: "it is certain and inevitable that a person who uses God's name to confirm his falseness will not elude God's revenge".[6] Although this remark concerned the Magdeburg law, used in Polish towns, the same lack of penal punishment for perjury can also be observed in land law.[7]

The oath according to medieval procedural law was sworn in public in a ritual and sacred form, which depended on confession. Catholics swore inside or in front of a church on their knees with two fingers on the cross. It was also possible, especially in case of clergy, to take the oath with a hand on the Gospel, rather than the cross. The Orthodox usually swore in front of the Orthodox Church with their left hand on the doors and making the sign of the cross with their right hand.[8] Armenians, according to the Armenian Statute of 1519, swore the oath inside church, with their fingers on the cross, while the opposite party had to pour water three times on the hands of the oath-taker.[9] Jews took the oath standing bearfoot on a stool, with their face towards the east and a Jewish hat on their head.[10] Even the oath at the sun, typical for the pre-Christian period, was still in use, although in narrowly limited types of cases.[11] Despite the different

---

[6] 'Kto bierze na daremno imię boże a swego fałszu nim potwierdza, pewna, a nieomylna rzecz jest, iż pomsty od Boga nie ujdzie', Groicki, Bartłomiej: *Porządek sądów i spraw miejskich prawa majdeburskiego w Koronie Polskiej.* Ed. Koranyi, Karol. Warszawa 1954, p. 143. Sources quoted in the main text of the article are translated into English while the original text is in the footnote. Marcin Jaskier, other legal writer of the Magdeburg law from the beginning of the 17th century argued, that perjury was under jurisdiction of secular courts. According to Jaskier, penalties for perjury were: infamy, deprivation of honour and capability to be a witness. However, in Poznań in the 16th century the cases of perjury concerned false witnesses, not oath-taking, see: Maisel, Witold: *Poznańskie prawo karne do końca XVI wieku,* Poznań 1963, pp. 192-194.

[7] Uruszczak, Wacław: Korektura praw z 1532 r. Studium prawno-historyczne, vol. 2, Kraków 1991, p. 82.

[8] Borowski (as in 3), pp. 52-60.

[9] *Corpus Iuris Polonici.* Vol. III. Ed. Balzer, Oswald. p. 461 (Article 124 of the Armenian Statute); Borowski (as in 3), p. 61.

[10] Zaremska (as in 3), pp. 229-243.

[11] Some elements from the oath at sun were incorporated into Jewish and Ruthenian oaths. An

rituals, the form of the oath remained similar. It contained an invocation to God, a statement of the fact which was the subject of proof, and a religious punishment in case of perjury. Until later medieval times, any mistake in swearing the oath resulted in the failure of that proof. In the 14th and 15th centuries, this severe rule was gradually moderated (by introducing the possibility of three or even four chances to swear the oath) and it was eventually dropped. Yet in 1498 there was an example of a case lost due to a stumble in the form of the oath. A plaintiff swore the oath, but failed to speak the form of the oath properly: "plaintiff [...]swore the oath, but did not speak the words properly, i.e. she stumbled".[12] The deputies of the land court did not know what do to and remitted the case to Sanok land court, which decided the case in favour of her oponent due to a wrongful oath-taking (*ob malam iuramenti praestitionem*).[13]

Polish land law granted a wide ability to take an oath. Juveniles and persons deprived of a good reputation (*bona fama*) were not capable of taking the oath. It was also unacceptable, at least in medieval procedure, that a person from outside the accepted religions (or excommunicated) could swear the oath.[14]

Various types of oath may be distinguished using different criteria. The first distinction is based on the party of litigation: the oath of purgation taken by the defendant and the oath of condemnation taken by the plaintiff. Another depends on the number of persons taking the oath. Apart from the oath of a sole party, a more solemn form of a party with a certain number of oath-helpers was also used in serious cases. The Latin term for witnesses (*testes*) used in records to describe oath-helpers might be misleading. Presumably they did not have, or at least did not have to have, factual knowledge about the case; they confirmed the credibility of the

---

example of such oath from the second half of the 18th century was found by Stanisław Szczotka: Stosowanie przysięgi na słońce w polskim sądownictwie wiejskim XVIII wieku. In: *Czasopismo Prawno–Historyczne* (1949), vol. II, p. 452-458. In its full form it was used in cases of exoneration of nobleman's honour, Borowski, p. 61; Semkowicz, *Przysięga*, p. 350, 372. The oath at the sun was also used by soldiers in the 17th century, Semkowicz, Władysław: *Jeszcze o przysiędze na słońce w Polsce*, Kraków 1938.

[12] 'Actrix (...) iuramentum praestitit, sed verbis bene non expressit alias *zayakalaszye*', Prochaska, Antoni (ed): *Akta Grodzkie i Ziemskie z czasów Rzeczypospolitej Polskiej z archiwum tak zwanego bernardyńskiego*, vol. XVII, Lwów 1901, p. 348, no. 2982.

[13] Prochaska (as in 12), p. 351, no. 2997.

[14] Borowski (as in 3), p. 21-26.

party instead.[15] However, another point of view has been presented by Rebecca Colman, who proposed, that in the small closed societies medieval people lived in, oath helpers must have had some degree of knowledge about the facts they sworn to.[16]

The number of oath-helpers varied from one to twelve, depending on the type of case. It was only partly regulated by the written law, most situations were subjected to the customs.[17] For example, the Statutes of Casimir the Great from the 14th century, demanded six oath-helpers in purgation from the accusation of a theft of a pouch, three or six oath-helpers in cases of forging an entry to the court records, one or two oath-helpers in cases of a debt (depending on the value of the dept).[18] The particular Masovian land law demanded six oath-helpers in cases where a nobleman was injured by peasants in a tavern, or in purgation of a nobleman accused of deliberate cutting off a limb of a peasant.[19] In the medieval land law, an oath-taker had to nominate the double or triple number of candidates and opposite party chose the oath-helpers. According to the act of the diet of 1496 regarding crime of robbery of a nobleman's home, the plaintiff had the proximity to proof and, when there was no other evidence available, he nominated 18 candidates for oath-helpers. According to the act the defendant had to choose "six noblemen of good reputation and with land possessions in that district, where the crime was committed".[20]

Additionally, a special list with their names was created when the oath was adjudicated. The oath was usually taken during the next court session

---

[15] Balzer (as in 4), p. 159; Rafacz (as in 4), pp. 160–161; Kutrzeba (as in 4), p. 95. A form of the oath-helper in Polish towns with the Magdeburg law was noted by Groicki: 'The oath taken by N. about given possessions or committed homicide of N. is true and just. So help me God' [*Przysięga, którą uczynił ten N. około darowanego imienia abo zadanego sobie mężobójstwa N. jest prawdziwa i sprawiedliwa. Tak mi Panie Boże dopomagaj*], Groicki (as in 6), p. 144.

[16] Colman (as in 1), pp. 576-577.

[17] Rafacz (as in 4), p. 161

[18] Balzer (as in 4), pp. 162-163.

[19] Grodziski, Stanisław; Dwornicka, Irena; Uruszczak, Wacław (ed.): *Volumina Constitutionum* (henceforward: VC), vol. II, part 1, Warszawa 2005, pp. 389-390. Wounding of a nobleman in a tavern by peasants, with whom he has sat, eaten and drunk, was an interesting example of exclusion of criminal responsibility. The peasants were not responsible for that kind of offence because of the 'fault' of the nobleman, who revelled with persons of low estate.

[20] 'Si citatus fuerit ad iudicium castrense non aliter convici debeat, nisi testibus decemocto nominates, e quibus electis sex nobilibus bonae famae, et possessionatis illius districtus aut palatinatus, ubi tale crimen patratum', VC, vol. 1, part 1, Warszawa 1995, p. 79.

or by other time appointed in the sentence of the court, and by that time nobody outside from the list could have become an oath-helper.[21]

3. The Oath in Polish Jurisprudence and Practice of Land Law Courts in the Early Modern Period

As already mentioned, the oath was a proof specific to the medieval trial, full of supernatural elements. The evolution of litigation in the early modern period headed towards the principle of material truth in hearing of evidence, which diminished the significance of the oath. Although land trial was reformed and partially codified by the *Formula processus*, the oath maintained an important place in the catalogue of proofs until the partition of the Polish-Lithuanian Commonwealth towards the end of the 18th century. The procedure of adjudicating the proximity to proof remained one of the crucial elements in the law of evidence, even though it was significantly changed in the 16th century. Basically, the *Formula processus* set an obligation for the plaintiff and the defendant to offer to the judges the proofs they would like to carry.[22] The party which presented better proofs confirming their statements should have been granted the proximity to proof. If the proofs offered were similar, the defendant was privileged with the right to carry the proof, even though there were some exceptions to that rule. As far as 'quality of proof' is concerned, this issue was not regulated by land law procedure. Jan Łączynski, a recorder in Cracow land court and the author of a work which briefly summarized the competences of the king's courts and court procedure stated, that the best proofs were: admission of a claim or guilt, capture a person red-handed with stolen goods and authentic official documents.[23]

Under these circumstances, it seems that the oath should play insignificant part in law of evidence. This point of view was presented by some representatives of Polish jurisprudence at the end of the 16th century. They claimed that the role of the oath should only be complementary, i.e. it should be used if there was no better evidence. Stanislaw Sarnicki, in his

---

[21] Balzer (as in 4), p. 163, p. 165; Rafacz (as in 4), pp. 164-167.
[22] VC, vol. 1, part 1 (as in 20), p. 392.
[23] Łączyński, Jan: *Kompendium sądów Króla Jego Mości*, Ed. Kolankowski, Zygmunt. In: Kolankowski, Zygmunt: *Zapomniany prawnik XVI wieku Jan Łączyński i jego „Kompendium sądów Króla Jego Mości". Studium z dziejów polskiej literatury prawniczej*, Toruń 1960, pp. 101-103.

private assemblage of the bill of rights (1594), which he hoped would become the basis for a future codification, stated:

"The judges try not in their, but in God's court [...] and because human reason is sometimes not capable of judging everything, when the judge becomes full of doubt and does not know what to do, he refers to the oath, that is, to God's reason."[24]

As we can see, the elements of *judicium Dei* were still present in this reasoning, but Sarnicki clearly assigns a merely subsidiary role to the oath. A similar opinion was held by Łączyński who assumed that only in cases where no documents existed, the oath should be adjudicated.[25]

However, there were also contrary opinions about the significance of the oath in the practice of the land law trials. Łukasz Górnicki, a talented late renaissance writer and the possessor of two royal complexes of premises, wrote about a case he has had with a wood thief. While he had been going home in a company of the court clerk through the forest which was a part of the royal premises in his administration, he had come up against a nobleman and his servants cutting down trees and loading the wood. Despite offering a proof from witnesses, including the official clerk, Górnicki lost the case – the judge adjudicated an oath of purgation to the defendant with a good reputation.[26] Another example set by Górnicki concerned cases of personal injury. According to customary law it was one of the exceptions, where the plaintiff had a proximity to the proof. Górnicki pointed out the abuse of law in these cases. According to him, it sometimes happened that a victim sued not the real offender, but another person with greater material status.[27] There are other indications of this practice in Masovia, a region of settlement for many of petty nobility and many of cases of wounding. Masovian nobility during their local assemblies (dietines) postulated changes in the law of evidence to prevent such abuse. They expected, that the proximity of proof would be granted to the

---

[24] 'Aby się znaczyło, że sędziowie nie swój sąd ale Boży sądzą, a i że na miejscu Bożym sąd się pokazuje i jawnie się pokazać może, że nie wszystkiego rozsądzić mogą i człowieczy rozum nie stanie go na to, aby miał sobą przywłaszczać coby miał wszystko rozsądzić. Przetoż, gdy zabrnie, a wątpi czego się ma trzymać, do przysięgi, to jest do Bożego rozsądku strony odsyła', Sarnicki, Stanisław: Statuta i metryka przywilejów koronnych, Kraków 1594, p. 792.

[25] Łączyński (as in 23), p. 101.

[26] Górnicki, Łukasz: *Pisma*. Ed. Pollak, Roman, vol. II, Warszawa 1961, p. 398.

[27] Górnicki (as in 26), pp. 411-412.

defendant, instead of the plaintiff in cases of minor personal injuries.[28] These sources show, that sometimes the oath created an easy opportunity to win the trial. There was no criminal punishment for perjury and not everyone seemed to be scared of punishment at the Last Judgement.

Court records indicate that despite quoted opinions of the legal writers, the oath was still the most frequently used form of proof. However, some changes since the medieval trial may be observed. The first concerns the form of oath which became less formal and sacral. The whole act of swearing, although still solemn, was held in the court room, rather than a place worship, in presence of the judges, the usher (*ministerialis*) who read the formula of the oath and the opposite party.[29] Its presence was a consequence of the principle of the public trial in land law procedure and it was *conditio sine qua non* of taking the oath. Absence of the opposite party was treated in the same way as negligence of peremptory summon and resulted in loosing the case.[30]

A different form of the oath, based on the claim of the plaintiff, was set every time by the judges.[31] Regarding the consequences of mistakes during the swearing of the oath formula these were no longer treated as a failure of proof.[32] Last but not least, the oath gained a slightly different significance in the law of evidence. It could still have been a proof *sui generis*, as in medieval litigation, but sometimes it became a sort of a second, formal stage of the hearing of evidence. The best example is scrutiny (*scrutinium*). It was an obligatory form of inquiry conducted either by the court clerk or by the parties in the most serious cases of a criminal or semicriminal nature, as homicide, armed robbery, and abduction. After reading the scrutiny, the judge adjudicated the oath to one of the parties. A

---

[28]Biblioteka Polskiej Akademii Umiejętności i Polskiej Akademii Umiejętności w Krakowie (The Library of the Polish Academy of Knowlegde and the Polish Academy of Science), 8331, f. 77; 8337, f. 11, 15, 56v., 61, 64v., 88v., 95v.; Archiwum Główne Akt Dawnych w Warszawie (Central Archive of Historical Records in Warsaw, henceforward: AGAD), księgi różańskie grodzkie relacje oblaty, vol. 5, f. 492v., 814; vol. 12, f. 38.

[29] Borowski (as in 3), p. 55; Balzer (as in 4), p. 155; Rafacz (as in 4), p. 173; Kutrzeba (as in 4), p. 97; AGAD, księgi ziemskie warszawskie *decreta iudicii,* vol. 12, p. 39, 58.

[30] An example from the beginning of 17th century: AGAD, księgi ziemskie warszawskie *decreta iudicii,* vol. 12, pp. 94-95.

[31] In the practice of the Masovian land courts from the 17th century the form of the oath of condemnation was in Latin and of the oath of purgation in Polish. If one of the parties found the formula erroneous, it could be a reason for appeal, AGAD, księgi ziemskie wieczyste relacji wyszogrodzkie, vol. 10, f. 315v.

[32] Balzer (as in 4), p. 156; Rafacz (as in 4), p. 173.

sentence taken by the Płock land court in 1591 might serve as an example. The defendant was accused of homicide and both parties conducted their scrutiny. The judges examined scrutiny of the plaintiff and the defendant and decided that it was a case of self defence. For further confirmation they adjudicated the oath with six oath-helpers for the defendant.[33] In this case the oath was a subsidiary proof; its task was to consolidate the scrutiny. Masovian court records from the end of the 16th century provide other examples of the oath being a formal completion to the hearing of the evidence, preceded by both scrutiny[34], and other proofs such as visit to the scene of the crime (*visio*) or documents.[35]

4. The Institution of Oath-Helpers

As far as the institution of oath-helpers is concerned research was only partially successful as laconic entries in court records turned out to be main problem. They usually contained a mere information about the number of oath-helpers, e.g. "*metterciae cum duobus testibus*".[36] It is rather an exception than a rule, that the names of the oath-helpers were put in a record of the case. The first question regards the ability to be an oath-helper. Masovian land law stated that a close relative of the oath-taker cannot be the oath-helper. Another restriction was a necessity to have a good reputation what probably meant not to be deprived of honour by a court sentence. Yet another regulation referred to a situation, when the opposite party would try to win the litigation by an intimidation of the oath-helpers. It was possible to take the oath with a fewer number of oath-takers than it was established in court sentence in such cases.[37]

---

[33] 'Iudicium praesens visiis huiusmodi scrutiniis ex utraque productis [...] attento eo quod quod ex scrutinio citati manifeste apparet eundem olim Paulum Mnichowski in defensione vitae suae occidisse iuri communi inhaerendi decrevit iudicialiter eidem citato metseptimo cum sex testibus sibi in genere similibus allegatione suam in sequentis terminis terrestribus Plonenses medio corporali iuramenti comprobare', AGAD, księgi ziemskie płockie wieczyste relacji, vol. 22, f. 378 v.-379, 434-435.

[34] AGAD, księgi ziemskie wieczyste relacji wyszogrodzkie, vol. 9, f. 638-642; vol. 10, f. 197, 348 v.-349, 640 v.-642.

[35] AGAD, księgi ziemskie płockie wieczyste relacji, vol. 22, f. 443v.–448, 526v.–528; księgi ziemskie wieczyste relacji wyszogrodzkie, vol. 10, f. 285–286, 300–301v.

[36] AGAD, księgi ziemskie wieczyste relacje wyszogrodzkie, vol. 10, f. 51. Other examples from that court record: f. 443, f. 445v.

[37] VC, vol. II, part 1 (as in 20), p. 383.

Although due to brief records it was impossible to ascertain whether these regulations were used in practice. Another interesting issue is ability of women to be an oath-helper. Despite some scholars have denied females this right in Polish procedural law[38], it seems to be an open question. There was no direct indication in the sentences regarding sex of the oath-helpers. For example, the plaintiff Barbara Chyczewska had to take the oath with two noblemen: *"mettertius cum duobus Nobilibus suae conditioni paribus"*.[39] Form *nobilibus* used in this sentence does not settle this issue, therefore it needs further research. The records provide information about estate affiliation of the oath-helpers. They had to belong to the same estate as the oath-taker. A condition of similar estate of the oath-taker and oath-helpers was usually set in the court records. Most of the cases in the land courts concerned nobility, therefore the oath-helpers usually belonged to this estate.[40] However, there are also examples of oath-helpers from other estates in land courts. A peasant Jan Zalkowicz sued a nobleman Jan Sieromski for personal injury. The Płock land court adjudicated an oath for the plaintiff *'cum duobus testibus sibi in genere similibus'*.[41] This case also indicates that in certain situations a nobleman could convict on the basis of the oath taken by the members of lower estates.

A decline of the necessity of formal restrictions concerning oath-helpers in the early modern period is another issue that needs further research. Court records searched for this article did not contain any lists of oath-helpers. It might be assumed that, contrary to medieval litigation, they were not used any more at the end of the 16th century; at least as far as Masovian region is concerned. Neither there are indications of objections against oath-helpers.[42] Thus, it seems that some of highly formalized rules were abandoned during the 16th century.

---

[38] Balzer (as in 4), p. 164; Kutrzeba (as in 4), p. 95-96. Contrary opinion: Rafacz (as in 4), p. 164.

[39] AGAD, księgi ziemskie wieczyste relacji wyszogrodzkie, vol. 10, f. 423.

[40] An example from a single court session of the Wyszogród land court in 1591 proves that rule, AGAD, księgi ziemskie wieczyste relacje wyszogrodzkie, vol. 10, f. 65, 99-99v., 194-195, 197, 237-237 v., 239.

[41] AGAD, ziemskie płockie wieczyste relacje, vol. 22, f. 368. Other examples of that rule from that record of the Płock land court: f. 368v., 524.

[42] The objections were sometimes raised against witnesses. The plaintiff Wojciech Dzierzanowski demanded annulment of the defendant's scrutiny due to a fact that one of the co-accused persons participated in it as a witness, AGAD, księgi ziemskie wieczyste relacji wyszogrodzkie, vol. 9, f. 648.

Court records provide information regarding the number of oath-helpers and type of cases this form of proof has been used for. As it was indicated earlier in this article, this issue was only partially regulated by the positive law. Moreover, the dispositions of law were not necessarily applied in practice. In 1591 a nobleman Marcin Sawłowski accused a peasant Grzegorz Pączek of wounding committed in a tavern. Despite regulations of written law[43], domanial court adjudicated the oath with two oath-helpers in favour of Pączek. Sawłowski appealed to land court, which increased the number of oath-helpers to six and demanded an additional oath from the tavern-keeper as seventh oath-helper:

"This court has changed the sentence of the village court and orders, that according to the Masovian law the defendant Gregory Paczek should take an oath with six witnesses and a keeper of the tavern where the defendant was wounded."[44]

In cases of homicide setting an oath with six oath-helpers was a common practice of land courts in Masovia by the end of the 16th century.[45] As far as personal injury is concerned, various judicial decisions were made. The Wyszogród land court adjudicated as well an oath with two oath-helpers[46] (in accordance with an act of the diet from 1538) as an oath with one oath-helper[47] or a sole oath of the party.[48] Similar differences can be also observed in other types of claims, e.g. cutting out forest[49] or damages

---

[43] See fn. 19.

[44] 'Iudicium praesens meliorando decretum illiud iudicii villanici eadem inculpato Laborioso Gregorio Paczek inherendo constitutionis exceptarum pallatinatus Mazoviae juramento corporali cum sex testibus simulque et eo hospite apud quem in taberna actor vulneratum esse affectum', AGAD, księgi ziemskie wieczyste relacji wyszogrodzkie, vol. 10, f. 644-644v. It is possible that in this particular case the tavern-keeper was added as the person, who was supposed to have factual knowledge about the incident.

[45] AGAD, księgi ziemskie wieczyste relacji wyszogrodzkie, vol. 10, f. 197, 348v.-349, 640 v.-642; księgi ziemskie płockie wieczyste relacji, vol. 22, f. 378 v.-379, 434-434 v.

[46] AGAD, księgi ziemskie wieczyste relacji wyszogrodzkie, vol. 10, f. 64v.-65, 191v.-193v., 196v., 237, 242, 423, 513v.-514, 643 v., 672 v.. The act of 1538: VC, vol. I, part 2, Warszawa 2000, p. 176.

[47] AGAD, księgi ziemskie wieczyste relacje wyszogrodzkie, vol. 10, f. 323.

[48] AGAD, księgi ziemskie wieczyste relacje wyszogrodzkie, f. 49–53, 192v., 237v.-239, 424-427, 678, 681.

[49] Examples of the oath with two oath helpers: AGAD, księgi ziemskie wieczyste relacje wyszogrodzkie, vol 10, f. 237, 443, 444-444v.; księgi ziemskie płockie wieczyste relacje, vol. 22, f. 523. The oath with one oath-helper: AGAD, księgi ziemskie wieczyste relacje

caused by kettle[50]. Judicial decisions made by land courts in Płock and Wyszogród were not strictly correlated with a value of the claim. For example, during the same court session, in one case of cutting down a forest the judges decided, that the oath of a sole party would be enough (damages set at 100 *grzywien*), but in another they adjudicated the oath with two oath-helpers (damages set at 50 *grzywien*).[51] It is worth mentioning, that in these cases both parties belonged to a similar estate and had a similar social and economical status. As we can see, it was left to the judges' discretion in most cases. Despite those differences, there is an indication, that a certain extent of compensation for damage could be one of the circumstances influencing a more solemn form of the oath. In one of the cases, the plaintiff claimed, that the customary law demanded not the sole oath of the party, but rather with oath-helpers due to the extent of the damage (1000 *grzywien*).[52]

5. The Cultural Context of the Oath

Contemporary procedural law no longer uses a proof of oath as it has disadvantages which are obvious for us. Was the oath a convenient way of winning a trial regardless of elementary justice for the nobility in the early modern period? Perhaps, on the contrary, the necessity of swearing an oath resulted in psychological discomfort and fear of the consequences of perjury? The cultural context of the oath can be observed in the case of oath-helpers. As already mentioned, court practice seems to be far from unitary, as far as the records used for this article are concerned. Robert Bartlett made an interesting point regarding the oath and the oath-helpers in medieval society. According to him, the demand and the number of

---

wyszogrodzkie, vol. 10, f. 239. Examples of the sole oath of the party: AGAD, księgi ziemskie wieczyste relacje wyszogrodzkie, f. 197v., 448, 677v., 678v.-679.

[50] The most common decision of the Wyszogród land court was an oath with two oath-helpers, AGAD, księgi ziemskie wieczyste relacja wyszogrodzkie, vol. 10, f. 194v., 195v.-196, 349v., 350, 443, 446v., 677, 679-679v., 681 v. However, we can also come across in the same court record an oath with one oath-helper: f. 193-194, 350, 443 v., 445-445v. and two oath-helpers: f. 349v., 444. The Płock land court in the same type of claims constantly adjudicated an oath with two oath-helpers, AGAD, księgi ziemskie płockie wieczyste relacje, vol. 22, f. 371v.-372, 374v., 376v.

[51] In cases of damage caused by kettle a similar issue may be observed. The judges adjudicated a sole oath of the party in a case, where value of the claim was 100 *grzywien*, whereas in other, with damages estimated at 60 *grzywien*, they adjudicated an oath with two oath-helpers.

[52] AGAD, księgi ziemskie wieczyste relacji wyszogrodzkie, vol. 10, f. 512-513.

oath-helpers depended on individual status of an oath-taker.[53] However, in cases mentioned above the persons had similar social position. We may therefore wonder whether it depended on 'soft' elements, such as degree of individual credibility, well known in a local community. Although records do not show any clear confirmation proving this hypothesis, there are some puzzling notes. In one of the cases a nobleman Jan Nowowieski, was accused of seizuring of a horse by another nobleman. He was granted a proximity to proof, and the court adjudicated him an oath with one oath-helper. Despite the sentence being clearly in his favour, Nowowieski appealed against it to the Crown Tribunal. He claimed, that the land court should have granted him a sole oath without any oath-helpers.[54]

The most probable explanation for this behaviour is that restriction in the shape of the extra oath-helper could have been understood by the parties as a humiliating sign of their diminished credibility. The same court record provides further examples of appeals taken by the parties, who had to swear an oath not solely, but with oath-helpers.[55] Another example of that approach to the issue of oath-taking may be a case of a quarrel between two magnates: Aleksander Koniecpolski and Jeremi Wiśniwiecki about the possession of Hadziacz. In 1646, their contention was to be decided by the diet court. Wiśniowiecki did not appear during a court session, but his representative lodged a motion to adjourn a trial because of his illness (*dillatio verae infirmitatis*). In accordance with article 13 of *Formula processus,* a person using this kind of adjournment had to prove the illness by taking the oath during next session of the court[56], unless the opposite party released him from this duty. Wiśniowiecki counted on the latter possibility so much, that he was supposed to give orders to his private units taken to the diet that in case he was forced to take the oath, they would burst into the senate and hit everybody, who was in favour of Koniecpolski.[57] However exaggerated, it is obvious that the necessity to take the oath in such circumstances was humiliating for proud magnate. Apart from the issues of credibility, there could be also a question of

---

[53] Bartlett (as in 1), pp. 30-31.
[54] AGAD, księgi ziemskie wieczyste relacji wyszogrodzkie, vol. 10, f. 293-293v.
[55] AGAD, księgi ziemskie wieczyste relacji wyszogrodzkie, vol. 10, f. 309v.-310, 513-514.
[56] VC, vol. 1, part 1, (as in 20), p. 393.
[57] Dyjariusz Bogusława Kazimierza Maskiewicza. In: Sajkowski Andrzej (ed.): Pamiętniki Maskiewiczów, Wrocław 1961, p. 228.

conscience. Zbigniew Ossoliński noted in his diary from the first half of the 17th century in somewhat moralizing tone:

"I have paid much attention not to leave any problems to my children, especially these, where an oath would have been necessary after my death. I did not wish for that kind of heritage left after me, even if the oath would have been the fairest one."[58]

There are also traces of the institution of oath and oath-helpers being abused. Łukasz Górnicki deplored: "There are lots of people, who walk around during court sessions and call: 'Who needs oath-helpers? I'm ready to swear an oath, just pay me.'"[59] The custom of offering services as an oath-helper lasted, as one author in the middle of the 18th century observed similar behaviour by petty declassed nobility during a session of the Crown Tribunal (court of appeal for nobility). However, he also noted the reason why 'buying' oath-helpers took place in cases of homicide: "It was difficult to find 11 oath-helpers among honest nobility as they would not dare to take somebody's death on their conscience."[60]

6. Conclusions

An oath in procedural Polish land law during the early modern period maintained its significance as a proof. Its essence remained the same as in the medieval litigation, i.e. an appeal to the divine presence in order to confirm a truth of a statement. Despite allegations of representatives of jurisprudence concerning a subsidiary role of the oath in the law of evidence, it stayed one of the most frequently used proofs. It is worth

---

[58] "Miałem i to na baczeniu najwięcej, abym był żadnych z nikim trudności potomstwu, a zwłaszcza takowych, które by się miały ich przysięgą po mej śmierci kończyć, nie zostawił. Więc i sobie takowej po sobie sukcesyji nie życzyłem, którąm bym miał i najsłuszniejszą przysięgą przyczyniać", Ossoliński, Zbigniew: *Pamiętnik*. Ed. Długosz J., Warszawa 1963, p. 166.

[59] "A postępując dalej idę do owych świadków, co ich owo na rokach siła się ozywa i chodząc wołają: 'komu świadków potrzeba, awom ja gotów przysiądz, jeno zapłać'", Górnicki (as in 26), p. 414.

[60] "Że zaś między uczciwymi osobami trudno było zebrać jedenastu świadków delatorowi, do siebie dwunastego, którzy by chcieli ważyć na czyjąś śmierć sumienie swoje", Kitowicz, Jędrzej: *Opis obyczajów za panowania Augusta III*. Ed. Pollak, Roman. Vol. I, Wrocław 2003, p. 220.

mentioning that slight changes of the oath in the early modern period may be observed. It seems that formal requirements regarding this form of proof were lessened, as well in a sole oath as in an oath with oath-helpers e.g. it became less sacral, and mistakes in swearing the form of the oath did not result in loosing the trial. In some cases, where other proofs were available, the oath became a second, formal stage of the hearing of the evidence. Courts after deliberation over presented proofs, especially over their quality, adjudicated a proximity to proof, that is, which party would take the oath to ultimately confirm guilt or innocence.

Brief records of adjudicated and taken oaths left many issues far from conclusive answers. An ability of women to be oath-helpers, exact form of oath taken by oath-helpers are among them. The information provided by the court records showed that there was no unitary practice regarding the number of oath-helpers. The same judges in a similar case could adjudicate a sole oath of the party as well as an oath with one or two oath-helpers. Sometimes even positive law regulations were not strictly applied by the courts.

One of the most interesting aspects of the oath is the cultural context of this institution, such distant from our mentality. Some of the sources indicated, that the oath with oath-helpers might have been treated as questioning a credibility of the oath-taker. This seems to be the most probable explanation of the situation where parties, despite sentences in their favour, have appealed from them due to a fact that oath with oath-helper was adjudicated rather than the sole oath of the party. Additionally, there was also a matter of religious imperative connected with a sin of perjury. No wonder, that some people showed anxiety about taking oath. Even in England by the end of the 17th century, when an oath was no longer a proof, but it was sworn during giving testimonies, the witnesses were warned of religious consequences of perjury.[61] Probably the pressure was even greater in cases of oath-taker or oath-helper. The party faced with a necessity of taking the oath sometimes has renounced a proximity to proof in favour of their opponent.[62] There are also indications of cynical abuse of the oath and using it as a simple way of winning a trial or

---

[61] Willen, Richard S.: Rationalisation of Anglo – Legal Culture: The Testimonial Oath. In: *The British Journal of Sociology* (1983), vol. 34, No. 1, pp. 116-117.
[62] AGAD, księgi ziemskie wieczyste relacje wyszogrodzkie, vol. 10, f. 53–54 v., 678 v., 680 v. The same can be noticed in the medieval Poland, see: Dąbkowski, Przemysław: *Litkup. Studium z prawa polskiego*, Lwów, 1906, pp. 58-60.

providing additional income. This leads to the conclusion, that the approach to the oath was a personal matter. For some it was an act without any greater meaning: that was very easy to make in their favour. For others it was a matter of their conscience and credibility, and one which had to be taken after great deliberation.

To Have and to Hold – Driving Licences as Important Legal Documents for the Normal Course of Life

Helmut Landerer

Driving licences developed into important "legal documents"[1] for the normal course of life in Germany within the 20th century. "To have and to hold"[2] a driving licence implies also a very significant difference in automobile societies, in which we live today.[3] During the 20th century, this legal right, which entails actually the opportunity of using motorised vehicles on public streets, turned into a meaningful symbol of being part of society likewise passports. Very often, this legal document is kept next to the passport in the wallet, purse or without deeper thought in the glove compartment of the car.

Both documents have unlike reasons for their introducing, which is different from their related symbolic content. The passport,[4] certifying the identity and nationality for the freedom of movement, also symbolises the citizenship or in a broader sense being part of a society. However, the driving licence proves that the holder has the legal capacity to drive, i. e. reached the age limit, visited a driving school and passed the test. It was introduced by the legislator, being accountable for society, in order to ensure road safety. Moreover, the licence developed for the user to a cultural, social, legal and economic symbol. It is virtually spoken the

---

[1] Law appears in various forms: For pictures, symbols and law respectively legal history in general: Kocher, Gernot: Zeichen und Symbole des Rechts, München 1992; Köbler, Gerhard: Bilder aus der deutschen Rechtsgeschichte von den Anfängen bis zur Gegenwart, München 1988, chapter: Recht und Form in der Gegenwart, pp. 356-370.

[2] Title of a novel of 1900, written by the American author Mary Johnston.

[3] At the latest, West Germany's automobile society could be detected since the 1960s. The standard of living of the average household of all income classes included from then on also an own automobile. E.g. in 1964 more than 80 % of all cars were the owned by labourers. See Schildt, Axel: Vom Wohlstandsbarometer zum Belastungsfaktor – Autovision und Autoängste in der westdeutschen Presse von den 50er bis zu den 70er Jahren, In: Dienel, Hans-Liudger; Trischler, Helmuth: Geschichte der Zukunft des Verkehrs. Verkehrskonzepte von der frühen Neuzeit bis zum 21. Jahrhundert, Frankfurt am Main 1997, pp. 287-309, in this case p. 293-296.

[4] For further details regarding passports and citizenship see the standard work of: Fahrmeir, Andreas: Citizenship, the rise and fall of a modern concept, New Haven et al. 2007, pp. 2 and 46-50.

opening key to the stage door of individual motorised mobility, adulthood and freedom apart from public transport.

On the one hand, if you query today's teenagers about the importance of being 18 years old, you will get the answer, that it is more relevant to obtain the licence than reaching the majority age or having the capacity to marry or even to vote. Obtaining the licence and later driving a car is an individual private decision, often flanked by economic or professional considerations. But the legal framework itself had also an impact on this development.

On the other hand, losing one's driving licence is not only a barrier in (auto-)mobile societies, it could also form an obstacle in career.[5] Aside from this individual point of view, the legislator intends to reduce the number of accident victims when excluding unqualified persons from using cars.

This article will explain why the legal right to drive a car transformed into a charged symbol of adulthood, freedom and a "must have" for everyone today. The answer could be found using an interdisciplinary approach of legal and social history. The focus lies on Germany at the end of the 19th and the beginning of the 20th century. The licence's importance has emerged long before the mass of society over 18 had a licence and could afford buying a motorbike[6] or car. The first part of this article is dealing with bicycle-cards, because they paved the way to the driving licence. Secondly, the article is concentrating on obtaining a driving licence and the legal age of 18. Afterwards, the revocation of a driving licence will also show its development into one of the most important legal documents of our time.

---

[5] Especially for professional drivers, the revocation of the driving licence could be a cause for a dismissal of job. E.g. a decision of 16 June 1986 regarding a field manager: LAG Schleswig-Holstein: Fristlose Kündigung eines Außendienstmitarbeiters wegen Führerscheinentzuges. In: Neue Zeitschrift für Arbeitsrecht (1987), p. 669f.

[6] In this paper, the motorbike will not be examined separately. Art. 14 *Bekanntmachung, betreffend die Regelung des Verkehrs mit Kraftfahrzeugen*, 3 February 1910, constituted the legal age of 18 also for *Krafträder*, so that we could subsume the motorbike under the term *Kraftfahrzeug*. Not until the interwar period, more different types of motorised two-wheelers were produced and diffused later in society. E.g. new licences when turning 16 years old were introduced.

1. Licences for Bicycles – Symbols of Law

If we look at road traffic dominated by the car from a legal historical perspective, we have to consider the railroad and the bicycle. The railroad stood model for the absolute liability, in German *Gefährdungshaftung*. The regulation of the bicycle in the form of age-specific norms and licences paved the way for the driving licence.

The history of the bicycle started with the *Laufmaschine* invented in 1816/17 by Karl Drais (1785-1851). Especially since the 1860s the principle of the two-wheeled locomotion has been improved, e. g. with the pedal-cycle, the development of the safety bicycle in the 1880s and the use of pneumatic tyres.[7] The different types of bicycles, such as safety bicycles and high wheelers, remained luxury goods for several years. In Cologne, for instance, increasing numbers of two-wheeled vehicles in the form of the high wheelers had been significantly common on the streets since the end of the 1860s.[8]

The "silent speed"[9] of the bicycle seemed exceptional to the other participants of road traffic, such as horsemen, pedestrians, coachmen and playing children. The (legal) uncertainty and the frequency of accidents grew.

There is often a discrepancy between the subjective fear and the objective potential danger of new technology. This numerous recognised hesitation towards new technology could also be noticed with regard to the bicycle. The media presence of a new technology, which is in turn a sign for its topicality, influenced the legislator. He had to cope with present and future issues arising from the bicycle. His aims were to ensure road safety and to create and perpetuate legal certainty for the users and the other participants in traffic.

Countless local and regional ordinances regarding the bicycle existed in Germany in the last quarter of the 19th century. Different means to regulate

---

[7] Merki, Christoph: Verkehrsgeschichte und Mobilität, Stuttgart 2008, pp. 47-52.

[8] Schubert, Werner: Die Anfänge eines modernen Verkehrsrechts im Radfahrrecht um 1900. Von den regionalen und einzelstaatlichen polizeilichen Radfahrordnungen bis zu den reichseinheitlichen „Grundzügen, betreffend den Radfahrverkehr" vom April 1907. In: Zeitschrift der Savigny-Stiftung für Rechtsgeschichte, Germanistische Abteilung (2005), pp. 195-241 in this case p. 197.

[9] Original: *„lautlosen Schnelligkeit"*, Brüdermann, Stefan: Die Frühzeit des Fahrradverkehrs in Nordwestdeutschland und die Verkehrsdisziplinierung. In: Technikgeschichte (1997) No. 4, pp. 253-267 in this case p. 255.

the two-wheeled vehicle were implemented in these local *Polizeiverordnungen*. For instance one of the first ordinances, the *Kölner Polizeiverordnung* of 9 October 1869, banned the bikes from almost every road.[10] Similarly, the *Berliner Polizeiverordnung* of 15 April 1884, which was in effect until 1896, also banned bicycles from nearly the whole inner city. Only persons over 16 were allowed to ride bicycles on public roads.[11] This age restriction presumably represented the first step in the process of a broad regulation of road traffic by age. The aim was to secure the streets.

In the last quarter of the 19th century, in many parts of Germany, permission, the so-called *Radfahrkarte,* had to be applied for to ride a bike. A typical[12] way to control bicycle traffic was to exclude persons who were not considered old enough. Hence, the application was very often tied to age: a person could obtain a licence when turning 12, 14, 15, 16 or 18 years old.[13] Aside from professional age-regulations for horseback riding, driving a carriage or for railroads and shipping – in case they existed – the age-based law regarding the bicycle was a modern way to regulate this new means of transport for individual users. Thus, we can conclude that the bicycle required daily road traffic to change. The legal symbol *Radfahrkarte* could be interpreted in two ways, on a public and a private level. It was introduced by the legislator in order ensure road safety. Along the way, a symbol of independence, status and ability to drive combined with the age limit emerged *à la longue.*

On the one hand, legal regulations had to be found to discipline all participants in traffic. Age-specific law was a generalizing instrument to include and exclude persons from using the new technology bicycle. On the other, the age-based law indicated an increasing interest and desire for this means of transport. The legislator literally formed a "roadblock" of the legal age in addition to the *Radfahrkarte*. If someone wanted to participate in road traffic with the bicycle, that person had to fulfil these criteria. But instead of preventing potential users, these barriers stimulated the wish to have an own licence and later hold an own two-wheeler. Obtaining the licence turned into a kind of decoration and distinction. It was crucial if someone wanted to be part of the in-group. Therefore, my assumption is

---

[10] Schubert (as in 8) p. 197 and 221.
[11] Schubert (as in 8) p. 203.
[12] "Typical" in this way means that regarding legal history, we can discover many rigid age-norms, which were often means to an end to regulate society.
[13] Schubert (as in 8) pp. 211f.

that the rigid age-restriction contributed importantly to the spread of the bicycle.

How can this thesis be proved? Any reliable statistics and numerical data about bicycles hardly exist.[14] But the bicycle transformed after 1900 from a luxury good to a means of transport for the masses. In 1903, thirty percent of one million estimated owners of bikes were labourers.[15] The number of registered *Radfahrkarten* is an indicator, that the new technology was adopted by society. In June 1897, in Braunschweig for instance 4000 *Radfahrkarten* were handed out. 10 years later, 30.000 bicycles existed among the 135.000 inhabitants of Braunschweig.[16] However, the number of users (certificated *Radfahrkarten*) exceeds the amount of bicycles. The latter is only partially significant, because many persons shared a bicycle in this time.

At the end of the 19th century, transport policy for a short time focused mainly on the bicycle.[17] Moreover, the bicycle had developed to an economic factor for the producer and for the user, who often rode it also to reach his job. A submission of the Vice Chancellor to the Federal Council of the Empire in 1903 implied that the economic factor of the bicycle had increased in the last decade. The authorities' objective was to unify law and regulate bicycle traffic for the whole German Empire.[18]

Finally in 1907, the *Grundzüge betreffend den Radfahrverkehr* was published. The federal states adopted these and included them in their ordinances.[19] *Radfahrkarten* were still mandatory to participate in traffic. From an age of 14 years, a person could apply for a *Radfahrkarte* which can be interpreted

---

[14] E.g. in 1903, 1 million bicycles should have existed in Germany. See Schubert (as in 8), p. 198. According to Kirchberg, in 1932 about 15 million and end of the 1930s 20 million bicycles existed in Germany. See Kirchberg, Peter: Die Motorisierung des Straßenverkehrs in Deutschland von den Anfängen bis zum Zweiten Weltkrieg. In: Niemann, Harry; Hermann, Armin (Ed.): Die Entwicklung der Motorisierung im Deutschen Reich und den Nachfolgestaaten, (Stuttgarter Tage zur Automobil- und Unternehmensgeschichte, Vol. 2), Stuttgart 1995, pp. 9-22 in this case p. 19.

[15] Schubert (as in 8) p. 198.

[16] Ibid.

[17] Brüdermann (as in 9) p. 262.

[18] Original: „Da nach Ausdehnung der wirtschaftlichen Bedeutung, welche der Radfahrverkehr im Laufe des letzten Jahrzehnts gewonnen hat, der Wunsch der Interessenten auf eine Ausgleichung der Verschiedenheiten der geltenden Polizeivorschriften berechtigt erschien [...]." In: No. 128, Drucksachen zu den Verhandlungen des Bundesrates des Deutschen Reichs, Session 1903, Vol. II., 5 November 1903.

[19] *Reichsanzeiger* from 8 April 1907 , see Schubert (as in 8) p. 237.

as the right to ride a bike in the German Empire; for younger persons the father or guardian had to apply for it.[20] *Radfahrkarten* were still compulsory until 1922.[21]

In summary, the state had the duty to regulate the bicycle and to discipline their riders subjecting both to legal norms. Regulation of the bike by the legislator is a sign for its development from an improved invention to a real means of transport. Within a few years it was replaced by the automobile, not in numbers, but in its technical, social, cultural and legal significance. Following the bicycle, the more perilous motorised car had to be domesticated too.[22]

2. Obtaining a Driving Licence and the Legal Age of 18

Uncountable books and articles deal with the "invention" and the technical aspects of the automobile in 1885/86. But we are more interested in the spread[23] of the motor car. What reasons led to the broad use of this new means of transport? In the following, I will concentrate on the driver. Without interested consumers and – more or less capable – drivers, the car would not have gained popularity in society in the way it did: The driving capacity, which is certified by the licence, was also necessary for its acceptance by society, and therefore one aspect of the legal regulation to enhance safety.

The increasing number of registered cars induced rising accident victims. In short, the driver and his automobile developed into a danger for society and for life and limbs of the individual.[24] Therefore, the driver and his

---

[20] No. 47, Drucksachen zu den Verhandlungen des Bundesrates des Deutschen Reichs, Session 1907, Vol. I., 1 March 1907, here Art. 3 para. 3, in original: *"Für Personen unter 14 Jahren erfolgt die Ausstellung auf Antrag des Vater, Vormundes oder sonstigen Gewalthabers."*; Schubert (as in 8) p. 212.

[21] Art. 21 para. 11 c) In: Volkmann, Kurt: Die Straßenverkehrsordnungen, Berlin and Leipzig 1929, p. 129.

[22] Brüdermann (as in 9) pp. 253, 260, 262.

[23] The development of the automobile from an invention into a consumer good and the first distribution of the automobile took place in France and not in Germany, because the automobile was promoted much more and better in France. For further interest see Möser, Kurt: Benz, Daimler, Maybach und das System Straßenverkehr. Utopien und Realität der automobilen Gesellschaft, (LTA-Forschung, No. 27), Mannheim 1998, pp. 27-32.

[24] Zatsch, Angela: Staatsmacht und Motorisierung am Morgen des Automobilzeitalters, (Schriften zur Rechts- und Sozialwissenschaft, Vol. 7), Konstanz 1993, p. 227.

machine had to be domesticated.[25] The regulation of car and driver is similar to the domestication of bicycle and rider, as decades before, but stricter because of the higher danger of the car. For instance, a driving test for bicycles had never existed.

Society does often not begin to deal with a technology until years and decades after its first introduction or its eminent improvements. In the 19th and 20th century, the time span from the "invention" to its daily application decreased considerably.[26] Only once a new technology becomes statistically relevant does its problems have to be solved and its risk dealt with. In the German Empire, for instance, official statistics about accident victims in road traffic have been recorded – interruptedly – since 1906.[27] The growing number of registered automobiles and accidents eventually obliged the legislator to act. On the one hand, law is an efficient means to ensure road safety. On the other, it indicates that a technology is significant for society, when law is addressing it. The assonant controversial question if the automobile was enforced from top down by a plan or if it did become accepted piecemeal will not be discussed here.[28]

If we generally regard the legal regulation in consequence of the industrial revolution, it is obvious that new technologies like the railroad, steam boiler, industrial facilities and their potential danger had to be controlled and domesticated *by law*.[29] These inventions were either controlled during the process of their creation or after they turned into prosperous innovations and spread. Railroad and bicycle paved the way for the automobile. The decisive difference between the individual road traffic and the public transport is the (potential) number of active users. Therefore, the legal regulation of the automobile, regarding the driver, traces back more to the bicycle than to the railroad. As mentioned above, the regulation of the bicycle actually stood model for the motor car. At

---

[25] E.g. the discussion about the motor vehicle liability insurance in Germany was examined from Gadow, Olaf von: Die Zähmung des Automobils durch die Gefährdungshaftung. Eine Analyse der Entscheidungen des Reichsgerichts zu § 7 des Gesetzes über den Verkehr mit Kraftfahrzeugen vom 03.05.1909, (Schriften zur Rechtsgeschichte, Vol. 95), Berlin 2002.

[26] Timm, Albrecht: Einführung in die Technikgeschichte, Berlin and New York 1972, p. 59.

[27] Zatsch (as in 24) p. 227; Fraunholz, Uwe: Motorphobia. Anti-automobiler Protest in Kaiserreich und Weimarer Republik, Göttingen 2002, p. 63.

[28] See e.g. Möser, Kurt: Geschichte des Autos, Frankfurt am Main et al., pp. 194-198.

[29] Vec, Miloš: Kurze Geschichte des Technikrechts. Von den Anfängen bis zum Ersten Weltkrieg. In: Schulte, Martin (Ed.): Handbuch des Technikrechts, Berlin et al. 2003, pp. 3-60 in this case pp. 23-30.

first, the automobile prevailed in the background, because its emerging character of the "largest techno-social system on earth"[30] was evidently not visible at first glance. The car actually seemed less revolutionary than the railroad.[31] In retrospect, the automobile entailed that largest system of a special infrastructure: New roads (e. g. motorways), petrol stations, car dealers, garages, auto liability insurances, driving schools, Emergency Medical Services had to be developed. A new legal system arose, consisting of traffic rules and road traffic acts, criminal law, traffic police, special taxation laws, driving licences, age-specific norms etc.

After the turn of the century local decrees for the regulation of the bicycle were the inspiration for the regional *Polizeiverordnungen* to regulate motor traffic, apart from specifications for the automobile.[32] In Germany, many federal states and cities developed police rules, local laws or regulations regarding the motor car. The *Berliner Polizeiverordnung* of 15 April 1901 stood model for the Prussian provinces, so that a certain standardisation prevailed in Prussia and later in the regulations of the German Empire. The ordinance of Berlin included the age-specific norm of 18 and the requirement of a licence to drive a car. In 1906, the Federal Council of the Empire issued a code of model regulations.[33] The different states adopted and included the model regulation in their particular ordinances in order to attain legal unity.[34]

The motor car act for the empire of 1909 *(Gesetz über den Verkehr mit Kraftfahrzeugen)* states that a person wanting to participate in traffic had to obtain a licence issued by the competent administrative authority.[35] The act

---

[30] Möser, Kurt: The dark side of 'automobilism', 1900-30: Violence, war and the motor car. In: The Journal of Transport History (2002) Issue 2, pp. 238-258 in this case p. 238.

[31] Stieniczka, Norbert: Wegbereiter auf bereiten Wegen? Das Automobil als konservatives Symbol für Modernität. In: Schneider, Ute; Raphael, Lutz; Hillerich, Sonja (Ed.): Dimensionen der Moderne, Festschrift für Christof Dipper, Frankfurt am Main et al. 2008, pp. 403-421, pp. 413f.

[32] Schubert (as in 8) p. 240. E. g. The Kraftfahrgesetz of Braunschweig and Prussia followed the legal regulations of the bicycle. See Brüdermann (as in 9) p. 260.

[33] *Grundzüge des Bundesrates, betreffend den Verkehr mit Kraftfahrzeugen vom 3. Mai 1906.* They came into force on October 1, 1906. No. 66, Drucksachen zu den Verhandlungen des Bundesrates des Deutschen Reichs, Session 1906, Vol. I., 21 March 1906.

[34] Gadow (as in 25) p. 45.

[35] See § 2, *Gesetz über den Verkehr mit Kraftfahrzeugen vom 3. Mai 1909*, (in short: Kraftfahrzeug-gesetz), RGBl. 1909 p. 437. The part according the auto liability insurance came into force on 1 April 1909, the rest on 1 April 1910. In: Oberländer, Ernst: Aus dem Automobilrecht, 5th edition, Berlin 1914, p. 5.

also established the absolute liability for the whole German empire. The law itself did not include an age-norm. The age limit was actually introduced by the according ordinance, which came into effect on 1 April 1910.[36]

Finally one hundred years ago, the two conditions to travel by car – the legal age of 18 and the driving licence – became mandatory in all of the German Empire. Other countries had similar regulations. The Convention of Paris had just a year before established these two requirements to drive a car on the international level as well.[37] The harmonisation of legal regulations was necessary, because traffic does not stop at frontiers. One aim of the mentioned regulations was certainly to secure road traffic.

The licence and age limit should guarantee responsibility, certain physical and moral attributes, technical skills, the capacity to drive and a minimum standard of education regarding traffic rules. In the eyes of the authorities, the document was a symbol of safety.

At the beginning of the 20th Century, the automobile itself symbolised amusement, luxury and conspicuous consumption, sport, voyage and engineering progress. So for individual users, the licence was symbolically charged: between freedom and flexibility, means to an end and means of transport, profession and progression and so on. Bit by bit, the document became more important for the professional life. Chauffeurs, cab drivers and country doctors needed the licence for their profession. Also tradesmen, factory owners and landholders used automobiles as motorists themselves or hired professional drivers.[38] To sum up, the symbol of the legal document is split in safety and freedom, each with broader sense on a public and a private level.

In automobile history, the structural change in traffic is very often only indicated by the number of registered cars. For this purpose the level of motorisation is measured in automobiles per thousand inhabitants.[39] This dimension of mass motorisation is clearly significant. I argue however, that in addition we have to look at the number of registered licences. The

[36] See § 14, Bekanntmachung, betreffend die Regelung des Verkehrs mit Kraftfahrzeugen, 3 February 1910. In: Oberländer (as in 35) p. 23.
[37] Art. 2. Conditions for drivers, International Convention on Automobile Traffic, Paris 11 October 1909.
[38] Krämer-Badoni, Thomas; Grymer, Herbert; Rodenstein, Marianne: Zur sozio-ökonomischen Bedeutung des Automobils, Frankfurt am Main 1971, p. 9-13.
[39] E. g. See Kirchberg (as in 14) p. 17.

number of licence holders – as possible users – demonstrates the beginning
importance of the motor car.

year	permitted licences p. a.	accumulated number of licences	total stock of automobiles
1907	not available	not available	10.115
1908	not available	not available	14.671
1909	not available	not available	18.547
1910	36.077	36.077	24.639
1911	39.636	75.713	31.696
1912	26.993	102.706	39.943
1913	31.329	134.035	49.760
1914	29.219	163.254	60.876
1915	11.636	174.890	not available
1916	2.947	177.837	not available
1917	3.130	180.967	not available
1918	2.820	183.787	not available
1919	23.592	207.379	not available
1920	26.924	234.303	32.450
1921	46.194	280.497	59.588
1922	52.668	333.165	80.937
1923	50.484	383.649	98.587
1924	121.431	505.080	130.346
1925	202.534	707.614	171.445

Registered driving licences and total stock of registered cars. (1907-1925)[40]

[40] Material for statistics: Kaiserliches Statistisches Amt (Ed.): Statistisches Jahrbuch für das
Deutsche Reich, Vol. 34 (1913), Berlin 1913, p. 129; Seherr-Thoss, Hans-Christoph Graf von:
75 Jahre ADAC 1903-1978, Tagebuch eines Automobilclubs, second edition, München 1978,
p. 76, and 241; Fack, Dietmar: Automobil, Verkehr und Erziehung: Motorisierung und Sozia-
lisation zwischen Beschleunigung und Anpassung 1885-1945, Opladen 2000, p. 134 and 218;
Gadow (as in 25) p. 40f.; Flik, Reiner: Nutzung von Kraftfahrzeugen bis 1939 – Konsum-
oder Investitionsgut? In: Walter, Rolf (Ed.): Geschichte des Konsums. Erträge der 20. Ar-
beitstagung der Gesellschaft für Sozial- und Wirtschaftsgeschichte 23.-26. April 2003 in
Greifswald, (Vierteljahrschrift für Sozial- und Wirtschaftsgeschichte, Beihefte, Vol. 175),
Wiesbaden 2004, pp. 249-269, here p. 250. For the number of registered automobiles from
1920-1925, of which omnibuses were subtracted, since 1922 without Saarland, see Merki,
Christoph Maria: Der holprige Siegeszug des Automobils 1895-1930. Zur Motorisierung des
Strassenverkehrs in Frankreich, Deutschland und der Schweiz, Wien et. al. 2002, p. 115.

After 1910[41], when the licences were first registered nationwide in Berlin, the number of licences grew to a greater extent and much faster than the amount of registered cars, which can be proved by statistics. In the pre-war year of 1913, when the total stock automobiles had been just under 50.000, the accumulated number of licences had been more than 130.000. From 1910-1925, altogether more than 700.000 driving licences were issued, whereas less than 175.000 cars existed in 1925. Of course it might be complicated to find out how many licences were issued and withdrawn, or if anyone who owned a licence actually used his or her car.[42] Nevertheless the number of licences is an indicator, which shows that an invention is culturally adapted, i.e. also by law.

The requirement to obtain a licence to drive an automobile has emerged as an appeal to take lessons in driving and pass the driving test in order to have at least the legal right to travel by car. In the early years of the motor car, considerably more people obtained a driving licence than possessed an automobile themselves. A significant part of the holders of driving licences were chauffeurs,[43] who used it in their profession.[44]

Certainly, only a minority could afford to buy an automobile, whereas the bicycle was already changing from a sport-vehicle for dandies to daily transportation for the average worker. It was not until the late 1950s that the main part of society could afford a motor car in Germany.[45]

---

[41] In 1910, the *Sammelstelle für Nachrichten über Führer von Kraftfahrzeugen (SNFK)*, subordinated at the *Berliner Polizeipräsidium*, was created. That administration collected information about the drivers and the licences. The files do not exist any more. For more detailed information see Haberlandt, Ludwig: Aus der Chronik des Kraftfahrt-Bundesamtes, Berlin [1988], p. 29.

[42] E.g. in four years from 1910-1913, 814 driving licences were withdrawn and in 2450 cases the agency refused to issue a licence. BArch R 1501/113998.

[43] Chauffeurs could enhance their position in the master-servant social structure due to their mechanical knowledge. See Borg, Kevin: The "Chauffeur Problem" in the Early Auto Era: Structural Theory and the Users of Technology. In: Technology and Culture (1999) No. 4, pp. 797-832.

[44] Merki, Siegeszug des Automobils (as in 40) pp. 326-329.

[45] The USA and GB were the first automobile societies before the Second World War. Germany: There exist many indicators and time frames, for the majority of society to afford cars: See Edelmann, Heidrun: Vom Luxusgut zum Gebrauchsgegenstand. Die Geschichte der Verbreitung von Personenkraftwagen in Deutschland, (Schriftenreihe des Verbandes der Automobilindustrie, Vol. 60), Frankfurt 1989, p. 224-229; Flik, Reiner: Von Ford lernen? Automobilbau und Motorisierung in Deutschland bis 1933, Köln et al. 2001, p. 3. At the latest, about 1970, we can speak of an automobile society. More than half of the working class' households owned a car by then. See Sachs, Wolfgang: Die auto-mobile Gesellschaft. Vom Aufstieg und Niedergang einer Utopie. In: Brüggemeier, Franz-Josef; Rommelspacher, Tho-

From a retrospective view, we can argue that law had a bearing on promoting the car – turning it from an object of luxury into a transport vehicle for the masses.[46] In addition to safety aspects, the introduction of the age-norm of 18 and the driving licence can also be interpreted as signs of the changing of a technological invention into an accepted innovation and its integration into everyday life (course). Law addresses new means of transport only when they become relevant for society and economy.[47] Next to the social and technical change, a new legal system arose concerning road traffic and these new means of transport. Beyond that, reaching the legal age of 18 has become closely associated with obtaining a driving licence in Germany's (auto-)mobile society. The opportunity to obtain a driving licence established for the most part of society the desire to drive and finally own an automobile. That had a big impact on the broad diffusion of the car after the Second World War. Even when the access to public means of transport and airports is meanwhile a more important factor, road traffic and automobile are still dominating in various forms: Children are prepared or socialised beginning with safety education in the kindergarten and school. They ride bikes, apply for a motorcycle licence until they have the desired driving licence for automobiles.

3. To Hold a Licence – or the Revocation of the Driving Licence

To apply for a licence, to take driving lessons and pass the driving test were only one aspect. The other side of the picture implies holding the licence. Hence, the jurisdiction regarding the suspension of the driving licence in the early 20th century will be analysed. What happened to delinquents in road traffic?

---

mas (Ed.): Besiegte Natur. Geschichte der Umwelt im 19. und 20. Jahrhundert, second edition, München 1989, pp. 106-123 in this case p. 115.

[46] Other reasons like taxation laws, e. g. luxury tax and gasoline tax affected this development too. See Edelmann (as in 45); Kopper, Christopher: Der Durchbruch des PKW zum Massenkonsumgut 1950-1964. In: Jahrbuch für Wirtschaftsgeschichte (2010) No. 1, pp. 19-36.

[47] The growing number of accidents did eventually require the legislator to deal with the driver and the uncertain insurance questions. In Germany the auto liability insurance was introduced to deal with the problems of liability. For the discussion and development of the Gefährdungshaftung, see the dissertation of Gadow (as in 25).

number of cases	jurisdiction or result c. 1906/1907
58	The car drivers got neither police penalty, nor had there been a trial. Only in 8 cases of this was the driver dead.
42	Dismissal of the legal proceeding
10	The sentence was one of acquittal
2	The hit-and-run driver could not be investigated
1	Police penalty
17	Sentence i.e. jail sentence from 8 days to 1.5 years
15	There had been no adjudication before 1 April 1908
145	**Total number of worst cases of loss of life**

A statistic of 1906 and 1907 regarding automobile accidents shows that the jurisprudence was in favour of the car drivers. In proportion of registered cars, there had been many automobile accidents and high death rates. In the year 1906/07, more than 4800 accidents were recorded by questionnaire by the local police authorities. 2419 of these caused personal injury. The 145 worst cases if loss of life results were analysed.[48]

Which causes could lead to the revocation of the driving licence round WWI? Article 4 of the Motor car act of 1909 says:

"If the assumption is proved by facts, that a person is unqualified to drive motorised vehicles, then the according administrative agency can revoke his/her licence for life-time or a certain period of time. After the revocation of the permission, that means the legal right, the driving licence has to be handed over to the agency. The revocation is effective for the whole empire."[49]

Beside some changes, this act is still in force, today in Article 4 of the road traffic act, so called *Straßenverkehrsgesetz (StVG)*. Causes were e.g. drink-driving, a physical or mental handicap or a lack of morality. Facts of

---

[48] Becker, G[ustav]: Ueber Automobil-Unfälle in Deutschland 1906 – 1907, Vortrag auf Grund amtlicher Ermittlungen gehalten auf dem I. Internationalen Congress für Rettungswesen in Frankfurt a. M. am 12. Juni 1908, Berlin 1908.

[49] Own translation of article 4, *Gesetz über den Verkehr mit Kraftfahrzeugen vom 3.5.1909*, RGBl. 1909 pp. 437ff. In original source: „*Werden Tatsachen festgestellt, welche die Annahme rechtfertigen, daß eine Person zum Führen von Kraftfahrzeugen ungeeignet ist, so kann ihr die Fahrerlaubnis dauernd oder für bestimmte Zeit durch die zuständige Verwaltungsbehörde entzogen werden; nach der Entziehung ist der Führerschein der Behörde abzuliefern. Die Entziehung ist für das ganze Reich wirksam.*"

the case were e.g. speeding, reckless driving or to cause an accident with injured or death casualties. The licence could also be revoked from criminals, even if the criminal act had nothing to do with the driving licence.

A decision in 1914 of the administrative court of Baden could serve as an example for the revocation of a licence: Speeding, reckless driving and using the wrong side of the street were the causes, why a car driver killed two playing children and injured one child. He was sent to prison for three months. His driving licence was revoked for lifetime, because he was seen by the administrative court to be unqualified to drive.[50]

It seems that for motorists the "driving licence" document is even more important than the legal right to drive a car. Very often motorists put the driving licence *(Führerschein)* on a level with the so called *Fahrerlaubnis*, the legal right to drive. In the English language, a difference in the term does not exist as in German. E.g. in 1974, a 38-year old car driver ate his driving licence, when he had to show it to the police after an accident.[51] This is of course a strange example, but it shows that the legal document and the legal right are often mixed up.

The revocation of a licence is an exclusion from taking part in road traffic. A special kind of administrative law grants and revokes the permissions to drive. Today, specialist road traffic solicitors plead the cases of those who ran into trouble with traffic authorities.

Individual freedom for the user and public safety on streets seem to be diametrically opposed. Road safety which is the aim of the legislator is in contrast to the one-eyed perspective of many delinquents. People who are banned from driving for a certain period of time, often try to take their suspension in vacation, e.g. lorry-drivers and cab drivers require the driving licence for their profession. In fact, the revocation of the driving licence could be a cause for a dismissal from employment. The loss of the licence is also a symbol of not being part of society, of having a wrong life cycle, which does not confirm to the typical one. Summarised, we can conclude that the exclusion of mobility by the revocation of a driving licence has an impact for the normal course of life. The question of having a licence or not, underlines too the importance of that legal document.

---

[50] VerwGerH, 23 September 1914, Architekt E. R. in Pf. g. Staatsverwaltungsbehörde (Bezirksamt Pf.). K., See No. 37, Badische Rechtspraxis und Annalen der Großh[erzoglichen] Badischen Gerichte (1916) Vol. 18, der Annalen Vol. 82, pp. 90f.
[51] Seherr-Thoss (as in 40) p. 628.

4. Conclusion

Having the legal capacity to drive a car when reaching the age of 18 – or in other countries with 16 or 17[52] – and actually driving a car transformed. It has changed from an opportunity for a wealthy minority and professional chauffeurs around 1910 to a "must" for everyone today at least in industrialised countries. This right is symbolised within the legal document – the driving licence.

At first glance, due to accompanied driving, it seems that young person's drive cars earlier. Accompanied driving momentously reduces the risk for new drivers, as experience has shown. In Germany, the model of accompanied driving at age 17 *(Begleitetes Fahren)*, tested in some of the federal stated, will enter into force on 1 January 2011 in all of Germany. 17-year-old persons will then be able to drive a car if accompanied by a designated thirty years old person until their 18th birthday.[53] Regarding road safety, the lack of adulthood of the driver is more than compensated by the age and operating experience of the "tutor".

What is the impact? Driving alone without a tutor, also symbolising freedom is still tied to adulthood. In fact, the stage fever to enter the next act, driving a car, declined for some parts of the youth. Especially in cities, a proportion of the youth hold off on or even pass on obtaining the licence. For parts of the youth, mobile communication is more important than mobility by car. Young persons have to assign priorities regarding their salary or allowance.[54]

The decline of mobility by car for parts of the youth is a blueprint of the development since the 1970s. On the face of it, it seems that nowadays the legal right which entails actually the opportunity of using motorised vehicles decreased for a part of society. Of course it is often faster, cheaper, safer and more comfortable to use public means of transport.[55] We could therefore consider post-materialism, environmental or economic reasons or

---

[52] E.g. in the UK, the qualifying age for a car licence of 17 years was introduced by the Motor Car Act 1903. See Mahaffy, Robert Pentland; Dodson, Gerald: The Law Relating to Motor Cars, London 1910, p. 2.

[53] This person will have to meet certain requirements: they must be at least thirty years old, have held a driving licence for five years and must not have more than three penalty points in the Central Register of Traffic Offenders.

[54] Tully, Claus: Für das Auto bleibt kaum Geld. Fakten und Überlegungen zur Mobilität von Jugendlichen. In: Frankfurter Allgemeine Zeitung, 31 August 2010, No. 201, p. T4.

[55] Krämer-Badoni (as in 38) p. 59.

people who will not travel by car everyday or even do not own a car. However, the causes are irrelevant in this case.

Forecasting the further development is not the task of a historian. Nevertheless, the driving licence is still important for the professional life and social standing. It remains an important document for the most part of society. In the style of Norbert Stieniczka, it can be observed that someone who does not obtain a driving licence nowadays might be suspected to be critical towards technology.[56] The technological product automobile has developed into a part of the social normal life course.[57] Moreover, in the Automobile Society road traffic is important for everyday life, for the institutional life course[58] and a crucial part of the legal system that deals with it. Ensuring independence, mobility by car is also important for older people. The disputes about revoking old people's licences show that the right implied in the legal document emerged to a kind of basic right, the freedom to choose and drive motorised vehicles.[59]

My investigations have shown that driving licences are more than a piece of paper. Two levels of its symbolic character can be identified: The causes of the introduction of *Radfahrkarten* and driving licences combined with age limits and other restrictions were to prove the competence of the driver and to enhance road safety. In few words, that was *ex ante* the aim of the state. Today the individual symbol of the document expressed in flexibility, freedom, adulthood and mobility for the user prevails: The legal roadblocks developed into a normative archetype for life course, which have to be achieved on the one hand and which give reasons for freedom of automobility on the other. In short, that is the position of the individual user, which can be identified only *ex post*. New drivers are proud of passing driving school, driving test and getting the licence, i.e. proving their

---

[56] Original: „Wer heute keinen Führerschein besitzt, dem wird schnell unterstellt, er habe auch sonst eine technikferne oder gar technikskeptische Einstellung und Lebensweise." Stieniczka (as in 31) p. 421.

[57] Sachs (as in 45) p. 118.

[58] The so-called institutional life course, which divides life in the three phases of education, professional life and retirement, has emerged since the end of the 18th century, See Kohli, Martin: Die Institutionalisierung des Lebenslaufs, Historische Befunde und theoretische Argumente. In: Kölner Zeitschrift für Soziologie und Sozialpsychologie (1985), pp. 1-29.

[59] Landerer, Helmut: Alter, Recht und Straßenverkehr seit dem Ende des 19. Jahrhunderts – Zugangsbeschränkungen, Schutzbestimmungen und Ausschluss von Mobilität mit Hilfe von Altersstufen. In: Ruppert, Stefan (Ed.): Lebensalter und Recht. Zur Segmentierung des menschlichen Lebenslaufs durch rechtliche Regelungen seit 1750, (Studien zur europäischen Rechtsgeschichte 249), Frankfurt am Main 2010, pp. 295-322, here pp. 317-320.

competence and responsible participation in traffic. That important step to adulthood is inhered in the legal document. The safety aspect of the licence takes a backseat after some time of having the licence in favour of its individual symbolic character. It is often ignored by users until the licence is withdrawn.

Licences in road traffic developed into important legal documents of daily life. That development traces back to our focus around 1900, when licences and age-specific norms were established for bicycles and automobiles.

Kapitel III
„Medien des Rechts"

Mirror of Changing Law:
The *Journal des Tribunaux* in the *fin de siècle*

Bart Coppein

1. Introduction

Legal journals throughout early-modern history have had an important role in bringing law to the stage. Journals determined their own specific focus on jurisdictions and areas of law and helped mostly also in shaping the identity of the social group of legal practitioners. That way it becomes clear that a legal journal had always an underlying vision on law and that its choices were never neutral. Some insight into the history of law journals has already been achieved, but much research awaits future legal historians.[1] For Belgium, the German legal historian Ernst Holthöfer made an exhaustive inventory of the law reviews in the 19th and 20th centuries.[2] A first general analysis was recently published by the Belgian scholar Dirk Heirbaut, who characterized the Belgian law reviews as *"instruments of legal practice and linguistic conflicts"* and denied, just as Holthöfer had concluded before him, that there had ever existed real scientific law reviews in his country.[3] About the *Journal des Tribunaux* – the subject of this article – there exists only an unpublished master thesis and some small case studies besides the anniversary commemoration articles in the review itself.[4]

Abbreviations: col. = column; p. = page; J.T.= Journal des Tribunaux; POB = Parti Ouvrier Belge.

[1] Stolleis, Michael (ed.): *Juristische Zeitschriften. Die neuen Medien des 18.-20. Jahrhunderts* (Studien zur europäischen Rechtsgeschichte, 128). Frankfurt am Main, 1999; Stolleis, Michael and Simon, Thomas (eds.): *Juristische Zeitschriften in Europa* (Studien zur europäischen Rechtsgeschichte, 214). Frankfurt am Main, 2006.

[2] Holthöfer, Ernst: *Beiträge zur Justizgeschichte der Niederlande, Belgiens und Luxemburgs im 19. und 20. Jahrhundert* (Rechtsprechung. Materialien und Studien. Veröffentlichungen des Max-Planck-Instituts für Europäische Rechtsgeschichte Frankfurt am Main. Band 6). Frankfurt am Main, 1993, pp. 147-192.

[3] Heirbaut, Dirk: "Law reviews in Belgium (1763-2004): instruments of legal practice and linguistic conflicts". In: Stolleis and Simon (as in 1), pp. 343-367.

[4] Carré, Véronique: *Le Journal des Tribunaux d'Edmond Picard (1881-1899). Approche d'un journal judiciaire au dix-neuvième siècle*. Unpublished master thesis, Université Libre de Bruxelles, Faculté de Philosophie et Lettres, Brussels, 1986; Lesaffer, Randall: "Le Journal des Tribunaux (1904-1914). De Belgisch-Nederlandse betrekkingen vanuit het standpunt van de Belgische

We will consider in this article the terms 'legal journal' and 'law review' as synonyms of each other. It is not easy to find a sufficient definition and the literature does not present a uniform opinion whether law reviews should show on the one hand a more scholarly character or may on the other hand be especially oriented towards practice, although research results seem to go mostly in the second direction.[5] We prefer therefore the pragmatic attitude of Heirbaut, who calls a law review "*a publication about law for lawyers, published with some regularity*". More or less placing himself at the same point of view, the French scholar Jean-Paul Barrière suggests as main characteristics for a professional journal "une périodicité assez longue [...] contenant mises au point scientifiques (au sens large), essais, débats, comptes rendus d'ouvrage et de publications ou informations liées au domaine de la revue".[6]

Both definitions are appropriate to the *Journal des Tribunaux*. It was founded on 14th December 1881 by the Brussels editor Fernand Larcier (1852-1889), the well-known Belgian lawyer and jurist Edmond Picard (1836-1924) and his *confrères* Alexandre de Burlet (1841-1891), Victor Bonnevie (1849-1920) and Octave Maus (1856-1919).[7] Thus, the majority

nationalisten". In: Stevens, Fred and Van den Auweele, Dirk (eds.): *Uutwysens d'archiven. Handelingen van de XIe Belgisch-Nederlandse rechtshistorische dagen. Leuven, 22-23 november 1990.* Louvain, 1992, pp. 107-139; Lesaffer, Randall: "De justitie en de media". In: Heirbaut, Dirk, Rousseaux, Xavier and Velle, Karel (eds.): *Histoire politique et sociale de la justice en Belgique de 1830 à nos jours.* Bruges, 2004, pp. 357-368. See in the *Journal des Tribunaux* itself amongst others the following commemoration articles: Cambier, J.: "Histoire du Journal des Tribunaux". In: *J.T.*, 50 (1935) 3419; Sterckx, D. a.o.: "Un siècle de J.T.". In: *J.T.*, 101 (1982) 5200, pp. 262-267.

[5] Simon, Thomas and Stolleis, Michael: "Juristische Zeitschriften in Europa". In: Stolleis and Simon (as in 1), p. 5.

[6] Heirbaut (as in 3), p. 343, note 1; Barrière, J.-P.: "Un genre à part: les revues juridiques professionnelles". In: Pluet-Despatin, J., Leymarie, M. and Mollier, J.-Y. (eds.): *La Belle Epoque des revues 1880-1914.* Caen, 2002, p. 269.

[7] See for the latest research results about Picard our own publications, in which the elder literature is fully integrated and completed with original archival input and a thorough analysis of the extensive oeuvre of Picard. It concerns: Coppein, Bart: "Edmond Picard (1836-1924), avocat bruxellois et belge par excellence de la deuxième moitié de la XIXe siècle". In: Bernaudeau, Vincent. a.o. (eds): *Les praticiens du droit du Moyen Age à l'époque contemporaine. Approches prosopographiques (Belgique, Canada, France, Italie, Prusse).* Rennes, 2008, pp. 225-237; Coppein, Bart: "Edmond Picard, actor and witness of the socialization of law in Belgium at the end of the 19th century". In: Hornyák, S. a.o. (eds.): *Turning points and breaklines* (Yearbook of Young Legal History, 4). München, 2009, pp. 151-166; Coppein, Bart: *Edmond Picard (1836-1924), actor en getuige van een veranderend Belgisch rechtsdenken in Europees perspectief aan het einde van de negentiende eeuw.* Unpublished PhD thesis, Katholieke Universiteit Leuven, Louvain, 2010. A book version is scheduled for the end of 2010. See about Ferdinand Larcier and his publishing

of its board of editors was formed by lawyers; Picard became the first editor in chief. The first issue dated from 15th December 1881.[8] Without doubt, the *Journal des Tribunaux*, which still exists today as the most famous Belgian French-speaking general law review and has become above all a scholarly-liked work instrument for practitioners that is rather embarrassed by its deviant past, is certainly for the first two periods of its history one of the most interesting Belgian and even European law reviews and did not follow at all the normal pattern of such a specialized and 'isolated' journal. Hence, it has been called rightly *"a rebellious journal"*.[9] If one looks closer, it appears indeed that this law review had a special character and mirrored very well the new visions on law in Belgium.

What was exactly the mission statement of the *Journal des Tribunaux?* Why did it seem necessary to some lawyers to found that journal and what was its unique selling position compared to other general law reviews? How big was the influence of the editor in chief? Who was its audience and which were the consequences of this choice? Which subjects were reported and gave the journal its typical character? How representative were some points of view for the broader community of jurists? To keep the study manageable, we are forced to limit our analysis to the period until the First World War, the major event that closed in fact finally the *Ancien Régime* in Belgium as it did also in other Western-European countries.[10] Moreover, we will privilege the first period of the journal and only briefly study the second period.

2. Methodology

Whoever wants to write a press study has to think first carefully about his methodology. Although commonly used, press is not an easy source to deal with. Two main possibilities appear: or one prefers a quantitative

---

house, which was continued after his death by his widow: "Mort de Ferdinand Larcier". In: *J.T.*, 8 (1889) 633, col. 849-850. See about the other three mentioned persons, who were all lawyers at the Brussels' court of appeal: "Mort de Me Alexandre de Burlet". In: *J.T.*, 10 (1891) 787, col. 377-382; *Biografisch repertorium van België vanaf 1830. Letter B.* Brussels, 1956, p. 104; Maus, Madeleine: *Trente années de lutte pour l'art: les XX, La Libre Esthétique 1884-1914.* Brussels, 1980.
[8] Carré (as in 4), p. 11.
[9] Heirbaut (as in 3), p. 352.
[10] Mayer, Arno: The Persistence of the Old Regime. Europe to the Great War. New York, 1981.

analysis or one goes for a qualitative approach. If desired, a combined approach is also possible.

A quantitative method means essentially counting and focuses on the external aspects of a journal. Usually a rather limited number of journal issues is selected by a random sample survey, which is not always fully representative and cannot bring all the nuances and details to surface. Such an approach can have some advantages, e.g. the easiness of comparing journals with each other. Yet, it can show also serious disadvantages.

Let us illustrate this with an example from the unpublished master thesis of Véronique Carré. She tried to calculate the average number of columns for each section par year during the period when Picard was editor in chief of the *Journal des Tribunaux*. The main problem of her final result appears to be the difficultness to distinguish clear sections. Because there were not always section titles above the articles and some section titles did also not fully cover the therein published articles, she had to decide mostly herself under which section she would classify articles. It must be stated simply that other scholars could have made other choices. If we look at this method critically, we do not see ourselves enough difference between sections as 'parliamentary debates', 'analyses of legislation' and the real 'editorials', who all expressed the (political) opinion of the journal.[11]

Personally, we preferred for our research a qualitative approach, which really could accent the intrinsic positions of the journal. Especially the aforementioned opinion articles were privileged, where as the extensive jurisdiction was skipped almost totally. Although this method could not exclude some subjectivity, e.g. in the choice of the read articles, the final result was much more detailed and precise.

One of the biggest problems was of course the great presence of anonymous articles, as is the case in many journals of that period. Only the most important articles were signed, usually by the editor in chief, but not always. Some articles could be demystified through bibliographies, but the great majority stayed as anonymous as before. Fortunately, a lot of articles could be attributed to the first editor in chief through their very own style. For the other articles, those were possibly written by other members of the board of editors; one can suppose certainly that they express also the opinion of the editor in chief and could not have been published without his permission.

---

[11] See for the mentioned table: Carré (as in 4), p. 41.

Another problem was the great gap between facts and opinion: The articles usually only contained a certain opinion, as the facts were mostly already known by contemporary readers using other information sources. This means that twenty-first-century scholars must find other ways to remedy their lack of knowledge, either by reading general daily newspapers either by using, if possible, the available literature. Rarely, it will be necessary to combine this with detailed archival research.

3. The Foundation Period: Edmond Picard as Editor in Chief (1881-1900)

The question that first deserves an answer is of course why Picard and his companions founded the *Journal des Tribunaux*. In 1881, there existed already a general French-speaking law review in Belgium with a rich tradition, namely *La Belgique judiciaire*. What was wrong with that journal and what would the challengers do differently? *La Belgique judiciaire* was founded in 1842 by four lawyers of the Brussels' court of appeal, but its board of editors was controlled very soon by magistrates and university professors. In its mission statement, the editors had explicitly expressed their ambition to renew the Belgian legal science and to link up with the glorious past of Viglius d'Attya, Joos de Damhouder, Gabriel Mudaeus and so many other great 'Belgian' jurists.

Special attention would be paid to legal history, critical commentaries of legislation and the publication of jurisdiction.[12] Yet, after forty years of existence, the conclusion could not be other than that *La Belgique judiciaire* had not managed to realise this dream. The journal was modelled after the French *Gazette des Tribunaux*[13] and filled it columns mostly with Belgian and foreign jurisdiction, which makes clear that it was indeed mostly meant for legal practitioners.

Moreover, the journal published sometimes extremely detailed articles of scholars and, at the beginning of the new juridical year, the tedious opening speeches of the presidents of the Court of Cassation and the three courts of appeal. In other words, *La Belgique judiciaire* had become a very classic law review, which followed the French pattern and was treated by its

---

[12] [Lavallée, H.; Arntz, E.; Orts, A. and Bartels, J.]: ["Au lecteur"]. In: *La Belgique judiciaire*, 1 (1842-1843) 1, col. 1-6.
[13] This journal was published in France from 1775 until 1789 and again from 1825 until 1955, when it was continued by its opponent, the *Gazette de Palais*. Barrière (as in 6), p. 281, note 10.

readers above all as a practical work instrument. Typical was that they mostly kept their volumes bound in books in their libraries, for which the used small tabloid format was indeed ideal. *La Belgique judiciaire* could not claim to be a real journal, which reported in short articles the judicial actuality and which revived Belgian legal science. Additionally, some issues were unfortunately published with great tardiness, mostly because it took some time for the authors to finish their essays.[14] The foundation of the *Journal des Tribunaux* must thus be seen as a reaction to the 'fossilization' of *La Belgique judiciaire*. If things had gone differently for this journal and if the wish of the original editors had been respected, it seems realistic to suppose that the *Journal des Tribunaux* would never have been founded at all. During the years 1860 and 1870 Picard was a respected contributor of *La Belgique judiciaire*, but it appears clearly that at the end of this period his collaboration was fading away.[15]

With the *Journal des Tribunaux* the founders really wanted to renew legal journalism and hoped to be a legal equivalent of a general newspaper.[16] This becomes very clear if one looks closely to the content. Already in the first numbers they opted for a rather rigid structure. Each section had its fixed place in every number. The first page was usually reserved for the editorial or other opinion articles, such as summaries of parliamentary debates or commentaries on legislation. At the bottom of that page normally begun the so-called 'feuilleton'. This could contain almost everything, going from jurisprudence to legal novels. The second page presented the most important Belgian jurisdiction, whilst relevant foreign jurisdiction and sometimes also jurisprudence were signalized at the third page. The continuation of the feuilleton was printed beneath the second and third pages. The fourth and last page gave the legal chronicle and the advertisements.[17] In the beginning the *Journal des Tribunaux* was only

---

[14] Heirbaut (as in 3), pp. 347-348.

[15] The first article from Picard in *La Belgique judiciaire* dated from 1862 and his regular contributions ended in 1879: Claudius [= Picard, Edmond]: "Examen de quelques questions relatives à la profession d'avocat". In: *La Belgique judiciaire*, 20 (1862) 91, col. 1441-1447; Picard, Edmond: "Paradoxe sur l'avocat". In: *La Belgique judiciaire*, 37 (1879) 80, col. 1265-1269. In the years 1880 Picard published his last two articles in that journal: Picard, Edmond: "Essai sur la criminalité d'après la science moderne". In: *La Belgique judiciaire*, 39 (1881) 12, col. 188-192; Picard, Edmond: "Embryologie juridique des droits intellectuels". In: *La Belgique judiciaire*, 43 (1885) 47, col. 737-750.

[16] Carré (as in 4), p. 24.

[17] Carré (as in 4), pp. 18-21 and 101-110.

published once a week at Thursday. From the 1st January 1884, a supplementary Sunday edition was added. From 1890, issues were not produced during the summer months while the courts were closed, which was compensated by double numbers thereafter.[18]

If the *Journal des Tribunaux* acquired under the guidance of Picard its typical character, this was essentially due to four major stresses, which were expressed especially in the articles at the first page but certainly also throughout. Contrary to *La Belgique judiciaire* that guarded carefully its political neutrality, the *Journal des Tribunaux* pronounced explicitly the ambition to vulgarize law, supported actively the battle for the extension of suffrage, stressed always the need for social legislation, pleaded for an independent Bar and privileged new developments in law. We cannot treat all these cases in detail, but will only illustrate the most important tendencies and points of view.

3.1 Bringing Law to the People

With the *Journal des Tribunaux*, Picard and his co-editors hoped first of all to create a *rapprochement* between the judicial world and the common people. Law seemed for the common people something strange that they did not know and in which they were in fact not even interested. As a result, law had lost it social function and was not adapted anymore to the new needs of society. In the opening article of the first issue, Picard formulated the ambitious goal to close that gap or at least to try to do so:

"The judicial activity has in Belgium this specific character that it is happening in a certain way somewhere far away, in an almost closed world, unknown by all, except by those who are staying there. [...] However, it is important that the judicial life should be common to the whole nation. Only the nation can give the feeling of law. When citizens are not interested anymore in it, law looses its force, because one does not understand the meaning nor the utility."

Therefore, Picard promised to cover subjects that could interest the masses and to use a very simple language.[19] For that reason the *Journal des*

---

[18] "A nos lecteurs. Avis important". In: *J.T.*, 2 (1883) 99, col. 777; Carré (as in 4), pp. 22-23.

[19] Quote translated from French: "*L'activité judiciaire présente en Belgique ce caractère singulier qu'elle se meut en quelque sorte à l'écart, dans une région presque fermée, ignorée de tous, excepté de ceux qui s'y trouvent. [...] Il importe cependant que la vie judiciaire soit commune à la nation entière. Seule elle peut*

Tribunaux was also printed on the courant great size of daily newspapers, which meant 48 x 32 cm, – although it always rained complaints from readers about the unwieldiness thereof – and sold on the streets and in cafés.[20] Yet, that original ambition was much too high to have any chance to succeed. The failure could have been predicted, knowing that a significant part of the Belgian population was illiterate, did not know French, could not afford to buy such an expensive journal, or was simply still not interested.[21]

Nevertheless, Picard continued his original conception. In 1894, he gave a lecture for the *Fédération des Avocats*, which was literally reproduced in the *Journal des Tribunaux*. Therein he repeated that there was a gap between the law and the people on which that law was founded. The people did not trust the law anymore, which had become a specialised matter for the legislator and a cast of jurists. According to Picard, exactly this alienation had caused the social issue of his time. The only possible solution for him was a return of law to the people, by which law would become immediately more just. In other words, the social battle of the labourers was first a legal battle and not a political one:

"What must be conquerred, is the Law that one part of the nation does not have as that part should have it. To that part has only been given an imperfect law, in which the equity is violated, in which there is a crying injustice."

Every member of the Fédération des Avocats should oppose permanently those unfair situations and help spread law outside the courts.[22]

---

donner le sentiment du droit. Quand les citoyens s'en désintéressent, la loi perd sa force parce qu'on n'en comprend plus le sens ni l'utilité." Picard, Edmond: "Au lecteur". In: J.T., 1 (1881) 1, p. 1. See also: Carré (as in 4), pp. 9-10; Lesaffer: "De justitie en de media", pp. 357-359.

[20] Picard, Edmond: "Question de format". In: *J.T.*, 5 (1886) 294, col. 1-4; Picard, Edmond: "La mission d'un journal judiciaire". In: *J.T.*, 11 (1892) 849, col. 1-4; [Picard, Edmond]: "La nouvelle vie judiciaire". In: *J.T.*, 2 (1883) 95, col. 713-715. See also: Carré (as in 4), p. 15.

[21] One issue of the *Journal des Tribunaux* costed 20 cents, where as the price of daily Belgian newspapers such as *Le Soir*, *Vooruit* or *Le Peuple* was between 1 and 5 cents. Carré (as in 4), pp. 11-12 and 134; Sterckx (as in 4), p. 262. At the outbreak of the First World War still a tenth of the Belgian population was illiterate. Strikwerda, Carl: *A House Divided. Caholics, Socialists and Flemish Nationalists in nineteenth-century Belgium*. Lanham, 1997, p. 34.

[22] Quote translated from French: "Ce qu'il faut conquérir, c'est le Droit qu'une partie de la nation n'a pas comme elle devrait l'avoir. On ne lui a concédé qu'un droit imparfait où l'équité

3.2 Herald of the Socialization of Law

Following on this will to vulgarize law, the *Journal des Tribunaux* supported closely the socialization of law, as appears clearly in its pleas for extension of the census suffrage and the promulgation of social legislation.[23]

Concerning the suffrage issue, Picard published an extensive *Histoire d'une réforme législative*, that argued for a universal suffrage, in the journal during the summer of 1882.[24] Especially from 1886 on, the *Journal des Tribunaux* joined actively the debate.[25] At the beginning of the 1890s the campaign of the Parti Ouvrier Belge (POB) for universal suffrage revived and Picard helped by appearing as a celebrated speaker at an endless string of meetings. A stenography version of the speech he held in the Brussels *Maison du Peuple* on 26th February 1891 was published integrally at his demand in the *Journal des Tribunaux*. Towards his labourers' public he confirmed that he had always been a supporter of a real and simple universal suffrage:

"Regarding myself, as ever (it seems that I should be surprised and inquiet because I did not change my opinion about it, contrary to so many others), I support the pure and simple Universal Suffrage. I do not see so much evil in it. [...] I do not want to throw some teeth of it nor to cut off its claws or its crest. I do want it as it is: completely nude, in its natural beauty. [...] That

---

est violée, où l'injustice est criante." Picard, Edmond: "La vulgarisation du Droit". In: J.T., 13 (1894) 1105, col. 1427-1430. The same evolutions can be stated for the Dutch journal Paleis van Justitie, at least from its founding in 1872 until its change of editorial accent in 1893. See about this journal: Jansen, Corjo: "Popularisering van het recht in Nederland. Enige beschouwingen over de kloof tussen recht en volk in het laatste kwart van de 19ᵉ en in het begin van de 20ᵉ eeuw". In: Tijdschrift voor Rechtsgeschiedenis, LXIII (1995) 1-2, pp. 120-121 and 126-130.

[23] See about this concept: Coppein: "Edmond Picard, actor and witness of the socialization of law in Belgium", pp. 151-153. See in general for this paragraph also: Carré (as in 4), pp. 45-67.

[24] Picard, Edmond: "L'évolution des lois électorales en Belgique depuis 1830". In: J.T., 1 (1881-1882) 28, col. 441-443; 29, col. 457-460; 30, col. 473-476; 31, col. 489-493; 32, col. 505-510; 33, col. 521-525; 34, col. 537-540; 35, col. 553-557; 36, col. 569-572; 37, col. 585-589; 38, col. 601-605; 39, col. 617-620; 40, col. 633-638; 41, col. 649-654; 42, col. 665-670; 43, col. 681-684; 44, col. 697-701 en 45, col. 713-717. See also: Carré (as in 4), pp. 50-51.

[25] Carré (as in 4), pp. 117-123. See e.g. the following articles in the J.T.: [Picard, Edmond]: "Interdiction de la manifestation du 13 juin". In: J.T., 5 (1886) 336, col. 673-677; "Affaire De Fuisseaux". In: J.T., 5 (1886) 337, col. 692-699; "Affaire Anseele. Actes d'accusation". In: J.T., 5 (1886) 338, col. 708-710; "Affaires Defuisseaux [sic] et Anseele". In: J.T., 5 (1886) 338, col. 705-710; "Lettre ouverte à Me Englebienne". In: J.T., 5 (1886) 358, col. 1029.

is because it appears as the expression of a great historical and social law, to which nothing can resist." [26]

In 1892 the editorials of the *Journal des Tribunaux* – mostly written by Picard himself as he confessed later – were totally devoted to the revision of the Constitution and the extension of suffrage. The parliamentary discussion was followed from week to week and extensively commented. The journal could not be satisfied with less than universal suffrage:

"The Force that will give triumph to the Universal Suffrage is in the Nation. It is not only one class anymore who is claiming it, but there are thousands of bourgeois' souls, inspired by a zeal of Justice and Fraternity." [27]

Consequently the editorial board opposed vehemently against a phased attribution, warning that there would be no peace in the country as long as it was not totally conquered. That the period of the census suffrage had brought general welfare for the Belgian population was strongly denied.

---

[26] Quote translated from French: *"Quant à moi, depuis toujours (comme ça m'étonne et m'inquiète de ne pas changer là-dessus, alors que tant d'autres changent), je suis pour le Suffrage Universel pur et simple. Je n'y vois pas tant de malice. [...] je ne veux pas lui arracher quelques dents, lui rogner ses griffes ou sa crinière. Je le veux tel qu'il est: tout nu, dans sa beauté naturelle. [...] C'est qu'il apparaît comme l'expression d'une grande loi historique et sociale, à laquelle rien ne résiste."* Picard, Edmond: "La législation sociale. La Revision constitutionnelle. Le suffrage universel". In: *J.T.*, 10 (1891) 782, col. 297-308 and 302-303 (quote). This speech was partially reprinted in the festschrift that was published for the 65th anniversary of Picard: *In Memoriam. Manifestation du 21 Décembre 1901 en l'honneur de Me Edmond Picard.* Brussels, 1902, pp. 135-140. See also: Carré (as in 4), pp. 60-62.

[27] Quote translated from French: "La Force qui fera triompher le Suffrage Universel est dans la Nation. Ce n'est plus seulement une classe qui le réclame, ce sont des milliers d'âmes bourgeoises, saisies d'un élan de Justice et de Fraternité." [Picard, Edmond]: "A la bataille". In: J.T., 11 (1892) 872, col. 401-404; [Picard, Edmond]: "Le marchandage universel". In: J.T., 11 (1892) 873, col. 417-420; "Personnel à renouveler". In: J.T., 11 (1892) 874, col. 433-437; [Picard, Edmond]: "Forces perdues". In: J.T., 11 (1892) 875, col. 449-453 and 451 (quote); "Renouveau Clérico-Doctrinaire". In: J.T., 11 (1892) 877, col. 481-485; [Picard, Edmond]: "La poussée nécessaire". In: J.T., 11 (1892) 878, col. 497-500; "Sunt verba rerum". In: J.T., 11 (1892) 881, col. 545-549; [Picard, Edmond]: "Le 1er mai". In: J.T., 11, (1892) 882, col. 561-564; Picard, Edmond: "Le bilan du suffrage censitaire". In: J.T., 11 (1892) 883, col. 577-584; Picard, Edmond: "Les prétendus dangers du suffrage universel". In: J.T., 11 (1892) 884, col. 593-601 and [Picard, Edmond]: "La propagande par l'action". In: J.T., 11 (1892) 920, col. 1233-1237. Picard confessed himself his autorship of most of these anonymously published articles: Picard, Edmond: Quarante-huit heures de pistole. Conte moral. Brussels, 1893, pp. 15-16.

The blessings had only gone to a small minority to the detriment of the great majority of the people. In reality the country stood at the border of the abyss by the electoral self-interest of the bourgeoisie.

The year 1893 brought the culmination with the arrest of Picard himself and the final parliamentary acceptance of the tempered universal suffrage – compromise in which every male citizen now obtained at least one vote, but some got two or three depending on conditions of wealth, education or family life. Strangely enough, only the first event that was of course closely linked to the second was reported in the columns of the *Journal des Tribunaux*. Picard had to stay 48 hours in prison, because he was accused of the murderous attack on the Brussels mayor Charles Buls, for which he seemed to have called in a speech on a meeting for universal suffrage. He was arrested in the early morning of 18th April 1893, exactly the same day on which the parliament tacked in the evening. In fact, there was no legal ground for Picard's arrest, which therefore can only be understood as a political choice of the government in a prerevolutionary climate.[28] However, the silence of the *Journal des Tribunaux* on the tempered universal suffrage itself is remarkable, but is probably a consequence of its ambiguous attitude towards that compromise. On the one hand, the journal and particularly its editor in chief had always fought for a real universal suffrage *à la française* (one man, one vote) and could not really be satisfied with the moderate version that had finally resulted, although it was certainly a progression regarding to the census suffrage. Every man possessed now the right to vote, but men were still not equal. On the other hand, they knew very well that nothing more could be achieved in the short term, but they expected already a great change of the political landscape with the general plural suffrage and hoped that it could stimulate earlier or later the promulgation of the real universal suffrage.

In the following years, there appeared hardly articles about the extension of the suffrage in the *Journal des Tribunaux*. The explanation is probably the political mandate of the editor in chief. In 1894, Picard became a socialist senator, mandate he kept until 1908. It seems very possible that he chose to keep some distance and preferred not to position himself anymore in the *Journal des Tribunaux* on political subjects. If one looks at his activities in the

---

[28] "L'arrestation de M. Edmond Picard". In: *J.T.*, 12 (1893) 966, col. 497 en 967, col. 513-522. See about this event also: Heirbaut (as in 3), p. 354.

Senate, it appears immediately that he never gave up the ideal of the real universal suffrage.[29]

Not surprisingly, the *Journal des Tribunaux* was also characterised by a great social conscience. Many articles attested to the great frustration about the very slow advance and the manifest unwill of catholic and liberal politicians to really deal with the labourers' problems and warned that there would be revolutionary situations if nothing should change.

When the parliament agreed, for instance, after an endless treatment in 1883 finally with the abolition of the so-called *livrets d'ouvriers*, the *Journal des Tribunaux* was not able to rejoice. That it had taken so much time to decide such an easy measure and that there were still supporters of this unjust system, although no other industrial country possessed such an obligation, proved once again that politicians did not realise at all the gravity of the social problem. Therefore the journal feared violent revolts, which would be the inevitable consequence of such an attitude: "the unavoidable labourers' questions which are rising everywhere as the threat of a new 93, - threat today, tomorrow a sure explosion if one does not open at time the air valves of this formidable steam boiler". A myopic government that constantly ignored the social problem would undergo the same destiny as the French King Louis XVI.[30]

In his editorial of 2nd May 1886, Picard was simply scandalized about the reaction of the Beernaert Cabinet on the labourers' revolts of March that year. He denounced that the social problem had never got the attention it deserved and praised the army general in chief, who had sanguinary repressed the revolts, for his warning to the government that violence

---

[29] Coppein: "Edmond Picard, actor and witness of the socialization of law in Belgium", pp. 158-159.

[30] Quote translated from French: "les inéluctables questions ouvrières qui, partout ailleurs, se dressent comme la menace d'un nouveau 93, - menace aujourd'hui, demain explosion certaine si l'on n'ouvre à temps les soupapes de la formidable chaudière". "L'impuissance parlementaire". In: J.T., 2 (1883) 73, col. 353-356; "Les livrets d'ouvrier". In: J.T., 2 (1883) 74, col. 369-373 and 369 (quote). The livret d'ouvrier contained the personal data of a labourer and all relevant information about his earlier jobs; a labourer had to give it to the employer for who he worked. The risk of power abuse lay herein that the employer could refuse to give back the livret at the employee. In that case the latter could not work for another employer and was condemned to stay working in the same place. By the Act of 10th July 1883 the livrets d'ouvrier lost their obligatory character. Chlepner, B.: Cent ans d'histoire sociale en Belgique. Brussels, 1956, pp. 93-95; Delbroek, Bart: "Werkboekjes in de 20e eeuw: de charmes van een vergeten bron". In: Brood & Rozen. Tijdschrift voor de geschiedenis van sociale bewegingen, 11 (2006) 2, pp. 8-13.

would not solve the situation. He considered the parliament's apathy outrageous:

"In the Parliament, a manifesto which is a plea of the capital against the recriminations and exigencies of the labour! Nor at right nor at left the least cry of humanity. Not more sagacity than charity; [...] all are unified in one same thought, punish!"

Hence, he explicitly incited the government to deal without delay with the real solutions of the labourers' crisis. The daily misery of labourers needed an immediate solution, which did not only ask for a profound study, but above all the will to change things.[31]

During the following years, the *Journal des Tribunaux* kept the theme constantly under the attention and always again repeated the same argument. Regarding the elections of 1888, the journal implored its readers to turn away from the former sterile ideological discussions – which were above all an obstacle – and to side with the necessary social reforms. Jurists were not allowed to stay neutral and had to subscribe the exigence for concrete social laws:

"That is why we, men of law, expect reforms in the domain of Law, not scholastical revisions of lawbooks, not humanitarian or revolutionary utopian dreams, but laws which attack the social abuses of the everywhere privileges or the power of money which neglects the human equality and fraternity."[32]

---

[31] Quote translated from French: "Au Parlement, un manifeste qui est un plaidoyer du capital contre les récriminations et les exigences du travail! Ni à droite ni à gauche le moindre cri d'humanité sortant de l'âme de qui que ce soit! [...] Pas plus de sagacité que de charité; [...] tous rapprochés dans une même pensée, sévir!" [Picard, Edmond]: "La législation de la peur". In: J.T., 5 (1886) 328, col. 545-549 and 546 (quote). See also: Nandrin, Jean-Pierre: "La genèse du droit du travail en Belgique. Plaidoyer pour la chronologie". In: Dauchy, Serge, Monballyu, Jos and Wijffels, Alain (eds.): Auxtoritates. Xenia R.C. Van Caenegem oblata. De auteurs van de rechtsontwikkeling (Iuris Scripta Historica, XIII). Brussels, 1997, p. 266.

[32] Quote translated from French: "C'est pourquoi nous, hommes de droit, nous attendons des réformes dans le domaine du Droit, non pas des revisions scolastiques de Codes, non pas des utopies humanitaires et révolutionnaires, mais des lois s'attaquant aux abus sociaux du privilège partout où le pouvoir de l'argent méconnaît l'égalité et la fraternité humaines." [De Burlet, Alexandre]: "Les élections et la législation progressive". In: J.T., 7 (1888) 535, col. 785-786 and 786 (quote); "La législation progressive et le ministère". In: J.T., 7 (1888) 536, col. 801-804.

Also in the issue of 14th July 1889 the government policy was evaluated as insufficient and the Beernaert Cabinet was once again called to accelerate the process of reform. The judgement of the *Gazette de Francfort*, which had written that Belgium was in terms of social legislation one of the most reactionary European countries and stood on the treshold of a revolution, was assentingly quoted.[33] The same point appeared in an article about the resignation of Bismarck. The German chancellor was especially praised for his social policy, contrary to the situation in Belgium. The Beernaert Cabinet had at least the merit to do something, but it went all so slowly and was intrinsically unambitious.[34]

In 1891, Picard formulated the idea that only a real universal suffrage could bring fundamental changes concerning social legislation, military service, improvement in education and so on, because representatives of the bourgeoisie, to which he counted also himself, did not know really the sad and hard conditions of the labourers' life and were not inclined to alter these problems:

"We are members of the privileged class, we participate since sixty years at the advantages of a legislation [...] made in profit only of the bourgeoisie. [...] But which laws have been made for the labourers? Really almost nothing. [...] For you the ten, twelve and sometimes fourteen hours of soul-destroying drudgery, in deplorable physical conditions, with a frightening mortality and often, with cruel and horrible catastrophes."[35]

As remarkable as this confession was in the same year the special attention for the papal encyclical *Rerum novarum*. The most important fragments were litterally reproduced and commented by Picard. He saluted benevolently the adequate description of the labourers' problem, but

---

[33] "La législation ouvrière". In: *J.T.*, 8 (1889) 637, col. 913-916.
[34] "La législation socialiste". In: *J.T.*, 9 (1890) 699, col. 353-356. See also: "La législation progressive et les élections". In: *J.T.*, 9 (1890) 723, col. 737-740.
[35] Quote translated from French: "Nous sommes dans la classe privilégiée, nous participons depuis soixante années aux avantages d'une législation [...] faite au profit de la seule bourgeoisie. [...] Mais quelles lois a-t-on faites pour les ouvriers ? Vraiment presque rien. [...] A vous les dix, douze et parfois quatorze heures de corvée abrutissante, dans des conditions physiques lamentables, avec une mortalité effrayante et souvent, avec les cruautés horribles des catastrophes." Picard, Edmond: "La législation sociale. La Revision constitutionnelle. Le suffrage universel". In: J.T., 10 (1891) 783, col. 313-324 and 321-322 (quote) and 784, col. 329-338.

condemned the catholic remedies as irrelevant and too soft.[36] Looking back in 1900, the *Journal des Tribunaux* marked 1886 as the definite caesura for the break-through of social legislation in Belgium and stated especially from 1894 onwards an acceleration of the efforts and the results, which had to be attributed to the first Minister of Industry and Labour Albert Nyssens and the Christian-Democratic and socialist members of parliament.[37]

3.3 Herald of an Independent Bar

Besides this rather left-wing ideology, the identity of the *Journal des Tribunaux* was determined by a special attention to the bar in all its aspects, from the more social life of the *confraternité* to the defense of the professional interests. Not surprisingly, the majority of its subscribers – in 1884 already more than 1000 – were lawyers.[38] Therefore, the journal was unevitably forced to present its point of view about what contemporary authors called "*la crise du Barreau*". In fact it concerned a broadening of the lawyers' profession. Because the number of lawyers increased constantly in this period and because there were not enough trials to allow every lawyer to earn his living that way, many lawyers searched other resources. Mostly they became directors at one of the then massively emerging companies, which needed such legally-educated specialists. However, that those administrators wanted to stay enrolled on the *tableau*, did not want to give up their lawyers' title and even wanted to plead, caused a serious discord in the ranks of the Bar.[39] One part of the Bar, that represented obviously the majority, did not see a problem at all in this combination, referred to the changed context, and supported total freedom. The other part, conducted by the *anciens* of the bar, but not as numerous, considered this evolution as a grave threat for the lawyers' independance and feared that it would influence at the end the whole Bar. Therefore it asked the persons concerned to make a clear choice, either lawyer or administrator. It argued that the social mission of the lawyer excluded the combination of this profession with a pecuniary lucrative mandate.[40]

---

[36] [Picard, Edmond]: "La législation sociale et l'encyclique". In: *J.T.*, 10 (1891) 809, col. 729-739 and 810, col. 745-756.

[37] "Les lois sociales en Belgique". In: *J.T.*, 19 (1900) 1569, col. 665-667.

[38] Carré (as in 4), pp. 88-95; Heirbaut (as in 3), p. 354 and note 78.

[39] Jamar, P.: "La Belgique et le Barreau". In: *Entretiens sur la Belgique contemporaine*. Brussels, 1904, pp. 222-223.

[40] Jamar (as in 39), pp. 223-224. The magistrates experienced the same problem: "Magistrature

As Picard was himself an established lawyer, he had written before with his confrère Gustave Duchaine a highly recommended deontological manual and had himself an extremely prosperous practice, one must not doubt that he used the *Journal des Tribunaux* as the instrument to reject the broadening tendency.[41] When in 1886 the *Fédération des Avocats* was founded for instance, the journal remarked that it should recruit its members especially within the 'real Bar'.[42] It was only a logical consequence that the journal became very soon the official medium of the Fédération. In 1899, Picard strongly condemned Charles Graux, who had declared in his authority as *bâtonnier* that the Bar had simply to accept *"l'invasion des affaires commerciales et industrielles"* and the changing customs that resulted thereof, such as the possibilty to obtain *honoraria* before the court. Picard deplored heavily such unwise exclamations of Graux and called to fight with all possible means that evolution.[43] Also in the next year, there appeared many condemning articles, in which every lawyer was charged to respect himself the traditional deontology:

"Everybody of us must orient every day in his relations within the Court his sorrows to the maintenance of a professional ideology of nobility and disengagement. We can still, if we want, throw ourselves before the threatening mass of opportunists of the commercial Bar: Sursum corda!"[44]

3.4 Stimulator for 'avant-garde law'

Also in a lot of other aspects, which we can not treat here in detail, the *Journal des Tribunaux* showed itself a mirror of its time. It must be said that many of these subjects were also hobbyhorses of the editor in chief.

---

et Finance". In: *J.T.*, 22 (1903) 1825, col. 754-757.

[41] Duchaine, Gustave and Picard, Edmond: *Manuel pratique de la profession d'avocat en Belgique.* Paris and Brussels, 1869, 548 p.

[42] "Fédération des barreaux belges". In: *J.T.*, 5 (1886) 335, col. 657-658.

[43] Graux, Charles: "Allocution de Me Charles Graux. Bâtonnier de l'Ordre des Avocats". In: *J.T.*, 17 (1898) 1427, col. 1129-1134; [Picard, Edmond]: "Barreau d'Affaires". In: *J.T.*, 18 (1899) 1520, col. 1266-1268 and 1267 (quote).

[44] Quote translated from French: "Chacun de nous doit chaque jour dans les relations du Palais, orienter ses soucis vers le maintien d'un idéal professionnel de noblesse et de désintéressement. Nous pouvons encore, si nous le voulons nous jeter en travers de la foule menaçante des arrivistes du Barreau d'affaires: Sursum corda!" "Ancienne et nouvelle profession". In: J.T., 19 (1900) 1557, col. 465-467 and 467 (quote). See also: "Sur l'avenir du Barreau". In: J.T., 19 (1900) 1563, col. 570-573 ; "Institut de jurisprudence". In: J.T., 19 (1900) 1579, col. 826-829.

Remarkable was for instance the great attention for the new branch of intellectual law, going from comparative studies of international legislation to extensive reports of specialized congresses.[45] And what to think about the major interest that was given to art trials?[46] On the other hand, penal trials were normally not reported, with the sensational Peltzer trial as the only exception for which a special daily edition of 23 issues was published.[47] That the famous polemic about a possible abolition of the Pandectes course in the university law curriculum was fought in 1889 in the journal was also not astonishing.[48] In general, legal education appeared to be a cherished subject.[49] The same must be said about legal philosophy[50] and the now problematic but then modish concept of race.[51]

---

[45] Carré (as in 4), pp. 68-70. See e.g.: "VIIIe congrès de l'association littérarie et artistique internationale à Anvers". In: *J.T.*, 4 (1885) 269, col. 1163-1172; "Le congrès international de droit commercial à Anvers". In: *J.T.*, 4 (1885) 270-271; "Congrès international de la propriété industrielle de Paris en 1889". In: *J.T.*, 8 (1889) 650, col. 1121-1132; Combe, E.: "Le droit d'auteur". In: *J.T.*, 17 (1898) 1375, col. 275-277.

[46] Heirbaut (as in 3), p. 354.

[47] Carré (as in 4), pp. 77-80. In the Peltzer trial a men (Léon Peltzer) was accused of the murder of the husband of his brothers (Armand Peltzer) mistress. The two Peltzer brothers were condemned to death punishment. Picard defended in particular Armand Peltzer.

[48] The main protagonists in the 1889 debate were Albert Nyssens and Polynice Van Wetter, the first being a professor at the Catholic University of Louvain and catholic politician; the second being a professor in Roman Law at the Ghent State University. At the end of the Pandectes course only disappeared in 1969 in Belgium as an obligatory course. [Nyssens, Albert]: "Le droit romain et les Pandectes". In: *J.T.*, 8 (1889) 633, col. 850-856; Mahaim, Ernest: "Le droit romain et les Pandectes". In: *J.T.*, 8 (1889) 635, col. 892-893; Van Wetter, Polynice: "Quelques observations sur le cours de Pandectes". In: *J.T.*, 8 (1889) 661, col. 1297-1302; Nyssens, Albert: "Les Pandectes. Réponse de l'ancien étudiant". In: *J.T.*, 8 (1889) 664, col. 1345-1350; Van Wetter, Polynice: "Les Pandectes". In: *J.T.*, 8 (1889) 671, col. 1457-1463. See on this polemic also: Stevens, Fred: "Het rechtsonderwijs in België in de 19e eeuw". In: *Handelingen IXe Nederlands-Belgisch rechtshistorisch congres 'Rondom Feenstra'*. Leiden, 1986, pp. 69-70 and note 29.

[49] See e.g.: Picard, Edmond: "La législation sur les examens universitaires et la nouvelle Ecole libre d'Enseignement Supérieur". In: *J.T.*, 13 (1894) 1054, col. 529-534; Otlet, Paul: "Sur l'enseignement du droit. Points de vue tout à fait généraux". In: *J.T.*, 14 (1895) 1134, col. 449-458; Des Cressonnières, Jacques: "Sur l'enseignement du droit". In: *J.T.*, 17 (1898) 1424, col. 1081-1088.

[50] See e.g.: Picard, Edmond: "Embryologie juridique". In: *J.T.*, 3 (1884) 141, col. 609-620, 412, col. 625-636 and 143, col. 641-648; Picard, Edmond: "Essai d'une nouvelle méthode d'Encyclopédie du Droit". In: *J.T.*, 14 (1895) 1114, col. 129-140 and 1115, col. 145-150; Hennebicq, Léon: "Sens de mots: droit naturel et philosohie du droit". In: *J.T.*, 14 (1895) 1146, col. 650-655; Hennebicq, Léon: "Eléments abstraits du droit naturel". In: *J.T.*, 14 (1895) 1176, col. 1161-1172.

[51] See e.g.: Hennebicq, Léon: "La race et le droit. Esquisse de mythologie juridique". In: *J.T.*,

4. A New Tradition: Léon Hennebicq as Editor in Chief (1901-1914)

Picard resigned as editor in chief at the end of 1900 and was succeeded by a board of eleven editors, in which his former *stagiaire* Léon Hennebicq (1871-1940), lawyer at the Brussels court of appeal, became very soon the leading figure.[52] For this second era in the history of the *Journal des Tribunaux*, we will only treat the first decade until the First World War.[53] Although some readers were complaining that the new board of editors did not have enough respect for the old progressive spirit of Picard and became too conservative,[54] the *Journal des Tribunaux* presented in fact itself as a true heir. Just like in the first two decades of its existence, many articles dealt with the socialization of law and social legislation.[55] Likewise, the defense of the professional deontology and the independance of the bar was continued.[56] Of course, it appeared inevitable that new themes arose. This was caused essentially by the major events of that period, but equally a consequence of the personal interest of the new editor in chief. Most remarkable of all seemed the greater focus on nationalistic articles. The language problem in Belgium and the existence of a Belgian national identity, two facts which were hardly reported before 1900, became now a

---

15 (1896) 1236, col. 745-754 and 1237, col. 761-762; Hennebicq, Léon: "La race et le droit". In: *J.T.*, 18 (1899) 1482, col. 609-620, 1483, col. 625-635, 1484, col. 641-652 and 1485, col. 657-663.

[52] Picard, Edmond: "Le passé et l'avenir du Journal des Tribunaux". In: *J.T.*, 19 (1900) 1610, col. 1346-1350; "L'avenir du Journal des Tribunaux". In: *J.T.*, 20 (1901) 1611, col. 2-4.

[53] See also Sterckx (as in 4), p. 263.

[54] "Jeunes réactionnaires que vous êtes". In: *J.T.*, 21 (1902) 1711, col. 258-261.

[55] See e.g., amongst many other articles, for the period until the First World War: "Justice de classe". In: *J.T.*, 20 (1901) 1629, col. 305-308; "Les habitations ouvrières". In: *J.T.*, 24 (1905) 1958, col. 130-132; "Exposés des théories d'avant-garde". In: *J.T.*, 25 (1906) 2080, col. 717-721; "Le lock-out verviétois". In: *J.T.*, 25 (1906) 2097, col. 998-1001; "Le droit nouveau". In: *J.T.*, 27 (1908), col. 242-245; "Vers la Justice sociale". In: *J.T.*, 28 (1909) 2292, col. 89-91; "La Justice dans le Droit". In: *J.T.*, 29 (1910) 2370, col. 34-38; "Des effets sociaux des abonnements d'ouvriers sur les lignes de chemins de fer belges". In: *J.T.*, 30 (1911) 2451, col. 66-69; "Les tendances du syndicalisme". In: *J.T.*, 31 (1912) 2597, col. 1202-1205 and "Liberté individuelle et justice sociale". In: *J.T.*, 32 (1913) 2640, col. 593-597.

[56] See e.g.: "Referendum sur l'incompatibilité existant entre l'exercice de la profession d'avocat et les fonctions d'administrateur de sociétés anonymes". In: *J.T.*, 21 (1902) 1748, col. 865-880; "Avocat et administrateur délégué". In: *J.T.*, 23 (1904) 1866, col. 18-21; Duchaine, Paul: "Le barreau et les incompatibilités". In: *J.T.*, 24 (1905) 2025, col. 1289-1304; "La liberté de l'avocat". In: *J.T.*, 27 (1908) 2237, col. 625-627.

popular subject in the journal,[57] as well as the Congo Freestate, that became in 1908 a Belgian colony – an event that was strongly supported.[58] The threat of a new war created discussions about the obligatory neutrality statute of the country and the need for alliances.[59] More than before was also pointed the lack of efficiency and the weakness of the parliamentary system and the need for a *Conseil d'Etat*.[60]

Finally other current themes, for instance the entry of women to the bar, found their place in the columns of the journal.[61] The last issue of the *Journal des Tribunaux* before the war was published on 23rd July 1914. At the outbreak of the war, the editor in chief Léon Hennebicq became a war volunteer. The publication only recommenced after the armistice. Hennebicq should stay editor in chief until his death on 5th May 1940. On 12th May could still appear a commemoration number that was fully devoted to him, but then the publication of the journal was again suspended for four years.

5. Conclusion

Whoever reads nowadays the *Journal des Tribunaux* and expects to find therein in one way or another the heritage of the traditions set by Picard and Hennebicq, will be rather disappointed. On the contrary, one will have the impression to look in a succesor of *La Belgique judiciaire*, that other

---

[57] See e.g.: "Le nationalisme et le droit". In: *J.T.*, 20 (1901) 1615, col. 66-70. "Notre langue". In: *J.T.*, 20 (1901) 1661, col. 818-821; Van den Borren, Charles: "Le sentiment Flamand". In: *J.T.*, 20 (1901) 1690, col. 1321-1331; Hennebicq, Léon: "La question du langues". In: *J.T.*, 24 (1905) 1971, col. 354-358; Smeesters, C.: "L'âme belge et la vie contemporaine". In: *J.T.*, 26 (1907) 2186, col. 1114-1127; "La nouvelle loi flamande". In: *J.T.*, 27 (1908) 2220, col. 322-325.
[58] See e.g.: "La Belgique et l'Etat du Congo". In: *J.T.*, 20 (1901) 1647, col. 593-597; Hennebicq, Léon: "L'annexion du Congo". In: *J.T.*, 22 (1903) 1820, col. 666-670; Hennebicq, Léon: "Un pamphlet anti-colonial". In: *J.T.*, 25 (1906) 2048, col. 210-214.
[59] See e.g. Graux, P.: "La neutralité de la Belgique et l'annexion du Congo". In: *J.T.*, 23 (1904) 1938, col. 1211-1221. See for a detailed analysis: Lesaffer: "Le Journal des Tribunaux (1904-1914)", pp. 116-138.
[60] See e.g.: "L'institution d'un Conseil d'Etat". In: *J.T.*, 20 (1901)1634, col. 386-390; Hennebicq, Léon: "Le Conseil d'Etat devant le regime parlementaire". In: *Journal des Tribunaux].T.*, 20 (1901) 1643, col. 530-533; "La crise parlementaire". In: *J.T.*, 20 (1901) 1686, col. 1258-1261; "Le parlement et les lois". In: *J.T.*, 21 (1902) 1744, col. 786-789; Janssens, Raymond: "De l'institution d'un Conseil d'Etat". In: *J.T.*, 21 (1902) 1757, col. 1019-1029;
[61] "La Femme-Avocat". In: *J.T.*, 20 (1901) 1619, col. 130-134; Gheude, Charles: "La Femme-Avocat". In: *J.T.*, 20 (1901) 1630, col. 322-326; La Fontaine, Henri: "La Femme et le Barreau". In: *J.T.*, 20 (1901) 1641, col. 513-516.

French speaking journal that had finally faded away in 1939 after a long death. This is not an error, but was a deliberate choice of the third editor in chief, Charles Van Reepinghen (1903-1966), who took over the guidance of the *Journal des Tribunaux* from its resurrection on 5th October 1944. Since then much more place than before has indeed been given to jurisdiction and doctrine, whilst (political) opinion articles were not published anymore. For instance, not a word was said about the royal question that strongly divided Belgium until 1950. Very symbolic also were the decisions of Van Reepinghen to reduce immediately the size of the journal to the smaller tabloid-format, which fitted perfectly to be bound in books, and to only sell the journal through subscriptions. [62]

This remarkable shift illustrates perfectly that the *Journal des Tribunaux* was in its first two periods certainly a rebellious and self-willed legal journal that mirrored perfectly the changing law of the *fin de siècle* and the early twentieth century. In that time, Belgian society was confronted with fundamental transformations, particularly the political and legal integration of the labourers. The journal did then not hesitate to join the debate and explicitly supported the labourers' cause, as appeared clearly in its pleas for universal suffrage and social legislation. One may not make a mistake: such points of view were very unusual and extremely daring, especially for a law review – we do not know of a similar European equivalent[63] –, and many Belgian jurists promoted a far more conservative opinion. The same must be said for the program of vulgarization of law, which was continued until the Second World War in spite of the lack of success. This left-wing ideology was combined with a special attention for the interests of the Bar and brought the journal a great popularity amongst the French-speaking (Brussels) lawyers. In the second period a nationalistic accent was added. It can not be denied at all that the influence of the first two editors in chief, Edmond Picard and Léon Hennebicq, was profound: they totally permeated the journal with their colourful personalities and gave it a vanguard position. The present journal has intentionally given up that unique selling position and tries to bring law on stage in a neutral way by restricting it to itself. Nevertheless, such a play is as meaningful as the former direction, when the *Journal des Tribunaux* chose above all to interact

---

[62] "1914-1918". In: *J.T.*, 33 (1914/1918) 2740, col. 937; Carré (as in 4), pp. 1-2; Heirbaut (as in 3), p. 355 and note 89; Sterckx (as in 4), pp. 264-267.
[63] For this we rely on the works mentioned in note 1.

and connect law and society. Legal journals appear to be symbols which always reflect their own time and context.[64]

---

[64] The author would like to thank Adelyn Wilson for reading an earlier version of this text.

Frieden durch Sicherheit: Notarielle Urkunden als Konstrukt zur Beweissicherung*

Sarah Bachmann

Häufig begegnet uns die „schöne und bewegende Metapher des Psalmisten" (G. Dilcher) von Frieden und Gerechtigkeit, die einander küssen.[1] Nicht zu Unrecht, vermag sie doch in einprägsamer Weise ein Bild der Auffassung unserer Kultur von Frieden und Recht zu zeichnen. Ein Bild, das die friedvolle zwischenmenschliche Interaktion auf die Basis einer gerechten Ordnung stellt. Vor diesem Hintergrund beschäftigten sich die bisherigen Forschungen überwiegend mit der Verquickung von Frieden und Recht, wobei den Überlegungen meist eine Gleichsetzung von Recht und Gerechtigkeit zugrunde gelegt wurde.[2] Der 1929 von Gustav Radbruch[3] in den Blick genommenen ersten (wichtigsten) Aufgabe des Rechts zur Friedensschaffung durch Sicherheit kam in der neueren rechtshistorischen Forschung[4], neben der viel beachteten zweiten, der Schaffung von Gerechtigkeit, bislang eine eher untergeordnete Rolle zu.[5]

---

* An dieser Stelle sei Prof. Dr. Tilman Repgen für Kritik und Anregungen gedankt.

[1] 85. Ps. 11. Die Bibel. Altes und Neues Testament. Einheitsübersetzung, Freiburg, 2006.

[2] Dilcher, Gerhard: Friede durch Recht, in: Träger und Instrumentarien des Friedens im Hohen und Späten Mittelalter. Johannes Fried. Sigmaringen 1996, S. 203ff.; Walde, Elmar: Die peinliche Strafe als Instrument des Friedens. Ebd., S. 229ff.; Hattenhauer, Hans: Pax et iustitia. Göttingen 1983.

[3] „Die Gerechtigkeit ist die zweite große Aufgabe des Rechts, die erste aber ist die Rechtssicherheit, der Friede." Radbruch, Gustav: Aphorismen zur Rechtsweisheit. Göttingen 1963, S. 26 (Nr. 77).

[4] Bezeichnend für die geringe Präsenz der „Sicherheit" in der rechtshistorischen Forschung ist das Fehlen eines Lemmas „Sicherheit" im HRG.

[5] Kleinschmidt, Harald: Öffentlichkeit, Legitimität und Sicherheit in der europäischen Tradition des Mittelalters und der Frühen Neuzeit. (http://www.desk.c.u-tokyo.ac.jp/download/es_6_Kleinschmidt.pdf, 03.03.2010); Rümelin, Max: Die Rechtssicherheit. Tübingen 1924. Meist erstreckten sich die Überlegungen zur Friedensschaffung und Wahrung durch Sicherheit nur auf den staatsphilosophischen, politischen oder militär- bzw. polizeihistorischen Bereich. Stellvertretend: Härter, Karl: Sicherheit und Frieden im frühneuzeitlichen Alten Reich. In: Zeitschrift für Historische Forschung 2003 (Bd. 30), S. 413ff. mwN; ders.: Religion, Frieden und Sicherheit als Gegenstand guter Ordnung und Policey: Zu den Aus- und

Einer der Gründe ist sicherlich in einer perspektivischen Verengung des Blickwinkels auf die Verbindung von Frieden und Recht zu sehen.[6] Verstärkt wurde diese Begrenzung durch die Fokussierung auf das Element der Sicherheit im traditionellen Friedensbegriff.[7] Dies hatte zur Folge, dass das Verständnis von Friede mit juristischer Eindeutigkeit und Einseitigkeit gleichgesetzt wurde.[8] Die bisherigen Überlegungen gingen – völlig zu Recht – davon aus, dass das maßgebliche Werkzeug zur Friedensschaffung eine bestehende Rechtsordnung und deren zivilisierte Durchsetzung sei. Rechtssicherheit setze „Schutz und Garantien voraus, die auf konkreten Rechtsgrundlagen beruh[t]en und durchsetzbar sein müss[t]en"[9]; es bestehe also ein offensichtliches Abhängigkeitsverhältnis zwischen dem zu erreichenden Frieden und einer Schutzgewalt, die eben diesen Frieden garantiert und schützt. Rechtsstaatlichkeit und Rechtssicherheit seien danach unabdingbare Grundvoraussetzungen der Friedensschaffung und - sicherung.

Die Richtigkeit dieses Gedankenganges steht außer Frage, dennoch bedarf er einer Ergänzung, denn das friedenstiftende Recht kann überhaupt nur dort angewandt und durchgesetzt werden, wo seine Geltung unzweifelhaft nachweisbar ist. Das nackte Recht selbst kann keinen Frieden schaffen, erst durch seine Anwendung sind unsichere, friedensgefährdende Situationen sicher zu lösen. Eben diese Überlegung entwickelte sich im 15. Jahrhundert zu einer maßgeblichen Triebkraft der Reichsreformbe-

---

Nachwirkungen des Augsburger Religionsfriedens und des Reichsabschieds von 1555 in der reichsständischen Policeygesetzgebung. In: Der Augsburger Religionsfriede 1555. Wolfgang Wüst, Georg Kreuzer, Nicola Schümann. Augsburg 2005; ders.: Von der Friedenswahrung zur „öffentlichen Sicherheit": Konzepte und Maßnahmen frühneuzeitlicher Sicherheitspolicey in rheinländischen Territorien. In: Rheinische Vierteljahresblätter 67 (2003), S. 162ff.; Fritz, Gerhard: Sicherheitsdiskurse im Schwäbischen Kreis im 18. Jahrhundert, in: Repräsentation von Kriminalität und öffentlicher Sicherheit. Bilder, Vorstellungen und Diskurse vom 16. bis zum 20. Jahrhundert. Karl Härter, Gerhard Sälter, Eva Wiebel. Frankfurt am Main 2010 genannt.

[6] Hermann, Hans-Georg: Art. Friede, in: Albrecht Cordes, Heiner Lück, Wolfgang Stammler. Handwörterbuch zur deutschen Rechtsgeschichte (Aufl.2), Berlin 2009, Sp. 1807ff.

[7] Besonders deutlich wird dies in den Arbeiten Fichtes (Grundzüge des gegenwärtigen Zeitalters, in: Sämtliche Werke Bd.7, Leipzig 1845, S. 165) und Hobbes (Leviathan I, 13. EW Vol. 3 (1839; ND 1966), S. 165).

[8] Janssen, Wilhelm: Art. Friede, in: Geschichtliche Grundbegriffe. Historisches Lexikon zur politischen-sozialen Sprache in Deutschland, Bd.2. Otto Brunner, Werner Conze, Reinhart Koselleck. Stuttgart 1992, S. 543ff.

[9] Conze, Werner: Art. Sicherheit, Schutz, in: Geschichtliche Grundbegriffe. Historisches Lexikon zur politischen-sozialen Sprache in Deutschland, Bd. 5. Otto Brunner, Werner Conze, Reinhart Koselleck. Stuttgart 2004, S. 831ff., 831.

strebungen, die dem bis dato bestehenden Selbsthilferecht einen effektiven Rechtsschutz durch die Zivilisierung der Konfliktlösung entgegensetzte.[10] Den materiellen Rechten des Einzelnen sollte in einem ordentlichen Verfahren zur Durchsetzung verholfen werden. Um aber materielle Rechte überhaupt geltend machen zu können, muss der Einzelne durch einen schlüssigen Tatsachenvortrag dem Gericht darlegen, dass die im Gesetz niedergelegten Anwendungs-voraussetzungen vorliegen. Ist ein solcher Nachweis nicht möglich, kann die Rechtssicherheit in ein direktes Spannungsverhältnis zur Gerechtigkeit treten. Wenn nämlich wegen des fehlenden Nachweises ein falsches, nicht mit der tatsächlichen, aber unnachweisbaren Rechtslage übereinstimmendes Urteil gefällt wird, das dann Rechtskraft erlangt. Um friedensgefährdende, rechtlose Situationen zu vermeiden, musste dem Menschen also ein Mittel in die Hand gegeben werden, das ihm im Zweifelsfall den Beweis seiner Rechte garantierte. Vor diesem Hintergrund ist die Sicherung der eigenen Rechtsposition durch Beweismittel als ein wesentlicher Faktor der Friedensschaffung und - bewahrung anzusehen. Anders ausgedrückt: Zur Herstellung und Sicherung von Frieden genügt eben nicht nur die theoretische Möglichkeit, sich auf Recht berufen zu können, und die abstrakte Aussicht, dieses Recht durchzusetzen. Erst durch die tatsächliche Anwendung, die Anwendbarmachung von Recht, wird seine Friedensfunktion entfaltet. Ein Werkzeug dazu bilden die Beweismittel. Durch sie wird die Position des Beweisenden gestärkt, er erhält eine Sicherheit, die ihm die Durchsetzung seiner Rechte ermöglichen und damit Frieden schaffen soll.

Dabei musste die Sicherheit aber nicht nur in dem Zeitpunkt, in dem der Konflikt bereits entstanden und damit unvermeidlich war, gewahrt werden. Auch im Vorfeld einer möglichen Instabilität konnte ihrer Schaffung eine entscheidende Rolle zukommen, worauf ich später noch einmal zu sprechen kommen werde.

Jenseits der Notwendigkeit von Beweismitteln und der Festlegung ihres Wirkungsbereiches für das Problem der Erzeugung und Sicherung von Frieden drängen sich zwei Fragen ganz besonders auf: Was macht ein Beweismittel überhaupt zu einem solchen? Und wie muss es beschaffen sein, um eine Beweiswirkung zu entfalten und damit dem Anspruch der Friedenssicherung gerecht zu werden? Auf diese Fragen möchte ich versuchen, eine Antwort zu finden. Sinnvoll erscheint es mir, den

---

[10] Conze, Sicherheit, Schutz, S. 831ff., 837 (Fn. 9).

theoretischen Überlegungen zur Friedenserzeugung und Sicherung durch Beweissicherheit die historische Entwicklung von Beweismitteln folgen zu lassen. Ein besonderes Augenmerk werde ich dabei auf schriftliche Beweismittel, namentlich notarielle Urkunden, die bis heute als eines der stärksten und sichersten Beweismittel gelten dürfen, legen. Im Anschluss widme ich mich der Frage, wie und weshalb notarielle Instrumente Sicherheit vermitteln und woher sie ihre Beweiswirkung beziehen. Am Ende soll eine kurze Zusammenfassung dazu dienen, die Ergebnisse erneut mit der Frage der Friedenserzeugung und -sicherung zu konfrontieren.

Grundannahme: Frieden durch Beweissicherheit

Der Friedensbegriff beinhaltet eine enorme Vielzahl verschiedener Aspekte: gesellschaftlich-zwischenmenschliche, (philosophisch) egozentrierte, staatliche, soziale, religiöse, um nur einige zu nennen. Schon in der Antike differenzierte man zwischen verschiedenen Bedeutungsgehalten, wobei der öffentliche, interkulturelle Frieden dominierte. Friedenserzeugung war eine Aufgabe des Herrschers bzw. der Herrschenden, die notfalls mit Gewalt durchgesetzt werden sollte.[11] Einen privaten Frieden, wie er heute allgemein anerkannt zur Grundvoraussetzung eines jeden gesellschaftlichen Friedens notwendig ist, war in der Antike nicht geläufig. Der Grund dafür lag im antiken Menschenbild, das ihn innerhalb seines Standes als Masse begriff, ohne in besonderem Umfang zwischen einzelnen Individuen näher zu differenzieren. Erst die Anerkennung des von der Gesamtheit losgelösten Menschen durch die jüdisch-christliche Religion ermöglichte es, den Grundstein für eine private Friedenseinung zu legen.[12] Der Mensch wurde als Ebenbild Gottes geschaffen (Genesis 1, 27). Erst diese verstärkte Betonung des Einzelnen, der als Abbild des Schöpfers existierte, ermöglichte eine private Friedenseinung neben der Erzeugung eines öffentlichen Friedens. Auch die Augustinische Friedenslehre[13], die

---

[11] Zur pax romana: Hooff, Anton: Pax Romana: een studie van het Romeinse imperialisme. Nijmegen 1971.

[12] Zum christlichen Friedensbild in Abgrenzung zum römischen: Hattenhauer, Hans: Europäische Rechtsgeschichte. Heidelberg 1999, Rn. 376.

[13] Augustinus, Aurelius: De civitate dei, XIX; s.a. Janssen, Friede, S. 543ff., 548 (Fn. 8); sowie weiterführend zur Augustinischen Friedenslehre: Geerlings, Wilhelm: De civitate dei XIX als Buch der Augustinischen Friedenslehre, in: Augustinus – De civitate dei. Christoph Horn. Berlin 1997, S. 211ff.

unser westliches Friedensverständnis wohl am nachhaltigsten geprägt hat, unterscheidet zwischen einer *pax domestica* und einer *pax civitatis*. Die Erkenntnis von der menschlichen Vernunftbegabung und der Gottesebenbildlichkeit schufen die Voraussetzungen für einen Frieden im privaten Bereich, die *pax* des Einzelmenschen – einen politisch-sozialen Frieden.[14]

Mit der zunehmenden Rationalisierung des Prozesses hatte sich bereits im Mittelalter, verstärkt aber in der Frühen Neuzeit, die Auffassung des friedenbringenden Nutzens rechtlicher Regelungen durchgesetzt. Die bis ins Hochmittelalter üblichen Ordale, bei welchen die Vorstellung zugrunde lag, Gott greife zur Herstellung von Gerechtigkeit in den Rechtsfindungsprozess ein, wurden durch ein formelles Verfahren abgelöst. Ausgehend von einem verstärkten Streben nach materieller Wahrheit trat immer mehr die Einhaltung prozessualer Formvorschriften in den Vordergrund.[15] War zunächst ein rigider Formalismus ausschlaggebend für den prozessualen Erfolg, wandelte sich die Aufgabe des Prozessrechts hin zum Schutzmechanismus einer ordnungsgemäßen Durchsetzung subjektiver Rechte.

Aus der obersten Zielsetzung des Zivilprozesses, subjektive Rechte des Einzelnen zu schützen, folgt unmittelbar, dass der Zivilprozess materielle Rechte zu verwirklichen hat.[16] In besonderem Maße gilt das für das Beweisrecht, dessen Zweck neben der Erzeugung von Rechtsgewissheit auch die Herstellung von Rechtsfrieden ist.

Verknüpft man die Idee eines privaten und eines öffentlichen Friedens mit der geschilderten Aufgabe des Beweisrechtes, so wird deutlich, dass der

---

[14] Eine Verbindung von privatem und öffentlichem zu einem einheitlichen Frieden wird aber erst mit dem aufkeimenden Vernunftrecht in der Aufklärung erreicht. Gemeinsam sei diesen Friedensaspekten, dass sie an das Vorhandensein einer Ordnung anknüpften, deren Existenz notwendige Voraussetzung für die Entstehung von Frieden ist. Ohne die Ordnung im Inneren sei schlicht kein Frieden nach außen möglich. Auch sei eine äußere Ordnung notwendige Voraussetzung für den inneren Frieden. S. Kant, Immanuel: Idee zu einer allgemeinen Geschichte in weltbürgerlicher Absicht, in: Akademieausgabe, Berlin 1902-1923 (ND 1968-1977), Bd. 8, 24, 22. Weiterentwickelt in: Kant, Zum ewigen Frieden, in: Akademieausgabe Bd. 8.

[15] Kohler, Marius: Die Entwicklung des schwedischen Zivilprozeßrechts, Tübingen 2002, S. 81f.

[16] Leipold, Dieter: 50 Jahre Zivilprozeßrecht – ein persönlicher Rückblick: Vortrag anlässlich der Verleihung der Ehrendoktorwürde durch die Juristische Fakultät der Demokritos Universität Thrazien am 08. Oktober 2008 (http://www2.jura.uni-freiburg.de/institute/izpr2/Bruns/Lehrstuhlinhaber/files/VortragKomotioni.pdf, 01.11.2010).

Verknüpft man die Idee eines privaten und eines öffentlichen Friedens mit der geschilderten Aufgabe des Beweisrechtes, so wird deutlich, dass der Gedanke, Beweissicherheit zu schaffen als ein wesentlicher Schlüssel zur Friedenswahrung anzusehen ist, der seinerseits auf zwei Grundannahmen basiert: Zum einen, dass der Frieden weniger gefährdet sei, wenn Tatsachen leichter zu beweisen seien, ihnen also keine Beweisschwierigkeiten entgegenstünden. Und zum anderen, dass sich die Gefährdung der Rechte des Einzelnen auf die Rechte und den Frieden des Kollektivs durchschlagen könne und dort den Gemeinschaftsfrieden bedrohe. Um Beweise des Einzelnen zu sichern und damit den Frieden zwischen den Streitenden, aber auch innerhalb der Gesellschaft zu wahren, bedurfte es also bestimmter, von der Gemeinschaft anerkannter Beweisformen.

Konzepte zur Schaffung von (Rechts-)Sicherheit:

A. Sicherheit durch Schriftlichkeit

Mündlichkeit im Mittelalter

Das mittelalterliche Rechtsleben war weitgehend von Mündlichkeit geprägt. Das hatte gegenüber dem im Hochmittelalter aufblühenden Urkundenwesen den entscheidenden Nachteil, dass dem individuellen Gedächtnis für die Beweisbarkeit einer Tatsache eine überragende Bedeutung zukam.[17] Um Beweise in Form von Erinnerungen auf lange Zeit zu bewahren, bediente man sich symbolischer, einprägsamer Handlungen. Aber Erinnerungen können täuschen und Zeugen versterben, so dass es in der Folge häufig zu Uneinigkeit und Streit kam. Zur Wahrung des Friedens sowohl im Prozess als auch zur Konfliktminimierung im Vorfeld bedurfte es sicherer und insbesondere dauerhafter Beweismittel.

Beweissicherheit durch Urkunden

Mit zunehmender Literalität und um der Vergänglichkeit des gesprochenen Wortes entgegenzuwirken, wählte man immer häufiger die Schriftform. Das Sicherheits- und Friedensbedürfnis der Menschen, das sich unter anderem im Versuch, Beweismittel zu bewahren, manifestierte, beförderte die Bemühungen, eine scheinbar unvergängliche Sicherung

---

[17] Eichler, Frank: Recht ohne Schrift. Zur Rechtspflege des Mittelalters in Deutschland. Hamburg 2010, S. 7.

durch die Verwendung von Schrift herzustellen – also Sicherheit durch Schriftlichkeit.[18]

Einordnung der notariellen Urkunden

Ab dem späten 14. Jahrhundert lassen sich neben besiegelten und privaten Urkunden auch notarielle Instrumente nachweisen. Bislang bemühte man sich, Urkunden über eine Zuordnung zum Aussteller zu kategorisieren. Man unterschied zwischen Urkunden, die in einer kaiserlichen oder päpstlichen Kanzlei ausgestellt wurden – sog. öffentliche Urkunden – und den Übrigen, die man als Privaturkunden zusammenfasste. Diese Einteilung konnte aber keine befriedigenden Ergebnisse liefern. Besonders deutlich wird dies bei den hier thematisierten notariellen Instrumenten, die nach dieser Terminologie zu den Privaturkunden gezählt werden müssten, obwohl sie sich in ihrem formalen dreigliedrigen Aufbau (Protokoll, Text, Eschatokoll) und in ihrer Beweiswirkung als glaubwürdige Urkunden nicht von Kaiser- und Papsturkunden unterschieden.[19]

Das häufig bemängelte Fehlen einer angemessenen Nomenklatur darf aber nicht dazu führen, dass alte falsche (!) Begrifflichkeiten mit Verweis auf das Wissen um die Unzulänglichkeiten der vorhandenen Ordnung weiterhin gebraucht werden wie dies schon von Oswald Redlich vorgeschlagen wurde.[20] Letztendlich konnten auch andere Kategorisierungsversuche nach Gültigkeitsdauer, Überlieferungsweg, quellenkritischem Wert oder rechtlicher Funktion (mit der Untergliederung in dispositive und deklaratorische Urkunden) nicht überzeugen.[21] Bei konsequenter Fortführung der Forderung Harry Bresslaus nach mehr Berücksichtigung der rechtlichen Wirkungsweise der Urkunden könnte sich jedoch eine Lösung der terminologischen Schwierigkeiten erreichen

---

[18] Zu den funktionalen Aspekten der Schriftlichkeit: Weitzel, Jürgen: Schriftlichkeit und Recht, in: Schrift und Schriftlichkeit. Hartmut Günther; Otto Ludwig. Berlin/New York 1994, S. 619ff.

[19] S. formelle Vorgaben der RNO abgedruckt in Grziwotz, Herbert: Kaiserliche Notariatsverordnung von 1512: Spiegel der Entwicklung des europäischen Notariats. München 1995; sowie zum Aufbau der Kaiser- und Papsturkunden: Bresslau, Harry: Handbuch der Urkundenlehre, Bd. 2. Berlin 1958, S. 76ff., 45ff.

[20] Redlich, Oswald: Privaturkunden des Mittelalters. Darmstadt 1911 (ND 1967), S. VI.

[21] So auch Trusen, Winfried: Zur Urkundenlehre der mittelalterlichen Jurisprudenz, in: Recht und Schrift im Mittelalter. Peter Classen. Sigmaringen 1977, S. 197ff., 201ff.

lassen.[22] Das gilt insbesondere, weil sich der Beweiswert von Königs- bzw. Kaiser-, Papst- und notariellen Urkunden auch im formalen Aufbau der Urkunden niederschlägt.[23]

Während im klassischen römischen Recht die Urkunden einer umfassenden und vor allem freien richterlichen Beweiswürdigung[24] unterzogen wurden, waren die mittelalterlichen Richter aufgrund der Legaltheorie[25] dazu angehalten, die Echtheit und Wahrheit der Urkunde anhand vorgegebener formaler Kriterien festzustellen. Hinter der aus dem kanonischen in das weltliche Beweisverfahren rezipierten Theorie stand das mittelalterliche Streben nach materieller Wahrheit, welches das frühere Verfahren, das auf die Erfüllung formaler Beweishandlungen gerichtet war, ablösen sollte. Die Form der Urkunde wurde zur Voraussetzung für die Echtheitsvermutung, die ihrerseits wiederum die Vermutung der Wahrheit des Urkundeninhalts nach sich zog.[26]

In dieser „Vermutungskette" ist der den Schriftstücken innewohnende Glaube zu sehen wie wir ihn in Deutschland noch heute vom Publizitätsgrundsatz der Eintragungen in Grund- und Handelsbüchern kennen. Diese Eintragungen gelten bis zum Beweis des Gegenteils als richtig. Ebenso verhält es sich bei den mit *publica fides* ausgestatteten Urkunden nach der mittelalterlichen Lehre. Die Urkunden „habet pro se praesumptionem (...) sine alterius adminiculo"[27] – für sie spricht also die Vermutung der Wahrheit, ohne dass es weiterer (die Wahrheitsvermutung untermauernder) Beweismittel bedurft hätte. Dabei darf aber nicht außer Acht gelassen werden, dass bei der faktischen Anerkennung der notariellen wie auch der Siegelurkunden die örtliche Gesetzgebung oder das Gewohnheitsrecht letztlich die ausschlaggebende Rolle spielten.[28] Und so

---

[22] Bresslau, Harry: Handbuch der Urkundenlehre, Bd. 1. (Aufl.3). Berlin 1958, S. 635f.

[23] Invocatio, Intitulatio, Narratio, Dispositio, Eschatokoll, Subscriptiones als unverzichtbare Bestandteile, die um weitere Bestandteile ergänzt und ausgebaut werden können.

[24] Kaser, Max: Das Römische Zivilprozessrecht. München 1996, S. 177.

[25] Endemann, Wilhelm: Die Beweislehre des Civilprozesses. Heidelberg 1860, S. 23ff.; Briegleb, Hans Karl: Einleitung in die Theorie der summarischen Processe. Leipzig 1859, S. 15ff.

[26] Trusen, Jurisprudenz. S. 205. (Fn. 21).

[27] C. I de fide instr.

[28] Schulte, Petra: Scripturae publicae creditur – Das Vertrauen in Notariatsurkunden im kommunalen Italien des 12. und 13. Jahrhunderts. Tübingen 2003 zu den Besonderheiten des (nord-) italienischen Notariats; Luschek, Fritz: Notariatsurkunde und Notariat in Schlesien von den Anfängen (1282) bis zum Ende des 16. Jahrhunderts. Weimar 1940; Schuler, Johannes: Notare Südwestdeutschlands: ein prosopographisches Verzeichnis für die Zeit von 1300 bis ca. 1520. Stuttgart 1987.

lassen sich nicht wenige Hinweise auf eine zusätzliche Bestärkung notarieller Urkunden in Prozessakten sowie im partikularen Recht finden. Im Reichsrecht sind die Parallelen in der Beweiswirkung wie im Aufbau zwischen notariellen sowie kaiserlichen und päpstlichen Urkunden aber unverkennbar.[29] Es wäre deshalb ratsam, die leider noch immer bestehenden Mauern zwischen der Geschichts- und Rechtswissenschaft niederzureißen und die Urkunden nach der beschriebenen Wirkweise sowie dem vergleichbaren Urkundenaufbau zu kategorisieren, und sie analog zu unserer heutigen juristischen Urkundeneinteilung als öffentliche – weil mit öffentlichem Glauben ausgestattete – Urkunden zusammenzufassen.

Sicherheit im Prozess

Für die Friedensschaffung durch Beweismittel waren öffentliche Urkunden von besonderer Bedeutung. Schon in hochmittelalterlichen Rechtsquellen hob man die „bezzer[en]"[30] Beweissicherungsmöglichkeiten durch Urkunden – gemeint waren hier nur Siegelurkunden, die Abfassung notarieller Urkunden war zu dieser Zeit im deutschen Reichsgebiet noch unüblich[31] – gegenüber dem Zeugenbeweis hervor.

Erst im Hochmittelalter mit dem Aufkommen der gelehrten geistlichen Gerichte begann auch ein Rinnsal der notariellen Urkunden zu fließen. Zu jener Zeit waren die Siegelurkunden bereits weit verbreitet. Entgegen häufig bekundeter gegenteiliger Auffassungen[32] hatten sich die notariellen Urkunden durchaus auf deutschem Gebiet etablieren können, wenn sie auch nie zu einer echten Konkurrenz für Siegelurkunden avancierten.

Im Mittelalter existierte der Begriff der Siegelmäßigkeit, der das Führen von Siegeln als besonderes und exklusives Vorrecht privilegierter Stände zum Ausdruck brachte, nicht. Grundsätzlich konnte also jeder, der ein Siegel führte, Urkunden besiegeln. Gerade darin lag nun der entscheidende Vorteil der notariellen Urkunden. Die Siegel machten die Urkunden nicht per se glaubwürdig. Vielmehr war der Umfang der Beweiswirkung

---

[29] So auch Trusen, Jurisprudenz. S. 203ff. (Fn. 21).

[30] „Wir sprechen daz briefe bezzer sin danne gezivge" Schwabenspiegel, ed. Lassberg, S. 36.

[31] Anlässlich von Streitigkeiten zwischen Kaiser Ludwig dem Bayern und Papst Johannes XXII musste der Erzbischof von Magdeburg eingestehen, „quia usus tabellionum in partibus nostris non habentur". (zitiert nach Harms, Wolf-George: Bibliographie zur Geschichte des deutschen Notariats. Würzburg 2007, Einführung S. 2 mwN).

[32] Z.B. Redlich, Oswald: Privaturkunden des Mittelalters. Darmstadt 1911 (ND 1967), S. 231; Bresslau, Urkundenlehre, Bd. 2., S. 662ff. (Fn. 19), der sich lediglich den von Kaiser und Königen beauftragten notariellen Urkunden widmet.

einerseits davon abhängig, für wen die Urkunde besiegelt wurde, andererseits von äußeren Faktoren, wie dem Ansehen und der Macht des Sieglers. Je nach sozialer Stellung des Siegelnden bedurfte es zur Erstellung glaubwürdiger Urkunden weiterer Siegel hochgestellter Persönlichkeiten. Deren Beschaffung war stets mit Mühe und erheblichen Kosten verbunden.[33] In dieser Lage gewann das Notariat als eine Institution, die jedermann zur Erstellung öffentlicher – also glaubwürdiger – Urkunden frei zur Verfügung stand, an Attraktivität.

Sollte eine notarielle Urkunde im Prozess widerlegt oder zumindest entkräftet werden, so war das mit außerordentlichen Schwierigkeiten verbunden, denn bei Leugnung ihrer Echtheit musste die zweifelnde Prozesspartei den vollen Beweis des Gegenteils führen. Anders als bei päpstlichen und kaiserlichen Siegelurkunden, bei welchen das Führen eines Gegenbeweises auf inhaltlicher Basis gänzlich unmöglich, ja sogar verboten war, bestand diese Möglichkeit bei notariellen Instrumenten durchaus. Denn gemeinhin galt der Grundsatz, dass nicht die Urkunde existiere, damit durch sie die Wahrheit lebendig werde. Vielmehr solle eine Urkunde die Wahrheit abbilden.[34] In der Praxis traten jedoch erheblich häufiger Fälle auf, in denen Urkunden wegen formeller Fehler (erfolgreich) gerügt wurden. Es darf aber nicht der Eindruck entstehen, dass die Vernichtung der gesteigerten Beweiswirkung öffentlicher Urkunden den gerichtlichen Alltag bestimmt hätte. Im Gegenteil: wegen der urkundlichen Vermutungswirkung gelang diese Beweisführung nur sehr selten.

Sicherheit und Konfliktprävention

Jenseits ihrer Verwendung vor Gericht konnten notarielle Urkunden auch eine friedenssichernde Wirkung außerhalb des prozessualen Geschehens entfalten. Dabei ist zwischen verschiedenen „Notartypen" zu differenzieren, nämlich solchen, die ihre Arbeit im Dienste einer Person oder Institution verrichteten, und jenen, die sich als freie Notare

---

[33] Kroeschell, Karl; Albrecht, Cordes; Nehlsen- von Stryk, Karin: Deutsche Rechtsgeschichte. Bd. 2, Köln 2008, S. 29.

[34] „In summa notandum est, quod iudex non debet alligare animum suum ad unicam probationis speciem, ut ff. de testi. l. iii. Exceptis ergo casibus, qui excepti sunt, non obest, sive instrumenta non fuerint confecta, sive facta perdita: dummodo fides alias esse posit comperta, fiunt enim scripturae non ut per eas veritas subsistat, sed ut per eas veritas probetur, ff. eod. l. In re, et ff. de pigno. l. Contrahitur, et C. eo. l. i., et l. Statum , et l. Instrumentis, et l. Cum instrumentis, et l. Emancipacione, et l. Non" Placentinus, Summa Codicis zu Cod. 4.21, ed. Calasso, S. 154.

verdingten. Die Letzteren – oder besser gesagt, deren Schriftstücke – sind für die Friedenssicherung von herausgehobener Bedeutung. Im Gegensatz zu Siegelurkunden[35] und institutionellen notariellen Urkunden, die ihre Beweistauglichkeit aus der Glaubwürdigkeit des Sieglers bzw. aus einer Institution zogen, waren die von freien Notaren ausgestellte Urkunden gleichsam neutral und konnten – anders als Zeugen, Siegel- oder institutionelle Notarurkunden – im Zweifelsfall helfen, Wogen zu glätten. Gerade ihre Neutralität machte sie im Alltag zu friedensstiftenden Mittlern.

Besonders anschaulich wird die präventiv-sichernde Wirkung notarieller Urkunden im Rahmen eines Reichskammergerichtsprozesses geschildert, der heute im Hamburger Staatsarchiv lagert.[36] Darin hatten die Großväter von Kläger und Beklagtem eine Abrede notariell beurkunden lassen und waren Jahre später über deren Inhalt in Streit geraten. Laut der Vorakte hatte man sich eine Abschrift der Nota des beurkundenden Notares anfertigen lassen, um Klarheit zu erlangen und Frieden zu wahren. Da der Notar „keyns andern frund" gewesen sei, habe man der „schrifft" Glauben schenken können, einen Prozess verhindert und damit „fridlich gemeinschafft" gewahrt. Allein die Gier des Enkelsohnes habe diesen dazu getrieben, Jahre nach dem Tode des Großvaters die Urkunde anzuzweifeln und zu prozessieren. Das notarielle Instrument hatte einen Prozess zwar offensichtlich nicht für alle Zeiten zu verhindern vermocht, war aber von den ursprünglichen Vertragspartnern als ausreichendes Werkzeug zur Sicherung der Abrede angesehen worden, so dass eine gerichtliche Konfliktaustragung hatte verhindert werden können.

Aber der Befund des friedenstiftenden, sichernden Charakters notarieller Urkunden lässt sich nicht nur an Einzelfällen festmachen, sondern ist vielmehr im Wesen des Notariats selbst verankert. Dies hebt die Reichsnotariatsordnung von 1512 hervor, indem sie die Abfassung notarieller Instrumente als ein Mittel zu Erhaltung des Friedens „(…) dardurch dy chandlung und willen der menschen (damit sye nit in vergessen gesetzt) durch mittel der Schrifft in ewiger gedechtniß behalten und durch glaubwirdig offen urkund bevestigt werden (…)"[37] umschreibt.

Und noch heute besteht ein wichtiger Teil notarieller Beschäftigung, neben der Funktion des Notares als Beweissicherer, in der Konfliktverhütung und der Vermeidung gerichtlicher Auseinandersetzung.

---

[35] Die Rede ist hier immer von der Besiegelung fremder Urkunden.
[36] Staatsarchiv Hamburg: Reichskammergericht 211-2, M 5, Acta priora, Bl. 11r.
[37] Vorrede Reichsnotariatsordnung, ed. Meyer, Salzburg 1971.

Denn das selbstsüchtige Ziel des Einzelnen, das sich allzu häufig im Streben, den anderen übervorteilen zu wollen, zeigt, lässt sich am besten dadurch lösen, das „zwischen die beiden [Parteien] oder aber vor sie ein(…) unparteiische[r] Dritte[r]" – eben ein Notar, gestellt wird.[38]

B. Sicherheit durch Glaubwürdigkeit

Das spätmittelalterliche und frühneuzeitliche Recht kannte verschiedene Beweismittel: Parteieid, Zeugen, Urkunden, Augenschein sowie sachverstän-dige Gutachter. Zur Sicherung des außerprozessualen Friedens waren jedoch nur solche Beweismittel brauchbar, die aufgrund einer neutralen Stellung von beiden Streitparteien als geeignet anerkannt wurden. Diese Neutralität war per se beim Zeugenbeweis sowie dem Parteieid ausgeschlossen. Brauchbar waren Urkunden und Gutachter also überhaupt nur dann, wenn sie von beiden Parteien gemeinsam aufgestellt bzw. beauftragt worden waren. Als Beweismittel bezogen sie ihre Glaubwürdigkeit ausschließlich aus dem einvernehmlichen Erstellen des Beweisstücks und dem fortbestehenden Einverständnis, dieses in seiner Aussage unwidersprochen zu akzeptieren. Ohne das Element der beiderseitigen Akzeptanz gingen Urkunden ihrer friedenssichernden, streitschlichtenden Eigenschaften im Rahmen der Konfliktprävention verlustig und behielten lediglich ihre Bedeutung im gerichtlichen Prozess.

Konnte die Vorlage einer beiderseitig akzeptierten Urkunde im Rahmen der Konfliktprävention noch ausreichen, um eine aufkeimende Auseinandersetzung abzuwehren, war der Einsatz einer einseitig, d.h. von einer Partei aufgestellten Urkunde, im gerichtlichen Verfahren auf ihre Funktion als prozessuale Erkenntnisquelle beschränkt. Das in das Verfahren eingeführte Beweismittel war nun dazu bestimmt, den Tatsachenvortrag einer Prozesspartei zu untermauern, eine Behauptung zu festigen.[39] Anders als die römischrechtliche freie richterliche Würdigung

---

[38] Torres Escámez, Salvador: La función notarial, función preventiva de litigios: el consejo y la mediación notariales como instrumentos (1. parte) in: Tribunal Arbitral de Barcelona: Anuario de justicia alternativa 2002 (Nr. 3), S. 75ff.; Ebd.: La función notarial, función preventiva de litigios: el consejo y la mediación notariales como instrumentos (2. parte), in: Tribunal Arbitral de Barcelona: Anuario de justicia alternativa 2003 (Nr. 4), S. 53ff; Kurze Zusammenfassung: Torres Escámez, Salvador: Die Mittlerfunktion des Notars vor und nach Konflikten, Kurzreferat zum 13. Europöischen Notartag, Athen 2001 (www.notar.at/uploads/salvadortorresescamezdtletztversion20401.pdf, 01.11.2010).

[39] Allgemein zur mittelalterlichen und frühneuzeitlichen Beweislehre: Meile, Josef: Die Beweis-

der Beweismittel, bei welcher ein hoher Grad an Wahrscheinlichkeit genügte, um vernünftige Zweifel am Bestreiten der Ausführung zum Schweigen zu bringen,[40] waren die spätmittelalterlichen und frühneuzeitlichen Urteiler aufgrund ihres starken Hanges zur rationalistischen Argumentation zur strengen Beachtung der Formalia angehalten.[41] Deren Einhaltung war die notwendige Voraussetzung dafür, dass das eingebrachte Beweismittel überhaupt eine Wirkung entfalten konnte.

Die Bedeutung eines Beweismittels für die Erzeugung friedenstiftender Sicherheit war jedoch höchst unterschiedlich zu bewerten. Im Vordergrund stand hier nicht mehr, wie es noch bei der Ausbildung schriftlicher Beweismittel der Fall war, die Beständigkeit des Sicherungsmittels, sondern seine Wirkung und damit die Frage, welches Mittel eine Rechtsposition am sichersten belegen und einen Streit friedlich beenden konnte. Genau genommen war es eine Frage der den Beweismitteln zugemessenen Glaubwürdigkeit. Für die Verhinderung von Zwistigkeiten musste eine Möglichkeit eingeräumt werden, bestimmte Behauptungen auf überzeugende Beweismittel zu stützen und damit sein Recht zu verteidigen – also Sicherheit durch Authentizität der Beweise zu garantieren. Je umfänglicher diese die Rechte des Vorbringenden sicherten, desto mehr vermochten sie Frieden zu gewährleisten.

Der Umfang der Sicherheit[42], die die notariellen Instrumente vermitteln konnten, richtete sich dabei nach der zugebilligten „publica fides". Danach erbrachten die Urkunden aber nicht lediglich – und das wird den heutigen Juristen verwundern – den Beweis der formellen Wahrheit, also einen Beweis wie wir ihn noch heute in §§ 437, 415 ZPO kennen, sondern auch den der materiellen Wahrheit, dass also auch der beurkundeten Tatsache selbst Glauben geschenkt werden musste.[43] Damit legte man den notariellen Schriftstücken das höchstmögliche Maß an Glaubwürdigkeit bei.

---

lehre des kanonischen Prozesses. Paderborn 1925; Endemann, Wilhelm: Die Entwicklung des Beweisverfahrens im deutschen Zivilprozess seit 1495. Bonn 1895; Bentham, Jeremias: Theorie des gerichtlichen Beweises. Berlin 1838.

[40] Kaser, Zivilprozessrecht. S. 177 (Fn. 24).

[41] Zur mittelalterlichen Legaltheorie: Kohler, Schwedischen Zivilprozessrecht, S. 82 (Fn. 15).

[42] Zur formellen und materiellen Wahrheit: Fried, Johannes: Wille, Freiwilligkeit und Geständnis um 1300: Zur Beurteilung des letzten Tempelgroßmeisters Jaques de Molay. In: Historisches Jahrbuch, Bd. 105 (1985), S. 388ff.

[43] Dass notarielle Urkunden über den formellen auch den materiellen Beweis zu erbringen bestimmt waren, belegen unter anderem die Ausführungen des Lehrers der Notariatskunst

Glaubwürdigkeit als Machtfrage?

Wieso aber schenkte man diesen Schriftstücken mehr Vertrauen als Personen und Privaturkunden? Ich möchte im Folgenden versuchen, eine Antwort auf diese Frage zu geben. Besonders hilfreich erscheint es mir dabei, die Parallelen in der Entwicklung von Siegelurkunden und notariellen Instrumenten aufzuzeigen.

Um die Bedeutung der Siegelurkunden ergründen zu können, muss man sich zunächst das Wesen eines Siegels verdeutlichen. Aus seinem ursprünglichen Zweck, ein Schriftstück oder ein anderes Beweismittel zum Schutze zu verschließen, hatte sich im Laufe des Frühmittelalters ein Instrument entwickelt, mit welchem sich eine Verbindung zwischen dem Urkundeninhalt und dessen Aussteller herstellen ließ.[44] Die herausragende Stellung der Siegelurkunden als glaubwürdiger Beweismittel war in der Autorität ihres Ausstellers zu suchen, als dessen materialisiertes Zeichen das Siegel fungierte. Durch das Anbringen des Siegels auf der Urkunde wurde sie vollzogen. Zugleich begründete es eine Vermutung, dass sich der Siegler durch das Anhängen des Siegels mit dem in der Urkunde niedergelegten Inhalt identifiziere und ihn damit beglaubige.[45] Vor dem Hintergrund der Verflechtung von Autorität und Glaubwürdigkeit wird auch verständlich, weshalb eine päpstliche oder kaiserliche Urkunde lediglich formell anfechtbar war und schwerste Strafen für den Fall drohten, dass der Beweis der formellen Unechtheit misslingen sollte.[46] Ein Angriff auf die Urkunde stellte einen mittelbaren Angriff auf den Siegler dar. In der Rückkopplung der Beweiswirkung an die Anerkennung des Siegelträgers liegt nun auch die Ursache für die unterschiedliche

---

Petrus de Unzola aus dem frühen 14. Jahrhundert, der in seinem Kommentar der Summa totius artis notariae des Rolandinus Passagerii die notariellen Urkunden den authentischen zurechnet und konstatiert, dass diese solche seien, denen man sehr glaubt und vollstes Vertrauen schenken könne (Nam illud dicitur autenticum, cui multum creditur, et cui fides maxima adhibetur). Jedoch sei dem Urkundeninhalt kein bedingungsloses Vertrauen entgegengebracht, sondern von verschiedenen formellen Voraussetzungen abhängig, die der Kontrolle zugänglich seien und daher das entgegengebrachte umfängliche Vertrauen rechtfertigten. (Unzola, Petrus. In: Rolandinus, Summa (Tractatus notularum), ed. 1546, fol. 406v.). Insgesamt zum Vertrauen in Notariatsurkunden auch Schulte, Petra: Scripturae (Fn. 28).

[44] Bresslau, Urkundenlehre, Bd. 2., S. 548ff. (Fn. 19); Bresslau, Urkundenlehre, Bd. 1., S. 686ff. (Fn. 22).

[45] Ebd. (Fn. 44).

[46]Bresslau, Urkundenlehre, Bd. 1, S. 643f. (Fn. 19); auch: Pitz, Ernst: Erschleichung und Anfechtung von Herrscher- und Papsturkunden vom 4.-10. Jahrhundert. In: Fälschungen im Mittelalter III, Hannover 1988 (MGH-Schriften 33, III), S. 69ff.

Gewichtung der Siegelurkunden höhergestellter Persönlichkeiten und der einfachen Bevölkerung. Die prozessuale Gewichtung einer beweisenden Urkunde wurde mit dem Rang und dem gesellschaftlichen Ansehen des Sieglers verquickt – die Glaubwürdigkeit war eine Frage der Macht.

Daneben stehen nun die notariellen Urkunden, die ganz unbestritten seit der Reichsnotariatsordnung von 1512, mit hoher Wahrscheinlichkeit aber bereits früher mit öffentlichem Glauben ausgestattet waren – wie an den Ausführungen Unzolas gezeigt wurde.[47] Das frühneuzeitliche deutsche Notariat wurde aus unterschiedlichen Quellen gespeist und lässt sich nicht auf eine einzelne Wurzel zurückführen. Entsprechend möchte ich im Folgenden versuchen, seine Entstehung zu rekonstruieren, ohne dabei Anspruch darauf erheben zu können, mehr zu leisten, als den vermeintlichen Ursprung zu streifen – dieser liegt völlig im Dunkeln – und auf ein lohnendes Forschungsfeld aufmerksam zu machen.

Die ersten Grundlagen des frühneuzeitlichen deutschen Notariats wurden bereits im antiken Rom gelegt. Das römische Recht kannte verschiedene „Schreibertypen" – Tabularii und Tabellionen – deren Urkunden sich in ihrer rechtlichen Wirkweise voneinander unterschieden.[48] Während sich die Tabellionen als Privatschreiber verdingten, deren Schriftstücke über keine gesteigerte Beweiswirkung verfügten[49], wurden die Tabularii der öffentlichen Verwaltung zugerechnet. Aus der Zugehörigkeit zu einer öffentlichen glaubwürdigen Institution bezogen die Tabularii die Befähigung, mit *publica fides* ausgestattete Urkunden aufstellen zu können.[50] Wir finden also schon hier eine Verknüpfung zwischen der Fähigkeit, glaubwürdig zu beurkunden und der Zugehörigkeit zu einer mächtigen Institution.

Nach dem Untergang Roms geriet die rechtliche Differenzierung der ursprünglich verschiedenen Schreiber zunächst in Vergessenheit.[51] Erst

---

[47] S.o. Sicherheit durch Glaubwürdigkeit: Fn. 43.

[48] Zum Unterschied zwischen Tabellionen und Tabularii: Oesterley, Ferdinand: Das deutsche Notariat, Bd. 1. Hannover 1842, S. 12ff.; Kaser, Max/ Knütel, Rolf: Römisches Privatrecht, (19.Aufl.) München 2008, S. 80f.; Schulte, Scripturae, S. 7 ff. (Fn. 28).

[49] Oesterley, Notariat, Bd. 1., S. 18f. (Fn. 48); Sachers, Erich: Artikel „Tabellio". In: RE 4A (1932) Sp. 1847-1863; Kaser, Privatrecht, S.80. (Fn. 48).

[50] Oesterley, ebd. (Fn. 49); Kaser, ebd.(Fn. 49); Sachers, Erich: Art. Tabularius. In: RE 4A (1932) Sp. 1969-1983.

[51] Zum fortbestehenden Schreiberwesen innerhalb der kirchlichen Organisation: Trusen, Winfried: Das Notariat und die Anfänge der rechtlichen Urkundenlehre in Deutschland, in: Gelehrtes Recht im Mittelalter und in der Frühen Neuzeit. Winfried Trusen. Goldbach 1997, S. 583ff., 584.

nach der Wiederentdeckung des römischen Rechts im Hochmittelalter und seiner wissenschaftlichen Bearbeitung durch die italienischen Rechtsgelehrten wäre eine erneute Unterscheidung möglich gewesen. Dennoch wurden bis heute keine mittelalterlichen Quellen gefunden, die die antike Differenzierung zwischen öffentlichen und privaten Schreibern wieder aufleben ließen. Im Gegenteil: Es muss davon ausgegangen werden, dass die mittelalterlichen Vertreter der Notariatskunst die Unterscheidung bewusst ignorierten.[52] Denn die Begründungen der Lehrer der *ars notariae*, die im Mittelalter zur rechtlichen Grundlage des Notariats wurden, beinhalten sowohl solche Vorgaben, die wir in den Vorschriften zu den Tabellionen finden, wie etwa das Verbot der heimlichen Erstellung der Urkunden und verschiedene formelle Vorgaben[53], als auch solche, die denen der Tabularii entstammen, wie zum Beispiel die Ein-ordung der Tabularii in den Kreis der *publica persona*, deren Urkunden *publica fides* beigemessen wurden.[54] Augenscheinlich wird die Vermischung auch in Rechtstexten zum Notariat, in welchen die Bezeichnungen Tabularii, Tabellio und Notar synonym verwandt werden.[55] Dass es sich dabei lediglich um ein Versehen – eine Verwechslung beider Institute gehandelt hat, wie dies von Voltelini[56] angenommen wurde, ist meiner Meinung nach nicht möglich. Vielmehr ist der Grund für die Zusammenführung der Institute durch die Rechtsgelehrten meines Erachtens in ihrem Bemühen zu suchen, ein bereits vorgefundenes Institut mit den römischen Rechtsquellen in Einklang zu bringen. Ein Institut wie es sich im Mittelalter aus Gerichtsschreibern entwickelt hatte. Aufgrund ihrer Zugehörigkeit zum Gericht und ihrer exponierten gesellschaftlichen Stellung war es Richtern

---

[52] Eine bereits in der Antike bestehende Gleichsetzung von Tabularii und Tabellionen wie sie beispielsweise von Conradi (Conradi, Francisci Caroli: Parerga: In Quibus Antiquitates et Historia Iuris Illustrantur. Helmstadt 1738, S. 458 zitiert nach Oesterley, Notariat, Bd. 1., S.16 (Fn. 48)) in 18. Jahrhundert behauptet wurde, ist wegen der bereits genannten unterschiedlichen Tätigkeitsbereiche und insbesondere aufgrund der verschiedenartigen Wirkweise der erstellten Urkunden nicht aufrecht zu erhalten.

[53] Sachers, Tabellio. Sp. 1847ff. (Fn. 49); Kaser, Privatrecht., S. 78-80. (Fn. 48).

[54] Kaser, Privatrecht, S. 80f. mit Anm. 59. (Fn. 48).

[55] Nam publicum instrumentum est, quod scriptum est per manum publicam, id est per manum notarii publici, hoc est tabellionis (...), Tancredus: Ordo iudiciarius pars III.13, ed. Bergmann, S. 248f.; Tabularii dicuntur qui faciendis publicis instrumentis publice praesunt in singulis civitatibus, Azo: Summa super Codicem zu Cod. 10.71/69, ed. 1506, fol.425r.

[56] Voltelini, Hans: Die Südtiroler Notariats-Imbreviaturen des dreizehnten Jahrhunderts, Teil 1. Innsbruck 1899 (ND Aalen 1973), S. XXIII.

vorbehalten, glaubwürdige Schriftstücke auszustellen.[57] Mit der Zeit wurde dieser Aufgabenbereich von Gerichtsschreibern übernommen, die die Urkunden zunächst stellvertretend ausfertigten.[58] Nach und nach scheinen die Schreiber zunehmend Beurkundungen vorgenommen zu haben, die in keiner Verbindung zum Gericht standen.[59] Die Frage, weshalb ihren Urkunden dennoch eine gesteigerte Glaubwürdigkeit zugemessen wurde, bleibt offen. Feststeht, dass die Schreiber bis zu ihrer gewohnheitsrechtlichen Verselbständigung ihre Macht, glaubwürdige Urkunden auszustellen, aus der Autorität der hinter ihnen stehenden anerkannten Institution bezogen. Mit der Lösung vom Gericht entfiel diese institutionelle Verbindung, die es den Gerichtschreibern zuvor erlaubt hatte, glaubwürdige Urkunden aufzustellen. Durch die Rückkopplung an die römischen Schreiber, und nicht etwa erst durch die ausdrückliche reichsrechtliche Anerkennung der gesteigerten Beweiswirkung in der Reichsnotariatsordnung von 1512, versuchte man die Wirkung dennoch zu legitimieren.

Inszenierte Glaubwürdigkeit

Aber auch das „neue" Notariat kam nicht gänzlich ohne eine obrigkeitliche Autorisation aus. Wollten Notare im gesamten Reichsgebiet zur Aufstellung öffentlicher Urkunden berechtigt sein, so bedurften sie einer Bevollmächtigung durch den Kaiser oder Papst. Anders als Winfried Trusen annahm,[60] wurde die frühere Zugehörigkeit zu einem Gericht nicht durch die ernennungsrechtliche Anbindung an Papst, Kaiser oder eine sonstige kreierungsbefugte Person oder Institution ersetzt, auf der die Anerkennung der gesteigerten Glaubwürdigkeit nun beruhen sollte. Diese neue Verbindung war gänzlich anderer Natur: Keine institutionelle Bindung wie dies bei den antiken Tabularii oder den mittelalterlichen Gerichtsschreibern der Fall gewesen war. Die Ernennung war zwar unverzichtbar für die Ausübung der notariellen Tätigkeit, sie umgrenzte jedoch nur den Bereich, in dem den notariellen Urkunden eine gesteigerte Beweiswirkung zuerkannt wurde – in diesem Fall den Machtbereich von

---

[57]Trusen, Winfried: Das Notariat und die Anfänge der rechtlichen Urkundenlehre in Deutschland, in: Gelehrtes Recht im Mittelalter und in der Frühen Neuzeit. Winfried Trusen. Goldbach 1997, S. 583ff., 584.

[58] Dolezalek, Gero; Konow, Karl Otto: Handwörterbuch zur deutschen Rechtsgeschichte III (1982). Sp. 1051.

[59] Trusen, Anfänge. S. 584 (Fn. 57).

[60] Trusen, Anfänge, S. 584ff. (Fn. 57).

Kaiser, Papst[61] oder sonstigem Ernennungsberechtigten wie beispielsweise einer Stadt. Sie lässt keine Rückschlüsse auf die Herkunft der Glaubwürdigkeit selbst zu. Anders ist nicht zu erklären, weshalb die unangezweifelte Autorität des Kaisers oder des Papstes im Rahmen der notariellen Tätigkeit z. B. durch im partikularen Recht zum Teil festgeschriebene zusätzliche Prüfungen der päpstlichen und kaiserlichen Notare oder sogar gänzliche Missachtung ihrer Urkunden in Frage gestellt werden sollte. Zwar war es zu jeder Zeit möglich, im partikularen Recht Regelungen zu erlassen, die den gemeinrechtlichen entgegenstanden, es würde der grundsätzlichen Anerkennung der kaiserlichen und päpstlichen Macht aber diametral zuwiderlaufen, eine von der kaiserlichen oder päpstlichen Autorität hergeleitete Glaubwürdigkeit anzuzweifeln oder gar vollständig zu verwerfen. Dass zwischen der Anerkennung der Beweiswirkung einer notariellen Urkunde eines kaiserlich ernannten Notares und der kaiserlichen Autorität selbst unterschieden werden muss, bestätigt sich auch in einer Stellungnahme des Hamburger Rates. Dieser hatte sich geweigert, ein notarielles Instrument, das von einem kaiserlich ernannten Notar aufgestellt worden war, anzunehmen und anzuerkennen. Maßgebliches Augenmerk legte der Hamburger Rat in seiner Rechtfertigung auf die Feststellung, dass man mit der verweigerten Anerkennung keinesfalls die Autorität des Kaisers selbst habe in Zweifel ziehen wollen, sondern ihn vielmehr als die „vann gott geordnete(..) hochste(..) Obrigkeit Inn seinem hertzen"[62] trage und sich lediglich gegen den Notar und die von ihm ausgestellte Urkunde wende. Insofern sei zwischen Kaiser und Notar strikt zu trennen.

Auch die Festsetzung der gesteigerten Glaubwürdigkeit durch die mittelalterliche Wissenschaft und die Übernahme dieser Wirkung über das Gewohnheitsrecht in die geltende Rechtsordnung bilden lediglich das Ergebnis des Anerkennungsprozesses, liefern aber nicht dessen Begründung. Um die gesteigerte Beweiswirkung zu legitimieren, bedurfte es einer Verschiebung des Anknüpfungspunktes. Anstatt der früheren Kopplung an eine glaubhafte, mächtige Institution, die nun nicht mehr bestand, musste eine neue Stütze gefunden – inszeniert werden. Trotz der

---

[61] Ein besonders lohnendes Forschungsfeld ist daher die Frage, wie das Beweisrecht mit notariellen Urkunden in den Bereichen umging, in denen jeweils eine Partei die ernennende Autorität nicht anerkannte; beispielsweise im Handel mit Ländern außerhalb des Reichsgebiets oder auch auf dem Gebiet des (Seehandels-)Versicherungswesens.

[62] Staatsarchiv Hamburg: RKG 211-2, M 17, Conclusiones (Nr. 7), fol.12r.

Lösung der mittelalterlichen (Gerichts-)Schreiber von der die Glaubwürdigkeit vermittelnden Gerichtsinstitution behielt man die bislang anerkannte Wirkung der Gerichtsschreiberurkunden bei. Nach der Abspaltung basierte die gesteigerte Beweiswirkung nun nicht mehr auf dem Respekt vor einer hochgeachteten Macht, sondern gründete lediglich auf einem allgemeinen Konsens. Allein der Glaube an die Beweiswirkung gepaart mit der Erwartung, dass dieser Glaube auch von anderen geteilt werde, konnte dann eine solche Wirkung erschaffen.[63]

Das mittelalterliche Notariatswesen stand, wie wir bereits gesehen haben, in der Tradition der Gerichtsschreiber, welche glaubwürdige Urkunden erstellen konnten. Auch der formale Aufbau ihrer Urkunden glich dem, den das neugebildete Notariat aufstellte. Es liegt also nahe, ganz im eigentlichen Sinne des Wortes „Tradition" davon auszugehen, dass hier die anerkannte Wirkung der Gerichtsschreiberurkunden an das „neue" Notariatswesen weitergegeben und tradiert wurde. Durch den stillschweigenden Konsens und eine dauerhafte Übung wurde die institutionelle Neuordnung stabilisiert und gefestigt. Auch die im Hochmittelalter aufblühende Jurisprudenz hat diese Stellung wissenschaftlich anerkannt und im Rahmen ihrer Beschäftigung mit der Notariatskunst untermauert. Dass die Rechtsgelehrten dabei vielmehr auf die Legitimation der bestehenden Rechtswirklichkeit zielten und weniger auf eine exakte historische Rekonstruktion des römischen Rechts tritt an den Stellen klar zu Tage, wo sie zur Begründung der „neuen" Institution auf römisches Recht zurückgreifen, das sie größtenteils im ursprünglichen Umfang beließen, obgleich die Antike kein dem Notariat vergleichbares Institut gekannt hatte.[64]

In Anlehnung an die These Barbara Stollberg-Rilingers benötigt eine Ordnung keine Rechtfertigung ihrer Existenz im Sinne einer philosophischen, wissenschaftlichen Begründung. Ausreichend ist vielmehr eine gemeinsam geglaubte Fiktion.[65] Dennoch bestand ein nicht unbeachtlicher Teil der wissenschaftlichen Beschäftigung mit dem Notariatswesen im Mittelalter darin, das vorgefundene Notariat mit den römischen Quellen in Einklang zu bringen.

---

[63] Stollberg-Rilinger, Barbara: Des Kaisers alte Kleider: Verfassungsgeschichte und Symbolsprache des alten Reiches. München 2008, S. 9.
[64] So auch Schulte, Scripturae, S. 9 (Fn. 28).
[65] Stollberg-Rilinger, Symbolsprache, S. 9 (Fn. 63).

Eine Erklärung dafür ist im mittelalterlichen Rechtsverständnis zu suchen. Dieses manifestiert sich zum einen in der Vorstellung, dass das Recht nicht kreiert werden könne, sondern gleichsam als göttliches Recht bereits existiere – also lediglich gefunden werden müsse;[66] zum anderen kommt sie in der Idee der *translatio imperii* zum Ausdruck, die sich aus der Vier-Reiche-Lehre des biblischen Buches Daniel entwickelt hatte[67] und aufgrund derer sich das Heilige Römische Reich in der römischen Rechtstradition sah. Die Anknüpfung an das römische Recht bildete also eine zwingende Folge der herrschenden Rechtsvorstellungen. Der Versuch, das sich gewandelte Notariatswesen auf eine rechtliche, scheinbar traditionelle Basis zu stellen, widerspricht der These einer gemeinsamen Fiktion indes nicht, sondern untermauert sie sogar. Wie wir bereits gesehen haben, existierte ein dem Notariat vergleichbares Schreiberinstitut in der römischen Antike nicht. Auszuschließen ist, dass die großen Juristen des Mittelalters dies nicht erkannten. Um ihren Rechtsvorstellungen gerecht zu werden, konstruierten sie die Verbindung zum römischen Recht. Zusätzlich schufen sie mit der Anbindung an die Legaltheorie eine Möglichkeit, das theoretische Fundament auf eine objektiv nachweisbare Basis zu stellen. Die bloße Fiktion eines besseren Beweismittels erhielt auf diese Weise einen tatsächlichen Überprüfungsmaßstab, anhand dessen die Anerkennung der Wirkung auf eine formell-rechtliche Basis gestellt wurde.

Die Frage nach der rechtlichen Fundierung der Glaubwürdigkeit inszenierten die mittelalterlichen Rechtsgelehrten also mit Hilfe einer Konstruktion – der Zusammenfügung von Form und Wirkung.

---

[66] Loos, Fritz; Schreiber, Hans-Ludwig: Art. Recht, Gerechtigkeit. In: Geschichtliche Grundbe-griffe, Bd. 5., S. 231ff., 249ff. (Fn. 9).

[67] In Kap. 2 und Kap. 7 des Buches Daniel deutet Daniel einen Traum des Babylonierkönigs Nebukadnezar von einem Standbild aus verschiedenen Materialien, das von einem heranrollenden Felsen zerstört wird. Daniel deutet die vier Materialien dabei als vier Weltreiche. Nach der Zerstörung des letzten Weltreiches beginne der Jüngste Tag. Prägend für die Entwicklung der Idee der *translatio imperii*, der sog. Lehre von der Reichsübertragung war eine Interpretation dieser Bibelstelle durch Hieronymus im 4. Jh.. Dieser bezog die vier (unbestimmten) Reiche auf vier konkrete historische Reiche: zwei Reiche Babylons, das Reich der Makedonen und das römische Imperium. Aus der Vorstellung, das römische Reich sei das Letzte in der Folge vor dem Jüngsten Tage, ergab sich die unbedingte Notwendigkeit, das römische Imperium als nicht beendet zu betrachten.

Zusammenfassung

Ausgehend vom Ansatz Gustav Radbruchs, der Sicherheit als maßgebliche Voraussetzung zur Friedensschaffung ansah, wurde die in zahlreichen Forschungsarbeiten festgestellte Unverzichtbarkeit rechtlicher Regelungen zur Friedensschaffung und -sicherung um einen weiteren Aspekt ergänzt: die Notwendigkeit nachzuweisen, dass ein bestimmtes Recht überhaupt in Anspruch genommen werden kann. Nach dieser These besteht eine Möglichkeit zur Sicherung von Frieden in der Herstellung rechtmäßiger Zustände. Diese können aber nur dort geschaffen werden, wo unzweifelhaft nachgewiesen wird, dass das friedensstiftende Recht überhaupt greift. Um diesen Nachweis zu führen, bedurfte es sichernder Beweismittel. Zur Erhärtung dieser Theorie wurde die Entwicklung von den beschränkten Beweissicherungsmöglichkeiten des mittelalterlichen mündlichen Rechts durch Visualisierung hin zu langlebigen, schriftlich niedergelegten und damit sichereren Beweismitteln dargestellt. Ein besonderes Augenmerk galt dabei den mit *publica fides* ausgestatteten notariellen Instrumenten. Um die eigentümliche prozessuale Wirkung der notariellen Urkunden darzustellen, folgte eine kurze Gegenüberstellung von Siegelurkunden und notariellen Instrumenten, in welcher die Vorteile der Letzteren – die allgemeine Anerkennung der Glaubwürdigkeit, welche unabhängig vom Status des Notares oder seiner institutionellen Zugehörigkeit galt – herausgearbeitet wurden. Durch die dabei zu Tage tretende neutrale Stellung des Notares konnten seine Schriftstücke auch außerhalb gerichtlicher Streitigkeiten eine gewisse friedenssichernde Funktion erfüllen. Ausgehend von der institutionellen Entwicklung, die mit groben Strichen skizziert wurde, stellte sich die Frage, weshalb die glaubwürdige Wirkung der früheren Gerichtsurkunden auch nach der Loslösung der Schreiber vom Gericht und deren Verselbständigung fortbestehen konnte. In Anlehnung an den Gegenstand der Rechtsinszenierung drängt sich das Problem des zunächst scheinbar fehlenden Anknüpfungspunktes für die zuerkannte Glaubwürdig-keit des notariellen Urkundenbeweises auf. Dieser Konflikt konnte von den mittelalterlichen Rechtsgelehrten durch die Verschiebung des Bezugspunktes weg von einer glaubwürdigen Institution hin zur formellen Gestaltung der Schriftstücke, die im spätmittelalterlichen und frühneuzeitlichen Recht von überragender Wichtigkeit war, gelöst werden. Durch die künstliche Koppelung der vorgefundenen notariellen

Instrumente an die formellen Voraussetzungen der römischen Tabellionatsurkunden wurde nicht nur eine gesetzliche Normierung des neuen Bezugspunktes – der Form – ermöglicht, sondern vielmehr auch das rechtliche Fundament für die dauerhafte Anerkennung der gesteigerten Beweiswirkung gelegt. Erst durch diese Wirkung konnte den notariellen Instrumenten eine herausgehobene Stellung im System der Beweismittel zukommen. Als Beweismittel verhalf es dem Anwender zu einer sichereren, weil besser nachweisbaren Rechtsposition, die ihrerseits unverzichtbar für die Wahrung der Rechtsordnung war und damit maßgeblich zur Herstellung und Bewahrung von Frieden beitrug. Die allgemeine Anerkennung notarieller Urkunden und ihrer Beweiswirkung ist ein Baustein zur Herstellung und Sicherung von Frieden durch Recht, weil es dem Anwender durch den Nachweis einer notariell beurkundeten Tatsache zur Durchsetzung seiner Rechte verhelfen kann. Dass die urkundliche Wirkung nur inszeniert ist und sich nicht auf eine höhere Legitimationsbasis stützen kann, ist wegen ihrer allgemeinen Anerkennung für die Erzeugung von Frieden völlig unschädlich.

Und so möchte ich nun mit den Worten Rümelins schließen:

„Rechtssicherheit ist das Vorhandensein einer festen, tatsächlich durchgeführten Ordnung (...). Es kann vollkommen dahingestellt bleiben, ob es in irgend einem Sinn ein objektiv erweisbares richtiges Recht gibt, (...) [solange] „eine überindividuelle Instanz" [besteht], die, so lange nicht feststeht, was gerecht ist, wenigstens bestimmt was rechtens sein soll."[68]

---

[68] Rümelin, Max: Die Rechtssicherheit, Tübingen 1924, S. 3.

Rechtsformen in der Ingelheimer Rechtslandschaft

Alexander Krey und Regina Schäfer

1. Einführung und Quellenbestand

In Ingelheim nahe Mainz haben sich durch den Überlieferungszufall eine große Anzahl spätmittelalterlicher und frühneuzeitlicher Gerichtsprotokolle erhalten. Der Ingelheimer Grund, zuvor Fiskalbezirk des Königs, war seit dem späten Mittelalter an die Pfalzgrafen bei Rhein verpfändet.[1] Die Gerichtsschreiber des Grundes führten getrennte Protokollbücher für die Niedergerichtsbarkeit: sog. Haderbücher in den drei Hauptorten sowie über Oberhofsachen, darüber hinaus sog. Ufgiftbücher für Grundstücksüber-tragungen, und schließlich ein Kopialbuch. Die 13 bekannten Schreiber hatten nicht studiert, waren aber zum Teil vorgebildet; nachweisbar sind unter anderem vorherige Tätigkeiten als Sekretäre von Grafen, Hilfsschreiber in den Städten Mainz und Frankfurt oder als Notar.[2] Von 33 bezeugten spätmittelalterlichen Haderbüchern sind noch 18 der Jahre 1387 bis 1537 zugänglich.[3] Sie bilden damit den größten Bestand an dörflichen Gerichtsbüchern des Mittelalters im deutschsprachigen Raum.

Charakteristisch für die spätmittelalterliche Laiengerichtsbarkeit war eine Funktionsteilung, wonach die Urteiler – meist Schöffen – einen Spruch erarbeiteten, der erst mit der Verkündigung durch einen Richter, den Gerichtsherrn selbst oder einen vielfach Schultheiß genannten Vertreter verbindlich wurde.[4] Die Gerichtslandschaft[5] des Ingelheimer

---

[1] Vgl. Petry, Ludwig: Der Ingelheimer Grund vom 14. bis zum 18. Jahrhundert. In: Ingelheim am Rhein. Forschungen und Studien zur Geschichte Ingelheims. Hrsg. von François Lahenal u. Harald Weise. Ingelheim 1974, S. 63-76 passim.

[2] Vgl. zu den 13 Schreibern Schwitzgebel, Helmut: Kanzleisprache und Mundart in Ingelheim im ausgehenden Mittelalter. Diss. phil. Mainz 1958, S. 13-23.

[3] Blattmann, Marina: Beobachtungen zum Schrifteinsatz in einem deutschen Niedergericht um 1400. die Ingelheimer Haderbücher. In: Als die Welt in die Akten kam. Prozeßschriftgut im europäischen Mittelalter. Hrsg. von Susanne Lepsius u. Thomas Wetzstein. Frankfurt am Main 2008, S. 51-91, hier S. 55-57.

[4] Kroeschell, Karl; Cordes, Albrecht u. Nehlsen-von Stryk, Karin: Deutsche Rechtsgeschichte. Bd. 2: 1250-1650. 9. Aufl. Weimar 2008, S. 118; Willoweit, Dietmar: Gerichtsherrschaft und Schöffenrecht am Mittelrhein im 15. Jahrhundert. Beobachtungen anhand der Urteile des Ingelheimer Oberhofes. In: Seigneurial Jurisdiction. Comparative Studies in

Reichsgrundes hatte die Besonderheit, dass ein Schöffenkollegium[6] mehrere Gerichte, teils unter verschiedenen Schultheißen, besetzte.[7] Die Schöffen wurden folglich in gleicher Besetzung in unterschiedlichen Gerichtsforen tätig. Neben den drei Niedergerichten Ober- und Nieder-Ingelheim sowie Groß-Winternheim wurde aus dem Schöffenkollegium heraus auch der in der rechtshistorischen Forschung vor allem durch die Arbeiten von Adalbert Erler und Gunter Gudian bekannte Ingelheimer Oberhof[8] besetzt.[9] Die drei genannten Hauptorte des Grundes waren deshalb im Hinblick auf die Gerichtverfassung aufs Engste miteinander verwoben, wenn nicht gar als Einheit anzusehen.[10]

Das Ingelheimer Hadergericht war mit 14 überwiegend adeligen Schöffen des gemeinsamen Schöffenkollegiums besetzt. Sie kamen unter Vorsitz des örtlichen Schultheißen, der ebenfalls Schöffe war, bis zu sechsmal pro Woche zusammen; davon bis zu dreimal in Ober-Ingelheim, wo die Schöffen auch in Oberhofsachen tagten.[11] Im Regelfall tagte allerdings nur ein Ausschuss des Gerichts, vor dem

---

Continental and Anglo-American Legal History 4 (2000), S. 145-159, hier S. 149.

[5] Vgl. zum Forschungsbegriff der Gerichtslandschaft Amend, Anja; Baumann, Anette; Wendehorst, Stephan u. Wunderlich, Steffen: Recht und Gericht im frühneuzeitlichen Frankfurt am Main zwischen Vielfalt der Vormoderne und der Einheit der Moderne. In: Die Reichsstadt Frankfurt am Main als Rechts- und Gerichtslandschaft im Römisch-Deutschen Reich. Hrsg. von Anja Amend, Anette Baumann, Stephan Wendehorst u. Steffen Wunderlich. München 2008, S. 9-13, hier S. 9.

[6] Hübner tauchen im Reichsgrund mit einer einzigen Ausnahme nicht auf, vgl. Loersch, Hugo. Der Ingelheimer Oberhof. Bonn 1885, S. LXXV, Fn. 3.

[7] Die älteren Urteile des Ingelheimer Oberhofs. Bd.1. Hrsg. von Adalbert Erler. Frankfurt am Main 1952, S. 179.

[8] Vgl. hierzu Krey, Alexander: Ingelheimer Oberhof. In: Handwörterbuch zur deutschen Rechtsgeschichte. Bd. 2, Lfg. 13. 2. Aufl. Hrsg. von Albrecht Cordes; Heiner Lück; Dieter Werkmüller u. Christa Bertelsmeier-Kierst. Berlin 2011 (in Vorbereitung).

[9] Vgl. zu diesen Forschungen die Übersicht bei Kornblum, Udo: Adalbert Erlers Forschungen über die Ingelheimer Gerichtsbücher. In: In memoriam Adalbert Erler. Hrsg. von Karl Heinz Henn u. Ernst Kähler. Ingelheim 1994, S. 92-101 passim mit den Ergänzungen bei Blattmann (wie Fn. 3), S. 52, Fn. 4.

[10] Krey, Alexander: Die spätmittelalterliche Rechts- und Gerichtslandschaft des Ingelheimer Reichsgrundes. In: Die Ingelheimer Haderbücher. Mittelalterliches Prozessschriftgut und seine Auswertungsmöglichkeiten. Hrsg. von Franz J. Felten; Harald Müller u. Regina Schäfer. Ingelheim 2010, S. 43-63 passim; Vgl. auch Loersch (wie Fn. 6), S. LV u. LXXIII.

[11] Blattmann, Marita: Protokollführung in römisch-kanonischen und deutschrechtlichen Gerichtsverfahren im 13. und 14. Jahrhundert. In: Rechtsverständnis und Konfliktbewältigung. Gerichtliche und außergerichtliche Strategien im Mittelalter. Hrsg. von Stefan Esders. Köln u. a. 2007, S. 141-164, hier S. 156.

Klageerhebungen getätigt wurden, der Beweise verhörte, Fristen setzte, Klageverfahren stoppte und Freisprüche äußerte sowie Pfändungen und Gütereinsetzungen vornahm. Alle problematischen Fälle und Entscheidungen wurden „ad socios", d.h. bis zum Zusammenkommen des Vollgerichts vertagt. Auch der Ausschuss konnte aber auf Antrag der Parteien ein gültiges Urteil sprechen. Der Schultheiß fragte in diesen Fällen beide Parteien, ob sie mit dem anwesenden Gericht zufrieden seien, welches bei einer positiven Antwort dann das Urteil fällte.[12]

Anders als Adalbert Erler[13] und vor allem Gunter Gudian[14] meinten, können die Haderbücher durchaus für die rechtshistorische Forschung fruchtbar gemacht werden, da aus ihnen auch das Normen- und Wertgefüge sichtbar wird, mit dem die Schöffen operierten.[15] Marita Blattmann untersucht die frühen Gerichtsprotokolle vor allem im Hinblick auf den Übergang von der Mündlichkeit zur Schriftlichkeit.[16] In einem jetzt erschienen Tagungsband wurden die Gerichtsbücher in den Kontext mit zeitgleichen anderen Rechtsquellen, von Rechtsbüchern über städtische Gerichtsquellen bis zu herrschaftlich-normativen Quellen wie Weistümern und Dorfordnungen, gestellt.[17] Im Folgenden sollen Aspekte der Rechtsinszenierung vor allem am Beispiel eines Haderbuchs der Jahre 1476 bis 1485,[18] das für die Edition vorbereitet wird,[19] zur Darstellung kommen.

Im Rahmen dieses Beitrags wird hierbei zunächst ein elementarer Begriff der Rechtsinszenierung Verwendung finden, der auf die Sichtbarwerdung von Rechtsgewohnheiten in der mitunter formalen und rituellen Form vor Gericht abstellt. Die Eigenart der hier untersuchten Quelle als Niederschriften von Niedergerichtsitzungen bedingt, dass hierbei nicht abstraktes Recht wie möglicherweise in einem Rechtsbuch, sondern inszeniertes im Sinne von vor Gericht geübtem Recht sichtbar

---

[12] Vgl. Haderbuch 1476-1485, fol. 172r-v.
[13] Erler (wie Fn. 7), S. 55.
[14] Gudian, Gunter: Ingelheimer Recht im 15. Jahrhundert. Aalen 1968, S. 6.
[15] Vgl. zu diesem Ansatz die Hinweise bei Blattmann (wie Fn. 3), S. 64.
[16] Vgl. die Darstellung bei Blattmann (wie Fn. 3).
[17] Vgl. den Tagungsband: Die Ingelheimer Haderbücher. Mittelalterliches Prozessschriftgut und seine Auswertungsmöglichkeiten. Hrsg. von Franz J. Felten, Harald Müller u. Regina Schäfer. Ingelheim 2010.
[18] StadtA Ingelheim, Haderbuch 1476-1485.
[19] Das Institut für Geschichtliche Landeskunde an der Universität Mainz e.V. treibt unter der Leitung von Werner Marzi die Edition voran. Die Transkription des Gerichtsbuchs durch Regina Schäfer und Stefan Grathoff ist 2010 abgeschlossen worden.

wird. Da für das Gebiet des Ingelheimer Grundes kein Rechtsbuch oder eine andere Sammlung abstrakter Normen bekannt ist, lässt sich sogar sagen, dass sich das damals geltende Recht nur im prozessual in Erscheinung tretenden Regelwissen der Schöffen greifen lässt, das auf tradierten Rechtsvorstellungen[20] beruhte. Anders gewendet, lässt sich aber auch fragen, ob es möglicherweise im Kern nur jenes vor Gericht geübte Recht gab.[21] In diesem Beitrag sollen aber die letztlich damit zusammenhängenden und umstrittenen Fragen nach einer objektiven Rechtsordnung hinter den mittelalterlichen Rechtssprüchen der Schöffen[22] nicht in den Blick genommen werden. Vielmehr sollen konkrete Formen der Inszenierung untersucht werden. Das Beispiel der in den Prozess eingeschalteten und mitunter professionell agierenden Fürsprecher dient hierbei als Illustration der komplexen Situation vor Gericht. Zugleich offenbart das hier im Zentrum stehende Ober-Ingelheimer Haderbuch aber auch, dass nicht nur vor Gericht Rechtsgewohnheiten durch formalisierte Rituale im Rechtsalltag sichtbar wurden, sondern auch in alltäglichen Situationen, die ebenfalls beleuchtet werden sollen. Hierbei soll gezeigt werden, dass die konkreten Inszenierungsformen nicht bloße Hüllen des Rechts waren, sondern ihnen ein Eigenwert zukam, der darin bestand, Rechtsänderungen und -handlungen für die Rechtsgenossen sichtbar zu machen.

2. Parteien und ihre Vertreter vor Gericht

Für die Betrachtung des vor Gericht inszenierten Rechts ist zunächst von Bedeutung, wer die handelnden Personen am Gericht waren, wer also das Recht in Performanz brachte. Der Blick auf die verschiedenen institutionalisierten Vertretungsformen gibt hierbei Hinweise auf die komplexe Situation vor Gericht und insbesondere im Falle des Fürsprechers auch auf die Bedeutung der Form. Bemerkenswert ist zunächst, dass sich am Ingelheimer Gericht alle Schichten als Kläger wie

---

[20] Karl Kroeschell führte hierfür den Forschungsbegriff der Rechtsgewohnheit ein. Vgl. zur Diskussion: Kannowski, Bernd: Rechtsbegriffe im Mittelalter. Stand der Diskussion. In: Rechtsbegriffe im Mittelalter. Hrsg. von Albrecht Cordes. Frankfurt am Main u.a. 2002, S. 1-27, hier S. 16f. und zur Kritik Pilch, Martin: Der Rahmen der Rechtsgewohnheiten. Kritik des Normensystemdenkens entwickelt am Rechtsbegriff der mittelalterlichen Rechtsgeschichte. Weimar u.a. 2009, S. 273-312.

[21] Kroeschell; Cordes u. Nehlsen-von Stryk (wie Fn. 4), S. 129.

[22] Vgl. hierzu Kannowski (wie Fn. 20).

Beklagte trafen: Von der Bademagd bis zu den ortsgesessenen Adeligen und ebenso die Funktionsträger, vom Gerichtsschreiber über den Büttel und die Schöffen bis hin zum Schultheißen. Die Parteien vertraten ihre Sache hierbei selbst oder aber dies geschah durch einen Vertreter. In den Protokolleinträgen lassen sich insgesamt drei institutionalisierte Formen der Vertretung greifen. Neben diesen Formen gab es auch die Möglichkeit der kurzfristigen persönlichen Vertretung des Beklagten bei Herrennot oder Leibesnot, die entweder der Knecht oder auch die Ehefrau vornahmen;[23] dies soll hier außen vor bleiben.

Die Parteien hatten die Möglichkeit, auf verschiedene Formen institutionalisierter Unterhändler bzw. Vertreter zurückzugreifen. Zur Vervollständigung des Bildes dieser Möglichkeiten sei hier zunächst ein kurzer Blick in den außergerichtlichen Bereich geworfen: Beim außergerichtlichen Vergleich, der sog. „rachtung", entsandte jede Partei ein oder zwei bevollmächtigte Unterhändler oder „frunde", die unter einem Dritten oder Fünften als Schiedsmann die beiden Seiten vergleichen sollten.[24] Dieser Vergleich konnte schriftlich festgehalten werden.[25] Trotz dieser Möglichkeiten kam eine Fülle von Angelegenheiten vor das Gericht. Für die Jahre 1476 bis 1485 sind 240 Blatt mit Protokollierungen der Niedergerichts-barkeit erhalten. Auch wenn nicht mehr erhoben werden kann, wie viele aller tatsächlichen örtlichen Streitigkeiten vor Gericht kamen, so macht die große Anzahl der schriftlichen Zeugnisse für acht Jahre doch deutlich, dass mit einer hohen Rate der Vergerichtlichung gerechnet werden muss, insbesondere bei ausstehenden Zahlungen. In zahlreichen Fällen erfolgte die erste und vielfach auch zweite Heischung auf ausstehendes Geld, wobei die dritte dann aber fehlt, also der Streit nicht mehr weiter gerichtlich verfolgt wurde. Echte Endurteile sind deshalb selten. Zudem finden sich in den Protokollen viele Hinweise auf außergerichtliche Konfliktlösungs-versuche.[26] Die Beilegung des Konflikts außergerichtlich durch

---

[23] Bspw. Haderbuch 1476-1485, fol. 21 zur Vertretung durch den Knecht wegen Herren-not, fol. 8 u. 143v zur Vertretung durch die Ehefrau bei Krankheit.
[24] Haderbuch 1476-1485, fol. 194.
[25] So der Streit zwischen der Äbtissin von Engelthal und der ritteradeligen Magdalena von Venningen (Haderbuch 1476-1485, fol. 148).
[26] Vgl. hierzu Schäfer, Regina: Frieden durch Recht. Die Funktionen des Gerichts für die Gemeinde. In: Dorf und Gemeinde. Hrsg. von Kurt Andermann (Kraichtaler Kolloquien 8) (Erscheint 2011).

Schlichtung darf daher in ihrer Bedeutung für die Ingelheimer Gerichtslandschaft nicht unterschätzt werden.

Zum Zweiten ist der „Momper" zu nennen, der ein umfänglicher persönlicher Vertreter war. Momper wurden insbesondere von auswärtigen geistlichen Institutionen[27] und einheimischen Adeligen in Anspruch genommen, die sich um ihren verzweigten Besitz nicht persönlich kümmern konnten oder wollten.[28] Die Wahl des Mompers war frei, allerdings griff man meist auf das Umfeld zurück; mal setzte eine Witwe ihren Sohn oder einen Geistlichen ein,[29] mal ein Mann seinen Vater oder seinen Schwager,[30] mal nahm man den Hofmann,[31] doch auch Fürsprecher und Gerichtsschreiber sind bezeugt. Eine besondere Gerichtsvertretung von Frauen lässt sich, anders als Gunter Gudian für die Oberhofsachen anführte,[32] im Haderbuch nicht greifen. Es finden sich zahlreiche Frauen als Klägerinnen wie als Beklagte, über deren Familienstand teilweise nichts bekannt ist.[33] Nachweis-bar sind aber auch verheiratete Frauen[34] und Witwen.[35] Sie traten vor Gericht nicht anders als Männer auf. Allerdings lässt sich am Haderbuch auch ablesen, dass die Ehemänner über den Besitz verfügten, auch über jenen, welche die Frauen mit in die Ehe brachten, wobei diese aber ein Mitspracherecht hatten.[36] Die Aufgabe des Mompers wird im Haderbuch selbst mit den

---

[27] Genannt werden u. a. die Kartäuser von Mainz und St. Johann zu Mainz (Haderbuch 1476-1485, fol. 175r).

[28] Bspw. Hans Snyder als Vertreter des Schöffen Adam Wolff von Sponheim (Haderbuch 1476-1485, fol. 3r).

[29] Bspw. ernennt Else, die Witwe Peter Schreibers, ihren Sohn Heinrich zum Momper; Katharina Hiltz den Priester Heinrich Nickel (Haderbuch 1476-1485, fol. 174r).

[30] Cles Konne macht seinen Vater zum Momper (Haderbuch 1476-1485, fol. 175).

[31] Philipp, der Hofmann von Johann Boos von Waldeck handelt als dessen momper bevor er durch den Gerichtschreiber ersetzt wird (Haderbuch 1476-1485, fol. 202).

[32] Gudian (wie Fn. 14), S. 77.

[33] Bspw. die häufig erwähnten Grede von Oestrich und Anne Kitz (Haderbuch 1476-1485, fol. 40).

[34] Bspw. Hepchins frauwe Keth oder Barbel, die Frau von Hans von Worms (Haderbuch 1476-1485, fol. 171v u. 40v).

[35] Bspw. Grede, die Witwe Clesgin Benders (Haderbuch 1476-1485, fol. 3).

[36] Die Besitzwechsel fanden nicht vor Gericht statt und kamen nur im Streitfall vor Gericht. Das Verfügungsrecht des Mannes wird aber deutlich (bspw. Haderbuch 1476-1485, fol. 8v, 230). In einem Fall äußerte der Mann mündlich eine Klausel, wonach der Verkauf nur gelten solle, wenn seine Frau dem zustimme, da aus ihrem Besitz das Gut stamme (ebd. fol. 8v, 25r-v). Diese Klausel führte der Verkäufer an, um im Nachhinein den getätigten Verkauf rückgängig zu machen. Das Gericht folgte der Argumentation und hob den Kaufvertrag auf (ebd. fol. 27v-28).

Worten umschrieben, er sei „gemacht, jne zuvergene und zuverstene und sine sachen jm Riche ußzurichten, weß er zu dhun hait, als were er selbs gegenwertig hie".[37] Die Einsetzung geschah öffentlich vor dem Schultheißen und mindestens einem Schöffen und galt bis auf Widerruf durch eine der beiden Seiten.[38] Der Momper musste die Übernahme der Vertretung durch „Verbotung"[39] kund tun und damit zustimmen.[40] Kam es zum Amtskonflikt wie im Falle des Gerichtsschreibers, der zugleich Vertreter eines Adeligen war, musste dieser auf Forderung der Schöffen das Amt des Mompers ruhen lassen.[41]

Als letzte und für die Inszenierung des Rechts vor Gericht im Rechtsleben besonders bedeutsame Form der Vertretung lassen sich in vielen Einträgen Fürsprecher greifen. Ihnen kam nur eine Funktion im Gerichtsprozess als Vertreter im Worte zu und sie wurden von einer Partei beauftragt. Der Gerichtsschreiber vermerkte dann formelhaft A „hat sich verdingt", B „das wort zu thun unnd hat sin underdinge verbott alß recht ist".[42] Die Verpflichtung erfolgte damit durch eine öffentliche Anstellung, durch Verbotung vor dem Gericht. Sie musste grundsätzlich zu Beginn eines jeden Prozesstermins geschehen und folglich immer wieder erneuert werden.[43] Unmittelbar nach der Einsetzung wurde der Fürsprecher im Prozess tätig und brachte etwa die Anklage bzw. die Entgegnung vor. Einen solchen rechtskundigen Vertreter nahmen die unterschiedlichsten Parteien in Anspruch – einzelne Dorfbewohner in komplizierten Streitfällen z.B. um das Erbe, Vertreter von geistlichen Institutionen, aber auch Schöffen und der Oppenheimer Amtmann. Oft standen sich vor dem Dorfgericht damit zwei Fürsprecher gegenüber. Aufgrund seiner Natur als Vertretung in Wort nicht aber in Person waren Kläger und Beklagter zumindest

---

[37] Haderbuch 1476-1485, fol. 199v u. fol. 198.
[38] Haderbuch 1476-1485, fol. 202: „biß off ir beyer widderruffen".
[39] Vgl. zur Rechtsinszenierung der Verbotung die Ausführungen weiter unten.
[40] Vgl. Haderbuch 1476-1485, fol. 202 zur Einsetzung Johann Diels zu Winternheim durch Konrad, einen Maler von Kirchberg, vor dem Ober-Ingelheimer Schultheiß Adam Wolff von Sponheim und Schöffe Clese Raub.
[41] Haderbuch 1476-1485, fol. 202: „Daß habenn die scheffenn Sybeln gegonnet, also wan sie jne davon heyssent stehen, so soll die momparschafft abe und jne alleyne gehorsamm und gewertig sin."
[42] Bspw. Haderbuch 1476-1485, fol. 172v.
[43] Vgl. Buchda, Gerhard u. Cordes, Albrecht: Anwalt. In: Handwörterbuch zur deutschen Rechtsgeschichte. Bd. 1. 2. Aufl. Hrsg. von Albrecht Cordes; Heiner Lück; Dieter Werkmüller u. Ruth Schmidt-Wiegand. Berlin 2008, Sp. 255-263, hier Sp. 256.

manchmal nachweislich persönlich vor Gericht anwesend.[44] Waren mehrere Personen Kläger bzw. Beklagte, konnten sie einen gemeinsamen Fürsprecher haben, der dann für seine „heiptlude" gemeinsam handelte.[45] Auffällig ist, dass einzelne Namen im Zusammenhang mit der Bestellung als Fürsprecher signifikant häufig auftauchen – sich mithin sagen lässt, dass bis zu vier Personen gleichzeitig als wenigstens semiprofessionelle wenn nicht vollprofessionelle Fürsprecherelite am Gericht greifbar sind,[46] die allerdings nicht, wie mitunter üblich, zum Kreis der Schöffen zählten.[47] Der Fürsprecher konnte je nach Bestellung die Klageeinreichung übernehmen, die Pfändung fordern oder umfangreich bei Hauptverhandlungen vertreten. Neben den verschiedenen Beweismitteln durch Begehungen, Kerbhölzer und Urkunden, Zeugenaussagen und Eid war insbesondere das Öffnen und Verlesen des Gerichtsbuchs wichtig, das oft der Fürsprecher beantragte, dem in der mündlichen Verhandlungen eine wichtige Rolle zukam. Ebenso übernahm er die Funktion, eine Partei „zu den Heiligen zu geleiten", also bei der Eidesabnahme[48] vorzusprechen.[49] Ein Fürsprecherzwang bestand erkennbar nicht. Eine juristische Vorbildung der Fürsprecher ist nicht bekannt, wohl aber der Versuch, diese als Gegner im Prozess zu verhindern. So versucht ein Mann einen

---

[44] In einem Fall macht der dabei stehende Kläger, Philipp Hirt, nach der Aussage seines Vertreters noch eine gerichtskundige Bemerkung: „Ffurter ist Philips Hyrte zu geigen gestanden und hait gesagt, er woll myt recht behalten und beweren, dass die gulte yn maißen wie obgemelt von yne beiden also gegeben sij." (Haderbuch 1476-1485, fol. 38).

[45] Haderbuch 1476-1485, fol. 165v u. 228v.

[46] Genannt werden zunächst Antz Duppengießer (Haderbuch 1476-1485, fol. 3), Henne von Eltville (ebd., fol. 3), Drubein (ebd., fol. 15) und Hans Snider (ebd., fol. 3). Im Jahr 1478 taucht erstmals Johann Erk im Haderbuch auf, möglicherweise für Drubein, der nun nicht mehr genannt wird (ebd., fol. 82). Ab 1479 ist dann Henne Rudiger greifbar (ebd., fol. 103v).

[47] Bspw. sah es die Constitutio Criminalis Carolina von 1532 wahrscheinlich sogar als Regel an, dass die Fürsprecher aus dem Kreis der Schöffen gewählt wurden (vgl. Kleinheyer, Gerd: Tradition und Reform in der Constitutio Criminalis Carolina. In: Strafrecht, Strafprozess und Rezeption. Grundlagen, Entwicklung und Wirkung der Constitutio Criminalis Carolina. Hrsg. von Peter Landau u. Friedrich-Christian Schroeder. Frankfurt am Main 1984, S. 7-28, hier S. 12.

[48] Vgl. hierzu auch Oestmann, Peter: Der vergessliche Fürsprecher. In: Fälle aus der Rechtsgeschichte. Hrsg. von Ulrich Falk, Michele Luminati u. Matthias Schmoeckel. München 2008, S. 147-163, hier S. 164-156.

[49] Bspw. Haderbuch 1476-1485, fol. 8v (Fürsprecher Drubein); fol. 52 (Fürsprecher Henne von Eltville); fol. 72 r (Fürsprecher Hans Snider) u. fol. 103v (Fürsprecher Henne Rudiger).

Fürsprecher als Gegenpartei zu vermeiden, indem er vor Gericht geltend macht, dass jener ihm vorher zugesichert habe, „dasz wort widder yne nit zuthun und darumb genomme habe und daz nit helt".[50] In einem einzigen Fall ist von einem „anwalt" die Rede, wobei anhand der knappen Bemerkung nicht entschieden werden kann, ob hier ein Momper oder ein Fürsprecher gemeint ist.[51]

Gerade an der beschriebenen Gerichtsvertretung durch Fürsprecher zeigt sich die hohe Wertschätzung der rechtskundigen Personen am Gericht. Hier kann letztlich eine Form von Professionalisierung innerhalb einer von Laien durchgeführten Gerichtsbarkeit gegriffen werden, in der zumindest in den komplizierten Fällen ein Personenkreis als Fürsprecher fungierte, der dies professionell erledigte. Sicher waren sie keine Anwälte im modernen Sinne, sondern im Grundsatz Vertreter im Worte, gleichsam aber darf eine vertiefte Kenntnis der Rechtsgewohnheiten vor Gericht[52] angenommen werden, die gerade in komplizierten Fällen der Durchsetzung zuträglich war und den Fürsprecher zu einer Hilfsperson der gegnerischen Partei machte, die man auszuschalten versuchte.

Anderseits wird im Gerichtsbuch aber auch immer wieder eine elementare Rechtskundigkeit der Dorfbevölkerung deutlich. Diese zeigt sich gerade in den Fällen, die nicht durch Fürsprecher verhandelt wurden. So versucht man mit prozessualen Begründungen Streitigkeiten zu den eigenen Gunsten zu beenden, etwa weil die Gegenseite Gerichtstermine nicht gewahrt[53] oder nicht persönlich gewahrt habe,[54] die Unterhändler der Gegenpartei keine Vollmacht gehabt hätten oder die Gegenpartei mal persönlich und ein andermal durch Beauftragte vor Gericht erschienen sei.[55] Neben offensichtlichen, ‚bauernschlau' wirkenden Versuchen, etwa strittiges Gut schnell zu veräußern,[56] werden auch mündlich geäußerte Klauseln angebracht, etwa dass eine Gutsveräußerung der Zustimmung der Ehefrau bedürfe, wenn diese den Besitz

---

[50] Haderbuch 1476-1485, fol. 224r.
[51] Haderbuch 1476-1485, fol. 12: „Und begert dwile er eynen anwalt habe, register, briffe ader anders zu brengen und hofft, er soll eß billich thun."
[52] So auch für den Ingelheimer Oberhof Oestmann (wie Fn. 48), S. 157.
[53] Haderbuch 1476-1485, fol. 87v u. 190v.
[54] Haderbuch 1476-1485, fol. 82v.
[55] Haderbuch 1476-1485, fol. 21r-v.
[56] Bspw. Haderbuch 1476-1485, fol. 5v-6.

mitgebracht habe.[57] Umfassend geht es um Erbrechtsfragen, etwa ab welchem Zeitpunkt Miterben zuzulassen sind bzw. anteilig Schulden bezahlen müssen,[58] inwieweit das Erbe abgelehnt werden kann[59] oder aber um Gesamthandbesitz und die Anrechte von Haupt- und Nebengläubigern.[60] Anders gewendet: Auch wenn sich die Parteien im Prozess häufig gerade bei komplizierten Sachverhalten des Sachverstandes von Vertretern bedienten, so kann doch auch angenommen werden, dass die Bevölkerung mit den Rechtsgewohnheiten vor dem Dorfgericht im Grundsatz vertraut war. Fragt man, wer vor dem spätmittelalterlichen Ober-Ingelheimer Hadergericht Recht inszenierte, so waren dies nicht nur die mitunter professionell agierenden Fürsprecher, sondern ebenso die teilweise geschickt agierenden Dorfbewohner, die mitunter durchaus als rechtskundig anzusehen sind.

3. Formen der Rechtsinszenierung im dörflichen Alltag

In den Protokollierungen des hier vorgestellten Haderbuchs zeigt sich ein Spannungsfeld, das sich im Spätmittelalter zwischen tradierten Rechtsinszenierungen einerseits, die letztlich der Sicherung des Beweises einer Rechtshandlung dienen sollten, und dem Beweis durch schriftliche Fixierungen andererseits, die vor allem das Gerichtsbuch ins Zentrum rückten, formierte. Im Mittelpunkt der nachfolgenden Betrachtungen sollen deshalb die Beweismittel stehen.

Dem mittelalterlichen deutschrechtlichen Denken war eine freie Beweiswürdigung noch weitgehend fremd, weshalb formal richtig durchgeführte Beweise für die Schöffen zwingend waren und über die Beweisregelung ein Beweisurteil ergehen konnten.[61] Auf diese Weise konnten letztlich materiellrechtliche Fragen mithilfe des Beweisrechts entschieden werden. Dies zeigt sich auch im Ober-Ingelheimer

---

[57] Bspw. Haderbuch 1476-1485, fol. 8v; siehe dazu auch oben Fn. 36.
[58] Bspw. in einem umfangreichen Streitfall zwischen adeligen Erben (Haderbuch 1476-1485,
fol. 116-117v, Urteil fol. 152).
[59] Vgl. Haderbuch 1476-1485, fol. 212v-213 u. fol. 231v-232.
[60] Haderbuch 1476-1485, fol. 36v-37.
[61] Vgl. zum Verfahren am Ingelheimer Oberhof: Erler, Adalbert: Der Ingelheimer Oberhof. In: Ingelheim am Rhein. Forschungen und Studien zur Geschichte Ingelheims. Hrsg. von Johanne Autenrieth. Stuttgart 1964, S. 174-200, hier S. 187 f.

Haderbuch. Nach den Beweisangeboten der Parteien gibt das Ober-Ingelheimer Niedergericht meist eine Frist von 14 Tagen zur Beibringung der Beweise, beispielsweise mit den Worten: „Dwile sie von beydentheiln offs büch ziegen, so sollen sie eß auch brengen und das thun in 14 tagen."[62] Zulässige Beweismittel waren hierbei wie im Oberhofverfahren der Eidesbeweis, der Zeugenbeweis, der Urkundenbeweis und der Augenscheinbeweis.[63]

Betrachtet man nun die angebotenen Beweismittel der Parteien, so offenbart das Haderbuch zunächst eine große Bandbreite an mittelalterlichen rechtsrituellen Handlungen. Vor allem in einer illateraten Welt scheinen Rechtsinszenierungen in Form von Rechtsritualen notwendig, um die Rechtshandlung nach außen sichtbar zu machen. Rechtlicher Inhalt und Form werden so zu einer untrennbaren Einheit und bleiben im Gedächtnis verhaftet.[64] Im hier untersuchten Haderbuch beziehen sich die Parteien beispielsweise häufig auf die „lude eynßs winkauffs".[65] Der Weinkauf war ein ritueller Umtrunk bei Abschluss eines Rechtsgeschäfts unter Heranziehung von Geschäftszeugen.[66] Diese Zeugen konnten dann im Verfahren gehört werden. Selten wird auch die Hingabe eines Gottespfennigs als äquivalente Form der Sichtbarmachung des Rechtsgeschäfts greifbar.[67] Der Funktion der Manifestation eines an sich unsichtbaren Rechtszustandes dienten auch die, wenngleich seltener im Haderbuch protokollierten Kerbhölzer, die sog. „kerben".[68] Kerbhölzer waren schon im Frühmittelalter gebräuchlich und erhielten ihren Beweiswert durch das Einritzen von Zeichen in ein Stück Holz, das anschließend geteilt

---

[62] Haderbuch 1476-1485, fol. 6.
[63] Vgl. zum Oberhofverfahren: Kornblum, Udo: Das Beweisrecht des Ingelheimer Oberhofes und seiner malpflichtigen Schöffenstühle im Spätmittelalter. Diss. jur. Frankfurt am Main 1960,
S. 23.
[64] Erler, Adalbert: Rechtsritual. In: Handwörterbuch zur deutschen Rechtsgeschichte. Bd. 4. 1. Aufl. Hrsg. von Adalbert Erler, Ekkehard Kaufmann u. Ruth Schmidt-Wiegand. Berlin 1990, Sp. 337-339, hier Sp. 337 f.
[65] Bspw. Haderbuch 1476-1485, fol. 48.
[66] Fischer, Mattias Gerhard: Weinkauf. In: Handwörterbuch zur deutschen Rechtsgeschichte. Bd. 5. 1. Aufl. Hrsg. von Adalbert Erler †, Ekkehard Kaufmann u. Ruth Schmidt-Wiegand. Berlin 1998, Sp. 1234 f.
[67] Bspw. Haderbuch 1476-1485, fol. 25v.
[68] Haderbuch 1476-1485 fol. 40, 41 u. 157.

wurde.[69] Da nur diese beiden Stücke exakt zusammenpassten, konnten Schuldner und Gläubiger einander zugeordnet werden und der Rechtszustand letztlich über einen Augenscheinbeweis in den Prozess eingeführt werden.

Eine überkommene Rechtsinszenierung wird auch in der Wendung „also habe sie off die zijt den mantel off dem grabe laißen ligen"[70] erkennbar. Wollte die Witwe die Erbschaft ausschlagen und damit letztlich meist die Haftung für Schulden des Ehegatten nicht übernehmen, musste sie nach dem Tode für alle sichtbar ihren Mantel über dem Grab zurücklassen.[71] Da dieses Rechtsritual unter Zeugen und für die ganze Rechtsgemeinschaft erkennbar vollzogen wurde, konnte die Hinterbliebene im Prozess leicht den Zeugenbeweis anbieten.

Ein letztes Beispiel für eine Rechtsinszenierung wird in der häufig gebrauchten Wendung „der soll jme jne mit dem geren gebenn"[72] deutlich, die im Zusammenhang mit Pfändungen vorkommt. Vielfach findet sich formelhaft:

„Daruff ist er mit recht gewißt, weß er dess syne nust, so soll er dem schultheißen heymbergen heißenn, der soll jme jne mit dem geren gebenn, und soll jne der heymberger uber nacht haltenn unnd wydder an gericht bringen, dann geschee furter, waß recht sij (…) ."[73]

Die „Gere" war ein gefalteter Teil der Kleidung,[74] so dass „mit dem geren gebenn" wahrscheinlich andeutet, dass zur Inszenierung und Sichtbarmachung der Pfändung der Schuldner vom Heimbürgen am Rockschoß nachgezogen wurde[75]. Abermals wird hier ein Rechtsritual

[69] Schmidt-Wiegand, Ruth: Kerbholz. In: Handwörterbuch zur deutschen Rechtsgeschichte. Bd. 5. 1. Aufl. Hrsg. von Adalbert Erler, Ekkehard Kaufmann u. Ruth Schmidt-Wiegand. Berlin 1978, Sp. 701–703, hier Sp. 701 f.

[70] Haderbuch 1476-1485, fol. 17v u. 197v.

[71] Gudian (wie Fn. 14), S. 222 f. Vgl. ferner Ogris, Werner: Mantelrecht. In: Handwörterbuch zur deutschen Rechtsgeschichte. Bd. 3. 1. Aufl. Hrsg. von Adalbert Erler, Ekkehard Kaufmann u. Ruth Schmidt-Wiegand. Berlin 1984, Sp. 258 f., hier S. 258.

[72] Bspw. Haderbuch 1476-1485, fol. 164.

[73] Haderbuch 1476-1485, fol. 164.

[74] Vgl. Wachter, Ferdinand: Gere. In: Allgemeine Encyklopädie der Wissenschaften und Künste in alphabetischer Folge von genannten Schriftstellern bearbeitet. Erste Section. Hrsg. von Moritz Hermann Eduard Meier. Leipzig 1855, S. 371-373, hier S. 371 f, der auch Ingelheimer Oberhofquellen wiedergibt.

[75] Die Autoren danken Prof. Dr. Albrecht Greule, Regensburg für den Hinweis.

deutlich, das eine Rechtshandlung dermaßen verkörperte, dass sie öffentlich wurde und letztlich im Prozess Zeugen als Beweismittel eingeführt werden konnten. Für alle hier kurz vorgestellten Rechtsinszenierungen kann gesagt werden, dass sie letztlich den Zweck hatten, Recht mit einer konkreten Handlung zu verknüpfen und damit im Bewusstsein der Rechtsgenossen zu verstetigen. Obwohl im Bereich des Ingelheimer Grundes bereits relativ früh, seit 1366,[76] Gerichtsbücher nachweisbar sind, haben sich die rituellen Handlungen weiterhin behaupten können, wohl auch weil es – anders als beispielsweise bei Grundstücksübertragungen mit dem Ufgiftbuch – weder für Kaufverträge, Schuldverschreibungen noch für Erbausschlagungen eine regelmäßige Protokollierung von Seiten des Gerichts gab. Erb-, Kauf- und Schuldsachen wurden meist mündlich geregelt. Sie tauchen nur in den – allerdings zahlreichen – Fällen auf, wenn es zu Streitigkeiten kam und Zahlungen nicht getätigt wurden. Damit könnte erklärbar sein, dass beispielsweise die Übergabe eines Grundstücks „mit Halm und Mund" zwar im Ingelheimer Bereich nachweisbar ist, aber Protokolleinträge selten sind. So spiegeln sich paradoxer Weise gerade die besonders ritualisierten Formen des Besitzübergangs im Gerichtsbuch weit weniger als die hier vorgestellten, offeneren Rechtsinszenierungen wider.

An der Schwelle zur Neuzeit wird im Haderbuch ein weites Vordringen der Schriftlichkeit in den ländlichen Bereich sichtbar, so dass die überkommenen Rechtsformen vor allem mit nichtgerichtlichen, gleichsam aber schriftlichen Aufzeichnungen der Parteien in Konkurrenz gerieten und damit die Verstetigungsfunktion mitunter einbüßen konnten. Wenngleich Kerbhölzer im Haderbuch fassbar sind, so kommen doch nun auch Kerbbriefe, schriftliche Funktionsäquivalente, im ländlichen Bereich in Gebrauch. In der Quelle heißen sie unter

---

[76] Der ehemalige Gerichtsschreiber Conrad Emmerich Susenbeth erwähnt 1644, dass er Bücher von 1366 vorgefunden habe (vgl. Conrad Emmerich Susenbeth, Special-Extract über das vhralte Rethliche Herkomen auch recht undt gerechtigkeit des Adels- und Rittergerichts in Ingelheimb. Grundt, 1644, fol. 2v). Das Original der Handschrift befindet sich, bislang von der Forschung nicht wahrgenommen, in der Bibliothek des Germanischen Nationalmuseums in Nürnberg unter der Sig. Hs. 6194. Dort ist sie 1854 durch die Übernahme der Privatbibliothek von Freiherr Hans von und zu Aufsess, dem Museumsgründer, hingelangt. Eine Abschrift des 18. Jahrhunderts findet sich unter der Sig. F 2 Nr. 13/5 im HStA Darmstadt.

anderem „ußgesnytten zyttel".[77] Eine Protokollierung ist hier von besonderem Interesse, weil der komplette Wortlaut des Kerbzettels mitgeteilt wird.[78] Da von einem der Beteiligten zu lesen ist, dass er Knecht war, der Wortlaut des Zettels aber mit gerichtsbekannten Formeln und mit lateinischer Wendung am Ende versehen ist, liegt die Vermutung nahe, dass Gläubiger und Schuldner den Zettel nicht selbst angefertigt, sondern einen Schreiber beauftragt hatten. Möglicherweise wurde hier sogar der Gerichtsschreiber für Personen des Ortes außerhalb seines Amtes tätig.

An anderer Stelle wird erkennbar, dass sich die Parteien auch mitunter auf beides, Schriftstücke und Rechtsrituale, berufen konnten. In den Protokollierungen äußert sich dies durch Wendungen wie: „so das buch und winkauff verhort werden"[79], denen zufolge sowohl die Weinkaufszeugen als auch das Buch gehört werden sollen. An dieser Stelle deutet sich schon die überragende Stellung des Gerichtsbuchs als Beweismittel an. Eine große Anzahl der Einträge hat die Öffnung des Gerichtsbuchs zum Inhalt, nämlich dass eine Person „hait das buche … laißen offen".[80] Mit dieser Öffnung wurde die konkrete Protokollierung zum Beweismittel. Interessant ist hierbei, dass von Gerichts wegen keine Nachforschung im Haderbuch vorgenommen oder derartiges zumindest nicht protokolliert wurde. Vielmehr wird deutlich, dass die Parteien oftmals auf das Buch rekurrieren („nach lude des gerichtsbuchs"[81]) und danach ein Beweisbeschluss zur Öffnung ergeht. Prozessrechtlich war also die Zustimmung des Gerichts durch entsprechende Weisung zur Öffnung notwendig. Zum Beweisangebot und dem Beweisbeschluss findet sich im Haderbuch meist dann auch ein korrespondierender Eintrag, der die Öffnung festhält und damit den Eintrag zu einem Beweismittel werden lässt. Daneben finden sich an vielen Stellen auch Bezugnahmen der Parteien auf andere Schriftstücke, seien es „zittel"[82], „ußgesnitten bestenntniß zettel"[83], „briff"[84], „gerichts briff"[85], „verschri-

---

[77] Haderbuch 1476-1485, fol. 12v.
[78] Haderbuch 1476-1485, fol. 15r-v.
[79] Bspw. Haderbuch 1476-1485, fol. 22.
[80] Haderbuch 1476-1485, fol. 25.
[81] Haderbuch 1476-1485, fol. 109.
[82] Haderbuch 1476-1485, fol. 15v.
[83] Haderbuch 1476-1485, fol. 176.
[84] Haderbuch 1476-1485, fol. 39, 39v, 69.
[85] Haderbuch 1476-1485, fol. 28v, 63, 66v.

bunge"[86] schrifft,[87] oder „testament",[88] register"[89] oder „gifft buch"[90] und „kirchen buche".[91] Zudem wurde unterschieden zwischen einem Schriftstück, das nur ein „slechter zyttel" mit geringerer Beweiskraft darstellte und einer beglaubigten Gerichtsurkunde.[92] Und selbst der außergerichtliche Schiedsvergleich konnte, wie bereits erwähnt, in einer schriftlichen Festlegung münden, die sich ihrerseits in der Form an eine Urkunde anlehnte, die Inhalte der Einigung und das Datum festlegte, offenbar aber nicht die Rachtungsleute nannte. Dieses Schriftstück konnte bei der Gerichtssitzung vorgelegt und verbotet werden, was abermals den Kompromiss zwischen mündlichem und schriftlichem Recht verdeutlicht.[93]

4. Formen der Rechtsinszenierung vor Gericht

Ein besonderer Fall der Inszenierung von Recht könnte die sog. Verbotung gewesen sein, die in überragend vielen Einträgen protokolliert wurde. Anhand der zeitlich etwas früher gelagerten Ingelheimer Oberhofprotokolle entwickelte Peter Eigen, ein Schüler Adalbert Erlers, in den 1960er Jahren die Auffassung, die Verbotung sei ein Rechtsakt gewesen, in dem durch Gebühr die Schöffen verpflichtet werden konnten, sich einen Vorgang genau einzuprägen und später auf Verlangen mündlich kund zu tun.[94] Gegenstand der Verbotung hätte

---

[86] Haderbuch 1476-1485, fol. 165.
[87] In der Bedeutung Testament vgl. Haderbuch 1476-1485 fol. 12v.
[88] Haderbuch 1476-1485, fol. 72v, 218.
[89] Haderbuch 1476-1485, fol. 12, 69.
[90] Haderbuch 1476-1485, fol. 27v.
[91] Haderbuch 1476-1485, fol. 228v, 231.
[92] Haderbuch 1476-1485 fol. 121v.
[93] Haderbuch 1476-1485, fol. 148v: „Jtem diß ist die rachtunge zuschen myner frauwen der aptischen und frauwe Madlen von Fennyngen. Aym erßten so sollent sie geracht sin ummb allen verseße, kosten und schaden, wie der were. Also daß die von Fennyngen myner frauwen funffe phont heller jerlichs zinß zu sent Mertins tage fallende off dem yren vergewißen und vernugen sall, alsdann hie zu Jngelheim gewonheit und recht ist. Und des glichen eyn phondt heller jerlichs zinß off Clese Suffußen und III libras heller sall die von Fennyngen in XIIII tagen bare her uß geben. Und was Clese Suffuße von verseß wegen schuldig were, dar ummb sall er sich mit myner frauwen der apthissen vertragen. Geschen off Fritag nach sant Urbans tage anno etc. LXXX".
[94] Eigen, Peter: Die Verbotung in den Urteilen des Ingelheimer Oberhofes. Aalen 1966, S. 21; vgl. auch Zwerenz, Reinhard: Der Rechtswortschatz der Urteile des Ingelheimer Oberhofes, Diss. jur. Gießen 1988, S. 126.

hierbei alles sein können, was die Parteien für besonders erheblich hielten, ganz gleich ob es sich um das Verhalten der Parteien, des Gerichts oder anderer Beteiligter handelte.[95] Nach der Lesart von Peter Eigen war die Verbotung damit eine Rechtsinszenierung, die noch auf die mündliche Vorbringung und ein anschließendes Gerichtszeugnis abzielte. Aufgrund seiner Eigenart als Rechtsanfragestelle verstellen die Urteile des Oberhofs in gewisser Weise aber auch den Blick für die Rechtshandlungen der Untergerichte, weil sie hier, gefiltert durch den Vortrag der anfragenden Gerichte, durchscheinen. Auch aus diesem Grunde sind die Haderbücher eine wertvolle Ergänzung und tragen zu einem vertieften Verständnis des Rechtswortschatzes bei wie das Beispiel der Verbotung deutlich machen kann.

In dem hier herangezogenen Ober-Ingelheimer Haderbuch lässt sich die Verbotung in mindestens drei Varianten greifen: Erstens als herrschaftlicher Akt durch den Schultheißen, zweitens als gemeinschaftlicher Akt der beiden Parteien und drittens als einseitiger Akt einer der Parteien bzw. eines Fürsprechers. Die Verbotung wird in Folge eines Verfahrensschritts festgehalten, etwa nach einer Verweisung des Falles an das vollbesetzte Gericht,[96] einer Terminfestsetzung,[97] einer Aussage[98] oder einem Urteilsspruch.[99] Es gibt kaum einen Eintrag, in dem nicht wenigstens eine Verbotung vorgenommen wird. Zweifel an der unkritischen Übertragbarkeit der Schlussfolgerung Peter Eigens auf die Ober-Ingelheimer Niedergerichts-barkeit des späten 15. Jahrhunderts werden vor allem durch die Tatsache genährt, dass nur äußerst selten über eine Gerichtskundschaft das Verbotete in den Prozess eingeführt wird, dafür aber umso häufiger die Parteien das Buch öffnen lassen und damit die Verbotung möglicherweise vor allem das Begehren des Festhaltens im Gerichtsbuch darstellen könnte. Hinzu kommen die Fälle, in denen der Schultheiß als herrschaftlicher Vertreter ein Urteil verbotet und somit als Vertreter des Gerichtsherrn handelt und Gebot und

---

[95] Eigen (wie Fn. 94), S. 22.
[96] Bspw. Haderbuch 1476-1485, fol. 83: „Das ist gelengt ad socios. Das haint sie beide verbot."
[97] Bspw. Haderbuch 1476-1485, fol. 110v: „Des ist yme tag gestalt an das nehste gericht. Das haint sie beide verbot."
[98] Bspw. Haderbuch 1476-1485, fol. 85 für die Verbotung nur einer Partei: „Die sage hait Scher(er)hen(ne) verbot."
[99] Bspw. Haderbuch 1476-1485, fol. 84: „Das haint sie beide verbot." Oder fol. 24v „Das ortel hait Peder verbot."

Verbot festsetzt. Dies geschieht bei besonders hohen Klagesummen und in den Fällen, in denen der Gerichtsfrieden verletzt wurde.[100] In einem Verfahren Jeckel Monsters gegen Beierhenne von Algesheim beispielsweise heißt es: „Die ansprache hait der scholtes von unßers gnedigen herren und des gerichts wegen verbot."[101] Aus dem Quellentext geht hervor, dass der Schultheiß als Vertreter des Gerichtsherrn und des Gerichts tätig wird. Damit wird deutlich, dass die Verbotung nicht nur ein Instrument zur Verstetigung im Gedächtnis der Schöffen gewesen war.

Peter Eigens Vorstellung lässt sich noch am ehesten mit der im Haderbuch sichtbaren Verbotung durch eine oder beide Parteien in Einklang bringen. Auch hier wird ein Element der Öffentlichmachung eines Rechtsvorgangs sichtbar. Gleichzeitig aber wird deutlich, dass es den Parteien weniger um eine mündliche Gerichtskundschaft als vielmehr um den schriftlichen Gerichtsbucheintrag ging, was für einen gewissen Bedeutungswandel der Rechtsinszenierung der Verbotung spricht. Ebenso scheint aber, was bei Eigen nicht deutlich wird, ein Moment der Zustimmung der Beteiligten durch, das der Verbotung anhaftet. Vor allem mit der beiderseitigen Eintragung einer Verbotung, die formelhaft als „Das haint sie beide verbot"[102] oder „ambo verbot"[103] greifbar ist, werden – so die These – nicht bloß die Eintragung in das Gerichtsbuch und die Öffentlichmachung im trotz aller Schriftlichkeit im Kern immer noch mündlichen Prozess angezeigt. Stattdessen wird auch die Zustimmung der beiden Parteien im Sinne einer konsensualen Handlung sichtbar gemacht und festgehalten.

Im streitigen Verfahren wurde damit gemeinschaftlich eine Grenze gezogen, hinter die beide Parteien nicht mehr zurück wollten und wohl auch nach der Verbotung nicht mehr ohne Weiteres gehen konnten. Dieses Verfahren könnte damit vor allem dazu gedient haben, den Streit weiter einzugrenzen und auf das Problem zu verdichten. Unverkennbar ist aber trotz aller Wandlung auch der konstante Kern der Verbotung, dass nämlich letztlich durch diese Rechtsinszenierung ein Vorgang für die Rechtsgenossen öffentlich gemacht wird.

---

[100] Vgl. dazu Schäfer (wie Fn. 26).
[101] Bspw. Haderbuch 1476-1485, fol. 12.
[102] Haderbuch 1476-1485, fol. 25v.
[103] Haderbuch 1476-1485, fol. 24v.

5. Zusammenfassung

Das hier vorgestellte Ober-Ingelheimer Haderbuch gewährt den Blick auf eine differenzierte Rechts- und Gerichtslandschaft, die trotz des im Kern weiterhin mündlichen Verfahrens starke Bezüge zur Schriftlichkeit aufweist. Auffallend ist hierbei, dass gerade im Hinblick auf häufig fassbare Fürsprecher eine Professionalisierung innerhalb der Laiengerichtsbarkeit greifbar ist. Gerade diese zeichneten sich durch vertiefte Kenntnis der örtlichen Rechtsgewohnheiten aus, ohne aber studiert zu haben. Ebenso aber zeigt sich auch eine mitunter vertiefte Rechtskenntnis der dörflichen Bevölkerung, die neben den Fürsprechern zu den Akteuren der Inszenierung des Rechts am Ober-Ingelheimer Hadergericht gehörte.

In gewisser Weise wird auch ein Blick durch das Schlüsselloch in eine ländliche Umgebung offenbart, in der mithin althergebrachte Rechtsinsze-nierungen mit der sich immer weiter verbreitenden Schriftlichkeit in Konkurrenz geraten, mitunter aber zusammen im Rechtsleben Verwendung finden und eine reiche Fülle an Rechtsinszenierungen im dörflichen Alltag und vor Gericht sichtbar wird. Immer wieder begegnet dabei das Moment der Öffentlichmachung eines Rechtszustandes, das der Rechtsinszenierung im dörflichen Alltag eine wichtige Funktion zukommen ließ. Exemplarisch konnte anhand der Verbotung die Differenziertheit und Komplexität aufgezeigt werden, mit der eine solche Rechtsinszenierung im Rechtsleben in Erscheinung trat. Die hier vorgestellten Quellenbefunde zeigen nur einen kleinen Ausschnitt auf. Die jahrzehntelang in der Forschung vernachlässigten Haderbücher bieten umfangreiches Material zur Erforschung der dörflichen Rechts- und Gerichtslandschaft, das bislang noch nicht ausgewertet worden ist. Dieses Forschungsdesiderat gilt es aufzuarbeiten.

Roman Boundary Stones in Croatia: Legal Content and its Forms in Acts of Dispute Resolution

Ivan Milotić

1. Introduction

At the beginning of the 1ˢᵗ century AD Rome took complete control over the eastern Adriatic coast and introduced the system of government analogue to the one existing in Roman Italy. After the conquest, a task was put before the Roman provincial government in Dalmatia to control the tribal communities that existed there and to administratively incorporate them into the system of provincial municipal organisation. In any case, the Romans were aware that pre-Roman tribal communities, who had been living on the eastern Adriatic coast prior to their arrival and often inhabiting on fortified hills that were difficult to climb, had a long tradition of the community, self-government and legal autonomy[1]. In the 1ˢᵗ century AD these communities were typical *civitates* – small tribal, political, and territorial self-governing units whose structure the Romans could not and did not want to abolish[2]. The provincial government in Dalmatia acquired civilian characteristics soon after the Romans suppressed the great rebellion of tribal populations in 9 AD

---

[1] Sherwin-White, Adrian Nicholas: The Roman Citizenship. Clarendon Press. Oxford, 1973, pp. 252-253.

[2] For definition of *civitas* see: Cicero, De re publica VI,13,13; Abott, Frank Frost; Chester Johnson, Allan: Municipal Administration in the Roman Empire. Princeton University Press. Princeton, 1926, p. 4; Berger, Adolf, Encyclopedic Dictionary of Roman Law. In: Transactions of the American Philosophical Society, New Series, American Philosophical Society (1953) Vol. 43, No. 2, p. 389. Pliny the Elder documented that certain tribal communities (*civitates*) in Liburnian Dalmatia were awarded with *ius Italicum* which did not include distribution of municipal (*municipium*) or colonial (*colonia*) status. This meant: they were recognized as self governing units with partial recognition of their traditional rights. Plinius (Maior): Naturalis historia, CXXX, 139-140. *Ius Italicum* was the privilege of Italian cities granted to towns, settlements and communities outside Italy. It comprised different rights and powers both of public and private character: self-government, exemption from taxes (*immunitas*), exemption from the supervision by the provincial governor, transformation of lands to *res mancipi*, land ownership *ex iure Quiritium*, exemption from paying tribute (*tributum*) etc. See: Watkins, Thomas H.: Coloniae and ius Italicum in the early Empire. In: The Classical Journal, (1983) Vol. 78, No. 4, pp. 319-336.

(*Bellum Batonianum*). An early indication of the abandonment of its military features and transformation into civilian administration became apparent under Tiberius' legate Publius Cornelius Dolabella (14-20 AD). Apart from other things, he completed an overall survey of the region with a definition of boundaries and pertinent real property rights (water rights, rights of passage etc.) soon after the province was constituted. The result of this project was the issuing of a document which is analogue to what we define as the cadastre, which the sources record as *Forma Dolabelliana*[3]. *Forma Dolabellinana* was an official Roman document in the form of a catalogue of private and public real property rights. It was a basis of administrative division and boundary settlements. The issuing of *Forma Dolabelliana* raised many questions, and caused quarrels and disputes amongst adjacent communities that had been present in the region for a longer time. Some of these disputes and issues had been inherited from pre-Roman times, others appeared under the Roman administration in places where boundaries had not been determined definitely during the settlement of the province, or where the creation of new municipal organizations gave rise to litigation in the delimitation of territorial possessions. Disputes were raised over water rights as well, especially where the traditional rights were exercised by more communities on certain water source which *Forma Dolabelliana* ascribed to the territory of single community.

Boundary stones recovered on the territory of the Roman province of Dalmatia represent unique records of details and circumstances in which they were set up, as well as of disputes. They exclusively record the final adjudication which ended a dispute. As such, they are today valuable records of the Roman provincial administration in Dalmatia, predominantly in the Julio-Claudian period[4]. In this paper, it is our intention to discuss boundary and water rights disputes and settlements

---

[3] The Cambridge Ancient History, The Augustan Empire 43 B.C. – A.D. 69, vol. X. Cambridge University Press. Cambridge, 1996, p. 589; Wesch-Klein, Gabrielle: Okkupation und Verwaltung der Provinzen des Imperium Romanum von der Inbesitznahme Siziliens bis auf Diokletian. Ein Abriss. In: Provincia (2008) Vol. 10. LIT Verlag. Münster, 2008, p. 46; Rendić-Miočević, Duje: Cornelius Dolabella legatus pro praetore provinciae Dalmatiae, proconsul provinciae Africae Proconsularis. Problemes de chronologie, In: Akte des IV. internationalen Kongresses für griechische und lateinische Epigraphik, Vienna, 1964, pp. 338-347.

[4] Wilkes, John J.: Boundary Stones in Roman Dalmatia. In: Arheološki Vestnik, (1974) No. 25, 1976, p. 258.

in the context of Roman law, especially with reference to non-state organized mechanisms of dispute resolution. This analysis will rely upon epigraphic evidence preserved in the form of boundary stones, which have been recovered on the territory of Dalmatia. The analysis will also comprise of relevant epigraphic material and legal sources from other parts of Roman state.

2. The beginning of dispute resolution proceedings

Forma Dolabelliana raised many questions on how traditional boundaries should be incorporated into the Roman concept of land division and how traditional rights to water access on the territory of other communities should be exercised. Rome did not wish to interfere directly in such disputes. However, her primary interest was to find a convenient means for bringing an end to such controversies and to permanently determine the real rights which the parties in dispute would respect and recognize as just and acceptable. Judicial proceedings organized by the state were not a convenient means of dispute resolution in such circumstances because of the strict perception of justice and formal proceedings, which paid inadequate attention to decisive circumstances. A desire on the part of Rome was not so much to render a decision on the point at issue, as to preserve the stability of traditional legal relations.

Dispute resolution could be initiated by a decree (*ex decreto*) or edict (*ex edicto*) of the provincial governor:

"*ex decreto* Publii Cornelii Dolabellae legati pro praetore..."[5], "*ex dictu* P. Cornelii Dolabellae..."[6], "*...ob decretum* Aurelii Galli legati..."[7]. Several inscriptions indicate a command (iussu) of the provincial legate or senior Roman provincial military officials as the basis of the proceedings:

---

[5] Rendić-Miočević, Duje: op. cit (n. 3), p. 339 (n. 8); Wilkes, John J.: op. cit. (n. 4), p. 258 (n. 1), 259 (n. 3.).

[6] Cropus inscriptionum Latinarum (further: CIL) III, 9973; Dessau, Hermann: Inscriptiones Latinae selectae (further ILS). Weidmann. Berlin, 1902, n. 5953; Wilkes, John J.: op. cit. (n. 4), p. 260 (n. 6).

[7] CIL III, 3167; CIL III, p. 1515, n. 8663 and CIL III, p. 2326, n. 14239. Wilkes, John J.: op. cit. (n. 4), p. 265 (n. 16).

"...*iussu* A. Duceni Geminis..."[8], "...*iussu*...(?) legati Caesari Auigusti Germanici..."[9], "...*iussu* Luci Volusi Saturnini legati pro praetore..."[10], "....Bassus legatus Augusti pro praetore...*iudicare iussit*..."[11], "Lucius Funisulanus Vetonianus legatus pro praetore pontem et terminos *renovari iussit*..."[12].

There is even a record of one *praesidus provinciae Dalmatiae* who ordered the resolution of a dispute and appointed *iudices*[13]. In these cases, the dispute resolution was not always purely voluntary: parties in dispute generally had no discretion in the appointment of judges, and they could not control the proceedings or choose the material law relevant for the dispute resolution. This is best indicated by an inscription that records the appointment of *iudices* headed by a magistrate, based on the authority of the emperor himself[14]. The parties were obliged to participate in such proceedings and to conform to the final decision. F. F. Abott and A. Johnson denote this method of dispute resolution as *administrative arbitration*[15]. This method of dispute resolution is analogue to what we define as *mandatory arbitration*. In many ways it resembles what Cicero classified as *arbitrium honorarium* – arbitration ordered and constituted by a magistrate, holder of a certain administrative or military office[16].

Parties in dispute could reach an agreement on their own to settle the dispute. Under such circumstances, the intervention of a public authority was necessary to sanction their agreement. Parties could be instructed, or they would receive imperative commands from a provincial governor or senior provincial magistrate to reach an agreement to settle the dispute.

---

[8] CIL III, 2883 and 15045; Wilkes, John J.: op. cit. (n. 4), p. 260 (n. 7) and p. 262 (n. 8).

[9] Wilkes, John J.: op. cit. (n. 4), p. 262 (n. 10).

[10] CIL III, 8472; ILS 5948, Wilkes, John J.: op. cit. (n. 4), p. 265 (n. 17).

[11] Wilkes, John J.: op. cit. (n. 4), p. 266 (n. 20).

[12] Ibid.: pp. 266-267 (n. 21).

[13] Protector of the province Dalmatia. CIL III, 9860.

[14] "*Ex auctoritate imperatoris Vespasiani iudex datus*". Wilkes, John J.: op. cit. (n. 4), p. 268 (n. 25).

[15] Abott, Frank Frost; Chester Johnson, Allan: op. cit. (n. 2), p. 158.

[16] Cicero: Pro Q. Roscio Comoedo, 5, 15; Cicero: Disputationes Tusculanae, 5, 120. Broggini, Gerardo: Iudex Arbiterve, Prolegomena zum Officium des römischen Privatrichters, Forschungen zum Römischen Recht. Böhlau. Köln – Graz, 1957, pp. 212-215. Mitteis, Ludwig: Römisches Privatrecht bis auf die Zeit Diokletians, Bd. 1. Duncker & Humblot. Leipzig, 1908, pp. 46-47 (n. 16).

Such a method of constituting the arbitration is indicated on boundary stones by the words *"ex conventione"* – literally *"by agreement [of the parties]"*: *"ex conventione (eorum)* finis inter...[determinata]"[17], "iudex [name]...*ex conventione* datus"[18]. One boundary settlement text explicitly states: *"finis...secundum conventionem utriusque partis...iussu Auli Duceni Gemini legati Augusti pro praetore"*[19]. If *"ex conventione"* constitution of arbitration were chosen, it was possible for the parties to have certain control over the proceedings and to select judges by their own will. However, public authorities still had to confirm the appointment.

3. Appointment of iudices (arbitrators)

Appointment of *iudices* was an essential requirement of the dispute resolution proceedings. They are always recorded as *iudices dati*[20], which indicates that their selection and appointment was either ordered by public authorities or conducted through the consent of provincial magistrates. Though indicated as *iudices*, they were not equivalent to judges in state-organised judicial proceedings because their position and powers were similar to those of arbitrators. Inscriptions suggest that in most cases they were administrative or military officials to whom duty to resolve disputes was conferred by a decree or edict of the provincial governor, or by an imperative command, or by an agreement of the parties sanctioned by a public authority. We read of a centurion, centurion and *princeps posterior legionis*[21], veteran and former centurion[22], *praefectus castrorum*[23], and *tribunus militum*[24] acting as *iudices*. They were selected on an *ad hoc* basis rather than from the list of citizens qualified to

---

[17] CIL III, 15053; Wilkes, John J.: op. cit. (n. 4), p. 259 (n. 3).
[18] CIL III, 2882; Wilkes, John J.: op. cit. (n. 4), p. 259 (n. 4) and CIL III, 9832; Wilkes, John J., op. cit. (n. 4), p. 263 (n. 12).
[19] Translation: "Boundary settled according to the agreement between both parties based on the command of Aulus Ducenus Geminus, Augustan praetorian legate". Wilkes, John J.: op. cit. (n. 4), p. 262 (n. 9).
[20] CIL III, 2882; CIL III, 9938, CIL III, 9832; CIL III, 9860; Wilkes, John J.: op. cit. (n. 4), p. 268 (n. 25).
[21] CIL III, 2882; CIL III, 9973; ILS 5953; CIL III, 2883; CIL III,15045; CIL III, 9832; CIL III, 9864a; CIL III, 12794.
[22] CIL III, 8663.
[23] CIL III, 8472; ILS 5948.
[24] Wilkes, John J.: op. cit. (n. 4), p. 268 (n. 25).

assume the function of juror in judicial trials (*album iudicum*)[25]. In most cases they acted as single judges, but there are several records of arbitral commissions (*consilia*).

There is one mention of members of the commission whose number was odd[26]. If the arbitral commission was appointed, it would always consist of an odd number of persons[27]. In several cases where the final arbitral decision contains full names of arbitrators as members of arbitral committee, we can read the pattern of how they were chosen: The parties in dispute were entitled to appoint an equal and even number of arbitrators each, and the administrative officer would then appoint one, three or more arbitrators to add to the total number, respecting the necessity of an odd number of arbitrators. This pattern encouraged an active participation of parties in dispute and ensured that the arbitrators were familiar with traditional rules. In formulas of the inscriptions it is sometimes attested that a single arbitrator rendered the award after he heard the commission (*consilio athibito*). *Consilio athibito* probably means that the arbitrator heard arguments and claims of both parties in a dispute and their representatives at the same time. Very similar circumstances of decision-making in private proceedings not organized by the state, which chronologically coincide with Dalmatian boundary stones, can be found in Pliny's letter to Annius Severus. Pliny, in the capacity of an arbitrator as a good man (*arbiter bonus vir*), described how he rendered the award:

"*Adhibui in consilium* duos quos tunc civitas nostra spectatissimos habuit, Corellium et Frontinum. His circumdatus in cubiculo meo sedi. His circumdatus in cubiculo meo sedi. *Dixit Curianus quae pro se putabat.*"[28]

---

[25] „...*der Arbiter nicht aus dem Album*". Wlassak, Moritz: Römische Processgesetze – ein Beitrag zur Geschichte des Formularproverfahrens, 2. Abteilung. Duncker & Humbolt. Leipzig, 1891, p. 196 (n. 16).

[26] Judges are mentioned by their names: "Tiberius Claudius LIIII, Caius Avillius Clemens, Lucius Coelius Capella, Publius Reacius Libo, Publius Valerius Secundus iudices dati a Marco Pompeio Silvano legato Augusti pro praetore...". Their onomastic formulas indicates that some of them belonged to tribal communities that were parties in dispute, while other were not from the relevant territory and were objective and impartial element of the arbitral commission. CIL III, 9938; Wilkes, John J.: op. cit. (n. 4), p. 262 (n. 11).

[27] Ulpianus in D.4.8.17.6. suggests that if the parties had selected two *arbitri* in *compromissum*, praetor should intervene and appoint third *arbiter* for sake of preventing split decisions. Obviously in late classical period of Roman Law problems appeared with split decisions when there was even a number of arbitrators, which caused difficulties in decision making.

[28] "I summoned in commission two very prominent men of our state, Cornelius and

The *arbiter* in the Roman legal practice was usually an *expert arbitrator*.[29] He was never chosen arbitrarily; his appointment depended upon certain qualities. Specific features of the dispute requiring a specific set of skills, experience, knowledge or understanding of subject matter called for arbitrators with expert knowledge. Specific knowledge or skills and understanding of the subject matter often gave an increased confidence in the arbitration process. Boundary stones in Dalmatia exclusively record disputes on boundaries, water and passage rights, which may be indication that *iudices* (i.e. arbitrators) were selected from those persons in provincial apparatus or military forces who had a certain degree of knowledge of boundaries, land surveys and traditional real property rights. The inscription CIL III 2883 explicitly mentions that Aulus Resius Maximus, posterior centurion in the first cohort of legion XI, and Quintus Aebutius Liberalis fixed the boundary according to surveyed measurements by order of Aulus Ducenius Geminus, legate of the emperor with praetorian rank. Another inscription (CIL III, 2887) records boundary settlement conducted on the basis of the previous land survey on the ground. Inscription CIL III, 9938, on the other hand, records members of the communities in dispute who were not part of Roman army or provincial apparatus, but still acted as arbitrators. It is probable that in this case the Romans wanted the arbitrators to be persons who knew the state of affairs and all the factual background of the dispute.

Frontinus. Surrounded by them I sat in my chamber. Curianus [party in dispute] submitted what his thoughts were". Plinius, Epistulae, V, 1 Annio Severo. Roebuck, Derek; De Fumichon De Loynes, Bruno: Roman Arbitration. Holo Books. London, 2004, pp. 62-63; Ziegler, Karl-Heinz: Das private Schiedsgericht im antiken römischen Recht, Münchener Beiträge zur Papyrusforschung und antiken Rechtsgeschichte 58. C. H. Beck Verlag. München, 1971, pp. 159-161; Kaser, Max: Das Römische Zivilprozessrecht, Handbuch der Altertumswissenschaft, Abteilung 10, Rechtsgeschichte des Altertums. C. H. Beck Verlag. München:, 1966, pp. 28, 40, 58.

[29] Cicero: Pro Murena, 12, 27; Dilke, Oswald Ashton Wentworth: *The Roman Land Surveyors; An Introduction to the Agrimensores*. A. M. Hakkert. Amsterdam, 1992, p. 51; Mousourakis, George: *The historical and institutional context of Roman law*. Ashgate Pub LTD. Burlington, 2003, p. 128.

4. The constitution of the arbitral tribunal

A provincial governor's decree (*decretum*) or edict (*edictum*), administrative or military command (*iussum*) or agreement (*conventio*) was the basis of the tribunal's constitution. Whenever we read texts on boundary stones we recognize an arbitral *ad hoc* tribunal constituted for resolving a single dispute. These tribunals did not exist before because they were formed only for the purpose of resolving a single dispute in one certain legal case. The appointment of arbitrators was reserved only for this dispute and after the award the tribunal would be dissolved. The *modus operandi* of a tribunal was completely private and informal. Several indications of rendering the award after *consilio athibito* suggest that the elementary principles of judicial proceedings organized by the state were followed. Both parties were always heard before the decision was made. This is evident from the inscription CIL III, 9938 where it is explicitly emphasized that the award (*sententia*) was rendered in the presence (*in re presenti*) of tribal communities Asseriatium and Alveritarum, whose *res publicae* were parties in dispute over boundaries.

5. Parties in dispute

Inscriptions usually mention the parties in a dispute. The absence of their records in several rare cases should be ascribed to the fact that some of the inscriptions have been preserved in fragments only, resulting in the incomplete nature of their epigraphic content. Parties in dispute could primarily be identified as tribal communities. Inscriptions record them in two ways: either by their tribal name only (*Ortoplini, Parentini, Corinienses, Salviates, Stridonenses, Nediti*, etc.) or by the tribal *res publica* (*res publica Asseriatium, res publica Alveritarum*). In this context *res publica* should be perceived as an administrative term that corresponds to the term *civitas*. The expressions *res publicae* on boundary stones should be understood as self-governing tribal communities which were awarded with a certain degree of municipality[30]. Such an award should be perceived as an expression of consideration toward communities that Rome had incorporated into herself[31]. "Where communities of a

---

[30] Sherwin-White, Adrian Nicholas: op. cit. (n. 1), p. 47. On *res publica* in general see: Berger, Adolf: op. cit (n. 2), p. 679.
[31] Ibid.: pp. 58, 73.

different kind were incorporated, Rome was so far from destroying what little already existed of a *res publica* that she sought to amplify it"[32].

In dispute resolution proceedings tribal communities were recognized as parties entitled to stand before an arbitral tribunal and to take all the procedural actions necessary to protect their rights. Although some of them (especially those communities which did not reach the status of *res publicae* recognized by Romans) were not considered to be legal persons, in judicial or arbitral proceedings they were regularly awarded with the status of the party. In arbitral proceedings they had the full capacity (*ius standi in iudicio*) recognized on an *ad hoc* basis only in a single dispute[33].

6. Arbitrability

To identify arbitrability, types of disputes and their subject matter, it is necessary to quote the relevant parts of epigraphic sources:

(1) "...*[finis]* inter Begi et Ortoplinos..."; (2) "...*finis* inter Ortoplinos et Parentinos, *aditus ad aquam vivam*..."; (3) "...*finis* inter Neditas et [?]..."; (4) "*Finis* inter Neditas et Corinienses..."; (5) "...*finis* inter Ansienses et Corinienses..."; (6) "*Termini positi inter prata* legionis [...?] et fines roboreti Flavii Marciani per Augustianum Bellicum procuratorem Augusti"; (7) "...inter Onastinos et Narestinos *terminos* posuit..."; (8) "...inter Nerastinos et Pituntinos *termini* recogniti et restituti", "...diceret sententiam *de ponendis terminis*"; (9) "...*pontem et terminos* renovari iussit..."; (10) "...*fines* regeret et *terminus* poneret"; (11) "...*fines* inter Salviatas et Stridonenses determinavit"; (12) "...*[fines]* secundum *Formam Dolabellianam* restituit..."; (13) "*Finis* inter Seium severinum centurionem cohortis VIII voluntariorum et Baebidium TitIanum rigore rivi"[34].

---

[32] Ibid.: p. 72. Exceptionally, we read of a few cases where the disputants were private persons or military units, but on the whole they should not be considered as a representative sample upon which a conclusion can be drawn.

[33] See: CIL V, 698 and ILS 5946, 5948, 5951, 5973. On differences between *iudicium privatum* and *iudicium publicum* see: Kaser, Max; Hackl, Karl: Das römische Zivilprozessrecht. C. H. Beck Verlag. München, 1996, pp. 1-3.

[34] (1) "...boundary between the Begi and the Ortoplini...". Rendić-Miočević, Duje: op. cit. (n. 3), p. 339 (n. 8); Wilkes, John, J.: op. cit (n. 4.), p. 258 (n. 1); (2) "...boundary between the Ortoplini and the Parentini and access to live water...". CIL III, 15053; Patsch, Karl: Lika in römischer Zeit. In: Schriften der Balkankommission, Antiquarische Abteilung, (1900) No. 1, p. 22f.; Wilkes, John, J.: op. cit (n. 4), p. 258-259 (n. 2); (3) "...boundary

Boundaries (*fines*) were obviously the most disputed subject matter. Inscriptions suggest that several types of dispute could rise on boundaries, which subsequently meant the emergence of different types of proceedings and arbitral awards. Disputes over settling the boundary between two adjacent communities are documented in most cases. They consisted of a boundary settlement and the setting of the boundary stones. Boundaries, together with boundary markings, are sometimes mentioned as *termini* as well. In some exceptional cases, epigraphic data record real-estate disputes between two subjects which were not tribal communities: we read of boundary stones fixed between the legionary meadows and the oak woodlands of Flavius Marcianus.

The subject matter of a dispute and arbitrator's duty in the proceedings were defined by a governor's decree or edict. Regarding the boundaries, the governor could give instructions to determine the boundary, to settle the boundary, to recognize the position of the boundary if it was uncertain or forgotten but had existed on the territory previously, to set boundary stones, to restore boundary stones where they had previously existed, to renovate boundary stones or to make adjustments of the boundary according to *Froma Dolabelliana*.

A boundary settlement was sometimes followed by a constitution of some other rights. On one inscription we read the following: "Ex

---

between the Neditas and...?". Wilkes, John, J.: op. cit (n. 4.), p. 259 (n. 3) and p. 260 (n. 5); (4) "Boundary between the Nediti and the Corinienses..." CIL III, 2883; (5) "...boundary between the Ansienses and the Corinienses..." Wilkes, John, J.: op. cit (n. 4.), p. 262 (n. 9); (6) "Boundary stones were set up between the legionary meadows and the oak woodlands of Flavius Marcianus through Augustianus Bellicus, procurator of Augustus" CIL III, 13250; Wilkes, John, J.: op. cit (n. 4.), p. 264 (n. 14a-b); (7) "...set boundaries stones between the Onastini et the Narestini" CIL III, 8472; (8) "...between the Nerastini and the Pituntiti boundary stones were determined and restored..." CIL III, 12794; (9) "...to render award regarding the settlement of boundary stones" Wilkes, John, J.: op. cit (n. 4.), p. 266 (n. 20); (9) "...he ordered the restoration of bridge and boundary stones..." Wilkes, John, J.: op. cit (n. 4.), p. 266-267 (n. 21); (10) "to fix boundary and to set up boundary stones" CIL III, 9864a; (11) "...determined boundaries between the Salviati and the Stridonenses" CIL III, 9860; (12) "Boundaries in accordance with Forma Dolabelliana (he) restored" Wilkes, John, J.: op. cit (n. 4.), p. 268 (n. 26); (13) "Boundary between the estate of Seius Severinus centurion of the cohort VIII voluntariorum and Bebidus Titianus, along the course of the river". CIL III, 3163; Wilkes, John, J.: op. cit (n. 4.), p. 268 (n. 27). Exceptionally, the text of one boundary stone document opening of the public boundary road, constructed by Valerius Valens, which was previously closed off through decree of Aurelius (or Aufidius) Gallus, the legate. CIL III, 8663.

covnetione finis inter Ortoplinos et Parentinos aditus ad aquam vivam Ortoplinis passus D latus I"[35].

This inscription records a boundary settlement based on the agreement of the parties in dispute (the Ortoplini and the Parentini). At the boundary settlement a certain water source was assigned to the territory of Parentini, despite the fact that it had been traditionally used by the Ortoplini, who held a customary right to access the water source and to collect water. Once the boundary was settled, it was necessary to find an appropriate legal means by which access to water source and its exploitation by the Ortoplini could be secured. The inscription documents the constitution of the right to collect water on the territory of the Parentini in favor of the Ortoplini and parallel constitution of the right of passage to access the water source. We can identify water servitude as *servitus aquae haustus*, i.e. the right to take water from a fountain, a pond, or a spring located on another person's property[36]. This easement implied free access to the location, which is indicated by the mention of *aditus*. *Aditus* is always connected to some form of rustic servitude. It grants the right of walking (*ius adeundi*) to the location burdened with the servitude if the exercise of the servitude by the person so entitled would otherwise be impossible[37]. In the case of our inscription, the constitution of the right of passage (*aditus*) within *servitus aquae haustus* followed the Roman principle of real servitudes in which the entitled subject must enjoy his right *civiliter*, i.e. within reasonable limits. He had to have a high respect for the holders of real property rights, and had to lessen the effort to harm, or limit his interest or rights as much as possible[38]. Enjoyment within reasonable limits arises from the award of the judges and is inscribed on the boundary stone. The exercise of the right of passage (*iter*) is limited to a pathway 500 paces

---

[35] Translation: "According to the agreement the boundary between the Ortoplini and the Parentini. The access to the water source (live water) allowed to Ortoplini 500 paces long and 1 pace wide". CIL III, 15053.

[36] Berger, Adlof: op. cit. (n. 2), p. 708.

[37] Ibid.: p. 349.

[38] "Si cui simplici usu via per fundum cuiuspiam cedatur vel relinqatur, in infinito, videlicet per quamlibet eius partem, ire agere licebit, civiliter modo....". Cels., D.8.1.9. For the principle servitutibus civiliter utendum est see: Petrak, Marko: Römische Grundlagen des neuen kroatischen Sachenrechts. In: Schmidt-Recla, Adrian; Schumann, Eva; Theisen, Frank (ed.): Ius Commune Propriumque. Sachsen im Spiegel des Rechts. Böhlau. Köln – Weimar – Vienna: 2001, p. 349; Kolanczyk, Kazimierz: Pravo Rzymskie. Panstwowe Wydawnictwo Naukowe. Warsaw, 1973, pp. 319-320.

long and 1 pace wide (pace=lat. *passus*=1.48 m) that leads to the water source. Proceedings and adjudication concerning the constitution of water and passage rights are typical *adiudicationes servitutis*.[39]

7. The issue of the double arbitral procedure

A hypothetical question could be raised whether the parties in a dispute could at the same time initiate some other proceedings for the purpose of resolving an identical dispute between identical disputants. There are no records of such an issue in any of the epigraphic data in Dalmatia, but the issue is nevertheless worthy of elaboration. The classical Roman jurists had no clear understanding of this issue: Paulus explained the case in which the parties agreed upon *ex compromisso* arbitration and later, during the arbitral proceedings, one of the parties abandoned the arbitration and initiated proceedings before the state court[40]. Paulus understood this as legally possible, but a contractual penalty was imposed nonetheless. Herculanean tablets record a prohibition of initiating successive arbitral proceedings for an identical dispute between identical parties. If both parties abandoned the previous arbitration to initiate another, a penalty could be imposed on them[41].

Arbitral proceedings recorded on Dalmatian boundary stones are specific due to their mandatory character. Because of the interpolation of the public authority at the constitution of arbitral tribunal, analogies with proceedings organised by the state can be traced in procedural consumption. A classical Roman jurist proclaimed that good faith does not allow the same thing to be exacted twice[42]. Quintilian's principle was

---

[39] Kaser, Max:: Das römische Privatrecht, 1. Abschnitt. Das altrömische, das vorklassische und klassische Recht. C. H. Beck Verlag. München: 1971, p. 444; Guarino, Antonio: Diritto privato romano. Jovene. Napoli, 2001, pp. 718-719.
[40] Paul., D.4.8.30.
[41] "...ad alium ullum arbitrum interdum denuntiaretur neve iudicium moveretur a me heredeve meo cognitoremne darem procuratoremve meum ad quem ea res pertinet pertibebit: sive quidvis adversus ea factum eirt HS duomilia probos recte dari ...". Translation: "...do not let the dispute be brought before any other arbitrator during the arbitral proceedings and do not let the [private] judge to change by my decision or by the decision of my successor...If anything was done against this agreement, 2000 sesterces should be paid...". Tabulae Hercualnenses 82.
[42] "Bona fides non patitur, ut bis idem exigatur". Gai., D.50.17.57.

bis de eadem re agere non licet[43]. An action can not be brought over again in the same legal case[44]. If one of the parties within the mandatory arbitral proceedings abandoned the proceedings or tried to initiate parallel process, the magistrate could intervene and exercise his coercion powers. The Romans' main task was to safeguard the proceedings and guarantee the execution of the award. With this mechanism they sought to preserve the traditional relations regarding real property and to reduce the possibilities of a rebellion.

8. Arbitral award

Inscriptions on boundary stones consistently use the term *sententia,* meaning the final award. From the formal point of view, *sententia* denotes a legal act – the result of decision-making by which the dispute was finally resolved. The technical term used to denote the process of arbitral decision making is *sententiam dicere*[45]. This was the final and the most important duty of the arbitrator(s). Substantially, *sententia* on Dalmatian boundary stones could alternatively or cumulatively consist of a boundary settlement (*finis determinatio*)[46], setting the boundary stones (*terminorum ponere*)[47], recognition of boundary position (*finis definitio*)[48], recognition and restoration of the boundary and boundary stones (*finis determinatio et restitutio*[49]; *recognitio et restitutio*[50]), fixing the boundaries and setting up boundary stones for the first time (*finis regerere et terminorum ponere*)[51], renovation of boundary markings (*terminorum renovare*)[52] or boundary adjustments (*finis secundum Formam Dolabellianam restituere*)[53].

From the formal point of view, the word *sententia* becomes more customary for the decisions in private (non-state organized) proceedings.

---

[43] Quintilianus: Institutio oratoria VII, 6, 4.
[44] Kaser, Max: op. cit. (n. 28), pp. 59-60.
[45] „*...in re praesenti sententiam suam determinavit*" CIL III, 9938; „*[...] sententia...dixit*" CIL III, 8473; „*...sententiam diceret...*" Wilkes, John J.: op. cit. (n. 4), p. 266 (n. 20). See also: Tabulae Herculanenses 76; 77+78+80+53+92; 79.
[46] CIL III, 9938; CIL III, 9860.
[47] CIL III, 13250; CIL III, 8472; Wilkes, John J.: op. cit. (n. 4), p. 266 (n. 20).
[48] Wilkes, John J.: op. cit. (n. 4), p. 262 (n. 10).
[49] CIL III, 9973; ILS 5953.
[50] CIL III, 12794.
[51] CIL III, 9864a.
[52] Wilkes, John J.: op. cit. (n. 4), p. 266 (n. 21).
[53] CIL III, 3163.

On the other hand, *iudicium* is usually linked with decision of *iudex* in proceedings organized by the state (Roman formular process)[54]. However, the question of whether the award recorded on the Dalmatian boundary stones was of private or public law nature could be raised here. Subsequently, this raises the next question: Whether the execution of the award depended on the good will of the parties or whether it had be enforced by public authorities. After their appointment, the arbitrators (*iudices*) were allowed to act informally and in full private capacity. Their duty was to take into account all circumstances, decisive facts, traditional rulings and elementary principles of the Roman Law. Decision-making was regularly preceded by a survey of the land which was conducted by land surveyors (*agrimensores*) and was considered to be a purely private undertaking. The arbitrators' award (*sententia*) had to achieve a fair purpose, a result which both parties in dispute would consider as just and equitable. Although the *modus operandi* of the arbitrator(s) was purely private, their awards were treated as decisions in judicial proceedings organized by the state. The arbitrators were always appointed by public authorities – Roman highest military or civil officials – or their appointment was at least confirmed by Roman magistrates. Roman public authorities controlled the proceedings, and they could intervene into the dispute if necessary or at their discretion.

L. Mitteis noticed astutely that the arbitral decision made by arbitrators who were appointed by praetor (i.e. magistrate) contained public (magistrate's) authority[55]. This subsequently reflected on the nature of the award (*sententia*). The execution of the award in such cases was never left to the willingness of the parties in dispute, even when the parties themselves constituted the arbitral tribunal *ex conventione*, or when the award was rendered by their agreement. When Romans initiated the constitution of the tribunal, their aim was to resolve the dispute completely and to make the award binding for both parties. Romans wanted these disputes to be resolved in a fair and equitable way acceptable to the parties. Still, they could not risk the refusal of its execution. If the refusal of its execution occurred, magistrates were allowed to exercise *ius coercendi*. It empowered the magistrates to enforce

---

[54] Paul., D.4.8.19.1. Roebuck, Derek; De Loynes de Fumichon, Bruno: op. cit. (n. 28), pp. 20-21.
[55] Mitteis, Ludwig: op. cit. (n. 16), p. 47 (n. 18).

obedience to their commands using certain coercive or repressive measures (prison, fines, pledge etc.)[56]

9. Settlement of boundary stones and their role

The rendering of an arbitral award was followed by a settlement of material records. These records appear in form of inscriptions engraved in a stone surface (usually on a natural surface such as stone slabs or rocks) or, sometimes, on artificially shaped stone columns. They were positioned on the very spot which was the subject matter of the dispute: along the boundary line determined by the award, on the place where boundary stone existed previously, on the water source on which the right to collect water was constituted or along the pathway on which the access to water source was constituted. Being robust physical markers, they were placed on notable or especially visible points. Sometimes they were used to mark critical points of the boundary. These epigraphic records are the intended material expression (i.e. the form recognized by law and custom) of previous arbitral determinations. The arbitral award was proclaimed orally (*sententia dicta*) by the arbitrator(s), and at first it existed only as a verbal and hypothetical rule for the parties. The placement of its inscription on stone surface on exact relevant place was a realization of such hypothetical legal substrate.

The placement of inscriptions was intended to make public all the legal determinations in dispute: occurrence of the dispute, parties in the dispute, the subject of the dispute, arbitral mechanism of the dispute resolution, constitution of arbitral tribunal, appointment of arbitrators, award and its determinations. Boundary stones were permanent reminders for the parties in dispute of how they needed to act and what their rights and duties were. The boundary stones were means by which an abstract request was put before all third persons to respect real property rights as they were determined. The boundary stones were means of a proper introduction of all third persons on boundary and real property rights. This simple form was an instrument by which the legal essence – the contents of law within an arbitral adjudication – could *in concreto* become legitimized and recognized as binding and applicable.

---

[56] Mousourakis, George: A legal history of Rome. Routledge. London, 2007, p. 12; Berger, Adolf: op. cit. (n. 2), p. 393.

The form served the content of law to reach the addressees and to become legally operational in practice.

10. Conclusion

The value of Roman boundary stones in Croatia can be observed from several points of view. They are no abstract standards of behavior or hypothetical legal rules separated from the legal reality. Their origin and context of existence emerge from actual legal environment on the territory of Dalmatia in the Julio-Claudian period. All quoted inscriptions on boundary stones are products of the 1st century AD legal practice, in which the main goals were to suppress disputes as possible obstacles to Roman rule. The resolution of such disputes enabled full administrative incorporation of Dalmatia into the Roman system of provincial government. It enabled the realization of the Roman concept which encouraged provincial administrative units to exist and following the example set by the ones in the Roman Italy. Resolution of the disputes, especially of those that existed previously and those that were perceived as traditional, eliminated the animosity towards legal and factual Romanization.

Roman boundary stones in Dalmatia are unique records of arbitral dispute resolution with interventions by public authorities. In the field of law they are valuable records of the language of boundary settlements. The technical terms of arbitral dispute resolution indicate that the Romans strictly followed the principles of legality even when they wanted to end disputes among remote tribal communities who did not fully conform to the Roman supremacy. The rough form of boundary stones and their brief inscriptions do not reveal all the details of the arbitral proceedings. Their purpose was to record only the essential procedural elements and decisive fixtures which would be of practical use to the member of communities and to the third persons who would come in contact with this territory. From this aspect, the Dalmatian boundary stones are unique records on how the legal substance became effectual through its specific form.

Kapitel IV
„Legitimation und Verfahren"

Kurbayerische Visitationen im 17. und 18. Jahrhundert: Zur Inszenierung von Herrschaftsrechten zwischen Aktendeckeln

Birgit Näther

Die Ankündigung, sich im Zusammenhang mit der Inszenierung von Herrschaftsrechten kurbayerischem Verwaltungsschriftgut der Frühen Neuzeit widmen zu wollen, erscheint einigermaßen skurril. Dabei beschrieben schon die Zeitgenossen den engen Zusammenhang zwischen der Ausübung von Herrschaftsrechten und der Inszenierung derselben – so etwa der sächsische Kameralist Julius Bernhard von Rohr in seiner 1733 erschienenen 'Cermoniel-Wissenschaft der großen Herrn'. Im Kapitel „Von dem Staats-Cermoniel überhaupt" gibt von Rohr zu bedenken, es könne sich der „gemeine Mann […] nicht allein recht vorstellen, was die Majestät des Königes" sei. Durch die Präsentation von „Dinge[n], so in die Augen fallen" sei es für Untertanen aber leicht möglich „einen klaren Begriff von seiner Majestät Macht und Gewalt"[1] zu erhalten. Dieses Zitat weist auf einen Umstand hin, der in verschiedenen Forschungsarbeiten beobachtet und belegt worden ist: Zeremonielle Praktiken sowie repräsentative Kunst- und Bauwerke demonstrierten und inszenierten herrschaftliche Macht und Hierarchien. Gleichzeitig erschöpfte sich ihr Zweck, wie in konsequenter Folge des Zitats formuliert werden kann, nicht in einer bloßen 'Übersetzungsleistung'. Vielmehr dienten sie als expressive Instrumente der Herrschaftsausübung und Herrschaftssicherung.[2]

Diese Betrachtungen geben erste Hinweise auf den engen Zusammenhang zwischen der Ausübung von Herrschaft bzw. von Herrschaftsrechten und deren Inszenierung durch Symbolformen.[3] Dabei wird zur

---

[1] In: Rohr, Julius Bernhard von: Ceremoniel-Wissenschaft der großen Herren, Leipzig 1990 (Neudruck der Ausgabe von 1733), Teil 1/ Kapitel 1/§2 (hier S. 2).
[2] Daß es sich dabei keineswegs um ein ausschließlich vormodernes Phänomen handelt, zeigte 2010 eine Ausstellung im Deutschen Historischen Museum in Berlin: 'Macht zeigen – Kunst als Herrschaftsstrategie' verdeutlichte, daß Kunst auch in der Bundesrepublik zur Versinnbildlichung und Ausübung von Politik benutzt wird.
[3] Vgl. Neu, Tim; Sikora, Michael; Weller, Thomas: Einleitung, in: dies. (Hg.): Zelebrieren und Verhandeln. Zur Praxis ständischer Institutionen im frühneuzeitlichen Europa, Münster 2009,

Definition dieses Begriffes auf die Erläuterungen von Barbara Stollberg-Rilinger Bezug genommen, die unter Symbolen „eine besondere Spezies von Zeichen verbaler, visueller, gegenständlicher oder gestischer Art wie etwa sprachliche Methaphern, Bilder, Artefakte, Gebärden, komplexe Handlungsfolgen [...], aber auch symbolische Narrationen"[4] versteht.

Im Folgenden soll anhand von Beobachtungen zu Quellenbeständen kurbayerischer Visitationsverfahren der Frage nachgegangen werden, inwiefern auch im Bereich von Verwaltungsschriftgut symbolische Elemente auffindbar sind, die zur Ausübung von Herrschaftsrechten, sowie der Einübung und Stabilisierung von Herrschaftshierarchien gedient haben könnten.

1. Der Rahmen der Ausübung von Herrschaftsrechten: Akteure und Praktiken

Zur Erläuterung der Herrschaft innewohnenden Prinzipien wird häufig auf Max Webers Definition zurückgegriffen, wonach Herrschaft „die Chance [sei], für einen Befehl bestimmten Inhalts bei angebbaren Personen Gehorsam zu finden" und „den eigenen Willen auch gegen Widerstreben durchzusetzen"[5]. Überträgt man diese Definition auf die Verhältnisse Kurbayerns in der Vormoderne, so wird deutlich: Die Bezugspunkte landesherrlicher Herrschaft[6] – also die „angebbaren Personen" – waren sowohl diejenigen ohne Herrschaftsrechte, also die Untertanen, als auch solche mit verliehenen Herrschaftsrechten, wie etwa die Beamten aller Verwaltungsebenen, die wiederum gleichzeitig auch Untertanen waren. Die einzige Ausnahme bildete der Landesherr selbst, der zwar Herrschaftsrechte besaß und verlieh, aber im territorialen Zusammenhang nicht Bezugspunkt derselben war. Folglich kann Herrschaft also im Zusammenhang mit dem hier zu erörternden Gegenstand als Raum verstanden werden, in dem von allen an der Herrschaft beteiligten Akteuren

---

S. 16.

[4] In: Stollberg-Rilinger, Barbara: Symbolische Kommunikation in der Vormoderne. Begriffe – Thesen – Forschungsperspektiven, in: Zeitschrift für Historische Forschung, Bd. 31, Berlin 2004, S. 500.

[5] In: Weber, Max: Wirtschaft und Gesellschaft. Grundriß einer verstehenden Soziologie, Tübingen 1980, S. 28f.

[6] Die in den Teilen zwei und drei angestellten Betrachtungen widmen sich ausschließlich dem landesherrlichen Teil Kurbayerns. Adlige und kirchliche Grundherrschaften werden nicht in die Analyse einbezogen.

a priori vorhandene oder verliehene Herrschaftsrechte über alle Untertanen ausgeübt wurden.

Diese Erläuterungen zur Ausübung von Herrschaftsrechten sind allerdings insofern unbefriedigend, als sie zwar Akteursgruppen und ihren
Bezug zur Ausübung von Herrschaftsrechten beschreiben, aber den
durch sie und mit ihnen gestalteten praktischen Vollzug nicht zu erklären
vermögen.

Dabei ist unbestritten, daß der praktische Vollzug von Herrschaft
nicht im ‚luftleeren Raum' stattfindet. Um, wie Max Weber es formulier-
te, „für einen Befehl bestimmten Inhalts bei angebbaren Personen Gehorsam zu finden", d.h. um die von Herrschaft Betroffenen zu erreichen, mußten Strukturen und Verfahren entwickelt und etabliert werden,
die Herrschaft zur praktischen Umsetzung verhalfen. Dies galt insbesondere da nicht die Unumschränktheit der Macht als Signum der Epoche
gelten kann, sondern die Abwesenheit des Herrschers, die Dagmar Freist
mit dem Begriff der „Omniabsenz"[7] beschrieb und die nur durch eine
hinsichtlich ihrer Arbeitspraktiken, sowie der vertikalen und horizontalen
Organisation zunehmend ausdifferenzierten Administration überbrückt
werden konnte.

Die Behörden der Höfe waren entsprechend darauf angewiesen, ‚un-
terhalb' ihrer eigenen Institutionen personelle Bezugspunkte und eine
funktionstüchtige institutionelle Organisation vorzufinden, um die
Durchsetzung der landesherrlichen Herrschaft vor Ort realisieren zu
können. Ohne ein Netz von miteinander verzahnten, organisatorisch
und funktionell, sowie in ihrer Reichweite aufeinander abgestimmten
Verwaltungsinstitutionen war dies schlichtweg unmöglich. Der so beschriebene Lokalitätsbezug von Herrschaft ist trotz seiner Bedeutung für
die tatsächliche Herrschaftsdurchdringung eines Territoriums noch immer ein Desiderat der Forschung. Die Gründe hierfür liegen unter anderem in der lange Zeit forschungsleitenden Verengung des Fokusses auf
die institutionelle Verdichtung von Herrschaft bei Hofe im Rahmen des
Konzeptes des Absolutismus.[8] Zugleich muß erwähnt werden, daß der

---

[7] In: Freist, Dagmar: Einleitung: Staatsbildung, lokale Herrschaftsprozesse und kultureller
Wandel in der Frühen Neuzeit, in: Asch, Ronald G.; Freist, Dagmar (Hg.): Staatsbildung als
kultureller Prozeß. Strukturwandel und Legitimation von Herrschaft in der Frühen Neuzeit,
Köln 2005, S. 5.
[8] Vgl. zum Beispiel die Kritik bei Henshal, Nicolas: The Myth of Absolutism. Change and
Continuity in Early Modern European Monarchy, London 1996, S. 34f.

hier beschriebene Verwaltungsaufbau in seiner Funktionabilität als Ideal-typus zu verstehen ist und in Territorien kleinerer oder mittlerer Größe sicher eher umgesetzt werden konnte als in flächenmäßig ausgedehnten Ländern. In Letzteren konnten entlegene Gebiete oft nicht durchadministriert und lokale Verwaltungen kaum kontrolliert werden. So wurde, beispielsweise in der Habsburgermonarchie, vielerorts auf eine gewisse Verwaltungsautonomie der Einzelländer gesetzt. Wie der von Winfried Schulze zur Relativierung des Absolutismuskonzeptes so genannte „organisch-föderative[...] Absolutismus"[9] des Habsburgerreiches in seiner Praxis eigentlich funktionierte, genauer gesagt worauf seine spezifische Herrschaftsentfaltung angesichts fehlender Durchgriffsmöglichkeiten beruhte, ist Gegenstand verschiedener Forschungsdebatten.[10] Interessanterweise sind begriffliche Gemeinsamkeiten bei Verwaltungsorganisation und Verwaltungspraktiken in vielen Ländern Europas gut nachweisbar: Die Termini ‚Rentamt' oder ‚Visitation' finden sich nicht nur in Kurbayern, sondern auch in weiteren Gebieten des Alten und des Habsburger Reiches und lassen darauf schließen, daß es Lernprozesse und unter Umständen sogar regelrechte ‚Verwaltungs-Moden' gab.[11] Ob sie allerdings in Bezug auf ihre Umsetzung – ihre Struktur, inhaltliche wie personelle und instrumentelle Ausgestaltung, Positionen im Verwaltungsgefüge, Dauer der Einrichtung – tatsächlich vergleichbar sind, müsste durch vergleichende Studien geklärt werden, die bislang noch ausstehen.

Die Basis für die beschriebenen, Herrschaft zur Durchsetzung verhelfenden Praktiken bildete politisch-administrative Kommunikation, mittels derer Informationen[12] einerseits erlangt und andererseits weitergege-

---

[9] In: Schulze, Winfried: Das Ständewesen in den Erblanden der Habsburger Monarchie bis 1740. Vom dualistischen Ständestaat zum organisch-föderativen Absolutismus, in: Baumgart, Peter; Schmadeke, Jürgen (Hg.): Ständetum und Staatsbildung in Brandenburg-Preussen, Berlin 1983,
S. 263-279 (hier S. 263f.).
[10] Vgl. die Einleitung sowie spezieller die Beiträge von Michael Hochedlinger sowie Thomas Winkelbauer in: Mat'a, Petr; Winkelbauer, Thomas (Hg.): Die Habsburgermonarchie 1620-1740. Leistungen und Grenzen des Absolutismusparadigmas; Stuttgart 2006.
[11] Dies wurde jüngst auf der Tagung „Ordnung durch Tinte und Feder? Genese und Funktionen von Instruktionen im zeitlichen Längsschnitt" des Arbeitskreises „Höfe des Hauses Österreich" bei der Österreichischen Akademie der Wissenschaften sowie des FWF-Projekts „Herrschaftsverwaltung in Niederösterreich" der Universität Wien diskutiert. Eine Veröffentlichung der Tagungsergebnisse in der Reihe ist vorgesehen.
[12] Auch wenn an dieser Stelle auf eine umfängliche theoretische und praktische Einordnung des Informationsbegriffs verzichtet werden muss, so sind doch einige eingrenzende Hin-

ben werden konnten.[13] Um Kommunikation zwischen Fürsten, Beamten und Untertanen zu ermöglichen, entwickelten frühneuzeitliche Träger von Herrschaftsrechten spezielle Verfahren wie beispielsweise Berichte, Enquêten, Visitationen und Supplikationen.[14] Diese wurden, wie gerade skizziert, in vielen Territorien zu fest etablierten Elementen der Ausübung von Herrschaft. Von Bedeutung ist, daß die Verfahren vielfach eher hierarchisch-dialogisch als instruierend-monologisch angelegt waren, wie dies unter dem Vorzeichen ,absolutistischer' Herrschaft oftmals vermutet worden ist.[15] Im Sinne Arndt Brendeckes handelt es sich bei dieser „bottom-up-Kommunikation" durchaus um einen „im weitesten Sinne ,staatsbildenden' Vorgang [...], aus dem beide Seiten, das ,Oben'

---

weise erforderlich: Wie Arndt Brendecke in 'Imperium und Empirie. Funktionen des Wissens in der spanischen Kolonialherrschaft' (Köln 2009, S. 76) formuliert, ist der Begriff „eng mit der Entstehung empirischer Verfahren verbunden" und bezeichnet „sowohl den Anfang des Verfahrens (die Erhebung), als auch das dann folgende Dokument (den Bericht) wie auch schließlich das abstraktere Ziel des 'Informiertseins'" und verweist somit „auf die ganze Verfahrenssequenz zwischen Empirie [...] und Wissen". Übertragen auf den vorliegenden Beitrag handelt es sich um verfahrensgebundene, im weitesten Sinne herrschaftsbezogene Informationen über die am Verfahren beteiligten oder berücksichtigten Personen und Angelegenheiten. Die in den Akten enthaltenen Informationen geben dabei nicht zwangsläufig den Wissensstand der Beteiligten wieder, da Information und Wissen, nicht zuletzt aufgrund von verschiedenen Selektionsprozessen bei Beteiligung, Erhebung, Auswertung und Archivierung nicht deckungsgleich sein müssen.
[13] Vgl. Endres, Susanne: „Zu notdürftiger information". Herrschaftlich veranlasste Landeserfassungen des 16. und 17. Jahrhunderts im Alten Reich, in: Brendecke, Arndt; Friedrich, Markus; Friedrich, Susanne (Hg.): Informationen in der Frühen Neuzeit. Status, Bestände, Strategien (Pluralisiering & Autorität), Münster 2008, S. 301-334. Gottschalk, Karin: Wissen über Land und Leute. Administrative Praktiken und Staatsbildungsprozesse im 18. Jahrhundert, in: Collin, Peter; Horstmann, Thomas (Hg.): Das Wissen des Staates. Geschichte, Theorie und Praxis, Baden-Baden 2004, S. 149-174. Haas, Stefan; Hengerer, Mark (Hg.): Zur Einführung: Kultur und Kommunikation in politisch-administrativen Systemen der Frühen Neuzeit und Moderne, in: Haas, Stefan; Hengerer, Mark: Im Schatten der Macht. Kommunikationskulturen in Politik und Verwaltung 1600-1950, S. 7-22.
[14] Vgl. zu Visitationen z.B. Schnabel-Schüle, Helga: Kirchenvisitation und Landesvisitation als Mittel der Kommunikation zwischen Herrschaft und Untertanen, in: Duchhardt, Heinz; Melville, Gert (Hg.): Im Spannungsfeld von Recht und Ritual. Soziale Kommunikation in Mittelalter und Früher Neuzeit, Köln 1997, S. 173-186, hier S. 173. Zu Supplikationen vgl. z.B. Blickle, Renate: Laufen gen Hof. Die Beschwerden der Untertanen und die Entstehung des Hofrats in Bayern. Ein Beitrag zu den rechtlichen Verfahren im späten Mittelalter, in: Blickle, Peter: Gemeinde und Staat im Alten Europa (in: Gall, Lothar, Historische Zeitschrift. Beihefte neue Folge Bd. 25), München 1998, S. 241-266.
[15] Vgl. Holenstein, André: 'Gute Policey' und lokale Gesellschaft im Staat des Ancien Régime. Das Fallbeispiel der Markgrafschaft Baden(-Durlach). Bd.1, Epfendorf 2003, S. 282f.

und das ‚Unten', durch ihr Zusammenwirken gestärkt hervorgehen"[16]. Die Ausübung von Herrschaftsrechten war demnach zwar klar hierarchisch gebunden, allerdings waren die (mittelbaren) Möglichkeiten, Einfluß auf politische Entscheidungen und die Entwicklung von Verwaltungspraktiken zu nehmen, sicher größer als dies in älteren Forschungsarbeiten angenommen wurde.[17]

Im Folgenden soll die Betrachtung auf das Verfahren der politischen Visitation in Kurbayern beschränkt bleiben, bei der die Landesherren übergeordnete Behörden dazu instruierten, in einem konkreten, oftmals solennen Verfahren vor Ort untere Behördeninstitutionen hinsichtlich ihrer Amtsausübung zu überprüfen und darüber Bericht zu erstatten. Die Bezeichnung ‚politische Visitation' wird hier verwendet, weil das landesherrliche Verfahren seit dem ausgehenden 16. und beginnenden 17. Jahrhundert in Anlehnung an das kirchliche Visitationswesen etabliert wurde und weltliche wie geistliche Angelegenheiten umfasste. Daß es sich bei Visitationen in Kurbayern um ein poltisch-administrativ relevantes Verfahren handelte, belegt ihre vermutlich regelmäßige Durchführung: Pro Rentamt hat sich für alle zehn bis 15 Jahren jeweils eine Akte mit Einzelprotokollen der im betreffenden Jahr durchgeführten Visitationen archivarisch erhalten. Da die Akten in den 1830er Jahren noch vor ihrer Verzeichnung von einer Dezimierungsaktion im damaligen Archivskonservatorium Landshut betroffen waren, handelt es sich zeitgenössischen Berichten zufolge lediglich um ein Zehntel der ursprünglich vorhandenen Akten. Dies belegt, daß wesentlich mehr Akten vorhanden waren und das Verfahren, offenbar sogar unabhängig von Krisenzeiten, eine gewisse Regelmäßigkeit erreichte.[18]

---

[16] Brendecke, Arndt: Imperium und Empirie. Funktionen des Wissens in der spanischen Kolonialherrschaft, Köln 2009, S. 71.

[17] Vgl. Brakensiek, Stefan: Lokale Amtsträger in deutschen Territorien der Frühen Neuzeit – institutionelle Grundlagen, akzeptanzorientierte Herrschaftspraxis und obrigkeitliche Identität, in: Asch, Ronald G.; Freist, Dagmar (Hg.): Staatsbildung als kultureller Prozeß. Strukturwandel und Legitimation von Herrschaft in der Frühen Neuzeit, Köln 2005, S. 49-67.

[18] Sehr aufschlußreich hierzu: Schwertl, Gerhard: Die niederbayerischen Rentmeister-Umrittsprotokolle im Staatsarchiv Landshut, in: Rumschöttel, Hermann; Jaroschka, Walter (Hg.): Bewahren und Umgestalten. Aus der Arbeit der Staatlichen Archive Bayerns. Walter Jaroschka zum 60. Geburtstag. Mitteilungen für die Archivpflege in Bayern, Sonderheft 9, München 1992, S. 186-197. Angemerkt sei, daß im 18. Jahrhundert die normativ weiterhin vorgesehene Regelmäßigkeit der Durchführung faktisch wahrscheinlich nicht erreicht wurde, da ab circa 1720 große zeitliche Lücken entstehen. In der im Weiteren behandelten In-

Die im Weiteren genannten Funktionen beziehen sich durch die Beschränkung des Betrachtungsgegenstandes zwar vor allem auf die politische Visitation, treffen in Einzelaspekten allerdings auch auf die anderen genannten Verfahren zu. Als Hauptfunktionen der politischen Visitation können die folgenden drei genannt werden:

Zuvorderst, weil zugleich die Basis des administrativen Vollzugs bildend, ist die *Informationsfunktion* zu nennen. Durch die Herstellung von Kommunikation zwischen Fürsten, Beamten und Untertanen konnten Herrschende Informationen über die Lage in den Gemeinwesen erhalten. Die Informationsfunktion weist zudem auf die dialogische Struktur des Visitationsverfahrens hin: Wie zahlreichen Quellen zu entnehmen ist, entstand zwischen Fürsten, Beamten und Untertanen ein Kommunikationszirkel, in dem von allen Beteiligten, je nach spezifischem Anteil am Verfahren, sowohl Informationen gegeben als auch übereinander gewonnen werden konnten.

Daneben erfüllten politische Visitationen eine *Kontrollfunktion*, die mit der Informationsfunktion eng verknüpft war. Fürsten und deren Beamte überprüften mit Hilfe der Verfahren die jeweils untergeordnete behördliche Ebene auf deren (Dys-)Funktionalitäten. Dabei war eine organisatorisch und personell funktionierende, an den rechtlichen Rahmen gebundene, sowie um die Umsetzung von Anordnungen bemühte Amtswahrnehmung der Garant dafür, daß Herrschaft effektiv durchgesetzt und als legitim betrachtet werden konnte.

Darüber hinaus zeichnet sich das Verfahren durch eine *Repräsentationsfunktion* aus. Wie im Weiteren analysiert werden wird, trifft dies auf die Durchführung des Verfahrens vor Ort genauso zu, wie auf die mit dem Verfahren verbundene Verwaltungsschriftlichkeit. Die Symbolformen beider Seiten des Verfahrens dienten, so die Annahme, zur Inszenierung und Durchsetzung von Herrschaft.

Alle drei Funktionen sind mit der Herstellung und Etablierung von Kommunikationssituationen eng verbunden und weisen zugleich über diese hinaus. Es wird deutlich, daß auf der Basis einer Kommunikation,

---

struktion von 1774 wird denn auch beklagt, Visitationen seien „hin- und wieder 30: 40: 50: und noch mehr Jahre underblieben[...]". Dies bezieht sich, wie anhand der Bestandssituation und Archivierungsgeschichte nachweibar ist, auf die Zeit ab circa 1720 und ist entsprechend kein generelles Merkmal des seit circa 1580 in dieser Form durchgeführten Verfahrens.

die alle Akteursgruppen einband, Herrschaft überhaupt erst konkretisiert werden konnte. Im Weiteren soll vor allem die Repräsentationsfunktion der die Visitationen begleitenden Schriftlichkeit näher betrachtet werden. Die exponierte Bedeutung dieser Schriftlichkeit für die tatsächliche Verwaltungspraxis kann dabei als unbestritten gelten, wie neuere Beiträge zur Instruktionengeschichte nachgewiesen haben.[19]

So wurden in Instruktionen und Protokollen, sowie begleitenden Korrespondenzen Visitationen angeordnet beziehungsweise über ihre Durchführung Bericht erstattet und die Ergebnisse verarbeitet. Mit der schriftlichen Verarbeitung der Verfahren entstand zwischen Fürsten und Amtsleuten ein Austausch über die Intentionen der Fürsten und Oberbehörden[20], und die Möglichkeiten und Probleme ihrer Umsetzung vor Ort. Zudem liefern die Quellen wichtige Hinweise auf die vor Ort vorgenommene ‚Übersetzung' von Anweisungen auf lokale Erfordernisse und die Reflexion der Lage der Untertanen. Im Falle von Visitationen und Supplikationen in der Markgrafschaft Baden(-Durlach) hat André Holenstein nachweisen können, daß die in den Protokollen und Bittschriften enthaltenen Informationen die Gestaltung von Policeyordnungen beeinflussten.[21]

Zusammenfassend läßt sich feststellen, daß an die Stelle der Präsenz des Landesherrn vor Ort in der Frühen Neuzeit die Errichtung ausdifferenzierter Verwaltungsinstitutionen trat. Die physische Präsenz des einzelnen Herrschenden als Idealtypus wurde so durch die (tatsächliche) physische Präsenz vieler Herrschender ersetzt. Auf die Beamten wurden begrenzte Herrschaftsrechte übertragen, deren korrekte oder mißbräuch-

---

[19] Vgl. Hengerer, Mark: Instruktion, Praxis, Reform: Zum kommunikativen Gefüge struktureller Dynamik der kaiserlichen Finanzverwaltung (16. und 17. Jahrhundert), in: Haas, Stefan; Hengerer, Mark (Hg.): Im Schatten der Macht. Kommunikationskulturen in Politik und Verwaltung 1600-1950, Frankfurt/Main 2008, S. 78f.

[20] Für Kurbayern ist nachweisbar, daß Visitationsprotokolle nicht nur von den Oberbehörden, sondern auch vom Fürsten selber geprüft wurden. So sind beispielsweise im Umrittsprotokoll des Rentamts Straubing von 1630 eigenhändig vorgenommene Kommentare Maximilians I. nachweisbar, der bei den Visitationen zutage tretende Mißstände scharf rügte (StA Landshut, Bestand Rentkasten Straubing, P8). Aufgrund des Forschungsdesiderats ist bisher ungeklärt, ob weitere Fürsten dies genauso handhaben oder ob es sich hier um ein Spezifikum der maximilianischen Amtsführung handelt.

[21] Vgl. Holenstein, André: 'Gute Policey' und lokale Gesellschaft im Staat des Ancien Régime. Das Fallbeispiel der Markgrafschaft Baden(-Durlach). Bd.1, Epfendorf 2003, S. 282f.

liche Ausübung Gegenstand der Kontrolle war, oder zumindest sein sollte. Die in der Regel institutionell fest eingebetteten Amtsträger hatten
zur Aufgabe, dem omniabsenten, aber letztentscheidenden Herrscher
durch die Herstellung von Kommunikation zwischen Landesherr, Amts-
trägern und Untertanen einen steten Informationsfluß zu ermöglichen.
Ein Vehikel der Kommunikation – als Basis der Herrschaftsdurchdringung – waren dabei politisch-administrative Verfahren wie Visitationen.

2. Die konkreten Symbolformen kurbayerischer Visita-
tionsakten

Zu der mit politischen Visitationen verbundenen Schriftlichkeit zählen, neben der mit Bezug auf die Verfahren geführten Korrespondenz,
vor allem die zwei genannten Hauptquellen: Instruktionen und Visitationsprotokolle.

Die *Instruktionen*[22] wurden nach den Vorstellungen der Fürsten von den
Beamten des Hofrats angefertigt und enthielten Anweisungen und Vor-
schriften zur Durchführung von Visitationen. Zugleich bieten sie einen
Einblick in die Amtsführung der Beamten der Oberbehörden, deren
Selbstkonzepte und ihre Wahrnehmung der Mittel- und Unterbehörden.

Demgegenüber wurden die *Visitationsprotokolle*[23] von den Beamten der
mittelbehördlichen Rentämter[24] nach einer – in Kurbayern mit dem Begriff ,Umritt' periphrasierten – Visitation der ihnen unterstehenden lokalen Bezirke angelegt. Zu diesen lokalen Bezirken zählten Landgerichte,
Pflegen und landesherrliche Städte. Die Protokolle bieten einen Einblick
in die Amts- und Selbstwahrnehmung der Beamten der Mittelbehörden
sowie in deren ,Übersetzungsleistung' von Instruktionen in den konkreten Verfahrensvollzug vor Ort. Zusätzlich können anhand der Protokolle – wenn auch lediglich in vermittelter Form – Rückschlüsse auf die Lage der Untertanen gezogen werden. Da die Protokolle nach Fertigstel-
lung an die Hofkammer gesandt und von dort aus auch Hofrat und

---

[22] Exemplarisch sei hier auf folgende Bestände im Hauptstaatsarchiv München hingewiesen: Gl 381 Nr.16, MF 13100/2, StV 1158f. 12 bis 51, GR 1261/1.

[23] Exemplarisch sei hier auf folgende Bestände in den Staatsarchiven München und Landshut hingewiesen: Rentmeisteramt München Fsc. 33/125 bis Fasc. 40/139; Rentmeisteramt
Landshut P 11 bis 21.

[24] Das sind die niederbayerischen Rentämter Landshut und Straubing, sowie die oberbayeri-
schen Rentämter München und Burghausen. Das 1628 hinzukommende oberpfälzische
Rentamt Amberg findet hier keine Berücksichtigung.

Geistlichem Rat zur Prüfung vorgelegt wurden, enthalten sie je nach Überlieferung auch Vermerke der Oberbehörden. Diese Feststellung ist vor allem deswegen von Bedeutung, da anhand der Vermerke nachweisbar ist, daß die Protokolle tatsächlich Relevanz im ‚innenpolitischen' Alltagsgeschäft hatten: Sie wurden von den Oberbehörden ausgewertet und im Falle größerer Problematiken mit teils sehr umfangreichen und detaillierten Anweisungen an die Rentämter zurückgeschickt. So können diese Vermerke als Hinweis auf die Richtigkeit der Eingangsbehauptung gewertet werden, wonach zum Zwecke der Durchsetzung fürstlicher Herrschaftsrechte mit Hilfe von Verwaltungen Verfahren etabliert wurden, die Kommunikationsflüsse ermöglichten.[25]

Beide Quellentypen liefern bezüglich ihrer inhaltlichen Aussagen und der Rekonstruktion ihres institutionellen Werdegangs eindeutige Hinweise darauf, daß sie dezidiert auf die Durchsetzung von Herrschaftsrechten hin konzipiert waren. Es findet sich für diese Beobachtung allerdings noch ein weiterer Beleg, der nicht übersehen werden sollte: Die Symbolformen der Quellen.

Bei den Instruktionen ist augenfällig, daß diese in Bezug auf ihre äußere Form und die Auffächerung der Anweisungen eine vereinheitlichende und streng anordnungsorientierte Struktur aufweisen. Im diachronen Vergleich läßt sich eine Professionalisierung der Amtsführung vermuten, da die dargelegten Anforderungen und Anweisungen über einen Zeitraum von circa 150 Jahren systematischer angeordnet und zusammengefasst wurden. Der korrekten Abfassung und Schriftform wurde offenbar hohe Aufmerksamkeit geschenkt – es handelt sich um sehr umfangreiche Einzelquellen, die ein durchgehend klares Schriftbild ohne nennenswerte Korrekturen aufweisen. Wichtige Einzelsequenzen wurden in lateinischer Schrift hervorgehoben. Großer Wert wurde auch auf

---

[25] Wissenschaftliche Studien zu beiden genannten kurbayerischen Quellentypen sind bislang rar. Unter anderen Fragestellungen nähern sich den Quellenbeständen hauptsächlich Rankl, Helmut: Der bayerische Rentmeister in der Frühen Neuzeit, in: Zeitschrift für Bayerische Landesgeschichte, Bd. 60, München 1998, S. 617-648. Schwertl, Gerhart: Die niederbayerischen Rentmeister-Umrittsprotokolle im Staatsarchiv Landshut, in: Rumschöttel, Hermann; Jaroschka, Walter (Hg.): Bewahren und Umgestalten. Aus der Arbeit der Staatlichen Archive Bayerns. Walter Jaroschka zum 60. Geburtstag. Mitteilungen für die Archivpflege in Bayern, Sonderheft 9, München 1992, S. 186-197. Hinweise auf das Forschungsdesiderat gibt Kramer, Ferdinand: Verwaltung und politische Kultur im Herzogtum und Kurfürstentum Bayern in der Frühen Neuzeit. Aspekte der Forschung, in: Zeitschrift für Bayerische Landesgeschichte, Bd. 61, München 1998, S. 33-43.

die Hervorhebung der *Intitulatio* und *Publicatio* gelegt; der Name des Fürsten mit Titeln und Gottesgnadentum – also der gesamte Bezugsbereich seiner Herrschaftsrechte – wurde fett hervorgehoben und in meist zum Seitenende hin abnehmender Größe über etwa ein Viertel der Frontseite gestreckt. Die Unterschrift des Kurfürsten am Ende des Dokuments ist durch Tinte und Platzanteil hervorgehoben und hebt sich vom Rest des Textes insbesondere durch ihre Eigenhändigkeit ab, die durch eine Paraphe betont wird.

Bei der Auswertung der Symbolformen der Instruktionen soll einer Doppelüberlieferung besondere Aufmerksamkeit gewidmet werden: Von der letzten Instruktion aus dem Jahr 1774 sind zwei Fassungen erhalten, von denen eine zur Archivierung bei der Hofkammer verblieb, während die andere an die zu instruierende Mittelbehörde, in diesem Fall das Rentamt Landshut, ging. Beide Fassungen sind textlich identisch, unterscheiden sich aber in den symbolischen Formen: Bei der Landshuter Fassung[26] wurden *Intitulatio* und *Publicatio* in verwaltungsförmiger Art mit Ranken versehen.

Abb. 1: Instruktion von 1774, Version Rentamt, Detail Frontseite
Quelle: Staatsarchiv Landshut, Rentmeisteramt Landshut, A 1237

Bei der Fassung der Hofkammer[27] dagegen findet sich eine für Verwaltungsschriftgut sehr unkonventionelle Darstellung: Hier sind, bis auf die Buchstaben ‚I' und ‚t', fast alle Buchstaben des Eingangswortes ‚Instruction' aus schlangen- beziehungsweise wurmartigen Tieren mit Augen o-

---

[26] Bestand Staatsarchiv Landshut, Rentmeisteramt Landshut A 1237.
[27] Bestand Bayerisches Hauptstaatsarchiv München, GR 1262/1.

der ganzen Gesichtern in Kriechbewegung geformt. Ausnahmen bilden auch die Buchstaben ‚c' und ‚o', die als Mond und Sonne dargestellt sind, während das schlangenförmige ‚i' in der Mitte mit einem Stern bekrönt ist. Der eigentliche Text der Instruktion hingegen ist mit einer verwaltungsförmigen Ornamentik versehen, die, wie für die Oberbehörden üblich, etwas diffiziler ist als jene der Landshuter Fassung.

Abb. 2: Instruktion von 1774, Version Hofkammer, Detail Frontseite
Quelle: Bayerisches Hauptstaatsarchiv München, Generalregistratur (GR) Fasz.
1262/1

Bei der Auswertung der Visitationsprotokolle, einem sehr umfangreichen Quellenbestand, läßt sich im diachronen Vergleich eine starke Vereinheitlichung der äußeren Form feststellen. In den meisten der für die Zeit zwischen 1650 und 1750 überlieferten Protokollen ist die Abfolge der Inhalte ähnlich angeordnet. Die Anlage der Protokolle entspricht einer Art Dreisatz, in dem mittig das Ergebnisprotokoll präsentiert wird und die Außenränder mit Zusammenfassungen wichtiger Inhalte versehen wurden. Sofern es sich um Exemplare aus der oberbehördlichen Überlieferung handelt, kommen am Außenrand noch die erwähnten, zumeist mit anderer Tinte geschriebenen Anmerkungen der involvierten Hofbehörden hinzu.

Die Ordnung aller Protokolle zu einem Visitationsfolianten ist ein verbindendes Element: Zusammengefasst werden, in systematisch strenger Reihenfolge, die Instruktionen für die Unterbehörden, die Einzelprotokolle und, soweit vorhanden, die separat abgefassten Anweisungen der

Oberbehörden. Der Anfertigung und langfristigen Verfügbarkeit der Protokolle wurde dabei augenscheinlich viel Aufmerksamkeit geschenkt: Von den Ausgangsnotizen des Umritts, den so genannten Rapularen, wurden zwei Reinschriften angefertigt; eine zum Verbleib bei den Mittelbehörden und eine zur Versendung an die Oberbehörden.[28] Beide Fassungen wurden in beschriebener Anordnung in Folianten gebunden und, in den niederbayerischen Rentämtern fast ausnahmslos, mit Inhaltsverzeichnissen und metallenen Registerklammern versehen. Papierne Lesezeichen zeugen von der Weiterverwendung in den Verwaltungen.

Von der erwähnten Aufmerksamkeit zeugt auch die Schriftform der Protokolle: Sie sind in auffallend klarer Schrift verfasst. Aktendeckel und Sinnabschnitte wurden mit Bildelementen bedacht, besonderer Wert wurde hierbei auf die Ausgestaltung von Anreden, Personen- und Ortsbezeichnungen gelegt.

Diese Beobachtungen sind allerdings mit einer entscheidenden Einschränkung verbunden: Sie treffen vorzugsweise auf die niederbayerischen Protokolle zu, während beispielsweise die Protokolle des Rentamts München, welches strukturell und personell in die Verwaltung des Hofs eingegliedert war, oftmals der beschriebenen formalen Stringenz und Anordnung sowie der klaren schriftlichen Form entbehren. Bei diesen sind teilweise kaum lesbare Bestände mit ungeordnet zusammengehefteten Einzelprotokollen zu finden, die keine einheitliche Form aufweisen und unterschiedliche Handschriften erkennen lassen.

3. Die 'Inszenierung von Herrschaft zwischen Aktendeckeln' – Deutungsmöglichkeiten

Bei der Analyse der symbolischen Elemente des beschriebenen Verwaltungsschriftguts kann zur Systematisierung auf die von Barbara Stollberg-Rilinger aufgezeigten Elemente symbolischer Kommunikation zurückgegriffen werden. Hierzu zählen normierte äußere Formen, Wirkmächtigkeit und ein performativer Charakter, sowie das doppelte Hi-

---

[28] Vgl. Schwertl, Gerhart: Die niederbayerischen Rentmeister-Umrittsprotokolle im Staatsarchiv Landshut, in: Rumschöttel, Hermann; Jaroschka, Walter (Hg.): Bewahren und Umgestalten. Aus der Arbeit der Staatlichen Archive Bayerns. Walter Jaroschka zum 60. Geburtstag. Mitteilungen für die Archivpflege in Bayern, Sonderheft 9, München 1992, S. 186-197.

nausweisen über sich selbst durch Erinnerung an vergangenes und die Verpflichtung gegenüber zukünftigem Handeln.[29]

Diese Elemente konkretisieren sich, so die hier vertretene Annahme, im Rahmen der drei Hauptfunktionen von politischen Visitationen, wie sie eingangs beschrieben worden sind.

Nachgewiesen werden kann die Normierung der äußeren Form beider Quellentypen. Zu dieser Normierung gehören die strenge Anordnung der Inhalte und die Abfassung für den Gebrauch im Amtsalltag, und im Falle der Protokolle auch der Dreisatz der Anlage. Diese Elemente der Normierung sollten zur besseren und schnelleren Erfassung der enthaltenen Informationen dienen und so den Amtsvollzug erleichtern. Mit Bezug auf die äußere Normierung kann zusätzlich ein Einblick in die Selbstkonzepte der Akteure gewonnen werden: Über die äußere Sorgfalt und die langfristige Stringenz der Anordnung von Dokumenten inszenierten sich die Beamten als verläßliche Amtleute mit sachlichem Überblick.

Desweiteren weisen gerade die normierte äußere Form und die streng hierarchisierte Nennung der beteiligten Beamten auf den performativen Charakter beider Quellentypen hin: Sie repräsentierten organisierte Herrschaft nicht nur, sondern bewirkten diese gleichzeitig. Durch die stetig wiederholte schriftliche Abfassung von hierarchischen Ordnungen und das Einfügen der eigenen Amtsposition in diese wurden Beamte symbolisch auf ihre Plätze im hierarchisch angeordneten Herrschaftsgefüge verwiesen. Zudem wurden – ganz praktisch – Umfang und Grenzen der Kompetenzen von Beamten verdeutlicht und die daraus resultierenden Amtspflichten und Aufgaben für den einzelnen Amtsträger transparenter gemacht. Der Effekt war damit ein Doppelter: Durch das Verorten der Akteure im Gesamtsystem und durch das Ermöglichen eines konkreten Amtshandelns konnten die Beamten zu dem werden, was sie qua Bezeichnung bereits waren: beauftragte Amtsträger. Entsprechend weisen die Symbolformen beider Quellentypen über sich selbst hinaus auf den größeren Zusammenhang in dem sie stehen: Sie symbolisieren die Herrschaftsordnung, bekräftigen den hierarchiegebundenen Platz der Akteure

---

[29] Vgl. Stollberg-Rilinger, Barbara: Symbolische Kommunikation in der Vormoderne. Begriffe – Thesen – Forschungsperspektiven, in: Zeitschrift für Historische Forschung, Bd. 31, Berlin 2004, S. 503f. Das vierte Kriterium, die Aufführungsform, wird hier wegen der Fokussierung auf die Schriftlichkeit des Verfahrens nicht zur Analyse herangezogen.

und erinnern in ihrer stets ähnlichen Verwendung an Verwaltungstraditionen, die mit der Ausübung von Herrschaftsrechten korrelieren. An dieser Stelle sollen noch einmal jene Quellen in den Fokus gerückt werden, die auf den ersten Blick von der ansonsten den Kriterien symbolischer Kommunikation entsprechenden Anlage abzuweichen scheinen: die wenig verwaltungsförmige Symbolik der Münchner Instruktion und die gegen die sonst beobachtete äußere Normierung verstoßenden Visitationsprotokolle des Rentamts München.

Zu einer vergleichsweise sicheren Einschätzung kann man im letztgenannten Fall kommen. Hier könnten die Protokolle der weiter vom Hof entfernten Rentämter – insbesondere Niederbayerns – deswegen sorgfältiger in ihrer Anlage sein, weil die räumliche Distanz zum Herrscher durch die Aktenführung überbrückt werden mußte. Über diese ‚Inszenierung zwischen Aktendeckeln' konnten die Beamten ihr Selbstkonzept des sorgfältigen Amtmanns Fürsten und Hof übermitteln. In München hingegen war eine solche Inszenierung aufgrund der räumlichen und personellen Nähe des Rentamtes zum Hof nicht erforderlich – de facto war das Münchner Rentamt in die Oberbehörden eingegliedert. Diese Annahmen stützen also die hier vertretene These, wonach die formale Stringenz und Anordnung der Protokolle zur Inszenierung der Amts- und Selbstkonzepte der bearbeitenden Beamten gedient haben.

Der Entstehungshintergrund der Instruktion hingegen ist schwieriger zu klären, so daß bei der Bewertung Vorsicht geboten ist. Allerdings muß die Quelle, bei der es sich nach bisherigem Kenntnisstand um einen Einzelfund handelt, ernst genommen und nicht als ‚versehentliches' Handeln gedeutet werden: Denn selbst wenn der Schreiber beispielsweise aus Langeweile gehandelt hätte, würde dies eine Einschätzung dazu erfordern, warum ein amtliches Dokument derart verwaltungsuntypisch ausgestaltet wurde, – und das obwohl es dem Kurfürsten zur Unterschrift vorgelegen haben dürfte, und im Zuge des geschäftlichen Aktenlaufs nach der (nicht erfolgten) Visitation mindestens drei Oberbehörden mit dem Dokument in Berührung gekommen wären. Da das Dokument zudem fest archiviert wurde, scheint der Schreiber die Ausgestaltung im Vertrauen auf ein gewisses Verständnis bei den von Amts wegen Beteiligten und ohne Angst vor Sanktionierung vorgenommen zu haben.

Vielleicht kann sich der Deutung dieses Vorgangs folgendermaßen genähert werden: Der Instruktion folgte in keinem Rentamt jemals eine Visitation. Obgleich die Verdienste des Verfahrens in der Instruktion gepriesen wurden, waren 'Umritte' im 18. Jahrhundert durch die Steigerung des Umfangs an zu visitierenden Angelegenheiten schwerfällig geworden. Zudem baute man in der Folgezeit in Kurbayern die Verwaltung um und etablierte andere Verwaltungsinstrumente zur Durchsetzung der Informations-, Kontroll- und Repräsentationserfordernisse. In diesem Zusammenhang ist es auffällig, daß gerade die bei Hof verbleibende und nicht an die Beamten der unteren Verwaltungsebenen weitergereichte Instruktion diese wenig verwaltungsförmige Symbolik aufweist. Wenn vor dem Hintergrund der Entwicklung der kurbayerischen Verwaltungsorganisation und der Zukunft der Visitation als Verwaltungspraktik möglicherweise unklar war, ob auf die Durchführung der Visitation effektiv gedrungen werden würde, dann konnte die bei Hof verbleibende Instruktion ‚spielerischer' umgesetzt werden und so von einer zwiegespaltenen Haltung zu der Durchführung von Visitationen Zeugnis ablegen. Die an das Rentamt verschickte Version benötigte aber möglicherweise eine ‚amtlichere' Form, um an der grundsätzlichen Dienstverpflichtung der Beamten keinen Zweifel aufkommen zu lassen.

Die angeführten Beobachtungen zeigen, daß sich bei einer Auswertung von politischen Verfahren zur Ausübung von Herrschaftsrechten nicht nur die Betrachtung des konkreten Verfahrens selbst oder die inhaltliche Auswertung der sie begleitenden Schriftlichkeit lohnt, sondern auch deren Symbolformen interessant und aufschlußreich sind.

Wenn Herrschaft, wie eingangs beschrieben, in ihrer praktischen Durchführung an die Schaffung von Kommunikation zwischen allen von der Herrschaft Betroffenen gebunden ist, so wird durch die Kommunikation – ob in konkreten Verfahren oder dem zugeordneten Schriftgut – die Ausübung von Herrschaft nicht nur inhaltlich konkretisiert, sondern auch zelebriert. Der hieraus entstehenden Sinnverkürzung soll zum Schluß allerdings entgegengetreten werden: Die Auswertung der Symbolformen des Verwaltungsschriftguts zeigt, daß das begrifflich-analytische Nebeneinanderstellen von Form und Inhalt beziehungsweise eigentlicher und inszenierter Herrschaftsausübung eine sachlich unzutreffende Dichotomie impliziert, da es sich um zwei Seiten der gleichen Medaille handelt.[30] Die über symbolische Elemente erzielte Inszenierung von Herrschaft in verwaltungsförmiger Kommunikation ist in weiten Teilen

---

[30] Vgl. die diesen Zusammenhang analysierende Einleitung der Herausgeber in: Neu, Tim; Sikora, Michael; Weller, Thomas (Hg.): Zelebrieren und Verhandeln. Zur Praxis ständischer Institutionen im frühneuzeitlichen Europa, Münster 2009, S. 9-20.

deckungsgleich mit der inhaltlichen Ausrichtung und Gestaltung der Amtsakten. In beiden Formen konkretisiert sich die Ausübung von Herrschaftsrechten – von der Konzeption des hierarchischen Verwaltungsmodells und der Verortung der Beamten in ihr, über die deutliche Zuweisung von Rechten, Pflichten und Grenzen der jeweiligen Amtsausübung. Insofern wurde Herrschaft mit Hilfe symbolischer Formen zwischen Aktendeckeln nicht nur inszeniert – sie wurde durch diese vollzogen.

Law, Finances and Politics:
The Significance of Economic Contexts for the Formation of Norms

Lea Heimbeck

"Staging something" might mean that new legal ideas or concepts become part of public life. This might happen in form of treaties or conventions or of rules of customary law. Yet not only the content of these legal ideas is important but also the form they take when appearing on the public stage. Questions which seem to have a purely legal nature are always situated against a certain context. Yet, the meaning and the influence of this context for the formation of the legal norm (its appearing on stage) are quite important. Does the norm formation depend solely or mainly on such non-legal considerations? Or do legal ideas play such a decisive part that the economic context[1] is only significant during the enforcement of norms? Additionally, how do we know about this economic context and its interdependency with legal issues?

The relationship between legal norm formation and its economic context will be analysed against the background of international debt settlement after state bankruptcies.

In the 19th century several famous state bankruptcies occurred inside and outside of Europe.[2] However, an international legal regime governing debt settlement after state bankruptcies did not exist.[3] Consequently, there were numerous ways in which the affected states

---

[1] The issue of contextualism has been discussed broadly in philosophy. Yet, its understanding is quite different from the one used here. Contextualism relates to questions of knowledge and linguistics. The term "economic context" almost exclusively refers to the context of economic questions, aspects, and issues. The question of whether and in what way economic considerations function as context of (legal) issues is discussed neither in philosophical debates nor in economical or legal ones. Yet, at least social contexts were indeed discussed in some legal areas. See e.g. Berger, Ronald: The Social and Political Context of Rape Law Reform: An Aggregate Analysis. In: Social Science Quarterly (1991) Vol. 72 No. 2, pp. 221-38.

[2] See Table 6.2 in Reinhart, Carmen; Kenneth, Rogoff: This Time is Different. Eight Centuries of Financial Folly. Princeton, 2009 p. 91.

[3] Osterhammel, Jürgen: Die Verwandlung der Welt. Eine Geschichte des 19. Jahrhunderts. München, 2009 p. 1049.

tried to settle the insolvency.[4] The decision how to solve the situation was heavily influenced by economic (and political) considerations. Hence, this article will examine the weight these economic considerations had on the formation of norms of public international law covering state bankruptcies.

1. Subject Matter

The issue of debt settlement in public international law occurs only after state bankruptcies. These incidents vary legally from insolvencies of individuals and insolvencies of enterprises; additionally, several actors are involved both in the loan relationships as well as in the debt settlement process.

In contrast to insolvencies of individuals or enterprises states are said not "to go bust"[5] as they can levy higher taxes, or debase their currencies. Yet neither the affected states nor the creditors have doubts that states can indeed become insolvent. Therefore, the term of bankruptcy must be defined differently. A state is bankrupt if it denies paying its financial obligations to individuals when they exist without any legal doubt. It does not matter whether the state cannot or does not want to fulfil its obligations.[6] The actual moment of insolvency is not necessarily when the state is short of money but might be earlier. The government will decide upon this point based on economic, financial, political and social considerations.[7]

Already in the underlying loan contracts are several actors involved. First of all, a state which needed financial means tried to contract a loan agreement with a bank or a bank syndicate at a European financial market.[8] The legal nature of such contracts was disputed (a contract

---

[4] States intervened militarily, they created financial administrations, or they established trade embargos or other economic sanctions. Lippert, Gustav: Internationales Finanzrecht. In: Wörterbuch des Völkerrechts und der Diplomatie. Karl, Strupp, Vol. 3, Berlin 1925 pp. 884-925 in this case p. 924.

[5] See Szodruch, Alexander: Staateninsolvenz und private Gläubiger. Rechtsprobleme des Private Sector Involvement bei staatlichen Finanzkrisen im 21. Jahrhundert. Berlin, 2008 p. 21.

[6] Pflug-Nürnberg, Karl: Staatsbankrott und internationales Recht. München, 1898 p. 1

[7] Reinhart, This Time (as in 2) p. 51.

[8] As this investigation focuses on the formation of norms in public international law only debt settlement measures after state bankruptcies will be examined. Hence, a cross-border

under public[9] or civil law[10], or only a moral obligation[11]). The debtor state issued bonds to the bank which sold them to the public. These issues had fixed interest rates and guaranteed claims for the owner of the certificate. Henceforth, private investors had direct claims against the debtor state. Additionally, third states were also often involved in different functions. They were a) creditors of loan contracts with the debtor state, they b) took a guarantee in favor of the debtor with a bank, or c) they acted in favor of their nationals (banks and/ or private investors) on grounds of diplomatic protection.

Due to this quantity of involved legal subjects in the underlying loan relationships, many actors with different interests were also involved in the debt settlement. To make things even worse: Due to the lack of an international insolvency regime the actors were flexible in the legal means they used to cope with the bankruptcy. Private investors used forms of self-regulation to execute their claims[12] or they signed contracts with the debtor state to achieve satisfactory solutions. Many debtor states used their national legislation to introduce measures to consolidate their budget and to try to pay the outstanding claims back. At the same time many third states tried to minimize risks for investors by regulating bourses through national laws.[13] The debtor state and creditor states also signed international treaties establishing certain measures reducing the outstanding debt obligations, or consolidating the debtor state budget. Finally, factual debt settlement might also have created customary law.

---

situation is necessary because foreign states would not intervene in purely domestic debt issues in the debtor country.

[9] *See* Manes, Albert: Staatsbankrotte. Berlin, 1922 p. 147.

[10] Other Authors cite Lorenz von Stein as understanding loan contracts as being under private law. However, Stein did indeed say that even those contracts constitute a simple contractual obligation. Yet this obligation has a peculiar legal character under public law. *See* Stein, Lorenz von: Lehrbuch der Finanzwissenschaft, 5th ed., Vol. 2, Leipzig, 1886 pp. 10-1; Pflug-Nürnberg, Staatsbankrott (as in 6), p. 15.

[11] Manes, Staatsbankrotte (as in 9), pp. 152ff.

[12] In 1868 English investors formed the Corporation of foreign bondholders, an association which was to present all or many creditor claims together in order to execute more pressure on the debtor state. Mauro, Paolo: The Corporation of Foreign Bondholders. In: IMF Working Papers, WP/03/107 (May 2003), *available at* http://papers.ssrn.com/sol3/papers.cfm?abstract_id=879183, p. 13 ff.

[13] *See* Börsengesetz (5.07.1896), Hypothekengesetz (13.07.1899), Schuldverschreibungsgesetz (4.12.1899). Though national legislation reacted rather late in Germany; France had already introduced measures to protect investors a couple of years earlier.

International debt settlement issues had not only a complex underlying structure of involved legal subjects but they also affected several different legal regimes. Two questions may be raised: 1) Did the actors introduce international legal norms to settle claims after state bankruptcies? 2) What role did the economic context play in the creation of such norms? Did it have any influence? If so to what degree?

This issue will be studied by examining two specific case studies: Greece between 1821 and 1878 and Egypt between 1862 and 1904. These case studies were chosen because they took place in chronological order which will show a specific legal development; additionally, most creditor states were the same.

2. Greece (1821-1878): Economic Considerations as Reason for the Non-Formation of Norms

In 1824 and 1825 Greece took out its first two loans with English banks. The Greeks needed money to finance their war of independence.[14] However, by 1826 Greece had already stopped redemption of the loans. English private investors asked their government for diplomatic protection, which was denied. From the late 1820s onwards England, France and Russia themselves granted financial aids to Greece. But most important of all: Starting from that point of time all three countries guaranteed loans on behalf of Greece. In 1832 England, France and Russia guaranteed a £ 60,000,000 loan to Greece from Rothschild, London.[15] During the following decades Greece paid back all borrowed money only sporadically. Consequently, the three powers had to make payments (especially to Rothschild) on grounds of the guarantee for several decades.

In 1844 England started making naval blockades in front of the Greek coast and British troops occupied Piräus, the harbour of Athens. From 1857 until 1859 England, France and Russia established a temporal financial commission in Athens. Especially England and France wanted a thorough investigation of the state of Greek finances. The three states justified the establishment of the financial commission with a clause stipulated in the above-mentioned 1832 international treaty. After stating

---

[14] Woodhouse, C.M.: Modern Greece. A Short History. 5th ed., London, 1991 pp.138-9.
[15] Convention to the Sovereignty of Greece between France, Great Britain and Russia, and Bavaria, signed at London, May 7th 1832.

Greece's obligation to pay back the forwarded money on certain conditions, Art. 12 No. 6 reads as follows: "The diplomatic Representatives of the three Courts in Greece shall be specially charged to watch over the fulfilment of the last mentioned Stipulation."[16] In the commission England, France, and Russia each had one representative. Contrary to English suggestions the commission had only very limited powers. It was empowered to examine all state revenues, to suggest reforms concerning the Greek tax administration and its expenditure policies.[17] England criticized the Greek non-cooperation[18] but was not able to carry out real pressure on Greece due to the cautious policies of France and Russia. The commission published its report in May 1859.[19] It criticized corruption and inefficiency in the Greek administration and suggested both measures to consolidate the Greek budget as to pay the creditors by instalments. In 1860 Greece transformed those suggestions in national law. During all this time England still denied its nationals claims on diplomatic protection[20] and justified its actions on its own outstanding financial claims.

England's economic considerations were obvious: It had both outstanding bills from its several loans and arrears because of its payments to Rothschild due to its guarantee.

The relationship between the formation of legal norms and its economic context will be analysed with regard to a specific example: international (financial) commissions.

---

[16] Convention relative to the Sovereignty of Greece (as in 15).

[17] Kofas, Jon V.: Financial Relations of Greece and the Great Powers 1832-1862. New York, 1981 pp. 85, 95; Levandis, John Alexander: The Greek Foreign Debt and the Great Powers 1832-1898. New York, 1944 p. 51.

[18] Kofas, Financial Relations (as in 17), p. 92.

[19] Parl. Papers, General Report of the Commission appointed at Athens to examine the financial conditions of Greece. April 27th 1860, 1860 [2667].

[20] In 1848 Lord Palmerston gave a famous speech on the question of whether the British government supports its national's claims against debtor states. "It is therefore a simple question of discretion with the British Government whether this matter should or should not be taken up by diplomatic negotiation, and the decision of that question of discretion turns entirely upon British and domestic considerations." [. . .] ". . with a view to discourage hazardous loans to foreign Governments, [. . .], the British Government has hitherto thought it best policy to abstain from taking up as International Questions the complaints made by British subjects against foreign Governments which have failed to make good their engagements in regard to such pecuniary transactions". Lord Palmerston, January 1848, *See* Phillimore, Robert: Commentaries upon International Law. Vol. 2, Philadelphia, 1855 pp. 27-8.

In 1857 England, France and Russia established a financial commission on the basis of an international treaty (see above). Since 1815 international commissions began to be established in state practice. The first one was the commission for the Rhine; in 1856 the two commissions for the Danube followed and shortly after in 1865 the International Telegraph Union was created. Hence, in state practice there was a distinct development towards international institutionalization. However, the formation of such commissions and institutions was restricted to few arrears[21], e.g. the administration of international rivers, or the protection of intellectual property. No commissions concerning financial questions were formed.

Additionally, public international lawyers did discuss neither international commissions or institutions nor international financial commissions before 1857. In 1863 Travers Twiss mentioned the commission of war.[22] In 1844 August Wilhelm Heffter had discussed different kinds of international alliances or institutions with regard to postal, telegraphic, or railway issues, and to trade and waterway questions.[23] However, he did understand them as purely bi- or multilateral state contacts, and he doubted whether any legal development concerning these issues would happen: "Ist es auch noch nicht zu einem allgemeinen gleichförmigen Systeme hierunter gediehen, und nach Lage der Dinge vielleicht ein solches nicht zu ermöglichen [. . .]."[24] Heffter did not mention international commissions at all in his 1861 edition.

Also in his French edition from 1857 Heffter discussed the above-mentioned alliances and institutions.[25] Yet in the paragraph with the headline "Institutions Internationales pour l'Industrie" he just enlisted the different bi- and multilateral treaties states had signed to protect

---

[21] Vec, Miloš: Recht und Normierung in der Industriellen Revolution. Neue Strukturen der Normsetzung in Völkerrecht, staatlicher Gesetzgebung und gesellschaftlicher Selbstnormierung. Frankfurt a.M., 2006 pp. 22-8, 163.
[22] Twiss, Travers: The Law of Nations considered as Independent Political Communities. London, 1863 p. 383 ff.
[23] Heffter, August Wilhelm: Das Europäische Völkerrecht der Gegenwart. Berlin, 1844 pp. 467-71.
[24] Heffter, Europäisches Völkerrecht (as in 23), p. 467.
[25] Heffter, August Wilhelm: Le Droit International Public de l'Europe. Paris, 1857 pp. 448-546.

industrial products and innovations.[26] He did the same for "établissements" dealing with international trade and navigation.[27] Interestingly enough, Heffter discussed this subject-matter in the chapter about diplomatic intercourse between states. In other words: Those "Verbindungen" or "établissements" were only bi- or multilateral contractual relationships but they did not have any legal character themselves. Heffter did not even discuss such a possibility.

The issue of interdependency needs to be examined from two perspectives: 1) Did economic considerations (in other words the context) influence the establishment of the commission and therefore, the creation of norms? (Investigation period until 1857) 2) Did the (potential) creation of norms influence economic behaviour? (Investigation period after 1859)

Before 1857 norms concerning the establishment of international financial commissions did not exist. Yet, state bankruptcies had happened quite often in the first decades of the century. Hence, the question is whether actors did not want to introduce international legal norms to cover the subject; thus, to let it remain in a legal vacuum. This is hard to judge from today's perspective. Yet, as neither politicians nor economic or legal practitioners or scholars claimed the introduction of such norms, it seems that that was exactly the case. The economic (and political) context was so important that it determined not only the enforcement but also the creation of norms. This thesis is underlined by the examination of the post-1859 period. The factual establishment of the financial commission did neither introduce legal norms in state practice nor was it discussed by legal scholars (this will be shown in detail in the next case study). Thus, the creation of norms heavily depended on the context surrounding it: with regard to international waterways or intellectual property issues the context "permitted" the introduction of new norms, with regard to economic matters (or rather debt settlement matters) it did not. A possible explanation might be that a legal normation of such issues would have restricted creditor states' options with regard to such an important financial question too much. Additionally, even the big creditor states had been bankrupt several times in the past.

---

[26] Heffter, Droit International (as in 25), pp. 450-2.
[27] Heffter, Droit International (as in 25), pp. 452-6.

3. Egypt (1862-1904): The Formation of Norms: Initiated and Ruled by Economic and Political Considerations

From the start of the 19th century onwards Egypt continuously needed new capital. Due to enormous reforms and development processes the Khedive Mohammad Ali (1805-53) had increased state expenditure heavily. However, the issuance of bonds on European credit markets only began in 1862. From 1863 on, when Ismail Pasha became Egypt's new ruler, the amount of expenditure did not decline. Though he certainly wasted some money, he was also heavily hit by Napoleon III's arbitration award in favor of the Suez Canal Company which granted them £ 3,400,000.[28] Finally, Ismail modernized the irrigation system and built amongst others new railway networks. In October 1875 Ismail declared officially that Egypt had to reduce its interest payments by 50 %.

The Khedive then asked the English government to send a financial adviser who should support the Egyptian attempts to reorganize its financial administration.[29] Instead England sent an unofficial mission which would investigate the whole financial situation and suggest reforms. The so-called Cave-Report (published in February 1876) stated that the Egyptian financial status would not be utterly hopeless if the claims out of the treasury bonds were reduced.[30] Additionally, the report proposed several measures how to organize the Egyptian financial administration effectively.

Ismail Pasha then decided to establish an internationally controlled debt administration. Though the English government refused to officially send an envoy, it did not impede the plan. On May 2, 1876 the Khedive established the *Caisse de la dette publique de l'Egypte*. Each creditor country (England, France, Italy and Austria-Hungary) was to have one member in the *Caisse*. Whereas the French government sent an envoy, the English still refused to do so. Hence, the English commissioner was sent by the British investors.[31]

---

[28] Richmond, J.C.B: Egypt 1789-1952. London, 1977 p. 97.
[29] McCoan, J.C.: Egypt. London, 1882 p. 157.
[30] McCoan, Egypt (as in 29), Appendix p. 441.
[31] Bierschenk, Thomas: Die englische Ägyptenpolitik Anfang der 1880er Jahre und der Imperialismus. 2003 (1977), Working Papers No. 29, p.74.

The Khedive had introduced a special mood of redemption for the outstanding debt. Yet especially the English creditors were not satisfied with this method as it would privilege the French creditors.[32] Two envoys from England and France worked out a plan according to which the outstanding debt would be paid back, the Goschen-Joubert-Plan[33]. This plan proposed the introduction of two further positions (in addition to the *Caisse*): Two financial commissioners, one French, one English. One was to directly receive all state revenues, the other one to sign all payment instructions. The Khedive accepted these suggestions and published them by decree. On November 18, 1876, the Dual Control system was introduced.

Another significant incident was the establishment of Mixed Courts by decree of January 1, 1876. The Khedive himself had supported this measure for several years because the existing system of consular jurisdiction led the Europeans to serious abuses which the Egyptian state was unable to stop. The Khedive hoped to improve the situation by introducing courts which were staffed with both Egyptian and foreign judges. Even though the introduction of the courts did not have an immediate impact on the Egyptian financial administration or the debt settlement, it had a rather important effect on it. The *Caisse* was not only able to be a plaintiff before the court, but the Egyptian state could also be the defendant. In other words it was limited in its sovereignty. The *Caisse* sued the Egyptian government several times[34], when it thought its competences were violated.[35] Hence, the introduction of the Mixed Courts meant nothing less than a juridical control of the Egyptian state with regard to its debt settlement.

---

[32] There are two different sorts of debts: floating and consolidated ones. While floating debts are of a temporary nature – creditors can claim redemption at any time, consolidated debts are of a long-term nature and creditors do not have a right of cancellation or only a limited one. While English creditors mostly owned consolidated bonds, French creditors mostly had floating ones. Ismail Pashas plan would have privileged the latter. *See* Pflug-Nürnberg, Staatsbankrott (as in 6), p. 25.

[33] *See* Wilson, Keith M: The Game of Egyptian Finance. In: Fraser's Magazine (May 1879), pp. 533-47 (534-5).

[34] *See* judgment: McIlwraith: The Egyptian Government and the Caisse de la dette. In: Journal of the Society of Comparative Legislation (1896-7) No. 1, pp. 386-422.

[35] *See* Parl. Papers, Egypt No. 2 (1878), Correspondence respecting the Finances of Egypt, 1878-79 [C.2185] [C.2233], Inclosure 1 in No. 130, Vivian to Derby, February 2nd 1878; Bierschenk, Ägyptenpolitik (as in 31), p. 81.

Notwithstanding all these measures the state of Egyptian finances did not improve. Due to foreign pressure Ismail Pasha established a commission of inquiry in March 1878 which was to investigate Egyptian expenditure. This commission was staffed with five English men, one French person and one Egyptian. On the ground of new reform proposals the Khedive introduced a Minister Council in August 1878 in which an English person became minister of finance and a French person became minister of public affairs. Yet neither minister was officially supported by his respective governments.

From 1878 on the Egyptian opposition grew steadily. In September 1879 the Minister Council had to be closed. As a consequence the two financial advisors whose job had been suspended became active again. This time they had the official support of their respective governments.

On March 31, 1880 England, France, Germany, Italy, Austria, Italy and Egypt signed a treaty in which Egypt obliged itself to establish a commission of liquidation.[36] The commission both had to represent the creditor's interests and to secure Egypt's sovereignty. The main stipulation of this treaty was that Egypt could only issue new bonds with the agreement of the powers and Turkey.

Even though the English and the French government did not agree upon a common course of action (the question was whether they wanted to intervene militarily, or whether they wanted to let Turkey do this), both countries signed a joint note in January 1882 stating that they "resolve to guard, [. . .], against all causes of complication, internal and external, which might menace the order of things established in Egypt"[37]. This broad formulation opened the door to a possible military intervention.

In Egypt the Nationalist movement grew more and more and the conflict between the foreign powers and the Egyptians worsened. After a violent incident in Alexandria on June 11, 1882, the situation escalated. No solution was found at an international conference concerning the situation in Egypt in Constantinople in June/July 1882. On July 11, 1882

---

[36] Declaration between Austria-Hungary, France, Germany, Great Britain and Italy respecting the Appointment of a Commission for the Liquidation of the Egyptian debt, signed at Cairo, March 31st 1880.
[37] *See* Parl. Papers, Egypt No. 5 (1882), Correspondence respecting the Affairs of Egypt, 1882 [C.3230], Inclosure 2 in No. 42.

English ships bombarded Alexandria and English troops occupied Egypt within the following two months.

From 1882 until 1914 Egypt was occupied by England without being a formal Protectorate. This changed only in 1914. From 1882 until 1907 Evelyn Baring, 1st Lord Cromer, was British consul general in Egypt. Even though the international measures which had been instituted during previous years were not extinguished, Egypt's financial and economic recovery was mostly due to Lord Cromer's administration. He consolidated the Egyptian debt within 20 years by introducing several administrative reforms.[38] Both the *Caisse* and the Mixed Courts existed until the 1930s but they had lost their importance. Hence, the factual consolidation of the debt was not really reached due to means under international law but because of the financial capability of one expert.

In contrast to the Greek case, foreigners – being sent by their respective governments or by private creditors – were much more active in the Egyptian debt settlement. Within six years (from 1876 until 1882) several measures under international law had been introduced to consolidate Egyptian state finances.

Economic considerations seem to have played a minor role for England and France in the Egyptian case compared to their activities in Greece. If they intervened directly they usually justified their actions with the need for diplomatic protection of their nationals. In the Greek case they justified their intervention with the cited international treaty which obliged Greece to fulfil its financial obligations. Yet Egypt was also of economic interest to the western powers with regard to its cotton industry, especially during the American Civil War.[39]

Nevertheless, in both cases (Greece and Egypt) economic considerations did only play a minor role. In the Greek case it was just a very good justification for intervention as it was based on an international treaty.

However, Egypt was of the utmost significance for England and France with regard to it strategic position. The passage through the Suez

---

[38] Protectionism was abolished and domestic products were taxed the same way as foreign ones. Additionally, Europeans living in Egypt were taxed for the first time. Cromer sold private estates of the Khedive and his family to use the revenue for debt consolidation. By building the Aswan Dam Cromer increased the agricultural productivity of the country enormously.

[39] Issa, Mahmoud: The economic factor behind the British occupation of Egypt. In: Egypte contemporaine (1964) No. 55, pp. 43-57 (54).

Canal was the fastest way for England to reach India.[40] Additionally, England and France both wanted to keep the balance of power on the European continent. This would have been endangered if one of the two states had gained too much control on the African Continent. Therefore, both the political situation in Egypt as well as its territorial location played a major role in the political relationship between England and France.

The relationship between the formation of norms and its economic context shall be examined with regard to two examples focussing on legal apprenticeship: the *Caisse de la dette publique de l'Egypte* (→ international financial commissions) and the Mixed Courts (→ international jurisdiction).

a) International Commissions

Until 1895 no entries concerning "international commissions" or rather "international financial commissions" are found in standard books by public international lawyers. In 1896 Alphonse Rivier[41] referred to international commissions – though only to the ones administrating international water ways.[42] However, in 1899 it was also Rivier who mentioned the Egyptian financial commission for the first time.[43]

In 1898 Franz von Liszt[44] stated that permanent and general organizations in the state community did not exist. Yet he also emphasized that during the past decades permanent state representations had been established which should administrate certain common interests.[45] Apart from several other examples he specifically referred to the Egyptian debt administration stating that it got an international character through the law of liquidation:

---

[40] The journey from London to Bombay took four months taking the Cape route whereas it was shortened to 40 days using the Suez Canal. Landes, David: Bankers and Pashas. International Finance and Economic Imperialism in Egypt. New York, 1969 p. 81.

[41] Alphonse Rivier was a Swiss lawyer who was the general secretary of the Institut du Droit International for nine years. Rivier emphasized the fact that international law only developed between states with a common legal conscience.

[42] Rivier, Alphonse: Principes du droit des gens. Vol. 1, Paris, 1896 p. 565.

[43] Rivier, Alphonse: Lehrbuch des Völkerrechts. 2nd ed., Stuttgart, 1899 p. 311.

[44] Franz von Liszt who was student of Rudolf von Jhering published 11 editions of his treatise on public international law. He was quite innovative and supported the establishment of international institutions and the League of Nations.

[45] Liszt, Franz von: Das Völkerrecht. Berlin, 1898 pp. 92-3.

„[Die Commission de la caisse de la dette publique] erhielt den Charakter eines eigentlich internationalen Organs durch das Liquidationsgesetz vom 17. Juli 1880 ...'[46].

In 1904 Henry Bonfils[47] also mentioned the Egyptian debt administration. Yet he did not refer to it in the context of "international (financial) commissions", but in the context of state sovereignty. Even in cases where a debtor state could not fulfil its financial obligations towards other states, those states did not have the right to intervene in the debtor states inner sovereignty. Notwithstanding this general principle, there had been numerous examples in the past, e.g. the Egyptian debt administration. In case the financial administration of the debtor state was inefficient other states often let themselves "verleiten, durch ihren unmittelbaren Eingriff oder ihre Überwachung eine bessere Verwertung der Hilfsquellen des schuldnerischen Staates zu bewirken"[48]. The European states had intervened in that manner in Turkey, Tunisia, and Egypt. Interestingly enough, Bonfils dedicated two pages to the aspect of intervention in financial matters of another state in which he discussed exactly the issue of state bankruptcies after the issuance of bonds on European financial markets.[49] He even referred to Greece, Turkey, Egypt, and others. In an entire paragraph he summed up the financial intervention in Egypt – also mentioning the *Caisse*.[50] However, Bonfils did not use these historical facts to discuss issues of public international law, *inter alia* the aspect of international (financial) commissions. This is even more significant as he had mentioned this aspect in the chapter about state sovereignty. This means that Bonfils – contrary to Liszt two years earlier – did not see a development in the law of international commissions in public international law through the establishment of debt administrations after state bankruptcies.

---

[46] Liszt, Völkerrecht (as in 45), p. 94.
[47] Bonfils, a French lawyer, stated that international law emerged out of contacts between nations with a common civilization. He mentioned the international financial commissions in Turkey and Egypt as being in the field of public international law as Turkey became a member of the European Concert after the Treaty of Paris in 1856.
[48] Bonfils, Henry: Lehrbuch des Völkerrechts für Studium und Praxis. 3rd ed., Berlin, 1904 p. 135
[49] Bonfils, Völkerrecht (as in 48), pp. 160-2.
[50] Bonfils, Völkerrecht (as in 48), p. 161.

Only one year later, in 1905, Lassa Oppenheim[51] discussed the issue of international commissions very broadly. He explicitly made reference to the international financial commission in Egypt (as well as to Turkey and Tunisia) as an example for permanent ones.

"Besides temporary commissions, there are, however, permanent commissions in existence. They have been instituted by the Powers in the interest of free navigation on two international rivers and the Suez Canal; further, in the interest of international sanitation; thirdly, in the interest of foreign creditors of several States unable to pay the interest on their stocks [...]."[52]

Later Oppenheim stated that three international commissions in the interest of foreign creditors were in existence: in Turkey since 1878, in Egypt since 1880, and in Greece since 1897.[53]

In 1908 Emanuel von Ullmann[54] also distinguished between two different kinds of international commissions. One of them was permanent, cooperative bodies which had been established by an international act and which had an international mandate.

"Man versteht darunter aber auch ständige kollegiale Körper, die durch einen internationalen Akt mit einem internationalen Mandat ausgestattet eine gewöhnlich längere Zeit in Anspruch nehmende offizielle Wirksamkeit entfalten, oder dauernd für betreffende Zwecke bestellt sind."[55]

Ullmann then particularly pointed to international financial commissions as one example of such international commissions:

---

[51] Lassa Oppenheim who taught at the LSE and in Cambridge published one of the "standard" treatises of public international law. He was a vehement supporter of the establishment of international institutions.

[52] Oppenheim, Lassa: International Law – A Treatise. Vol. 1, London, 1905 p. 493

[53] Oppenheim, International Law (as in 52), p. 495.

[54] Ullmann who was a well-known lawyer at the beginning of the 20th century stated that nation states independence had to be limited in their self-interest as such a necessity lay in the "nature of practical relations and conditions". See Koskenniemi, Martti: The Gentle Civilizer of Nations. The Rise and Fall of International Law 1870-1906. 5th ed., Cambridge, 2008 p. 225.

[55] Ullmann, Emanuel von: Völkerrecht. Vol. 3, Tübingen, 1908 p. 236.

"Die Finanzkommissionen zur Wahrung der Interessen der ausländischen Gläubiger einzelner Staaten. [. . .] Die internationale Kommission zur Verwaltung der egyptischen Staatsschuld."[56]

These citations lead to interesting thoughts. When the Egyptian *Caisse* was formed in 1876 or rather when it got an international character in 1880, it did not have any legal setting in public international law. Yet after only about 20 years, legal apprenticeship became aware of debt administrations as legal bodies and it started to contextualise it in public international law. Franz von Liszt, Lassa Oppenheim and Emanuel von Ullmann explicitly referred to the Egyptian debt administration when discussing international law concerning international commissions. Yet as the issue of international commissions itself had not been considered earlier, the factual creation of international financial commissions initiated a development in public international law with regard to international commissions in general. Even though Henry Bonfils did not mention such debt administrations with regard to international commissions but only in the context of state sovereignty he was aware of their meaning in public international law. He also talked about international commissions in general, but he did not make a connection between these general thoughts about intervention in financial matters and the ones on the formation of international debt settlement bodies.

b) International Tribunals

An examination of the issue concerning international tribunals yields comparable results. Until the mid 19th century public international lawyers mainly discussed the subject of international arbitration which was fairly new.

In 1877 Théophile Funck-Brentano explicitly denied the existence of international courts and he doubted whether such establishments were possible at all.[57]

"Sans un code de droit des gens, [. . .], un tribunal international, chargé de régler leurs conflits, n'aurait aucune raison d'être. [. . .] Ainsi, on ne saurait ni imposer aux États un code de droit international, ni instituer

---

[56] Ullmann, Völkerrecht (as in 55), p. 237.

[57] This is not surprising though as Funck-Brentano and Sorel described in their treatise international law as diplomatic practice. *See* Koskenniemi, Gentle Civilizer (as in 54), p. 276.

un tribunal suprême des conflits internationaux sans porter atteinte à la souveraineté des États." [58]

In 1885 Pasquale Fiore[59] agreed with Funck-Brentano about the lack of an international authority judging over state disputes. Yet he stated the hope that one day such an authority might be established and that some international lawyers propose the establishment of an international tribunal as such an authority. Fiore referred to the Russian lawyer Leonid Kamarowski.

"Il [Kamarowski, LH] trouve [. . .] dans les tribunaux mixtes établis en Egypte les premiers précédents de Cours de justice qui par la nature des choses ont un caractère international." [60]

Yet Fiore also came to the conclusion that an international tribunal could only be established after the introduction of a binding international legal regime.[61]

In his 2nd edition from 1902 Franz von Liszt distinguished between two kinds of international courts[62]: On the one hand there were the "pure" ones which were strictly international, representing the international community itself.[63] On the other hand were the Mixed Courts which also formed part of the international jurisdiction. Mixed Courts were staffed with domestic and foreign judges to adjudicate disputes between foreigners or between a national and a foreigner.[64] Liszt cited two examples for such Mixed Courts: Turkey and Egypt and

---

[58] Funck-Brentano, Théophile; Albert, Sorel: Précis du Droit des Gens. Paris, 1877 pp. 440-1.

[59] Pasquale Fiore stated that the ultimate source of international law was the juridical conscience of the European people. He emphasized that individual freedom and human rights were under the collective juridical guarantee by all civilized states. Consequently, he hoped for the establishment of international institutions protection those rights though he was not very confident.

[60] Fiore, Pasquale: Nouveau Droit International Public. Vol. 2, Paris, 1885 p. 621.

[61] Fiore, Nouveau Droit (as in 60), pp. 623-4.

[62] In his first edition from 1898 Liszt also discussed "International Courts" in a specific chapter with regard to Mixed Courts in Turkey, Egypt, and Samoa but he did not speak about their legal character in general. Liszt, Völkerrecht (as in 45), pp. 99-103.

[63] Liszt, Franz von: Das Völkerrecht. 2nd ed., Berlin, 1902 pp. 145 ff.

[64] Liszt, Völkerrecht (as in 63), p. 144.

he discussed the Egyptian version broadly.[65] When speaking about the courts jurisdiction he also pointed to disputes arising out of insolvency settlements if affecting the interests of foreigners.

"Die Zuständigkeit der Gemischten Gerichte umfasst: a) Die Zivilgerichts-barkeit [. . .] γ) im Konkursverfahren, soweit dieses die Interessen von Angehörigen verschiedener Nationen berührt."[66]

The Egyptian Mixed Courts also ruled on claims against the Egyptian government when it was accused of having violated the stipulations out of the debt settlement treaties. The execution of the debt settlement clauses obviously affected foreign creditors. It is rather interesting that Liszt formulated the courts jurisdiction so broadly that it is not clear on first sight that it also covered actions against the Egyptian state with regard to debt settlement issues. Yet apart from the fact that foreign judges worked within the Egyptian legal system the fact that foreign judges had competences to intervene in Egyptian sovereignty by judging over debt settlement issues did in fact make the Mixed Courts international tribunals.

Henry Bonfils (1904) dedicated a whole chapter to the Egyptian Mixed Courts.[67] As with his explanations regarding the Egyptian *Caisse*, he talked broadly about the historical facts and described the courts' jurisdiction. He explicitly cited Article 11 of the Egyptian decree covering the courts' jurisdiction, which is very significant:

"[Die Gemischten Gerichte können nicht] über Hoheitshandlungen [. . .] erkennen, die von der Regierung in Ausführung von Verwaltungsgesetzen und –vorschriften und in Übereinstimmung hiermit getroffen worden sind."[68].

Yet this limitation did not cover rights of foreigners which these had received by treaties, laws, or conventions, „die durch solche Massregeln

---

[65] Liszt, Völkerrecht (as in 63), pp. 145-8.
[66] Liszt, Völkerrecht (as in 63), p. 147.
[67] Bonfils, Völkerrecht (as in 48), pp. 411-4.
[68] Bonfils, Völkerrecht (as in 48), p. 412.

erfolgten Verletzungen eines von einem Ausländer erworbenen, durch Verträge, Gesetze oder Abkommen anerkannten Rechtes"[69].

Without particularly stating it this clause meant nothing less than the admissibility of suits against the Egyptian government after violation of debt settlement stipulations.

However, it is of the utmost importance that Bonfils wrote a special chapter on "international tribunals" in the part of his book dedicated to public international law's future.[70] He expressed doubts on the formation of an international community between states but hoped that such a stage might be reached one day by establishing an international tribunal. Yet he limited the jurisdiction of such a court to questions concerning humanitarian law.[71] The structure of Bonfils' book leads to the following conclusion: Even though he was aware of the Egyptian Mixed Courts, he understood them neither as a current example of an international tribunal nor as an example how to structure such a tribunal in the future.

Lassa Oppenheim (1905) did not talk about international courts in general in his standard law book. Yet he mentioned the Egyptian Mixed Courts and just calling them "international tribunals"[72] without any further explanantion.

Emanuel von Ullmann (1908) named five sorts of international tribunals, one of which were the Egyptian and Turkish Mixed Courts.[73] Though according to Ullmann there were some legal uncertainties with regard to the courts judgments the courts themselves were internationally recognized.

"Allem Anschein nach dürfte nicht so sehr die Institution als solche und der ihr zugrunde liegende Gedanke der Wirksamkeit internationaler Organe auf einem wichtigen Gebiete internationalen Lebens als die Quelle neuerlicher Übelstände und Beschwerden anzusehen sein [. . .]."[74]

In other words: Not only did Ullmann himself understand the Mixed Courts as international tribunals, but he was of the opinion that the

---

[69] Bonfils, Völkerrecht (as in 48), p. 413.
[70] Bonfils, Völkerrecht (as in 48), pp.845-6.
[71] Bonfils, Völkerrecht (as in 48), p. 845.
[72] Oppenheim, International Law (as in 52), pp. 480-1.
[73] Ullmann, Völkerrecht (as in 55), p. 239.
[74] Ullmann, Völkerrecht (as in 55), p. 233.

international (legal) community had accepted the existence of such international bodies in public international law.

The statements of the named legal authors lead to the following conclusions: From 1885 on most international lawyers discussed the Egyptian Mixed Courts and presented their jurisdiction more or less broadly. Whereas Fiore in 1885 expressed the hope that international tribunals would be established one day and that the Mixed Courts might be a first step in this direction, von Liszt (1902), Oppenheim (1905) and Ullmann (1908) already understood the Mixed Courts as being international ones. Yet only Oppenheim and Ullmann explicitly said so. However, Bonfils in 1904 did not indentify the Egyptian Courts as international ones. Nevertheless, in general it can be seen that at the time when the Mixed Courts were established in the 1870s and 1880s they did not have a legal setting in public international law (neither in state practice nor in legal apprenticeship). Yet after only a couple of years they influenced public international law. Lawyers agreed upon the unjustified intervention in state sovereignty by establishing debt administrations[75], and the majority of lawyers also understood Mixed Courts as examples of international tribunals.

c) Conclusion: Significance of Context for the Formation of Norms

The development of legal scholars' appreciation of both the establishment of international financial commissions and Mixed Courts at the end of the 19th/beginning of the 20th century was quite similar.

Before the 1870s neither international commissions nor tribunals had been discussed in standard law books. Yet, the number of state bankruptcies had grown steadily between 1800 and 1874.[76] However, whereas at the beginning of the 19th century many European states had fallen bankrupt, the number of non-European debtors increased enormously during the century. Moreover, London and Paris became the main financial centres of the world only in this period. Hence, states began to issue bonds at foreign markets only after the middle of the century, and big European banks grew enormously.[77] Thus, there was a

---

[75] I stated this point only with regard to Henry Bonfils who wrote a chapter about „Intervention in financial affairs". Yet most lawyers named this kind of intervention directly or indirectly.

[76] Reinhart, This Time (as in 2), Table 6.2 p. 91.

[77] See Born, Karl Erich: Geld und Banken im 19. und 20. Jahrhundert. Stuttgart, 1977

distinct development in the financial world market. Furthermore, after the 1870s, Latin American countries became the main debtors and the number of European state bankruptcies declined significantly. Hence, the 1870s did not only constitute a major watershed with regard to legal scholars' appreciation of said legal institutes but also with regard to the economic context. Thus, there seems to be a manifest interdependency between the norm formation and its economic context.

Until the 1870s when the financial markets and their influence did not play a major role in the decisions of European politicians or moreover, when the negative consequences of international financial connections hit European states, European lawyers (and this was the majority of public international lawyers) did not discuss the issue of debt settlement. Thus, the context had an important influence as it hindered the introduction of legal norms. After the 1870s financial interactions between London, Paris and to a smaller degree Frankfurt and Berlin became more and more important. Moreover, it was now non-European states which were usually hit by bankruptcies. At that time public international lawyers (again mostly from creditor states) began discussing the subject broadly. This shows again the immense influence the economic context had on norm formation. Only in this case the context fostered the formation and not the non-formation as before the 1870s.

4. Reciprocal Instrumentalization of Legal Norms and their Economic and Political Context

In this article the relationship between the formation of norms and economic context was analysed. Yet, another question shall be raised. Economic considerations are always connected in one way or another with political ones. As we have seen such considerations, or to use the same term, such context influence legal questions. On the other hand legal questions may also influence the context surrounding it. Thus, of what kind is the mutual influence? My thesis would be that there exists a reciprocal instrument-talization of context and the creation of legal norms. [78]

---

pp.64-83; Cameron, Rondo: Geschichte der Weltwirtschaft. Vol. 2, Stuttgart, 1992 pp. 136 et seq.

[78] See general thoughts about the relationship between public international law and politics: Fischer-Lescano, Andreas; Philip, Liste: Völkerrechtspolitik. In: Zeitschrift für Internatio-

In the Greek case the creditor states instrumentalized law in using existing legal norms and principles, *inter alia* the ones on intervention, to legitimize their actions. That is what the creditor states did in Egypt, too. However, the creditor states did not use legal argumentation at all when establishing the different financial commissions and the Mixed Courts. This means that international commissions and jurisdiction succeeded out of an independent momentum free of using legal grounds as instruments to implement political goals.

From a historical point of view one might instead ask whether it was law which instrumentalized its economic and political context in the Egyptian case.

The question arises: Why did the said context instrumentalize law to act whereas law used economic and political interests to justify its formation with past economic and political considerations?

Maybe this difference is due to a change in public international law's function at the end of the 19th century. Because of the poly-centric processes started by global capital investments, there was a need for some sort of legal security. Only public international law was able to provide such a function of security and regularity. Additionally: Public international law needed to posses this function immanently; otherwise it was not able to offer mechanisms for conflict settlement. To meet these requirements public international law had an immanent need for legitimization. This need could only be satisfied by resorting to past state actions. In other words: There was a qualitative and quantitative increase of actions on international capital markets. This increase called for an adapted legal system. This adapted legal system received its legitimization through the underlying factual actions. Hence, this process of legitimization happened independent of its context. By instrumentalizing factual actions law outmanoeuvred economic and political considerations.

---

nale Beziehungen (2005) Issue 12 No. 2, pp. 209-49; *See* Luhmann who speaks about momentums in the rationization of systems between law and politics: Luhmann, Niklas: Die Gesellschaft der Gesellschaft. Frankfurt a.M., 1997; *See also* Schmitt's "Normativität des Faktischen". In: Schmitt, Carl: Hüter der Verfassung. Tübingen, 1931.

The Case of Patricide in the Century of the Codes

Ninfa Contigiani

The Legal Sources

Patricide is generally included in the penal codes of the 19th century as a separate murder case. A traditional legal content is transmitted to a new form of law. Law is by then reduced to the codified law, and criminal law is autonomous from procedural law. This crime is particularly significant for the problems and questions raised by the modifications of law.

In the 19th century the new juridical culture promoted by the philosophy of the Enlightenment developed. It spread throughout Europe through the implementation of the Civil Code as a manifestation of the centrality of law and of the re-construction of civil order starting from the individual and the social contract. Thus, the French Civil Code of 1804 and the Austrian Civil Code of 1811 considered as highly different institutional and historical development models, signal a clean cut from the past, from the point of view of the form. Indeed, the form of law is the true novelty when compared with *Ancien regime*, in which form and substance were not yet separated. On the contrary, with regard to the crime with which we are dealing in this article, it would seem that there is no such clear abandonment of the *Ancien regime* tradition. In other terms, as for patricide the separation is not so clean cut, whether regarding the form or the content.

From the point of view of Italy, the French and Austrian codification provides the pre-unitary Italian legislator with legislative solutions to assume or refuse, depending on the incrimination ideology that prevails in the different realities. It must be immediately said that not an equal value is given to the French and Austrian penal models within Italy. After Napoleon, during the Restoration, in the Lombardo-Veneto territory, the Italian translation of the universal penal Code of the Austro-Hungarian Empire comes into force in 1816. It is a code that will have, on this part of the country, an influence which is very different from that which the French code will have on other areas. Apart from the articles which severely repress political dissent (however not so different from the analogous articles of the Italian codes), the code is actually «written in a very progressive technique, that produces more precise and abstracting definitions, at least in the general section and in that dedicated to crimes (much less in contraventions)»[1], coherently with the juridical culture, linked to absolutist paternalism on one hand, and to the rights of the natural person, on the other. In this code there is no specificity of patricide envisaged with regard to murder.

On the contrary, we must notice that this crime is considered as autonomous in the penal legislation of all the other regional Italian states, influenced by the Napoleonic penal Code of 1810. The *Code pénal* clearly describes patricide in article 299:

«The murder of legitimate fathers or mothers, whether natural or foster, or of any other legitimate ascendant is qualified as patricide». The death penalty is inflicted, as written in article 302: «All those guilty of murder, of patricide, infanticide and poisoning, will be punished by death, without interfering the particular measures contained in article 13, regarding patricide»[2].

Patricide is seriously punished in Roman law too, where a specific law establishes the punishment of *culleo* for its perpetrators. In the 19th century, it is still distinguished from murder because the parental bond is considered as an essential element and not as a simple aggravating circumstance, within a point of view of case law and 'exceptionality', which goes against the gain of modern penal law[3]. In the French paradigmatic legislation, a first interesting element is the description of

---

[1] «Redatto secondo una tecnica molto più avanzata, che produce definizioni più precise e astrattizzanti, almeno nella parte generale e in quella dedicata ai delitti (molto meno in materia di contravvenzioni)»), states Da Passano, Mario: *Le definizioni nella storia del diritto penale italiano contemporaneo.* In 'Omnis definitio in iure periculosa?' *Il problema delle definizioni legali nel diritto penale* ed. by Cadoppi, Alberto. Cedam. Padova 1996, pp. 95-108, pp. 100-101.

[2] *Code pénal* (1810) article 299: «Est qualifié parricide le meurtre des pères ou mères légitimes, naturels ou adoptifs, ou de tout autre ascendant légitime»; article 302 «Tout coupable d'assassinat, de parricide, d'infanticide et d'empoisonnement, sera puni de mort, sans préjudice de la disposition particulière contenue en l'article 13, relativement au parricide».

[3] For the paradigm of the exception in modern criminal law see Meccarelli, Massimo: *Paradigmi dell'eccezione nella parabola della modernità penale.* In: «Quaderni storici» (2009) No. 131, pp. 193-521.

which relative could potentially be involved in the crime, a description that puts together different family ties: legitimate, natural, adoptions (this is not always true in Italy). Yet, what is more impressing is the «staging» of the execution of the death penalty, since it strongly recalls the past. It maintains – and at the same time renews – a real theatrical ritual. This is described in art. 13:

«The guilty party condemned to death for patricide, will be led onto the place of execution, in a shirt, bare-footed, and the head covered by a black veil. He will be put on stage while the court bailiff will give a public reading of the sentence; then his right hand will be cut, and he will immediately be executed»[4].

Actually, the *Code pénal* of 1810 omits a series of details of the traditional ritual which were still present in the draft of the criminal code of 1801 (of Gui-Jean Baptiste Target)[5], but despite that, during the meeting of the State Council, the amputation of the right hand causes great discussion, since it was considered as not being useful, if not harmful, by the conscience of the new legislators.[6]

However, modern penal codified law, openly contradicting the principle of humanity which was among its inspiring principles, fully maintained the theatrical characteristic of the execution of the parricide. This basically arrives from *Ancien Regime*: exemplary execution for the purpose of intimidation and deterrence.[7] The exemplariness is even

---

[4] *Code pénal* (1810) article 13: «Le coupable condamné à mort pour parricide, sera conduit sur le lieu de l'exécution, en chemise, nu-pieds, et la tête couverte d'un voile noir. Il sera exposé sur l'échafaud pendant qu'un huissier fera au peuple lecture de l'arrêt de condamnation; il aura ensuite le poing droit coupé, et sera immédiatement exécuté à mort».
[5] Projet de Code criminel, correctionel et de la police, présenté par la commission nommée par le Gouvernement, 1801, article 13.
[6] See Bouglé-Le Roux, Claire: *La Cour de cassation et le code pénal de 1810: le principe de légalité à l'épreuve de la jurisprudence*, 1811-1863. LGDJ. Paris 2005, p. 20 nt. 90: harmful, because it could move the people to pity the condemned; useless because it plainly violated basic human principles.
[7] The method of execution, although it underwent some changes over time, is the result of a long-standing tradition. Already in ancient Roman law the punishment for parricides, the *poena cullei*, was special and symbolic (see Tondo, Salvatore. *Leges regiae e paricidas*. Olschki. Firenze 1973; and also Nardi, Enzo: *L'otre dei parricidi e le bestie incluse*. Giuffrè. Milano 1980. In French juridical history the amputation or the injury of the right hand for parricides resulted from the Ancien Régime. According to Languì, André; Arlette, Lebigre: *Historie du droit penal*. Cujas. Paris 1979, vol. I, p. 127 ; Garnot, Benoît: *Un crime conjugal au 18 ème siècle*.

'encouraged' – rather than overcome – in the separate murder case that survives in the code and takes on its even greater symbolic 'speciality', because the rite of art. 13 is – now – reserved solely for patricide. In the past it was also foreseen for coniugicide, murder, for murder by poisoning, for death brought about under torture and abuse, in the logic of effectiveness that simply held together all the criminal behaviours recognized as 'atrocious'[8].

The Particular Juridical Object

The exacerbation of the exemplariness of execution is significant and it helps us understand. In the interpretative work of the legal doctrine and jurisprudence, this legislative choice serves to discriminate patricide from the other intra-family murders, so as to build a real 'crime system' (crime-archipelago).[9] Reconstructions of family violence will always start from a central standing point: the murder against the father that is against the head of the family.[10] The other murders (of the child by the father, of the husband by the wife, between spouses, between siblings) turn around the head figure which they depend on and they are 'perceived' as less severe.

In France, according to the authoritarianism of the relationship between the emperor and the legal culture (typical and constant feature of the Napoleonic era) Statute law itself 'commands' interpretation explicitly separating the murder of the father (or of the ascendant) by a child from its opposite. Indeed, the murder of a child committed by the father is declared a "simple murder", like coniugicide (art. 343-360). In Italy, on the contrary, it is the legal doctrine itself that distinguishes 'pure' and 'impure' patricide (or.: «*parricidio 'proprio' e 'improprio'*») the *intra-*

L'affaire Boiveau, Imago. Paris 1993, p. 143 ; see Lascoumes, Pierre; Poncela Pierrette; Pierre, Lenoël: *Au nome de l'ordre. Une histoire politique du Code pénal.* Hachette. Paris 1989, espec. pp. 109ff. for the debate in the National Convention on Lepeletier de Saint-Fargeau's proposal on the death sentence.

[8] For the history of 'atrocious' crime see Théry, Julien: «Atrocitas/enormitas». *Per una storia della categoria di "crimine enorme" nel basso Medioevo (XII-XV secolo).* In: «Quaderni storici» (2009), No. 131, pp. 329-375.

[9] See Sbriccoli, Mario: Crimen lesae maiestatis. Il problema del reato politico alle soglie della scienza penalistica moderna. Giuffrè. Milano 1974.

[10] Bouglé-Le Roux: *La Cour de cassation*, op. cit., p. 19 explicitly refers to the defence of the head of the family, rather than the defence of the person as such.

moenia deaths considered by the penal codified law as uniformly deriving from the one model of patricide.[11]

If read through the French filter, the Sardinian, Papal and Neapolitan codes are very significant. The *Codice per lo Regno delle Due Sicilie, Parte seconda: Leggi penali* (1819) writes that patricide deserves the death penalty (on the gallows) with the third degree of public example (art. 6 § 3, art. 352 § 1), for infanticide and coniugicide simple death (art. 352 § 3, art. 353).[12] As in the French model, in the definition of patricide, the line of descendents is totally eliminated, but the juridical bond of adoption is included; differently from France, also the ascendants of the mother are involved (art. 348). In addition, for the incrimination of patricide in the case of natural father, the legal recognition of the murderous son is needed.[13] In the text of this code is the definition of so called 'impure' patricide, art. 353:

«The wilful murder of the legitimate and natural child is also punished by death; as is that of the natural child when it is committed by the mother, as well as that of the legally recognised natural child when it is

---

[11] With the only exception of the Grand Duchy of Tuscany.

[12] On 17th February 1861 a law made the Sardinian penal code of 1859 enforceable in the Neapolitan regions. Upon its promulgation, the gradation of the exemplariness of capital punishment was the subject of a debate. See Da Passano, Mario: *Il problema dell'unificazione legislativa e l'abrogazione del codice napoletano.* In *Codice per lo Regno delle due Sicilie (1819). Parte seconda, leggi penali.* Cedam. Padova 1996, pp. LXIX-CLXIII and Da Passano, Mario: *Emendare o intimidire. La codificazione del diritto penale in Francia e in Italia durante la rivoluzione e l'Impero.* Giappichelli. Torino 2000, pp. 183 and 185 states that only under Murat do Italians mount opposition to the simple extension of the *code pénal* of 1810. His Committee for the translation of the Napoleonic texts proposes removing the amputation of the hand because it is never carried out in that Kingdom, see the book by Mastroberti, Francesco: *Codificazione e giustizia penale nelle Sicilie dal 1808 al 1820.* Jovene. Napoli 2001; see also Novarese, Daniela: *Dall'esperienza francese alla Restaurazione. La genesi del «Codice per lo Regno delle Due Sicilie», Parte seconda, Leggi penali (1819).* In: «Materiali per una storia della cultura giuridica» (1997), No. XXVII-1, pp. 33-52.

[13] See Mazzacane, Aldo: *Una scienza per due regni: la penalistica napoletana della Restaurazione.* In: *Codice per lo Regno delle due Sicilie,* op. cit., pp. XXVII-XLIV, p. XXXIII, but also the comprehensive reconstruction of Mastroberti, Francesco: *Tra scienza e arbitrio. Il problema giudiziario e penale nelle Sicilie dal 1821 al 1848.* Cacucci. Bari 2005. On the subject of legal definitions, see the interesting suggestions of Orrù, Giovanni: *Le definizioni del legislatore e le ridefinizioni della giurisprudenza.* In 'Omnis definitio', op. cit., pp. 147-161, pp. 153-154. The author maintains that it is not possible to provide unambiguous definitions, therefore the language of the legislator cannot be unambiguous. Not only for linguistic-logical reasons, but also and above all for ideological and social reasons.

committed by the father, and that of the adoptive child, the spouse, brother or sister in the second degree. If there has been premeditation, first degree of public example will be added»[14].

The important difference from the French model is the distinction between the failed and the attempted murder with decreased penalty (art. 354).[15]

The *Codice penale per il Regno di Sua Maestà il Re di Sardegna* (1839) is exemplary in terms of defence of the family. It even foresees a specific title (the ninth). This is significantly placed before the one regarding crimes against the person, placing the order of the household among protected 'public' goods, without equivocation[16]. Title IX includes the crime of adultery and concubinage (Chapter I, articles 523-529), though they are distinct as in the French codification. Subsection V is reserved for specific violations of the order of families, such as the insubordination of children (article 557)[17] and the excesses of paternal correction punished with reprimand and arrests according to the circumstances of the offence (article 560). A choice which is different from that made in the French code and which is stressed also by the punishment of ill-treatment between spouses activated by private action. On the contrary, the discipline of patricide[18] follows almost blindly the

---

[14] *Codice per lo Regno delle Due Sicilie, Parte seconda: Leggi penali* (1819) art. 353: «È anche punito colla morte l'omicidio volontario sul discendente legittimo e naturale, sul figlio naturale quando è commesso dalla madre, sul figlio naturale legalmente riconosciuto quando è commesso dal padre, sul figlio adottivo, sul coniuge, sul fratello o sulla sorella in secondo grado. Vi si aggiungerà il primo grado di pubblico esempio, se vi sia premeditazione».

[15] This equalisation faced strong opposition in Neapolitan jurisprudence, states Patalano, Vincenzo: *Sulle leggi penali contenute nella parte seconda del codice per lo Regno delle Due Sicilie del 1819*. In *Codice per lo Regno delle due Sicilie*, op. cit., pp. XLV-LXVIII, pp. LX-LXI, where the novelty of the distinction between failed and attempted crime in Romagnosi's theories is emphasized.

[16] That is in the absence of divorce, according to article 144 of *Codice civile per gli Stati di Sua Maestà il Re di Sardegna* (1837).

[17] But see also the *Codice civile* (1837), articles 214ff.

[18] *Codice penale per gli stati di Sua Maestà il Re di Sardegna* (1839) article 569: «L'omicidio volontario dei genitori o di altri ascendenti o di genitori naturali, quando questi abbiano legalmente riconosciuto il figlio uccisore, ovvero del padre o della madre adottivi, è qualificato parricidio» (TN: «Wilful murder of one's parents or other ancestors or of natural parents, if they have legally recognized the killer as their child, or against one's foster mother or father, is qualified parricide»). It is important to note that, differently from similar Neapolitan regulations, in the Kingdom of Savoy there is no distinction between

Code pénal of 1810, except for the amputation of the right hand (article 557) and the distinction between failed and committed crime. As happens in France, patricide will never be excusable (article 612) and homicide of the child by the parent together with coniugicide are referred to as wilful murders, since they are not even distinctly nominated. It is useful to remember that this code lasts for a longer time in the pre-unitary panorama, by virtue of the following history connected with the national unification, because the changes made by the legislator for the version of 1859 seem merely a specification and an improvement on the legislative technique.[19]

Finally, the *Regolamento sui delitti e sulle pene* (1832) of the Papal States establishes the widest discipline concerning the relatives involved in the case in point: the death sentence for patricide can involve ascendants, descendants, brothers, sisters – full and uterine – husband and wife.[20] Here the definition is totally comprehensive of the 'patricide system'. Instead of punishing the accused people in a qualitatively different way, the Pope prefers to 'intimidate' the highest number of possible interested people with Statute law, excepting the adoptive parents. This choice has to be considered, at least, predictable in the temporal kingdom of the Head of Roman Catholic Church.

All this must be read within the new context of reference of the repression of the crime of patricide and referred to the ideological foundation of incrimination. The basis of the building are represented by the family institution. The Napoleon Civil Code, without uncertainties, bypasses the equality of spouses gained with the French Revolution.[21] It takes on some traditional contents of the order of families in order to introduce them into the new economic perspective and especially into the new form of the law which has been reduced to Statute law, to the

---

mother and father as regards legal recognition. This is necessary for both of them, in order to favour the defence of the family over the father.

[19] See Vinciguerra, Sergio: *Breve profilo storico-giuridico del codice penale albertino.* In *Codice penale per gli Stati di S. M. il Re di Sardegna.* Cedam. Padova 1993, pp. VII-XXVIII, p. VII; see also Vinciguerra, *I codici penali sardo-piemontesi del 1839 e del 1859.* In: *Diritto penale dell'Ottocento. I codici peunitari e il codice Zanardelli.* Cedam. Padova 1993, pp. 350-393.

[20] *Regolamento sui delitti e sulle pene* (1832) article 276. Concerning this Code, see the general analysis in the book of Vinciguerra, Sergio (ed.): *I Regolamenti penali di Gregorio XVI per lo Stato pontificio (1832).* Cedam. Padova 1998, that has the merit to have drawn attention to the papal juridical experience.

[21] Actually, he removed the French revolution Act on divorce of 20th September 1792.

command of the sovereign. The diversity of the roles of members of the family community, the marked male primacy, the subjection of children[22] are substantial juridical content of the past but are now acting in the context of the codified system. This means that the 'sovereign written law' declares all citizens equal in formal terms, but in substance not all the individual rights act universally (whether the sovereign is the Nation or the Emperor is not important for this point).

The French Revolution created the conditions for the ascent of the Third Estate to the level of the other social classes, but it failed to achieve the goal of giving France a new civil order, as demonstrated by the three drafts of the civil code of Jean Jacques Régis de Cambacérès, which indeed remained drafts. The new legal order is designed solely by the Emperor Napoleon, who wants the free citizens as an instrument and source of support for his own power. For this reason, the *civil Code* 'prescribes' a precise hierarchy among the members of the family, which is structured similarly to the homeland and its sovereign: the woman entered on the hereditary axis, but her legal capacity is seriously limited by *patria potestas* or husband legal power, the legitimate children are equal as regards division of the patrimony, but they are object of the *ius corrigendi*[23] and its abuse by the father is not seen as criminally pursuable. In this way, the man, 'absolute owner' and head of the family[24], represents the vital nucleus of the first social cell that finds reflection in the State.

The *Code pénal* of 1810 that separates patricide, that excludes the line of the descendants from family members who could possibly be involved by it relegating the murder of the child to the case of simple murder, defends all this. There is, of course, a mark of *diminutio* that corresponds to the juridical forces of the sovereign-father[25], just as having foreseen the 'legal bond of adoption' declaims the 'political

---

[22] Who have, at least, obtained legal emancipation of the age of majority.

[23] See *Code civil des Français* (1804), articles 375 ff.

[24] On the limits of assumed Napoleonic 'absolute property' see Lacchè, Luigi: L'espropriazione per pubblica utilità: amministratori e proprietari nella Francia dell'Ottocento. Giuffrè. Milano 1995 and Cavanna, Adriano: Storia del diritto moderno in Europa: le fonti e il pensiero giuridico 2. Giuffrè. Milano 2005, last chapter.

[25] After 1870, the figure of the father and master is once again useful to the project of creating a new anti-liberal order. Battini, Michele: *L'ordine della gerarchia. I contributi reazionari e progressisti alla crisi della democrazia in Francia (1789-1914)*. Bollati Boringhieri. Torino 1995, p. 57.

nature' of the legitimate family, that is recognized by Statute law (it does not matter whether it is natural or adoptive).[26] However, the discipline of patricide defends the whole of the new civil order, through its founding element, because what matters is what is contained in statute law, and it is through the codified system that this order is planned. France of the Corsican Emperor has a new law, but it wishes to have new contents. The form of the law is very important, because it is a means of change, but it also concerns a view towards the future and a hegemonic will. The law of *Ancien Regime* could only care about the present, not having a new world to realise, the modern law (Statute law) orders looking forward.

In conclusion, it is clear that the stabilization of Napoleon was based on the family institution as a basic element of society[27], on a family conceived as central not only symbolically[28] but also as a first effective reference point for the State. It is a game of concentric circles through which the rest of society is built, from the *pater familias*[29], the sovereign of this form of 'little state'. This new centrality of the family, as basis of society which is uniform and without intermediates, contributes partially to the long life of the civil Code of Napoleon.

Moreover, «Regarding this, again, we should note the superiority of the *Code civil* over other possible juridical models. Therefore, dealing with social peace and order, it seems that one had to think rather than taking the *Code penal* as model. However, there are several reasons why this text has been rejected. Especially because, by its very name, the *Code penal*

---

[26] See *Code civil des Fraçais* (1804), articles 343-360.
[27] "Element" and not "body", foundation of society. In Napoleonic strategy, the family is considered an institutional *unicum* that has a rigid hierarchy of roles for functional reasons not as an intrinsically plural 'body', as 'primary society', although hierarchically ordered. The latter is the family model to which the anti-liberal reaction will refer after 1870, see again Battini, *L'ordine della gerarchia*, op. cit., *passim*.
[28] On the family as 'order' and 'stabilization' in classic liberalism, see Costa, Pietro: *Il progetto giuridico. Ricerche sulla giurisprudenza del liberalismo classico. Vol. I: Da Hobbes a Bentham*. Giuffrè. Milano 1974, pp. 317-318.
[29] According to the conclusions in the preliminary speech of Portalis, the main goal of the editors of the code was to «lier les mœurs aux lois, et de propager l'esprit de famille, qui est si favorable, quoi qu'on en dise, à l'esprit de cité» (TN: «link customs to law, and spread the spirit of the family, which is so favourable, no matter what people say, to the spirit of citizenship»); the family is indeed formally absent from the Titles of the *Code civil*, but it is undoubtedly one of the «deux grandes bases» (TN: «two great bases») of a legislative corpus designated to «diriger et à fixer les relations de sociabilité» (TN: «direct and fix the relations of sociability»), see Halpérin, Jean Louis: *Le code civil*. Dalloz. Paris 1996, p. 27.

appeared as the expression of police-law, and not that of social organisation. Then because of the role assigned to it – to repress antisocial behaviour – it will indicate rather what is understood by contrary to order, but not indicate what order is. Equally because, in the humanist-bourgeois concept of law, the penal law is but an extension of civil law. (...) the reference system is not exposed in the *Code penal*, but is in the *Code civil*[30].

The Italian case is profoundly different. In the legislation of the pre-unitary States, behind the apparent uniform reception of the French model, there is an ideological foundation of incrimination directed towards stabilisation, but looking towards the past. Before starting dealing with the crime, Giovanni Carmignani affirms that: «The voice of patricide had sometimes a wider, sometimes a narrower meaning, depending on the habits and the public virtues»[31]. In the political fragmentation of Restoration Italy, after the Napoleonic storm, the strong points able to guide the legislator are tradition on one hand, with the authority of the past, and juridical science on the other. Behind the civil and penal legislation, in the different Italian regional realities, there lies the Roman matrix of the crime of patricide, that sustains the reconstruction of all the murders qualified by family bond. However, «Society loses a citizen by murder as much as by patricide, (...)» underlines Giuseppe Giuliani, criminalist of the Papal States. He continues as follows:

---

[30] «A cet régard, encore, il convient de noter la supériorité du Code civil sur les autres modèles juridiques possibles. Et pourtant, agissant de paix sociale et d'ordre, il semble qu'on eût dût songer plutôt à prendre pour modèle le Code pénal. Mais existe plusieurs raisons qui ont fait écarter ce texte. Tout d'abord parce que, de par son nom même, le Code pénal apparaît comme l'expression du Droit-gendarme, non pas celle de l'organisation sociale. Ensuite parce que, de par le rôle qui lui est assigné – de réprimer les attitudes antisociales – il indiquerait plutôt ce qu'on entend par contraire à l'ordre, mais non pas quel est ce ordre. Egalment parce que, dans la conception humaniste-bourgeoise du Droit, le pénal n'est qu'une extension du civil. (...) il système de référence, lui, n'est pas exposé dans le Code pénal: il l'est dans le Code civil», see Arnaud, André-Jean: *Essai d'analyse structurale du code civil français. La régle du jeu dans la paix bourgeoise.* Lgdj. Paris 1973, p. 13.

[31] «La voce del parricidio ebbe, secondo il vicende dei costumi, e delle pubbliche virtù, ora più esteso ora più stretto significato». Carmignani, Giovanni: *Elementi di diritto criminale.* Francesco Sanvito. Milano 1865, p. 342.

«But (...) what man is more moved by the desire to commit crime than he who holds no respect for common blood? What most savage audaciousness is there in he who changes our friend faith of family affection into a tool of insidiousness and death? Which major difficulty is there in proving a crime, which goes against all presumption of nature, and which for the most part is committed within the impenetrable sanctuary of the domestic walls?»[32]

In Italy, where the power of the legislator is reduced, the jurist of Restoration reappropriates the role of "criminalist builder"[33] of categories and figures, in a context of a law that is transforming and that is even more limited by Statute law and the codified system. In this way, the patricide of the Statute law is defined and specified according to operative mechanisms and to a *modus procedendi* that immediately recalls the case of *crimen laesae maiestatis*[34]. On the model of patricide, archetype of the atrocious crime, is based the several typologies of patricide (i.e. fratricide, filicide and the coniugicide-uxoricide) as well as infanticide and induced abortion, also. They are distinguished, but thought as linked to one another through the bond of family-blood. Throughout Italy, regardless of all regional boundaries, natural blood bond is chosen as a founding element of the penal repression of murders in families. Patricide is presented by legal doctrine starting from the *point of view* of Roman law. It is a method, of course, but the Roman law *incipit* is rather reused and managed for the purpose of a *constitutive* treatment from which the law can start. The choice is therefore made not by chance, but it is useful to highlight the distinctive features of the crime. For everybody, it is the *quality of people* that makes the difference, with respect to the other murders. But, if the *quality of people* is the technical element

---

[32] «La società perde un cittadino nell'omicidio quanto nel parricidio» .... «Ma ... qual uomo più trasportato dal desiderio di delinquere [c'è] di colui, cui non rattiene il rispetto del comun sangue? Quale audacia più ferina di quella, che converte l'amica fede del famigliare affetto in istromento d'insidia e di morte? Qual maggiore difficoltà di quella di provare un delitto, che ha contro di sé la presunzione di natura, e che per lo più si commette nell'asilo impenetrabile delle domestiche mura?». Giuliani, Giuseppe: *Istituzioni di diritto criminale con notizie sullo stato attuale delle legislazioni penali pontificia e toscana.* Tip. Alessandro Mancini. Macerata 1856, vol. II, pp. 245-246.

[33] See Sbriccoli, 'Crimen læsae maiestatis', op. cit.; Lacchè, Luigi: *Latrocinium. Giustizia, scienza penale e repressione del banditismo in antico regime.* Giuffrè. Milano 1988, pp. 83 ff; Pifferi, Michele: Generalia delictorum. *Il 'Tractatus criminalis' di Tiberio Deciani e la "parte generale" di diritto penale.* Giuffrè. Milano 2006, pp. 367 ff.

[34] See Sbriccoli: 'Crimen læsae maiestatis', op. cit.

that specifies the violent action against another human being, which signals that quality is the blood bond.

Basing himself upon Roman law, Carmignani immediately makes several distinctions. The first one concerns the two general categories of the crime of patricide: the 'pure' and the 'impure' crime. Pure patricide is that one which is made on ascendants and descendants, while the impure patricide is made on spouses and on the other people named by the *Lex Pompeja*. But more elements must be considered for the accusation of patricide, since the quality of people «must be deduced only from the natural cognition, not from that one that can come from the positive laws, since the *lex Pompeja* declares to protect only the reasons of blood and nature»[35].

Giuseppe Puccioni clearly and resolutely confirms that if the French situation is considered: «the link that exists between the murderer and the murdered must find its origins in nature, not in Statute law»[36], but Domenico Fois specifies that it is «a bond that unites the legitimate father family»[37]. In other words, in the Italian experience what counts is the juridical nature of the bond and the level of intention of the murderer. The consequence is that those who kill their children or parents can be guilty of patricide, even if they are illegitimate, adulterine or incestuous. The only exception concerns the children of prostitutes because the father cannot be determined and therefore the blood bond is uncertain.

---

[35] «Si dee desumere dalla sola cognizione naturale e non da quella che può derivare dalle leggi positive, perciocchè la legge Pompeja dichiara di proteggere solo le ragioni del sangue e della natura», see Carmignani, *Elementi*, op. cit., pp. 343-344.

[36] «Il vincolo che lega l'uccisore all'ucciso deve avere origine dalla natura e non dalla legge», see Puccioni, Giuseppe: *Saggio di diritto teorico-pratico*, Tip. Luigi Niccolaj. Firenze 1858, p. 444.

[37] «Vincolo di sangue che unisce alla famiglia paterna». In this way Domenico Fois, who wrote just after the Restoration, kept the limits of what was universally recognized as an execrable crime within predetermined canons. The most execrable. What is actually important in his reduction is the introduction of the legitimate family, since it is taken for granted that it is the paternal one. In this way, completely obeying the Pompeja law, the jurist includes in the definition of parricide collaterals and kinsmen till the fourth degree of relationship, father- and mother-in-law, brother- and sister-in-law, stepfather or stepmother, stepson or stepdaughter, and includes in the list of descendants only natural children, that is those belonging to the family, excluding the illegitimate ones. See Fois, Domenico: *Dei delitti e delle pene e della processura criminale*. Dalla stamperia di Giacinto Bonaudo. Genova 1816, p. 159.

In Restoration Italy, lineage, nobility of lineage, and overall integrity of the name are still socially important cultural traits which were never driven away into the past because of the deep and widespread failure to adhere to revolutionary and, later, to Napoleonic ideals. The link with the traditional family, the family of blood has been – and still is – an 'anthropological' trait which variously marked Italian society over the centuries. Ever since national unification, the so called 'familysm', a totally Italian phenomenon, has unified a non-homogeneous and fragmented social fabric. This was possible also thanks to local patronage methods and relationships, different from the more dynamic and competitive relations that were developing in foreign nations. This certainly meant a network of social protection, guaranteed by the very peculiar power of blood relations, but this limited – at the same time – the development of a civic sense and a public conscience committed to the respect of Statute law, all within a panorama of a mature relationship with state institutions. When compared with the plainness of a protective, well-known and very close network, such as the family, the state has always been recognized not so much as a guarantor of rights, rather as an extraneous force, and at times a force of dispossession, whose need was very little understood since the family already provided people with protection. In this way, in Italy, even after the period of the enlightenment, a 'society of families'[38] and not of individuals developed, a society that was 'suspicious' of the State, that represented the common welfare, rather than respectful to it.

Beccaria used to assert that «[t]he family spirit is limited to the little things. The regulator spirit of the republics, master of the main principles, sees the facts and directs them towards the main classes which are important for the welfare of the majority of people»[39]. However, the sedimentation of centuries of legal culture justifies and explains the existence of the 'law of the codes' by limiting the repressive

---

[38] They can already be found in the early modern era, when the apex of the development of humanistic universalism went together with a territory which, lacking a national political representative, was subject to the dominion of *Signorie*, which were both splendid and tyrannical. All the works of Machiavelli describe this.

[39] «Lo spirito di famiglia è uno spirito di dettaglio e limitato a' piccoli fatti. Lo spirito regolatore delle repubbliche, padrone dei principii generali, vede i fatti e gli condensa nelle classi principali ed importanti al bene della maggior parte», see Beccaria, Cesare. *Dei delitti e delle pene*. Einaudi. Torino 1986, § *Dello spirito di famiglia*.

and restoring force of Statute law, also because its rigidity may produce paradoxical effects of impunity.

The Results Encountered in the Dynamics that Follow

Yet Beccaria had warned that «Countries and times of the most atrocious tortures were always those of the most bloody and inhuman actions because the same spirit of ferocity that drove the hand of the legislator, held that of parricide and of the assassin» because, the scholar explained, «it is not the cruelty of punishment, but the infallibility of the sentence» to be a barrier for the crimes.[40]

Following the wave of the Enlightenment, however, nothing much of such rational clearness seems to have passed in the 19th century criminal law legislation in relation to the repression of patricide.

In France, despite the raising of some doubts concerning the infliction of hand amputation, there were no objections among the lawgivers to the imposition of the death penalty for patricide. Moreover, the wording of article 299 does not seem to leave any room for judges to intervene. Indeed, the line of decisions of the criminal chamber of the Court of Cassation is proving quite consistent with the rigours of Statute law. In some cases, even the Court of Cassation (Supreme appellate jurisdiction) brings Statute law to extremes. Its action is carried out on two fronts: on the one hand, the "theory of the loan of crime" («théorie de l'emprunt de crime») aggravating the repression of criminal complicity in patricide[41], affects a number of people not covered by article 299; on the other, the definition of another jurisprudential theory acts, starting from 1838.

From that moment, indeed, the Court of Cassation does not accept the evaluation of the filiation bond between murderer and victim as a simple circumstance of aggravation of wilful murder, and considers it as «a constitutive element of a different crime»[42]. It is useful to remember

---

[40] «I paesi e i tempi dei più atroci supplicii furono sempre quelli delle più sanguinose ed inumane azioni, poiché il medesimo spirito di ferocia che guidava la mano del legislatore, reggeva quella del parricida e del sicario» [perché] « non è la crudeltà delle pene, ma l'infallibilità di esse» ad arrestare il crimine; Beccaria, *Dei delitti e delle pene*, op. cit. § *Dolcezza delle pene.*
[41] *Code pénal* (1810), articles 59, 60, 302.
[42] «Circostance costitutive d'un crime différent», see Bouglé, *La Cour de Cassation*, op. cit., especially pp. 20-26.

that French patricide is only that of the child towards the father, and that in 1832 the reforming law of the penal code intervened in order to point out the need for moderation. Indeed, the French system demonstrates itself to be very rigid by way of equalizing the attempt to the enacted crime[43] and refusing to grant extenuating circumstances in accordance with article 323 regarding the absolute unjustifiable nature of our crime.

A situation that has – as a direct consequence – the fact that inevitably all incriminations end up being the the death penalty and that excessive prosecutions and executions can be avoided only by pardon. Thus, consistently with the centrality of Statute law as primary instrument of government, of judiciary dynamics and of social and criminal phenomena, the solution lies with the *Code progréssif* (28th April 1832).[44] In the initial liberal environment of the July regime, it introduces the possibility of extenuating circumstances for crimes judgeable in the Court of Assizes, including patricide, leaving the task of recognising them or not to juries.[45]

In Italy too, interpretive activity of jurists does not focus on the measure of sentence. Instead, the question of patricide as deserving of the highest penalty is reinforced by the systematic approach of patricide to regicide, in Statute law. Because of this choice, the pre-unification Italian codified system appear rather rigid, except for not equalizing attempts to enacted crime, which distinguishes the Italian experiences

---

[43] The first text of article 2 of the future Napoleonic Penal Code can be found in the Act of 22nd Prairial year IV (10th June 1796), in the middle of post-Thermidor normalization. On this subject see Isotton, Roberto: 'Crimen in itinere'. *Profili della disciplina del tentativo dal diritto comune alle codificazioni penali.* Jovene. Napoli 2006, p. 349 and p. 351-352.

[44] A «code pénal progressif» following the expressions of Chauveau, Adolphe: *Code pénal progressif: commentaire sur la loi modificative du code pénal.* Chez l'ed. au Bureau de la jurisprudence criminelle. Paris 1832.

[45] This Act also deletes stigma, pillory, and any kind of maiming. On the introduction of extenuating circumstances as an act in the gradual trend towards abolition of the death penalty, see Chaveau, Adolphe; Faustin, Hélie: *Teorica del codice penale,* Pedone Lauriel. Napoli 1863, p. 40 ff. (orig. ed.: *Théorie du code penal.* Eduard Legarand. Paris 1843). Before 1832, i.e. in 1824, French legislation had already intervened in the discussion about extenuating circumstances and had extended this opportunity (which was very poor in the *Code pénal,* see article 463) to a greater number of crimes. See Moulin, Patricia: *Le circostanze attenuanti.* In Foucault, Michel (ed.): *Io, Pierre Rivière, avendo sgozzato mia madre, mia sorella e mio fratello...Un caso di parricidio nel XIX secolo.* Einaudi. Torino 1976 pp. 235-241, pp. 36 ff. (org. ed.: *Moi, Pierre Rivière, ayant égorgé ma mère, ma soeur et mon frère (...),* Gallimard. Paris 1973). In France this influenced the 'reallocation' of repressive power, which passed from the judges to the political-legislative power during the Revolution.

from the French model. However, in the Italian debate the prospect of legislative reform is not considered at all, because there is a different way of intervening on the rigidity of the system of patricide (as well as on criminal law in general). In point of fact, once the Statute law is issued, the slow interpretive work of the jurists, who are university professors and often lawyers, is that which re-shapes the matter at trial level, reconfiguring its substance.

Exemplary is the case of the Papal States. Its penal Code has the widest extent of incrimination. Yet, the observation of trials shows a significant quantitative difference between the number of formal charges (many), the number of reductions of charge in other crimes as well as the number of death sentences carried out (very few).[46] All this could seem to contradict a penal policy clearly aimed at punishing with the maximum possible force, considering the extent of the family circle involved in the law. However, the apparent contradiction becomes a clarifying clue.

The gap between charges and beheading carried out urges two reflections upon us: the first is true demands of justice. It is not difficult to imagine how many problems of public order there would be by adding up the capital punishments for patricide with those for all other capital offenses.[47] Despite the 19th century being the century that in Italy, as throughout Europe, finally abolishes the death penalty, until it was adopted, it was practiced – almost to its end – publicly with the old display of spectacular rituals.[48] The second consideration – that it is more interesting here – is the one that an important element of the phenomenon is the distance between declaration of the death penalty and effectiveness of the execution, more than that between incrimination and sentence. Paying attention to this, it becomes clear how this difference is a deeply significant transformation of the law into force (and even more so in a country that presents tremendous ambiguity and

---

[46] For details of this reconstruction, see Contigiani, Ninfa: *Il crimine di parricidio nel XIX secolo*. In «Materiali per una storia della cultura giuridica» (2007) No. XXXVII-1, especially pp. 42-45.

[47] See Lascoumes; Poncela; Lenoel, *Au nome de l'ordre*, op. cit., pp. 189-191.

[48] However, it is necessary to point out that executions are becoming an independent field, because they are considered surplus to the shame brought on by the publicity of the debates and by the sentence. In short, at one point the execution is not strictly necessary anymore, see Foucault, Michel: *Surveiller et punir. Naissance de la prison*, Gallimard. Paris 1975, p. 15.

misgivings towards the acceptance of written law and codified system, as was that of Pope Gregory XVI).

Indeed, it could have been very difficult «to conceive a justice in which the judiciary would say no right, no longer claimed, through its judgments, a hierarchy of values»[49] without moving the declaration of values into the rigidity of the form of Statute law, with a criminal justice policy that was especially a threatening statement, in accordance with that which was a common feature of the Italian Restoration. This gap does not allow abandoning the ductility of the *Ius commune* and all its forms because it leaves the legal culture of judges and lawyers the possibility to act for the better, above and beyond the written law itself. However, perhaps we can read 'Statute law' as the conclusion of an autonomous and separate development rather than a development of the traditional law. In this way, as far as pre-unitary Italian experience is concerned, we can understand how it was possible to leave the task of 'declaring' values and principles of the social order to the new Statute law. Thus, in our case Statute law affirms the absolute inviolability of family bonds, while justice of the courts describes the complex reality of domestic murders.

In a sense, we can recognize the practice of a gain which comes after the linguistic philosophy (and the theory of linguistic acts), according to which «in some conditions, the reality is really 'constituted', rather than only 'reflected' by the act of language: on one hand, an act of enunciation, on the other, a social reaction»[50]. In our case, the death penalty pronounced by Statute law is a juridical language act as the sentence is one of the judiciary language. This really is as good as a reflexion of quantitatively relevant criminal data to which the penal policy replies with repressive harshness. However, the non effectiveness of the penalty (which is achieved by commutations, reductions and cancellations through sovereign pardon) is the social reaction, meaning that the social intolerableness of that linguistic-judiciary act brings it back to the old and plural forms of law. So, even for the most part of the 19th

---

[49] «Concepire una giustizia nella quale l'apparato giudiziario non dicesse più il diritto, non affermasse più, attraverso i suoi giudizi, una gerarchia di valori», see De Kerchove, Michel: *Quand dire c'est punir. Essai sur le jugement pénal.* Faculté universitaires Saint-Luis. Bruxelles 2005, p. 23 and *passim.*

[50] «A certe condizioni la realtà si trova veramente 'costituita' piuttosto che solamente 'riflessa' dall'atto del linguaggio: un atto di enunciazione da un lato, ma reazione sociale dall'altro », see Kerchove, *Quand dire c'est punir*, op. cit., p. 18 and *passim.*

century, while in France the force of Statute law and codified system is definitely central, on the contrary, in the Italian peninsula all forms of law (both modern and past) still have much influence and power.

Zigeunerrecht und Zigeunergericht: Zur Fortwirkung überlieferter archaischer Konfliktbewältigungsformen in der Gegenwart am Beispiel des *Romani Kris*

Dóra Frey

1. Einleitung

In meinem Beitrag möchte ich über die Konfliktbewältigungsformen bei den Zigeunergruppen in Ungarn berichten. Diese Frage wurde bislang eher aus ethnographischer als aus juristischer Sicht erforscht. Die meisten Untersuchungen bezüglich dieses Themas stammen aus der Zwischen-kriegszeit oder unmittelbaren Nachkriegszeit.[1] Vor wenigen Jahren begannen auch Rechtssoziologen, sich damit zu befassen, darunter der früh verstorbene Wissenschaftler Sándor Loss.[2]

Die Zahl der in Ungarn lebenden Zigeuner ist sehr schwer festzustellen, da die offizielle staatliche Registrierung der ethnischen Herkunft oder Zugehörigkeit in Ungarn gesetzlich untersagt ist und diesbezügliche Angaben bei den Volkszählungen freiwillig sind. Bei der letzten Volkszählung 2001 haben 190.000 ungarische Staatsbürger sich als Zigeuner bezeichnet, von denen 48.700 explizit angaben, dass Ungarisch nicht ihre Muttersprache sei.[3] Von sozialwissenschaftlicher Seite wurden diese Zahlen wiederholt als unzuverlässig kritisiert (viele wollen die eigene Herkunft oder Zugehörigkeit aus Angst oder Scheu nicht preisgeben) und haben eigene Erhebungs- und Schätzungsmethoden entwickelt, obwohl auch darüber keine Einigkeit besteht, wer überhaupt als Zigeuner zu betrachten ist.

Eine Untersuchung aus dem Jahr 2003 schätzte die Zahl der Zigeuner auf 540.000 (was etwa 5,3 % der Gesamtbevölkerung entspricht).[4] Diese

---

[1] Die Zeitschriften Ethnographia und Néprajzi Közlemények enthalten einige Artikel be-züglich dieses Themas.

[2] Loss, Sándor: Romani kris a dél-békési oláhcigányoknál. Elmélet és gyakorlat. (*Romani Kris* bei den Oláh-Zigeunern in Süd-Békés. Theorie und Praxis) In: Ius humanum. Ember alkot-ta jog. Hrsg.: Szabó, Miklós, Miskolc, 2001, S. 9-22; S. 10.

[3] Dupcsik, Csaba: A magyarországi cigányság története (Die Geschichte der Zigeuner in Ungarn), Budapest, 2009, S. 273.

[4] Kemény, István – Janky, Béla – Lengyel, Gabriella: A magyarországi cigányság 1971-2003. (Zigeuner in Ungarn 1971-2003) Budapest, 2004, S. 11-12.

Zahl wird verlässlich erachtet, da bei der Berechnung auch berücksichtigt wurde, wer sich zwar nicht für einen Zigeuner hält, aber von seinem Umfeld als solcher betrachtet wird. Die regionalen Unterschiede in der Verteilung der Zigeunerbevölkerung sind sehr stark. So gibt es eine Vielzahl von Gemeinden (vor allem kleinere Dörfer), in denen Zigeuner die Mehrheit stellen und auch solche, in denen ausschließlich Zigeuner wohnen.

Dabei ist seit Beginn des 20. Jahrhunderts insofern eine grundlegende Veränderung der traditionellen Lebensform der Zigeuner zu beobachten, als die meisten von ihnen heute sesshaft sind.[5] Allerdings haben sich auch unter diesen neuen Bedingungen bestimmte Traditionen, wie etwa die traditionellen Konfliktbewältigungsformen, erhalten. Insgesamt ist das Bild der Zigeuner in Ungarn überaus heterogen: sowohl in kultureller als auch in sozialer Hinsicht bestehen große Unterschiede, und auch mit Blick auf Herkunft und Sprache herrscht Vielfalt.[6]

Die größte Gruppe, die so genannten *Romungros*, sind stark assimiliert, sprechen Ungarisch als Muttersprache und haben die Verbindungen zu ihren Traditionen weitgehend verloren – viele von ihnen halten sich für Ungarn und wehren sich vehement gegen eine Einstufung als Zigeuner.

Daneben gibt es eine erhebliche Zahl von Zigeunern, die noch einen Dialekt der Sprache Romani sprechen und einen mehr oder weniger starken Bezug zu ihren Traditionen haben: die *Oláh-Zigeuner*. Diese Gruppe kann als *Roma* bezeichnet werden und bezeichnet sich auch selbst oft so,[7] (in eigener Sprache: *rom*). Die *Oláh*-Zigeuner gliedern sich in mehrere Untergruppen (in der Fachliteratur schwankt ihre Zahl zwischen 10-12 Untergruppen; je nachdem, ob größere und heterogene Gruppen als Einheit betrachtet oder ob sie als zwei verschiedenen Untergruppen beschrieben werden). Die bedeutendste und am besten erforschte Untergruppe der *Oláh*-Zigeuner sind die so genannten *Lovári*-Zigeuner, die neben der Sprache (Lovarisch – ein Dialekt des Romani) auch ihre Traditionen in größtem Umfang beibehalten haben.

Eine dritte Gruppe der ungarischen Zigeuner, die so genannten *Beás*-Zigeuner bilden eine völlig eigene Kategorie. Sie sprechen eine archaische Version der rumänischen Sprache und unterscheiden sich von

---

[5] Fraser, Sir Angus: A cigányok (Die Zigeuner), Budapest, 1996, S. 287.
[6] Eine detaillierte soziologische Beschreibung: Kemény István (Hrsg.): A magyarországi romák (Die ungarischen Roma). Budapest, 2000.
[7] Dupcsik, zit. S. 278.

den restlichen Zigeunergruppen erheblich, sowohl sprachlich als auch in kultureller Hinsicht.

Es ist also schwer, allgemein über „die Zigeuner" zu sprechen. Die unterschiedlichen Teilgruppen sind ihrerseits unterschiedlich intensiv erforscht. Während über das Rechtsleben der *Beás*-Zigeuner, das sich wesentlich von den anderen Zigeunergruppen unterscheidet, bis heute nur lückenhafte Erkenntnisse vorliegen, sind die *Oláh*-Zigeuner – vor allem die bedeutenden *Lovári*-Zigeuner – vielseitig untersucht worden. Zu ihnen existieren, sowohl aus ethnographischer als auch aus soziologischer Sicht, viele Studien.

Angesichts dieses Umstands werde ich mich im Folgenden auf die Beschreibung der Konfliktbewältigungsmethoden der so genannten *Oláh*-Zigeuner konzentrieren. Wenn nachfolgend anstelle des in Deutschland eingebürgerten Begriffs der *Sinti* und *Roma* konsequent das Wort „Zigeuner" gebraucht wird, so trägt dies dem Umstand Rechnung, dass diese Minderheit in Ungarn offiziell so heißt und sie in der soziologischen und ethnographischen Fachliteratur auch so bezeichnet wird. Demgegenüber dient der Begriff „Zigeuner" weitgehend als Selbstbe-zeichnung der Betroffenen (die *Beás*-Zigeuner bezeichnen sich ausschließlich so) und wird auch nicht als abwertend empfunden – oder zumindest nicht abwertender als andere Bezeichnungen. Überdies ist die Bezeichnung „*Sinti* und *Roma*" mit Bezug auf Ungarn ethnographisch nicht korrekt, da in Ungarn keine *Sinti* leben, und nicht alle Zigeuner *Roma* sind – die bedeutendste Ausnahme bilden die *Beás*-Zigeuner.[8]

Bei der Untersuchung von rechtlichen Gewohnheiten und Konfliktbewältigungsregeln muss auf die stark von der Mehrheitsbevölkerung abweichende soziale und gesellschaftliche Lage der Zigeuner hingewiesen werden. Da die Zigeuner von der Mehrheitsgesellschaft während der ganzen Zeit des Zusammenlebens als Fremdkörper betrachtet und behandelt wurden, blieben sie außerhalb der gesellschaftlichen und staatlichen Strukturen.[9] Sie empfanden sich selbst auch als Außenseiter und entwickelten ihre eigenen Methoden für die Lösung von internen Konflikten. Obwohl die in Ungarn lebenden

---

[8] In diesem Zusammenhang ist jedoch anzumerken, dass sich die *Oláh*-Zigeuner öfter als *Roma* bezeichnen.Über die Diskussion der Bezeichnung: Dupcsik, zit. S. 278.
[9] Die Zigeuner lebten und leben oft auch räumlich von der Mehrheitsbevölkerung getrennt, am Rande oder neben den Siedlungen.

Zigeuner seit relativ langer Zeit sesshaft sind,[10] haben sie ihre sehr archaische, auf Stämmen aufbauende Gesellschaftsstruktur, weitgehend bis in die Gegenwart bewahrt. Dazu kommt die herausragende Bedeutung der Sippe in der patriarchalisch organisierten Familienstruktur. Neben diesen internen Faktoren sind auch die Beziehungen zum Rest der Gesellschaft bzw. das Fehlen von Kontakten zu dieser ausschlaggebend. So trug die ablehnende Haltung der Mehrheitsgesellschaft entscheidend dazu bei, dass die Zigeunergemeinschaft durch einen engen Zusammenhalt und eine starke Geschlossenheit gekennzeichnet ist.[11] Die Mitglieder einer Gemeinschaft waren sehr stark aufeinander angewiesen, dies machte die schnelle und effektive Lösung der aufgetretenen Konflikte unabdingbar.

2. Die Beziehungen zwischen den Zigeuner und der Justiz

Diese Faktoren führten auch zu dem gespaltenen Verhältnis der Zigeuner zu den staatlichen Justizorganen; dieses ist aus Sicht der Zigeuner durch starkes Misstrauen und eine intensive Angst vor dem Unbekannten geprägt.[12] Dieses Misstrauen verbunden mit den Traditionen der Zigeunergemeinschaften hatte zur Folge, dass die innerhalb der Gruppe entstandenen Konflikte bis Mitte des 20. Jahrhunderts – und in einigen Fällen bis heute – nicht „nach außen" getragen wurden und werden. Unter den Zigeunern besteht keine Bereitschaft, sich an die Polizei oder an die Gerichte zu wenden. Es ist bis heute ein Zeichen für die Eskalation eines Konflikts, wenn Zigeuner einander bei Behörden anzeigen. So erklärt sich auch die Unterrepräsentanz von Zigeunern in Zivilsachen. Obwohl darüber aus Datenschutzgründen keine Statistik geführt werden darf, fällt auf, dass Zigeuner kaum als Streitpartei auftreten,[13] wozu neben der genannten

---

[10] Eine Untersuchung im Jahre 1893 zeigte, dass nur etwa 3 % der Zigeuner in Ungarn nicht sesshaft war. Dupcsik, zit. S. 71.

[11] Tárkány Szűcs, Ernő: Magyar jogi népszokások (Rechtliche Volksbräuche in Ungarn) Budapest, 1981, S. 49.

[12] Loss, Sándor–H. Szilágyi, István: A „cigány per". In: Beszélő 2001/4. S. 94-100; S. 96.

[13] Da keine Statistik über die Abstammung der Parteien in Zivilsachen oder über die ethnische Zugehörigkeit der Angeklagten und Zeugen im Strafverfahren geführt werden darf, ist es schwer zu bestimmen, wie viele Zigeuner vor Gericht erscheinen. Zugleich stellt sich

Skepsis gegenüber justiziellen Institutionen auch wirtschaftliche und bildungsbedingte Faktoren beitragen.[14]

Erschwerend hinzu kommt ein weitgehendes Desinteresse der staatlichen Organe für die Binnenkonflikte der Zigeuner. Eventuelle Straftaten interessierten die Behörden früher nur in den Fällen, in denen auch Nicht-Zigeuner betroffen waren; jenseits dessen vertraten die Behörden den (halb-)offiziellen Standpunkt, dass sie es „untereinander regeln sollen".[15] Außerdem zeigen die Justizbehörden bis heute erhebliche Schwächen, wenn es um Konflikte geht, in die Zigeuner involviert sind. Bedingt durch kulturelle und sprachliche Probleme ist dieses Verhältnis von gegenseitigem Unverständnis und Misstrauen geprägt. Auf Seiten der staatlichen Behörden gelten Zigeuner als besonders schwierige „Kunden", weil sie die Fachsprache nicht beherrschen bzw. zum Teil nur sehr eingeschränkt verstehen, und ihr Rechts- und Gerechtigkeitsverständnis überdies signifikant von dem der Juristen abweicht.

Ende der 1990er Jahre begann eine Forschungsgruppe, bestehend aus Dozenten und Studenten der Universität *Miskolc*, damit, Strafprozesse mit Beteiligten zigeunerischer Herkunft im ungarischen Komitat *Borsod-Abaúj-Zemplén* (nach Schätzungen leben in dieser Region anteilsmäßig die meisten Zigeuner) wissenschaftlich auf möglichst breiter Basis zu erfassen; durch diese Studie konnten zahlreiche frühere Vermutungen, die bis dahin nicht wissenschaftlich belegt waren, verifiziert werden.

In diesem Rahmen wurde beispielsweise festgestellt, dass die zu Prozessen als Angeklagte oder als Zeugen geladenen Zigeuner sowohl durch ihr betont respektvolles Auftreten gegenüber dem Gericht als auch ihr Bemühen auffallen, sich der Gelegenheit angemessen zu kleiden. Dass die Bekleidung trotz des eindeutigen Bemühens oft auffällt,

---

dabei das Problem der Bestimmung: Wer kann und soll als Zigeuner betrachtet werden? Und nach welchen Kriterien soll diese Zuordnung erfolgen? Soll die Sprache den entscheidenden Ausschlag geben, oder eher, ob sich eine Person selbst als Zigeuner bezeichnet bzw. von seinem sozialen Umfeld als solcher identifiziert wird? Unter den traditionell lebenden Lovári-Zigeuner herrscht die Auffassung, dass nur diejenigen als Zigeuner gelten, die nach dem *Romani Kris*, dem so genannten Zigeunergesetz, leben. (Aussage von Ernő Glonzi, Interview am 26. April 2008.)

[14] Loss – H. Szilágyi, zit. S. 94.

[15] Erdős, Kamill: Cigány-törvényszék (Romani-Kris) (Zigeunergericht – Romani Kris) In: Néprajzi Közlemények. 1959. 203-214. S. 204 Neuauflage: Erdős Kamill cigánytanulmányai. Hrsg.: Vekerdi, József; Békéscsaba, 1989. S. 98-105.

resultiert daraus, dass in den traditionell lebenden Zigeunergemeinden eine andere Vorstellung von ordnungs- und gelegenheitsgemäßer Kleidung herrscht als dies bei der Mehrheit der Bevölkerung der Fall ist. Trotz dieser offen-kundigen Bereitschaft zur Kooperation ergeben sich bei Verhören immer wieder Verständigungsprobleme der Art, dass den Zigeunern das juristische Fachvokabular nicht geläufig ist und sie die verschiedenen abstrakten Termini und Fremdwörter dementsprechend miss- oder gar nicht verstehen. Ein anschauliches Beispiel für solch eine Diskrepanz zwischen dem Begriffsverständnis der Zigeuner und der Verwendung durch das Justizpersonal ist, dass Zigeuner auf die Frage nach ihrem Familienstand oft mit Nennung der Zahl ihrer Kinder antworten. Die juristischen Fachbegriffe bereiten den meisten Zigeunern Schwierigkeiten, weil es ihnen schlicht am Umgang mit diesen Begriffen mangelt. Diese Unzulänglichkeiten mit dem allgemein niedrigen Bildungsstand unter Zigeunern zusammen und werden durch die von ihnen gesprochene Regionalsprache noch verstärkt, was zu Missverständnisse führt. Dass der fehlende Umgang mit den Begriffen maßgeblich zu den Irritationen beiträgt, zeigt sich auch daran, dass sich die Kommunikation mit bereits Vorbestraften wesentlich einfacher gestaltet, weil diese Personengruppe „besser Bescheid" weiß. Insbesondere bei ehemaligen Häftlingen ist ein besseres Verständnis der Fachsprache zu beobachten, wenngleich sie dem Gericht oft weniger Respekt entgegen bringen.[16]

Die in den '90er Jahren eingeführte Robe für Richter, Staatsanwälte und Anwälte hat nach den Beobachtungen das richterliche Ansehen unter Zigeunern erhöht; wirkte aber auf viele auch beängstigend. Mehrere, zumeist ältere Zeugen hielten sie wegen der Bekleidung für Priester. Die Mitwirkung von Schöffen, obgleich diese in aller Regel völlig passiv sind, erhöhte durch die bloße Anwesenheit bei den Zigeunern das Prestige des Gerichts. Der Grund hierfür liegt darin, dass die meisten Schöffen zur älteren Generationen gehören, da vor allem Rentner diese Funktion ausüben.[17] Unter Zigeunern genießen ältere Menschen ein wesentlich höheres Ansehen als in der übrigen Gesellschaft; ihnen wird mit Achtung und Respekt begegnet und an den traditionellen Konfliktbewältigungs-methoden nehmen vor allem ältere Mitglieder der Gemeinschaft teil.

---

[16] Loss – H. Szilágyi, zit. S. 97.
[17] Loss – H. Szilágyi, zit. S. 97.

Aber auch mit Blick auf die Bewertung von Straftaten bestehen merkliche Differenzen zwischen der Rechtslage und der mehrheitlichen Rechtsauffassung einerseits und dem Gerechtigkeitsempfinden der Zigeuner andererseits. Aufgrund dieser Unterschiede ist es mitunter ausgesprochen schwierig – so die oft zu hörende Klage der Richter und Staatsanwälte –, wahrheitsgemäße Aussagen zum Tathergang zu erhalten, da sich Zigeuner, von einigen wenigen Ausnahmen abgesehen, weigern, gegeneinander auszusagen.[18] Das gilt umso mehr, wenn im Gerichtsaal viele Zigeuner anwesend sind; unter diesen Umständen richten die Aussagenden ihre Aussagen weniger an die Richter, als vielmehr an die anderen Anwesenden. Während der Studien in Miskolc machte man die Erfahrung, dass, wenn sehr viele Zuhörer oder Beteiligte in Raum waren, es oft schwer war, die Ordnung aufrecht zu erhalten, da sich die anderen Anwesenden ebenfalls – zumeist lautstark – äußerten und versuchten, die Befragung nicht auf den Richter, die Angeklagten und Zeugen zu beschränken, sondern alle im Gerichtssaal Anwesenden an einem „Gespräch" zu beteiligen.

Aufgrund der genannten Faktoren erweisen sich die Zigeuner in vielfältiger Hinsicht als „Problemfälle" für Richter und Staatsanwälte, da Selbstverständlichkeiten gerichtlicher Verhandlungen gerade nicht vorausgesetzt werden können. Oft muss etwa die Anklage erläuternd „übersetzt" werden, weil sie den Angeklagten unverständlich ist. Und auch die anderen Probleme etwa mit Aussagen und Zeugenverhören erschweren die Kommunikation. Dabei stoßen Eigenheiten wie zum Beispiel der Umstand, dass Zigeuner nicht gegeneinander aussagen, bei Richtern auf Unverständnis und werden als „Flause" gedeutet.[19]

Ein zusätzliches Hindernis für die den korrekten Ablauf justizieller Verfahren besteht darin, dass Zigeuner keine Strafverteidiger beauftragen können und deswegen die Verteidigung von Pflichtverteidiger übernommen bzw. in vielen Fällen gar nicht übernommen wird. Dieses Problem, die Zigeuner mit anderen Personen der unteren gesellschaftlichen, wirtschaftlich schlechter gestellten Schichten teilen, hat die paradoxe Folge, dass sich durch den schlechten Ruf der Pflichtverteidiger das Ansehen des Gerichts noch erhöht: die Angeklagten haben mehr Vertrauen zum Gericht als zum eigenen Verteidiger.

---

[18] Loss – H. Szilágyi, zit. S. 95.
[19] Loss – H. Szilágyi, zit. S. 97.

3. Besonderheiten des Rechtsverständnisses von Zigeunern

Neben den bereits erwähnten Unterschieden im Rechtsverständnis weicht häufig auch das Lebensbild der Zigeuner von dem der Mehrheitsbevölkerung ab und kann vom wissenschaftlichen Standpunkt aus – mit aller gebotenen Vorsicht in der Wortwahl – als archaisch bezeichnet werden. Im Rahmen dieses archaischen Systems diente früher der Ausschluss aus der Gruppe als schwerste, wenngleich äußerst selten verhängte „Strafe", was sich in der bis heute anhaltenden zentralen Rolle von Anerkennung durch und Stellung in der Gruppe widerspiegelt. Dadurch, dass nur diejenigen in der Gemeinschaft akzeptiert werden, die sich an die Regeln (die Normen der Gruppe und nicht die allgemeinen Gesetze) halten, war eine konformistische Haltung unbedingt notwendig. Auch sehr streng wurde die Familienehre, insbesondere die Ehre von Frauen, gewahrt. Bei allen Konflikten war es das oberste Ziel, die Wiederherstellung der Gerechtigkeit zu gewährleisten. Dies erforderte schnelle und effektive Lösungsmethoden, damit das Zusammenleben in der Gruppe keine anhaltende Störung erfuhr. Auch in Prozessen vor den staatlichen Justizorganen kommt es vor, dass das Geschehen so dargestellt wird – vor allem durch Zeugenaussagen –, dass nicht der Täter nach dem Tatbestand des Strafgesetzbuches verurteilt wird, sondern derjenige, der nach dem Verständnis der Zigeuner verantwortlich ist. Darüber hinaus kommt es auch vor, dass der Ehemann die eigene Ehefrau vor Gericht wissentlich zu Unrecht beschuldigt und falsch gegen sie aussagt, um auch für die Frau eine Verurteilung und Gefängnishaft zu erwirken. Auf diese Weise soll sicher gestellt werden, dass die Frau ihren Mann während seines Gefängnisaufenthaltes weder betrügen noch verlassen kann.[20] Entgegen aller gegenteiligen Mutmaßungen war die innere Konfliktlösung der Zigeunergruppen nur selten auf Blutrache angelegt[21] und sogar körperliche Strafen wurden möglichst gemieden. Zwar waren Racheakte natürlich nicht ausgeschlossen, allerdings wurden diese oft unter Beteiligung der ganzen Gruppe vollzogen. Die schwersten

---

[20] Loss – H. Szilágyi, zit. S. 98.

[21] Zur Blutrache bei den *Kaale*-Zigeunern in Finnland siehe: A finn „kaale" cigányok közösségi joga, a „vérbosszú" modell. (Gemeinschaftsrecht der finnischen „*Kaale*-Zigeuner", das Modell der Blutrache) In: Belügyi Szemle 1999. 7-8. S. 134-144.

Konflikte führten oft zu generationsübergreifenden Fehden. Diese Fehden werden seit geraumer Zeit aber nicht mehr von den Sippen geführt; in den letzten zwei Jahrhunderten handelt es sich vielmehr um Taten von Einzelnen oder höchstens von Familien.[22] Auch noch in den 1940er Jahren kam es in Komitat *Békés* zu Mord als Rache für ein früheres Tötungsdelikt. Die Täter und Opfer waren Mitglieder einer Großfamilie, die seit Generationen zerstritten war: Der Täter und das Opfer waren Cousins, der Vater des Opfers tötete vor mehr als einem Jahrzehnt den Vater des Täters.[23]

Derart drastische Taten blieben jedoch die Ausnahme. Denn das ganze System der Konfliktlösungsmethoden hat vielmehr zum Ziel, die Integrität der Gruppe zu wahren und ein friedliches Miteinander zu ermöglichen. Würde durch gegenseitige Vergeltung und Rache der Frieden einer Gemeinschaft dauerhaft gestört, so könnten die oben genannten Ziele nicht erreicht werden. Nicht zuletzt deshalb war es unerlässlich, die Konfliktlösungsmodelle schnell und effektiv zu gestalten, damit eventuelle Streitigkeiten rasch beseitigt wurden und das sehr enge Zusammenleben der Mitglieder der Gemeinschaft friedlich weitergeführt werden konnte.

Die internen Konfliktbewältigungsmethoden wurden durch die gesellschaftlichen Verhältnisse der Zigeuner geprägt. Die Zigeunersippen und -stämme sind gekennzeichnet durch einen engen Zusammenhalt und ein stark patriarchalisch ausgerichtetes Familienbild. Die alten Mitglieder der Gruppe genießen besonderen Respekt und Achtung. Privatsphäre und Privatleben gab es kaum, alle Probleme wurden in der ganzen Gruppe bekannt und ausdiskutiert, wobei diese Diskussionen in aller Regel zu einer Lösung der aufgetretenen Konflikte führten.[24] Die Zigeunergruppen blieben wegen der gesellschaftlichen Verhältnisse als sehr enge Gemeinschaften erhalten: die Zigeuner konnten sich in die Mehrheitsge-sellschaft nicht integrieren bzw. wurden dort nicht oder nur partiell aufgenommen. So waren sie sehr stark aufeinander angewiesen und konnten nur in der eigenen Gemeinschaft leben. Damit ist es zu erklären, dass der oben erwähnte Ausschluss aus der Gemeinschaft, als

---

[22] Tárkány Szűcs, zit. S. 494.
[23] László, Péter: Vérbosszú a magyarországi cigányok között (Blutrache unter den ungarischen Zigeunern) In: Etnographia 1947. S. 348.
[24] Tárkány Szűcs, zit. S. 494.

schwerste Strafform, trotz oder auch wegen seines archaischen Charakters in den Zigeunergruppen beibehalten wurde.

Dementsprechend, wie auch in der frühen Phase des germanischen Rechts, kommt der Ausschluss aus der Sippe einem Todesurteil gleich: allein war damals niemand lebens- und/ oder wehrfähig und somit der Umwelt völlig ausgeliefert. Bei den Zigeunern hatten diese Verhältnisse lange Zeit Bestand; die Gruppe leistete Schutz und sicherte die Versorgung in der Not. Damit ist der sehr starke Zusammenhalt der Gruppen zu erklären – dieser Zusammenhalt ist und war unter allen Umständen zu wahren, weswegen sich auch die schnellen und effektiven Konfliktlösungsmodelle entwickelt haben.

Zur Schlichtung der Konflikte nutzten die Zigeuner weder staatlich organisierte Gewalt noch eigens dafür vorgesehene Strukturen. Stattdessen wurden die Alten oder andere angesehene Familienoberhäupter zur Schlichtung der Konflikte berufen. So gab es in vielen Gemeinden eine Riege alter Männer, die immer wieder als Richter oder Schlichter berufen wurden. Im Gegensatz zu der bis heute verbreiteten Meinung waren die *Woiwoden* aber keine Richter in der Zigeunergemeinschaft.[25] Sie waren nicht einmal formelle Obmänner, sondern übernahmen die Rolle eines Sprechers der Zigeuner, um die Kommunikation mit der Mehrheitsbevölkerung zu erleichtern.[26] Wobei diese Rolle ihrerseits natürlich nicht ausschloss, dass ein *Woiwode* gelegentlich als Vermittler in Konflikten auftreten konnte, insbesondere weil der Posten des *Woiwoden* stets von einem angesehenen und vermögenden Mitglied der Gemeinschaft übernommen wurde.[27]

Das „Verfahren" zur Streitbeilegung verlief schnell, informell und kaum institutionalisiert; die Ergebnisse wurden zumeist akzeptiert und auch ohne zwingende Gewalt befolgt. Dies ist damit zu erklären, dass die Gruppenmitglieder nur dann durch die Gruppe akzeptiert wurden, wenn sie sich an die Regeln hielten – hierzu zählte auch, dass die Ergebnisse der Schlichtung von Konflikten akzeptiert werden mussten. Die „Richter" waren auch Mitglieder der Gruppe und zwar solche Mitglieder, denen man Vertrauen entgegengebrachte. Die „Urteile" oder

---

[25] Erdős, zit. S. 210.

[26] Zur Diskussion über die Stellung der *Woiwoden*: Dupcsik, zit. S. 45.

[27] Die begriffliche Verwirrung bezüglich der *Woiwoden* wird überdies dadurch verstärkt, dass auch die Nichtzigeuner, die mit der Aufsicht der Zigeunergemeinden und dem Eintreiben der Steuern von ihnen beauftragt waren, als *Woiwode* bezeichnet wurden.

Lösungsvorschläge wurden deshalb nicht als Machtinstrument wahrgenommen, sondern eher als „guter Rat", der den Konflikt beendete. In die Konfliktlösung wurden relativ viele Mitglieder der Gruppe einbezogen; diese starke Einbeziehung der Gemeinschaft hatte, im Gegensatz zu den heutigen Strafverfahren vor der ungarischen Justiz, den Effekt, dass sich die Streitparteien als Beteiligte und nicht als Gegenstand des Verfahrens fühlten. Das Urteil kam damit aus den „eigenen Reihen" und seine Einhaltung wurde von der ganzen Gruppe überwacht.

Diese informellen Verfahrens- und Vermittlungsweisen waren bei allen Zigeunergruppen bekannt und sind in Ansätzen bis in die Gegenwart erhalten. Vor allem bei Angelegenheiten, die Fragen der Ehre berühren werden Schlichter eingesetzt, wobei diese Schlichtungsverfahren in der tradierten Form praktiziert werden und auch bei den in Städten lebenden und wohlhabenden Zigeunern zur Anwendung kommen. Im Folgenden möchte ich eine relativ formalisierte und feste Verfahrensweise der *Lovári*-Zigeuner, das *Romani Kris*, vorstellen.

4. Das Romani Kris – Zigeunergesetz und Zigeunergericht

4.1. Der Begriff des Romani Kris

Der Begriff *Romani Kris* (auf *Lovárisch* bedeutet das Wort Zigeunerrecht und Zigeunergericht) besitzt zwei Bedeutungen: zum einen bezieht er sich auf das „Gericht" und die dort stattfindende Verhandlung; zum anderen wird darunter das Gesetz der Zigeuner, d.h. die Gesamtheit der Regeln, die ein Mitglied der Zigeunergemeinschaft befolgen muss, gefasst. Das *Kris* ist ein spezielles und vergleichsweise formalisiertes Verfahrens- und Regelwerk, das bei den *Lovári*-Zigeunern existierte und in Teilen bis heute besteht. Heute beherrschen schätzungsweise 50.000 – 100.000 Personen die *lovárische* Sprache und halten teilweise noch an den traditionellen Lebensformen fest. Als Roma – so bezeichnen sie sich in ihrer eigenen Sprache – gilt nur, wer nach dem Zigeunergesetz, dem „*Romani Kris*", lebt. Die meisten nach den Traditionen lebenden *Lovári*-Zigeuner leben in Südostungarn, vor allem im Komitat *Békés*, ihre traditionelle Beschäftigung war der Pferdehandel, viele leben auch heute noch davon. Hier wie aber auch im Ausland lebt die Tradition des

Romani Kris bis heute fort, wie die Forschungen von Sándor Loss belegen.[28]

Ein *Kris* ist weder ein Straf- noch ein Zivilgericht im eigentlichen Sinne, da es allgemein schwer ist, die vor Gericht verhandelten Streitigkeiten in juristische Kategorien einzuordnen. Es ist etwa zuständig für Handelsstreitigkeiten – heutzutage machen diese die Mehrzahl der Fälle aus, die im Zuge des Handels mit Pferden oder Gebrauchtwagen auftreten, nach juristischer Terminologie etwa Haftungsklagen. Im Komitat *Békés* betreiben auch noch heute sehr viele Zigeuner Pferdehandel und bestreiten damit ihren Lebensunterhalt. Deshalb beziehen sich die meisten der dort aufgezeichneten Beispiele auf diese Art von Streitigkeiten.

Auch für Fragen von Betrug, Fälschung oder Diebstahl, die nach unserem Verständnis zum Strafrecht gehören, ist das *Kris* zuständig. Der zweite Bereich, in dem ein Kris tätig werden kann, ist das Familienrecht, vor allem Fälle von Brautentführung und Ehebruch. Es besteht bis heute und wird in Zivilsachen sowie bei Straftaten mit geringer Schwere oft angewandt, anstatt eine Anzeige bei den Behörden zu erstatten. Damit soll vermieden werden, dass jemand, der der Gemeinschaft angehört, vor Gericht verantworten muss und gegebenenfalls eine Gefängnisstrafe bekommt.[29] Damit wäre ein Mitglied den – mit Misstrauen betrachteten – Justizorganen ausgeliefert bzw. bei einer Verurteilung für längere Zeit von der Erwerbstätigkeit ausgeschlossen, was zuletzt auch die Existenz der Familie gefährden kann.

Für Rechtsgelehrte und Wissenschaftler bereitet der Begriff „*Kris*" Schwierigkeiten, da er doch zugleich materielles sowie Verfahrensrecht bedeutet, und überdies auch das Gericht selbst bezeichnet. Des Weiteren fungiert die Versammlung von angesehenen Familienoberhäuptern nicht immer als Gericht und entscheidet nicht immer über Rechtsstreitigkeiten, oft erteilen sie nur gute Ratschläge für Mitglieder der Gemeinschaft.[30] Das *Romani Kris*, das Zigeunergesetz benennt darüber hinaus auch ein Verhaltensmuster – das Bündel von Regeln, das das Zusammenleben in der Gruppe ermöglicht. D.h. es spiegelt die Erwartungen der Gemeinschaft gegenüber ihren Mitgliedern wider.

---

[28] Loss, zit. S. 11.
[29] Loss, zit. S. 11.
[30] Aussage von Ernő Glonzi, Interview am 26. April 2008.

Diese Normen sind den Betroffenen seit ihrer Kindheit bekannt und das Kris sowie die anderen gemeinschaftlichen Konfliktlösungsmethoden sind für sie selbstverständlich und gewohnt. Neben eigenen Erfahrungen leben bei den Zigeunergruppen im Komitat *Békés* auch überlieferte Geschichten von früheren Verfahren weiter, die von älteren Familienmitgliedern erzählt werden; dies ermöglicht auch die Aufrechterhaltung und Weitergabe der Verhaltensmuster und Regeln. Auch Frauen besitzen genaue Informationen von vielen Verfahren, die weit in der Vergangenheit liegen und sich in den Zeiten abspielten als die Anwesenheit von Frauen bei einem Kris noch nicht üblich war. Durch die Erzählungen von anderen Familienmitgliedern sind auch sie an dieser wichtigen Tradition der Gemeinschaft beteiligt.[31]

4.2. Das Verfahren vor einem Zigeunergericht

Das *Romani Kris* hat seit langem tradierte, aber keine geschriebenen Verfahrensregeln, und auch die Verhaltensnormen sind nicht schriftlich festgelegt. Trotzdem sind die Regeln aufgrund der bereits beschriebenen mündlichen Überlieferung innerhalb der Gemeinschaft allgemein bekannt. Ein *Kris* wird nicht oft zusammengerufen, früher verhielt sich dies auch nicht anders, höchstens zwei bis dreimal jährlich oder nur ganz gelegentlich, bei Bedarf. Vorher festgelegte Termine oder Sitzungen gibt es nicht, es wird erst zusammengerufen, wenn es eine zu verhandelnde „Sache" gibt. Es besteht aus den höchstangesehenen Alten der Gemeinschaft, (gelegentlich wurden früher auch Angehörige anderer Stämme einbezogen) und dient von jeher ausschließlich der Beilegung von Konflikten zwischen *Oláh*-Zigeunern.

Bis Anfang des 20. Jahrhunderts wurden die Sitzungen im Freien gehalten, wobei der Wahl des Ortes keine besondere Bedeutung zukam; auch heute werden keine besonderen Anforderungen an die Lokalität gestellt, so dass eine Kneipe ebenso geeignet ist wie ein einfaches Zimmer. Es ist auch möglich, während eines Jahr- oder Monatsmarkts ein Kris zu halten, in einer abgelegenen Ecke des Geländes. Damals wie heute nehmen die Mitglieder in einer Runde Platz – ursprünglich auf dem Boden, später um einen Tisch – oder stellen sich bei einfacheren Fällen im Kreis auf. Dabei kommt der Kreisformation durchaus symbolische Bedeutung zu: die Mitglieder stehen oder sitzen sich auf

---

[31] Loss, zit. S. 19.

Augenhöhe gegenüber und können so unmittelbaren Blickkontakt zu jedem Einzelnen halten. Man verwendet einen sehr festlichen Redestil, der sich von der Alltagssprache deutlich abhob und auch sonst außerhalb des *Kris* kaum vorkam. Zum anderen ist der Kreis der möglichen Richter, ebenso wie auch der Kreis der Anwesenden, stark reglementiert. Die genaue Zahl der Richter ist hingegen nicht festgelegt und variiert von Fall zu Fall, beläuft sich aber zumeist auf 7 bis 8. Es soll mindestens zwei Richter geben, etwa 20 Personen waren früher das Maximum, heute werden so viele Richter aber gar nicht mehr berufen. Den Vorsitz eines *Kris* hat immer das älteste Mitglied inne, das auch als Richter (*lovárisch: Mujalo*) bezeichnet wird und dem zudem die Verkündung des Urteils obliegt, wenngleich er als *primus inter pares*, bei der Entscheidungsfindung keine hervorgehobene Rolle übernimmt.

Die Familienmitglieder der Beteiligten können Mitglied eines Kris sein, wohingegen Feinde der Parteien ausgeschlossen sind.[32] Lange Zeit war Frauen die Teilnahme am *Kris* generell untersagt; dieser Ausschluss wurde allerdings mit der Zeit insofern gelockert, als sie inzwischen als Streitpartei oder Zeuge auftreten können. Undenkbar ist hingegen nach wie vor, dass eine Frau als Richter tätig ist. Eine ebenfalls neuere Entwicklung betrifft die Mitwirkung von Nicht-Zigeunern – den so genannten *Gazsós*.[33] Ihnen wird mitunter die Möglichkeit eröffnet, als Zeuge aufzutreten.

Abgesehen von diesen Vorbehalten ist das ganze Verfahren öffentlich. Man war und ist bemüht, möglichst viele Mitglieder der Gemeinde einzubeziehen.[34] Indem die ganze Gruppe eingebunden wird, erhöhen sich zugleich die Legitimität des Urteils und seine Akzeptanz. Ein *Kris* ist also keine geheime Angelegenheit, sondern vielmehr eine Versammlung, die explizit auf die unmittelbare Lösung konkreter Probleme und Konflikte hinwirkt und dabei die Konfliktlösung zur Gemeinschaftssache erhebt. Zugleich wird ihm ein festlicher Anstrich gegeben, was sich darin zeigt, dass zu jedem *Kris* ein Festessen dazugehört, bei dem die Anwesenden (für ihre Verhältnisse) festlich

---

[32] Erdős, zit. S. 205.
[33] Loss, zit. S. 12.
[34] Bei einigen Stämmen geht dies sogar soweit, dass die Anwesenden auch in der Verhandlung und Entscheidungsfindung selbst mitwirken können. Erdős, zit. S. 205.

gekleidet erscheinen und den eigens dafür vorbehaltenen Redestil nutzten.

Feste Richter gibt es nicht, aber in allen Gruppen können einige Männer benannt werden, die oft in *Kris* gerufen werden. Meistens sind sie älter, Jüngere unter 30 Jahren werden selten als Mitglieder ausgewählt, aber sie sind dabei, um „die Gesetze zu lernen" und Erfahrungen zu sammeln.[35] Im Vordergrund stehen hierbei vor allem Anstand und Ehrbarkeit. Diese Ehre – nach eigenen Normen aufgefasst – wird auf *lovárisch* als *Patyiv* bezeichnet; ein ehrbarer Mann, der an der Urteilsfindung teilnehmen kann, gilt als *Patyivalo Manus*.[36] In einigen Familien wird die Richterrolle vom Vater auf den Sohn vererbt. Aber auch hier muss der Sohn seine persönliche Eignung eigens bestätigen.

Die Dauer des Verfahrens hängt von der Schwierigkeit der Entscheidung und von Zahl der Zeugen ab. Meist sind einige Stunden ausreichend, aber auch die Dauer mehrerer Tage ist möglich. Die Chronologie ist Folgende: Zuerst werden die Streitparteien angehört, auf sie folgen die Zeugen in Reihenfolge ihres Alters. Mitunter nehmen diese Befragungen beträchtlich viel Zeit in Anspruch, da alle, die angehört werden, beliebig lang vor dem *Kris* vortragen dürfen. Diese Ausführlichkeit dient der Aufdeckung aller relevanten Einzelheiten, so dass das Gericht prinzipiell auch an solchen Umständen interessiert ist, die nicht unmittelbar zum Fall gehören. Allein durch die Diskussion werden die Konfliktpunkte sichtbar und eine Lösung dadurch greifbar – zudem versucht man, durch die möglichst genaue und detaillierte Schilderung den Sachverhalt gut aufzuklären, damit die Mitglieder und Anwesenden ihn anlässlich des *Kris* nachvollziehen und nachempfinden können. Entsprechend sind die Erzählungen bildhaft, oft emotional aufgeladen und lautstark. Aus diesem Grund werden die an öffentlichen Orten geführten Verhandlungen von Außenstehenden oft als lauter Streit wahrgenommen. Für die Beteiligten bedeutet es hingegen, dass sie das Geschehene innerlich wieder erleben und versuchen, das von ihnen als die Wahrheit Aufgefasste den anderen plausibel zu machen.

Die Urteile sind unbedingt bindend und werden auch befolgt, Die Befolgung auch aus dem sonst drohenden Abbruch aller sozialen Kontakte und dem Ausschluss aus der Gemeinschaft. Eben dieser soziale Druck macht das *Kris* so effektiv: Auch ohne jegliche

---

[35] Loss, zit. S. 16.
[36] Aussage von Ernő Glonczi, Interview am 26. April 2008.

Vollstreckungsverfahren und öffentliche Gewalt werden die Entscheidungen befolgt. Die Entscheidung ist endgültig, Widerspruch ist nicht möglich, auch ein neues, anders zusammengesetztes Kris darf nicht anders entscheiden. Es kommt äußerst selten vor, dass das gefällte Urteil nicht akzeptiert wird und jemand versucht, „in Berufung" zu gehen.[37]

Die Mitglieder des *Kris* werden nicht bezahlt, auch die eventuellen Reisen organisieren und finanzieren sie selbst. Allein zu dem Festmahl nach der Urteilsverkündung, das fest zum Ablauf eines *Kris* zählt, werden sie eingeladen.[38] Die Teilnahme am *Kris*, vor allem wenn sie regelmäßig vorkommt, trägt aber zum gesellschaftlichen Ansehen bei und insbesondere die „gerechten" Richter sind hoch geschätzte Mitglieder der Gemeinschaft.

Der Rückgriff auf das *Kris* hat mehrere Ursachen. Die wichtigste besteht darin, dass auf diese Weise die Konflikte nicht außerhalb der Gruppe ausgetragen werden müssen. Es werden weder Staatsorgane eingeschaltet noch besteht die Gefahr, dass ein Mitglied der Gemeinschaft unter Strafe gestellt wird. Ein weiterer wichtiger Gesichtspunkt ist, dass die Beteiligten den Entscheidungen aus den eigenen Kreisen, den Urteilen von Männern mit *Patyiv*, mehr Vertrauen schenken. Eine nicht zu leugnende Tatsache ist, dass eine Verhandlung vor einem *Kris* schnell verläuft, wenig kostet und darüber hinaus schnell und unkompliziert zu vollziehen ist. Demgegenüber sind Klagen vor einem ordentlichen staatlichen Gericht für viele Zigeuner unerschwinglich. Allein die Kosten für Fahrten in die Stadt, Anwaltshonorare und Gebühren verhindern ihre Inanspruchnahme. Außerdem nehmen die Beschaffung der erforderlichen Dokumente und Nachweise sowie die Verhandlung als solche viel Zeit in Anspruch, so dass mindestens ein Familienmitglied (meistens der Mann) dadurch von seiner Arbeit ferngehalten wird.[39]

Wegen der Endgültigkeit und Unanfechtbarkeit der *Kris*-Urteile kommt das Verfahren nur als *ultima ratio* in Frage. Das erste „Vorverfahren" ist ein persönliches, informelles Gespräch der Beteiligten, bei dem sie versuchen, selbst den Streit beizulegen. Der informelle Charakter dieser Gespräche zeigt sich u. a. daran, dass diese

---

[37] Erdős, zit. S. 204.
[38] Loss, zit. S. 16.
[39] Loss, zit. S. 12.

heutzutage durchaus auch via Mobiltelefon erfolgen.[40] Den zweiten Schritt bildet das so genannte *Divano*, ein Streitbeilegungsverfahren, das dem Prinzip der Mediation entspricht. In diesem Rahmen sind die berufenen angesehenen Familienoberhäupter nur Vermittler und die Entscheidung ist für die Parteien nicht bindend, sondern kommt einer Empfehlung gleich, die versucht, einen Vergleich zustande zu bringen. Die Mitglieder stehen oder sitzen in einem Kreis und bemühen sich durch eine gründliche Diskussion des Falls selbigen zu lösen.

Kommt auf keinem dieser beiden Wege keine Einigung zustande, so wird ein *Kris* – möglichst sofort, spätestens aber innerhalb der nachfolgenden 2 bis 3 Tage – aufgestellt. Alle Teilnehmer beschwören mit dem *Soláx*, dass sie unter Verzicht auf Essen und Trinken zusammen bleiben bis ein Urteil gefällt ist. Aufgrund der besonderen Bedeutung, die dem Eidschwur[41] zukommt, ist der *Soláx* unbedingt bindend – er verhindert Aufschübe und garantiert eine zeitnahe Urteilsfindung.

4.3. Die Entscheidungen - Fallbeispiele

Es gibt wenige fest stehende Regeln, an die die Entscheidungen gebunden sind. Vielmehr bemühen sich die Richter um eine jedem Einzelfall angemessene gerechte Lösung, die den sozialen Frieden wiederherstellt und für Ausgleich zwischen den Parteien sorgt. Neben dem Tatbestand werden auch Besonderheiten des Falles, wie etwa die familiäre und finanzielle Situation der Parteien und andere Umstände, berücksichtigt. So wird beispielsweise minderbemittelten Schuldnern keine sofortige Zahlung abverlangt, sondern die Möglichkeit der Ratenzahlung oder auch der Aussetzung für eine bestimmte Dauer eröffnet.[42] Ebenfalls berücksichtigt wird das Vorverhalten der Beteiligten und auch die Häufigkeit von Anklagen fließt in die Urteilsfindung ein. Wer innerhalb eines Jahres mehrfach vor dem *Kris* gestanden hat, hat eine härtere Verurteilung zu erwarten. Parallelentscheidungen zur ungarischen Justiz werden hingegen möglichst vermieden; für Taten, die bereits durch die ordentliche Gerichtsbarkeit abgeurteilt wurden, wird niemand zusätzlich vor ein *Kris* gestellt.[43]

---

[40] Loss, zit. S. 12.
[41] Die Bedeutung und Besonderheiten des Eides werden nachfolgend in Teil 5 ausführlich behandelt.
[42] Erdős, zit. S. 209.
[43] Loss, zit. S. 15.

Die meisten Entscheidungen des *Kris* entsprechen dem Gerechtigkeits-verständnis der Zigeuner, was aber nicht zwangsweise mit der Meinung von Nichtzigeunern übereinstimmen muss. Zur Illustration sei der Fall zweier Einbrecher skizziert, der vor ein Kris gebracht wurde nachdem der aus der Haft entlassene – die Polizei hatte nur einen der Täter gefasst, vor Gericht gestellt und verurteilt – von seinem Komplizen eine Entschädigung für die im Gefängnis verbrachte Zeit forderte. Da dieser nach seiner Festnahme nicht gegen den anderen ausgesagt und ihn belastet hatte, war er allein zur Rechenschaft gezogen worden und musste eine Strafe verbüßen. Das angerufene *Kris* sprach ihm tatsächlich eine Entschädigung zu, und dies obwohl der Einbruch nicht erfolgreich gewesen war und die beiden keine Beute gemacht hatten.[44]

In ähnlich gelagerten Fällen ist es nicht unüblich, dass die verhängte Geldstrafe „geteilt" wird, wenn nur einer der Täter verurteilt wird, weil sie sich nicht gegenseitig belasten, sondern schützen, indem sie nicht gegeneinander aussagen. Sándor Loss hat einen Fall aufgezeichnet in dem von zwei Zigeunern aus dem Komitat *Békés*, die Stroh gestohlen hatten, nur einer gefasst und zu 100.000 Forint Geldstrafe verurteilt wurde. Die Strafe traf ausgerechnet denjenigen, der viel weniger Stroh entwendet hatte. Daraufhin wurde ein *Kris* zusammengerufen, das entschied, dass die beiden die Strafe im Verhältnis 20.000 : 80.0000 Forint zu bezahlen hätten, obwohl gegenüber der Polizei nicht eingeräumt worden war, dass zwei Täter den Diebstahl begangen hatten. Als Begründung wurde angeführt, dass es ausreiche, „wenn es die Zigeuner untereinander wissen."[45]

Die wichtigste Eigenschaft eines *Kris* besteht in seiner Flexibilität. Die ungeschriebenen Regeln können gut an die wechselnden Bedingungen angepasst werden, so dass die traditionellen Vorgaben problemlos auf moderne Konfliktlagen wie etwa Streitigkeiten aus dem Gebrauchtwagen-handel angewandt werden. Diese Anpassungsfähigkeit spielt eine große Rolle im Hinblick darauf, dass diese traditionelle gesellschaftliche Konfliktlösungsform bis heute erhalten geblieben und funktionsfähig ist. Das Verfahren und der Ablauf des *Kris* werden noch immer nach alten Formen und Ritualen ausgerichtet.[46]

---

[44] Erdős, zit. S. 209.
[45] Loss, zit. S. 22.
[46] Loss, zit. S. 12.

Eine peinliche Strafe oder sogar Todesstrafe war laut den Forschungen nie möglich.[47] Stattdessen wurde als Strafe meist eine Geldstrafe verhängt, also die Zahlung einer bestimmten Summe, die der Wiedergutmachung dienen sollte und zugleich, weil sie oft das Vielfache des ursprünglichen Wertes betrug, als Sanktionierung des Fehlverhaltens fungierte. Oft wurde und wird in den Entscheidungen eine bestimmte Handlung geboten oder die Rückgabe einer Sache angeordnet. Insbesondere bei familienrechtlichen Streitigkeiten ist diese Verfahrensweise verbreitet. Bei einer Brautent-führung etwa wurde der Entführer gezwungen, die Ehe mit der entführten Frau einzugehen. Bei „Ehrensachen" werden die Parteien aufgefordert, sich zu versöhnen oder dem für schuldig Befundenen wurde abverlangt, sich zu entschuldigen.

Zwar fällt ein Kris nie Todesurteile und verhängt auch keine Körperstrafen, es passiert aber oft, dass anhand des Urteils die Gemeinschaft selbst den Täter bestraft. Wenn Ehebruch festgestellt wurde, schnitt die Gemeinschaft der Frau die Haare ab (was die größte Schande ist, die einer Zigeunerin widerfahren kann) oder der betrogene Ehemann schnitt dem Täter ein Ohr ab. Dabei wurde das genaue Strafmaß durch die Gemeinschaft bestimmt – ein *Kris* ist zur Anordnung derartiger Körperstrafen nicht befugt. Insgesamt waren blutige Taten aber ausgesprochen selten. In aller Regel wurde die soziale Verachtung zum Ausdruck gebracht, indem die Täter bespuckt und beschimpft wurden.[48] Durch die Verurteilung – die Abwertung durch das Gericht, was im Fall eines *Romani Kris* eine Herabsetzung durch die ganze Gemeinschaft bedeutete – spielte die Missbilligung der Gemeinschaft oft eine viel bedeutsamere Rolle als die eigentliche Strafe dies erkennen ließ. Die Angst vor derartiger Verachtung, oder in besonders schweren Fällen auch vor einem Ausschluss aus der Gemeinschaft, trug dazu bei, dass die Ordnung in den Zigeunergemeinden auch ohne Polizei oder Gendarmerie aufrecht erhalten wurde. Nur jene wurden in der Gruppe geduldet und geachtet, die sich an die bestehenden Regeln hielten. Die oben angesprochene Familienehre war natürlich auch gekränkt, wenn ein Familienmitglied wegen einer Straftat von dem Kris verurteilt wurde.

---

[47] Erdős, zit. S. 207.
[48] Erdős, zit. S. 207.

5. Symbole und Rituale bei der Konfliktlösung

Nicht nur bei einem *Kris*, sondern auch bei anderen Akten mit Bezug zur Rechtsfindung sind Symbole in der Zigeunergemeinschaft sehr wichtig, wobei die Glaubenswelt der Zigeuner sehr heterogen und komplex ist: verschiedene Ebenen vermengen sich und die unterschiedlichen Symbole, die rituell gebraucht werden, sind nicht immer eineindeutig zuzuordnen. So bekennt sich die überwiegende Mehrzahl der Zigeuner zum Christentum, glaubt parallel dazu aber durchaus an übernatürliche Wesen wie Dämonen etc. Und auch andere Formen des Aberglaubens – zu nennen ist hier etwa der Glaube an die Wiederkehr des Geistes Verstorbener – sind weit verbreitet. Da sich die christlichen und heidnischen Symbole in ihrer Glaubenswelt und bei ihren Ritualen der Rechtsfindung vermischen, ist diese Symbolik oft nur schwer zu deuten. Hinzu kommt, dass einige der Elemente (zumindest theoretisch) miteinander kollidieren, so dass die Rituale oft einen fragmentarischen Charakter haben: Die Tatsache, dass die meisten Zigeuner getauft sind und sich als Christen bezeichnen, heißt nicht, dass sie regelmäßige Kirchengänger wären und die kirchlich gesetzten Pflichten strikt erfüllen würden.

Zwischen den unterschiedlichen Glaubensebenen besteht keine Hierarchie, sondern ein Nebeneinander, so dass, obwohl der überwiegende Teil der Zigeuner an Geister und Dämonen glaubt, christliche Symbole wie das Kruzifix und die Ikonen traditionell große Verehrung genießen. Eine besondere Rolle hat in der Glaubenswelt der Zigeuner auch die Kerze bzw. das Feuer, für das sie oft steht: Eine brennende Kerze verbietet zu lügen. Auf diesen Glauben wird bei der Ermittlung der Wahrheit immer wieder zurückgegriffen, und er trägt entscheidend dazu bei, dass das *Kris* und die anderen Verfahren funktionieren, ohne dass eine Ermittlungsbehörde oder ein Zwangsapparat einbezogen werden müsste.

Die symbolischen Akte begleiteten das Verfahren des *Kris* ebenso wie auch andere Rechtsakte; strenge Förmlichkeiten und Bräuche waren und sind einzuhalten, zu denen u.a. die oben genannten förmlichen und feierlichen Redewendungen gehören.

Eine gleichfalls besondere Stellung nimmt der Eid ein: die Parteien und Zeugen eines *Kris*, aber auch die Streitenden, die außerhalb eines Kris vor den Alten standen, mussten einen Eid leisten und schwören, dass sie nur die Wahrheit sagen bzw. im Fall eines Kris, dass alle bis dahin zusammen bleiben, bis in der Sache eine Entscheidung getroffen ist. Zur Eidableistung wurde ein (zumeist schwarzes) Tuch genutzt, auf dem eine Ikone oder zumindest die Abbildung eines Heiligen, der Jungfrau Maria oder Jesus gelegt und Kerzen angezündet wurden.

Es wird beschrieben, dass, sofern die Teilnehmer des *Kris* vor der Verhandlung eine Kirche betreten durften, sie dort, mit der Hand auf dem Altar, den Eid leisteten.[49] Hier kommen die brennenden Kerzen und die mit ihnen verbundene Überzeugung zur Geltung, dass sie Lügen jedweder Art verhindern. Die Vereidigung erfolgte kniend, mit der einen Hand auf dem Bild, mit der anderen Hand auf dem Herz. Meistens wurde bei dem Eid auf das Leben eines engen Familienangehörigen, also der Eltern, der Kinder oder der Geschwister geschworen – in jedem Fall auf das Leben einer sehr geliebten Person.[50]

Solch ein Eid war nicht zu brechen, alle glaubten fest daran, dass beim Eidbruch der Angehörige sterben würde oder ihm eine andere schwere Katastrophe wie Krankheit, Unglück oder andere Gefahr drohte. Mit dem Eid verfluchten sie sich selbst für den Fall des Eidbruches.[51] An diesen Eid hielten sich alle bzw. an den Glauben, dass ein Eidbruch ein großes Unglück mit sich bringen würde.

Diese Rituale werden zum Teil bis heute angewandt; so spielen die Heiligenabbildungen oder Kerzen weiterhin eine wichtige Rolle und auch der Eid wird nach wie vor in der Zigeunergemeinschaft sehr ernst genommen. Der feste Glauben daran trägt dazu bei, dass auch ohne ein besonderes, wissenschaftlich begründetes Beweisverfahren und ohne Zwangsmittel die Wahrheit ermittelt werden kann und dadurch die Konflikte gelöst werden können.

6. Fazit

Wie beschrieben, hat die auf dem kontradiktorischen Verfahren basierende staatliche Justiz in Fällen mit Beteiligten zigeunerischer

---

[49] Erdős, zit. S. 206.
[50] Bei den Pferdehändlern konnte es auch vorkommen, dass sie den Eid auf die Pferde leisteten, die ihre Existenzgrundlage bildeten.
[51] Rostás-Farkas, György: A cigányság hagyomány- és hiedelemvilága (Traditions- und Glaubenswelt der Zigeuner). Budapest, Cigány Tudományos és Művészeti Társaság, 2000, S. 60.

Herkunft mit vielen Probleme zu kämpfen; deren eigene Konfliktbewältigungsmethoden sind – dort, wo die traditionelle Gemeinschaft erhalten ist – weiterhin funktionsfähig. Fraglich ist, ob durch die Anwendung von Vermittlungsmethoden oder Mediation im Strafverfahren, also das Loslösen von dem strengen gerichtlichen Verfahren, eine Verbesserung zu erwarten ist.

Hier ist Skepsis angezeigt. Denn die Probleme der staatlichen Justiz mit den Zigeunern würden meiner Meinung nach auch nicht durch die breitere Anwendung der Vermittlungsmöglichkeiten gelöst; das Verfahren wäre aus Sicht der Zigeuner genauso formal wie ein „normaler" Prozess, das gegenseitige Vertrauen wäre nicht ad hoc herzustellen, der Mediator würde aus Sicht der Betroffenen – wie auch der Richter – als Fremder bzw. Außenstehender wahrgenommen werden, so dass gerade der gesellschaftliche Druck, der das *Kris* so effektiv macht, verloren ginge.

Die Konfliktbewältigungsmethoden der Zigeunergemeinschaft, vor allem bei den traditionstreuen *Lovári*-Zigeunern, bewahrten die archaischen Formen und werden teilweise bis heute praktiziert. Sie bieten eine alternative, wenngleich auch vom Staat nicht anerkannte und unterstützte Möglichkeit für die Bewältigung interner Konflikte. Das *Kris* und das Ansehen, das die dort urteilenden Alten der Gemeinschaft genießen, tragen dazu bei, dass die traditionellen Gruppen (und ihre Mechanismen) auch ohne Machtinstrumente und ohne Einmischung der Mehrheitsgesellschaft funktionsfähig bleiben. Die eingehende Erforschung der traditionellen Konfliktlösungsmethoden könnte zum Verständnis des Rechtsbilds und Rechtsempfindens der Zigeuner beitragen, was auch im Alltag der Justiz zu einem besseren Verständnis führen könnte. Natürlich ist dabei nicht zu vergessen, dass das *Kris*, und die anderen oben beschriebenen Methoden nur noch von einem kleineren Teil der Zigeuner in Ungarn praktiziert werden.

Das Kris wie auch andere vergleichbare gesellschaftliche Konfliktlösungsmodelle basieren auf dem Zusammenhalt der Gruppe, die ihrerseits sozialen Druck erzeugen und ausüben kann, um die Befolgung von Normen und Urteilen zu erringen. Dieser Mechanismus funktioniert allerdings ausschließlich in kleinen, geschlossenen und relativ homogenen Gruppen – auf Ebene der ganzen Gesellschaft sicher nicht.

Kapitel V
„Recht und Macht"

Law on the Diplomatic Stage: the 1725 Ripperda Treaty

Frederik Dhondt

1. "Balance of Power" between politics and law in history

The "Balance of Power", or the decentralised maintenance of stability between sovereign power centres, is one of the timeless metaphors for the theory of international relations. Indifferent whether we trace it back to Aristotle, to Polybius, to Islamic philosophy[1] or to the Italian *quatrocento*[2], it still occupies the mind today. "Detached from ideology, universally applicable, independent from short-term state considerations, it stresses the essential, timeless and inescapable, in international affairs: power and power relationships", to paraphrase Ernst Haas' words[3]. It is linked to the realist (if we think of Henry Kissinger's *Diplomacy*[4] or Raymond Aron's *Paix et guerre entre les nations*[5]), as well as to the interdependency-paradigm. Or, if we reframe it with Martti Koskenniemi's brilliant work: as well to apologists, as to utopists[6]. For the jurist, it explains how law can be derived from an anarchical society[7]

---

[1] Derived from the *al-Mîzân* (balance) at the final ordeal. Livet, Georges: L'équilibre européen de la fin du XVe siècle à la fin du XVIIIe siècle. PUF. Paris, 1976 p. 12.

[2] Wright, Martin: Theory and practice of the Balance of Power, 1486-1914: selected European writings. Dent. London, 1975.

[3] Haas, Ernst: The Balance of Power: Prescription, Concept, or Propaganda. In: World Politics V (July 1953), No. 3, p. 442-477.

[4] Kissinger, Henry: Diplomacy. Simon and Schuster. New York, 1994 p. 245. Kissinger built his eminent scientific career on his study of the 19th century-balance elaborated by Metternich and Castlereagh in Vienna (cf. Id.: A World Restored. Houghton Mifflin. Boston, 1973).

[5] Aron, Raymond: Paix et guerre entre les nations. Calmann-Lévy. Paris, 2004 [1962]. See also, as examples of realist balance-of-power thinking applied to law: Hoffman, Stanley, International Systems and International Law. In: World Politics XIV (1961), No. 1, p. 205-237; Morgenthau, Hans Jürgen: Macht und Frieden. Grundlegung einer Theorie der internationalen Politik. Bertelsmann Verlag. Gütersloh, 1963 p. 45.

[6] Koskenniemi, Martti: From Apology to Utopia: the Structure of International Legal Argument. Lakimiesliiton Kustannus - Finnish Lawyers' Publishing Company. Helsinki, 1989 p. 6.

[7] Bull, Hedley: The Anarchical Society: A Study of Order in World Politics. MacMillan.

inevitably characterised by the multiplicity of power centres[8], "involved in such intimacy of interrelationship as to make reciprocal impact feasible[9]".

The application of the concept to the eighteenth century, the "crossroads of international law", where medieval ideas of *causa justa* are abandoned, is a classic one[10]. To quote the British historian Herbert Butterfield:

"The eighteenth century looked back to the Roman Empire as a thing that must never be allowed to happen again. They realized [...] that there are only two alternatives: either a distribution of power to produce equilibrium or surrender to a single universal empire."

Through its multiple representations in pamphlet literature, philosophy, and even music[11], it conquered public opinion as well[12].

London, 1977.

[8] *"La théorie des relations internationales part de la pluralité des centres autonomes de décision, donc du risque de guerre"* (Aron, Raymond: Paix et guerres p. 28). We would hardly dare to suggest Mr. Aron was an interdependentist, but this phrase neatly frames the common starting point to both branches of theory, something shared by Hobbes and Kant as well.

[9] Sheehan, Martin: The Balance of Power: History and Theory. Routledge. London, 1996 p. 53.

[10] Mattei, Jean-Mathieu: Histoire du droit de la guerre, 1700-1819: introduction à l'histoire du droit international: avec une biographie des principaux auteurs de la doctrine internationaliste de l'Antiquité à nos jours. Presses Universitaires d'Aix-Marseille. Aix-en-Provence, 2006 introduction (s.p.); Kaeber, Ernst: Die Idee des europäischen Gleichgewichts in der publizistischen Literatur vom 16. bis zur Mitte des 18. Jahrhunderts. Gerstenberg. Hildesheim, 1971 [1907].

[11] Hume, David : The Balance of Power in Europe. Amsterdam, 1758; on the controversy between Kahle (La Balance de l'Europe considérée comme la règle de la paix et de la guerre. Berlin, 1744) and Justi (Die Chimäre des Gleichgewichts von Europa. Altona, 1758), see: Strohmeyer, Arno: Theorie der Interaktion. Das europäische Gleichgewicht der Kräfte in der frühen Neuzeit. Böhlau. Wien, 1994, pp. 40-56. 7-18. As a musical example, we can cite George Frederick Händel's 1713 celebration of the Peace of Utrecht: "Ode for the Birthday of Queen Anne" (9: "United Nations Shall Combine"), Chrysander, F.W. (Hrsg.): G.F. Händel's Werke. Deutsche Händelsgesellschaft. Leipzig, 1887, Plate H.W. 46a. Most recent recording: Berlin Academy for Ancient Music/Andreas Scholl, 2009 (Harmonia Mundi 9020401).

Butterfield, Herbert : The Balance of Power. In: Butterfield an Wight (eds.): Diplomatic Investigations: Essays in Theory of International Politics. Allen & Unwin. London, 1996 p. 142.

However, "the Balance" has a *histoire noire* of derision. An eminent example of this is Heinz Duchhardt's criticism, expressed in the *Journal of the history of International Law* in 2000. According to this most renowned scholar of 18th Century international relations, there was no such thing as an explicit conceptual "balance" in the treaty sources. Not even in the Peace of Utrecht, where it only figured in the British-Spanish, and the Spanish-Savoyan agreements[13]. Duchhardt cited the Peace of Vienna between Emperor Charles VI (1685-1740) and King Philip V of Spain (1683-1746) as a rare example of a post-1713-treaty literally retaking the formula. Conclusion ? "[T]he political metaphor of the 18th century did not at all succeed in being raised to the canon of the standard formulas of international law[14]", where amongst others the works of Evan Luard[15] and Wilhelm Grewe[16] classified it.

Why should I thus claim precious academic time discussing a mere political or even metaphysical metaphor? Randall Lesaffer demonstrated five years later, in an article in the same journal, that Duchhardt's analysis

---

[13] Treaty between Queen Anne of Great Britain and King Philip V of Spain, Utrecht, 13 July 1713, Published in: Dumont, Jean: Corps universel diplomatique du droit des gens. Pieter Husson & Charles Levier. Den Haag, 1731, nr. CLXIV, pp. 393-400; Treaty between King Philip V of Spain and Duke Victor Amadeus of Savoy, Utrecht, 13 July 1713, Parry, Clyve (ed.): The Consolidated Treaty Series. Oceana Publishing. Dobbs Ferry 1961-1986, v. XXVIII, p. 274, art. III ("CTS"); quoted in Duchhardt, Heinz: The Missing Balance, In: Journal of the History of International Law II (2000), pp. 69-70, footnotes 16 and 17. See also, in the same sense (the balance is a vague and ill-observed principle): Anderson, Mark S., Eighteenth-Century Theories of the Balance of Power, in: Studies in diplomatic history, essays in memory of D.B. Horn, edited by Hatton, Ranghild and Anderson, Mark S. Longman. London, 1970 pp. 183-198.

[14] Ibid., p. 72. See also the following quote from Charles Dupuis: "[L'équilibre] permet, dans la pratique, aux grands États de s'enrichir pourvu que chacun le fasse dans des proportions qui ne portent pas trop ombrage aux autres; il ne garantit que pour eux et entre eux le maintien d'un certain rapport de forces. Aux faibles, il ne laisse que l'alternative d'être épargnés, si leur maintien importe à tous, ou d'être dévorés, si leur absorption peut apaiser les discordes des forts. Ses complaisances pour les appétits robustes, sa souplesse ouverte à toutes les combinaisons, les aires de décence qu'il donne aux opérations les plus scabreuses, telles sont les conditions de son succès. Elles permettront aux adeptes de la philosophie d'applaudir avec une demi-inconscience aux pires scandales de la spoliation politique" (Dupuis, Charles: Le principe d'équilibre et le concert européen, de la paix de Westphalie à l'acte d'Algésiras. Perrin. Paris, 1909 p. 36).

[15] Luard, Evan: The balance of power: the system of international relations, 1648-1815. MacMillan. London, 1992 p. 1.

[16] Grewe, Wilhelm W.: Epochen der Völkerrechtsgeschichte. Nomos Verlag. Baden-Baden, 1984 p. 328.

was hasty and incomplete, pointing to at least five other treaties in the period concerned[17]. Peace Treaties, which Duchhardt examined, only tell us a part of the story, since treaties of *alliance* -bi- or multilateral- also reflect the underlying conceptions of the diplomatic actors. Moreover, to correctly appreciate the wordings of these formal documents, coming at the end of a negotiating process, the legal historian must venture into the archives of so-called "political" correspondence,

"[afin d'] échapper aux systèmes préfabriqués d'explication historique, de retrouver les peurs et les joies d'un temps, de déchiffrer les hésitations et certitudes d'une civilisation, en restituant le tremblement de l'histoire[18]".

At the occasion of this Forum of Young Legal Historians - putting *"the law on stage"*- I considered it appropriate to have a closer look at the diplomatic practice surrounding this so called "Ripperda"-treaty. During archival research, conducted in the State Papers Foreign, conserved at the National Archives in Kew[19], and in the Additional Manuscripts Collection of the British Library, I came across the reports of British diplomats from Paris, Vienna and Madrid. They shed a new light on the topic. I aim to demonstrate two theses:

(1) Balance of Power is a legal principle, born out of political circumstances. It gets its directing power from memorial construction. The conceptual treaty history of the balance dated back to long before the Treaty of Utrecht[20], and gained its force out of a memorial

---

[17] Lesaffer, Randall : Paix et guerre dans les grands traités du dix-huitième siècle. In: Journal of the History of International Law, VII (2005), p. 38, footnote 44: Treaty of the Quadruple Alliance - Vienna Treaty of Alliance between George II of Great Britain and Emperor Charles VI, 16 March 1731, CTS XXXIII, p. 318 – Treaty of Turin between Louis XV of France and Charles Emmanuel of Savoy-Sardinia, 26 September 1733, CTS, XXXIV, p. 97 - Bourbon Family Pact between Louis XV and Philip V of Spain, Escurial, November 1733, CTS, XXXIV, p. 125 – Vienna Peace Treaty between Louis XV, Charles VI and the Holy Roman Empire, 18 November 1738, CTS XXXV, p. 205.
[18] Bély, Lucien : La société des Princes. PUF. Paris, 1999 p. 29.
[19] Concerned with this theme: N.A., SP Foreign, Paris, 78-171 (Congress of Cambrai, March-December 1722), 172 (April-December 1723), 173 (January-April 1724), 174 (May-July 1724), 175 (July-December 1724), 176 (January-May 1725); 80-54 (Vienna, January-May 1725); 86 (May-October 1725); 94-93 (Madrid, May-November 1725); B.L., Add. Ms., 48981 (Townshend Papers).
[20] Lesaffer, Randall: Paix et guerre p. 39.

accumulation. *Tranquillité, libertés de l'Europe, balance* were synonyms for the rebuttal of universal monarchy. A club of great powers mended the system to fit the largest general denominator of interests. This is what Heinz Duchhardt called a *droit de convenance* in the beginning of his academic career[21]; however it has not been done much research yet[22]. In the long run, it might be interesting to integrate this *behavioural* concept with French sociologist Pierre Bourdieu's generalist schemes of *habitus*[23]. Did the discursive community of diplomats have a *legal habitus*, rather than a proper theory?

(2) This concept did not only serve *internally*, on the diplomatic αγορα (1), clothed by the veil of secrecy, but also as an *external image*, in the European public sphere, i. e. as a model of representation, with which the formal outcomes of relations between sovereigns ought to be in accordance (2). In other words, balance of power was not just a mere pretext or a mendable *causa justa* to wage war[24]. In the beginning of the eighteenth century, it had a permanent and stabilising function in the international system: it delivered the framework to safeguard and amend peace treaties.

The representation of the balance Duchhardt quoted in art. III[25] of the Ripperda Treaty made reference to the peace of Utrecht. The former treaty seemed to complete the latter peace agreement by ending the formal state of war between King Philip V of Spain (1683-1746) and Emperor Charles VI of the Holy Roman Empire (1685-1740). It is in this sense that we should understand French nineteenth-century scholar Arsène Legrelle's decision to take 1725 as the *terminus ad quem* of his

---

[21] Duchhardt, Heinz : Gleichgewicht der Kräfte, Convenance, europäisches Konzert. Friedenskongresse und Friedensschlüsse vom Zeitalter Ludwigs XIV. bis zum Wiener Kongress. Wissenschaftliche Buchgesellschaft. Darmstadt, 1976 p. 86.

[22] Duchhardt, Heinz : Balance of Power und Pentarchie. Schöningh. Paderborn, 1997 p. 19.

[23] "a system of dispositions, that is of permanent manners of being, seeing, acting and thinking"… "a set of acquired characteristics which are the product of social conditions" Bourdieu, Pierre: Habitus. In: Hillier and Rooksby (eds.): Habitus: a sense of place. Ashgate. Aldershot, 2005 p. 43 and 46.

[24] Mattei, Jean-Mathieu: Histoire du droit de la guerre, 1700-1819 p. 377.

[25] CTS XXXII, p. 44: "ad constituendum duraturum in Europa aequilibrium ea visa fuerit ut pro regula statuatur ne Regna Galliae et Hispaniae, ullo umquam tempore, in unam eandemque personam, nec in unam eandemque lineam coalescere unirique possent"

monumental *La diplomatie française et la Succession d'Espagne*. The two pretenders to the vacancy on the Spanish Habsburg throne in 1700 finally came together a quarter of a century later[26]. Article III of the 1725 Treaty served to create an appearance of bringing the situation into line with the Peace of Utrecht[27]. In reality, the secret clause to the Spanish-Austrian arrangement[28] projected a marriage between the Infant Don Carlos, eldest son of Queen Elisabeth Farnese (1692-1766), second spouse to Philip V of Spain[29], and the Archduchess Maria Theresia, eldest daughter to Emperor Charles VI. In view of the exclusion of women at the election of a King or Emperor of the Romans, Carlos would find himself sitting on Charlemagne's throne[30]. Were Philip's last remaining son, the Infant Ferdinand, to decease, he would inherit the Spanish monarchy too[31]. Even worse, if the sickly

---

[26] Legrelle, Arsène : La diplomatie française et la Succession d'Espagne: 1659-1725. Pichon. Paris, 1892, vol. IV pp. 738-771. Although Legrelle particularly enjoys painting a black picture of the German and Dutch interests in the War of the Spanish Succession, his primary source-work in the Quai d'Orsay and in Madrid remains excellent.

[27] For an overview of older works on Utrecht, see Duchhardt, Heinz : Gleichgewicht der Kräfte, pp. 41-68. However, one should complete it with the masterly cultural-anthropological study by Lucien Bély, incorporating insights from contremporary social sciences (Bély, Lucien: Espions et ambassadeurs au temps de Louis XIV. Fayard. Paris, 1990 905 p.).

[28] Du Mont, Jean : Corps universel diplomatique du droit des gens, v. VIII/2, nr. XXXVI, pp. 106-113 (Peace Treaty, 30 April 1725), XXXVII, pp. 113-114 (Treaty of Alliance, 30 April 1725), nr. XXXVIII, pp. 114-121 (Treaty of Commerce and Navigation, 1 May 1725). The attentive reader will remark the absence of a marriage clause in the published treaties. The union between Maria Theresia and Don Carlos was agreed on secretly and reported as such to the Commons by Horatio Walpole (1678-1757), ambassador in Paris and brother of Britain's Prime Minister Robert Walpole (Pearce, Edward : The Great Man: sir Robert Walpole, Scoundrel, Genius and Britain's First Prime Minister. Jonathan Cape. London, 2007 p. 231).

[29] "Comme le mariage du Prince des asturies avec l'ainée des archiduchesses accomodoit peu les interets de la Reine Catholique, et ceux de l'infant Don Carlos, il est vraisemblable que cette Princesse a d'abord pris la resolution de faire tourner la negociation en faveur de son fils", N.A., SP, 80-55, Common Relation of St. Saphorin and du Bourg to Charles Townshend, secretary of state for the Northern Department, Vienna, 11 May 1725, s.n.

[30] This happened with Maria Theresia's husband, Franz Stephan of Lorraine. See Zedinger, Renate : Franz Stephan von Lothringen (1708-1765). Böhlau Verlag. Wien, 2008.

[31] "Riperda parle ouvertement du marriage de Don Carlos comme d'une asseurée, et il dit que le Prince des Asturies est Etique, et qu'il ne peut pas vivre, l'on voit à quoi cela prepare…" (N.A., SP 80-55, St-Saphorin to Charles Townshend, private letter, Vienna, 11 May 1725, s.n.). Don Ferdinand (the later Ferdinand VI of Spain) was considered to be in a feeble state of both mind and body (Bély, Lucien : Les relations internationales en Europe,

Louis XV came to pass away before producing a legitimate male heir, the Spanish Bourbons could rule in Versailles, Madrid and Vienna. In other words, the spectre of Charles V' *Monarchia Universalis* rose again[32]!

2. Diplomacy and Legimitacy: the Ripperda Treaty (May 1725)

2.1. Forced to negotiate: Philip V and the lost territories

It is hard to understand the scandal provoked by the Treaty of Vienna, named after the 18th Century Dutch adventurer Jan Willem van Ripperda[33], without having regard to the preceding international acts. As the Treaty recalled in its preamble, Charles VI and Philip V were both competing for the Spanish crown after the decease of Charles II of Spain in November 1700[34]. At that time, the young candidates (17 resp. 15 years old) symbolised the larger power struggle between the houses of Bourbon and Habsburg, who both wanted to found a second branch in Madrid[35]. Thirteen years later, a separate Spanish house of Bourbon was

---

XVIe-XVIIIe siècles. PUF. Paris, 1992[3] p. 455.

[32] Bosbach, Franz : Monarchia universalis. Ein politischer Leitbegriff der frühen Neuzeit. Vandenhoeck & Ruprecht. Göttingen, 1988 p. 64.

[33] Johan Willem de Ripperda y Diest (1690-1737). A plenipotentiary for the Republic at the Congress of Utrecht, Ripperda converted himself to Catholicism as Dutch ambassador in Madrid (1715-1718) and served Philip V afterwards, rising to the position of most potent minister thanks to his achievements in Vienna. In December 1725, Ripperda was dismissed. He fled to the British ambassador William Stanhope's apartment, but was arrested there (in violation of international law, which accorded the privilege of inviolable asylum to the residences, see Réal de Curban: La Science du Gouvernement, t.5 p. 106). After eighteen months of detention in the Alcázar of Segovia, he escaped via Britain to Morocco. On the tumultuous life of Ripperda, see Campbell, John : Memoirs of the Duke of Ripperda: first embassador from the States-General to His Most Catholick Majesty, the Duke and Grandee of Spain; afterwards Bashaw and Prime Minister to Mully Abdalla, Emperor of Fez and Morocco, &c. Containing a succinct account of the most remarkable events which happen'd between 1715 and 1736. John Stagg & Daniel Browne. London, 1740; Syveton, Gabriel: Une cour et un aventurier au XVIIIe siècle. Le baron de Ripperda. Paris, 1896; van der Veen, Sytze : Spaanse Groniger in Marokko: de levens van Johan Willem Ripperda (1682-1737). Bert Bakker. Amsterdam, 2007.

[34] Maquart, Marie-Françoise: Le dernier testament de Charles II d'Espagne. In: Bély (dir.) : La présence des Bourbons en Europe, XVIe-XXIe siècles. PUF. Paris, 2000 pp. 111-123.

[35] Bérenger, Jean: Le conflit entre les Habsbourg et les Bourbons (1598-1792). In: Revue d'histoire diplomatique, 2002, pp. 193-232. Cruz González, Daniel: Une guerre de religion entre princes catholiques. Éditions de l'ÉHESS. Paris: 2006, 304 p.

installed in the Spanish Kingdoms[36]. The main clauses of the Peace of Utrecht, which consisted in reality of multiple bilateral agreements, were written by France and Great Britain[37], who co-managed European affairs during what Emmanuel Le Roy Ladurie has called "les trentes heureuses[38]". In a period stretching from 1713 to Frederick the Great's invasion of Silesia in December 1740, no major European war occurred. Although the Franco-British cooperation was more nuanced[39] than the previous label suggests, the association of both powers was exceptional. It dominated any new initiative.

Both Philip and Charles were unsatisfied with the outcome of 1713, but had to acquiesce temporarily, due to the overwhelming European power consensus supporting it[40]. They never concluded a formal peace and kept on quarrelling about two territories: Spain and Italy. Charles kept a Spanish and Italian council at his Viennese court. He was "governed" by his Spanish favourites Rialp and Folch de Cardona. Philip silently aspired to climb on the French throne once the young Louis XV disappeared. Less silent was his ambitious spouse, the turbulent queen Elisabeth Farnese, female heir to one of Italy's most prominent noble families. Italy had been a theatre of Franco-Habsburg confrontation

---

[36] See further: Bérenger, Jean: La question de la succession d'Espagne au XVIIe siècle. In: La présence des Bourbons en Europe, edited by Lucien Bély, pp. 75-91.; Frey, Linda and Marsha (eds.): The Treaties of the War of the Spanish Succession: an historical and critical dictionary. Greenwood Press. Westport (Conn.), 1995.

[37] Preliminaries between Queen Anne of Great Britain and Louis XIV, London, 27 September O.S./8 October N.S. 1711, Du Mont, VIII/1, nr. CXIX, p. 281. See Bély, Lucien: *L'art de la paix en Europe: naissance de la diplomatie moderne, XVI-XVIIIe siècle.* PUF. Paris 2007, pp. 465-466. [The abbreviation O.S. stands for Old Style or Julian Calendar, used in Britain until 1752, which differed about two weeks from the Gregorian Calendar, applied on the continent].

[38] Le Roy Ladurie, Emmanuel: L'Ancien Régime. T. 2: l'absolutisme bien tempéré (1715-1770). Hachette. Paris, 1991 p. 93. See also McKay and Scott, who label the Franco-British alliance

[39] For the evolution of British foreign policy towards a realignment with Austria after 1727: Black, Jeremy: George II, sir Robert Walpole and the collapse of the Anglo-French Alliance 1727-1731, Black. Newcastle, 2005 and Black, Jeremy: British neutrality in the war of the Polish Succession, 1733-1735. In: International History Review VIII (1986), pp. 345-366.

[40] Convention between the belligerent parties, by the mediation of the British plenipotentiaries for the evacuation of Catalunya and for an armistice in Italy, Utrecht, 14 March 1713, Du Mont: Corps universel diplomatique, VIII/1, nr. CLXVII, p. 327-330).

since Charles VIII's invasion at the end of the fifteenth century. During the War of the Spanish Succession, however, the Austrian Habsburgs replaced the Spanish branch in most of their dominions. Naples, Milan, Sardinia and the Toscan Presidia were held by Charles VI.

Neighbouring these Italian lands, the duchy of Parma and Piacenza, ruled by the childless duke Francesco Farnese (1678-1727), was to fall into Elisabeth's descendents, once his brother Antonio (1679-1731) disappeared without a legal male offspring. Thanks to dynastic intricacies[41], she could also claim the Grand-Duchy of Tuscany, where it was very likely that the de'Medici-dynasty would die out with Cosimo III (1642-1723) and his childless son Gian Gastone (1671-1737). The Emperor, who considered the territories to be masculine fiefs of the Holy Roman Empire, implying their return to the Emperor, who could then decide who to attribute the investiture, refuted both claims[42].

To complicate matters even further, the duke of Savoy had acquired the Isle of Sicily thanks to British mediation[43], on the basis of a unilateral

---

[41] Elisabeth's great-grandfather Cosimo III de'Medici, grandduke of Tuscany (1590-1621) constituted the link with Gian Gastone de'Medici. The claims to the double duchy of Parma/Piacenza were founded on Elisabeth's position as a daughter to Odoardo Farnese (1666-1693), brother of both Francesco and Antonio, who died before he could accede to the throne. I refer to the Genealogies in annex.

[42] The Emperor's competence to decide in these matters was not disputed by the other powers and recognized as such in the treaty of the Quadruple Alliance, art. V (*"Sacri Romani Imperii Feudus masculinis*; Rousset de Missy, Jean: Les intérêts présens des puissances de l'Europe, Fondez sur les Traitez conclus depuis la Paix d'Utrecht inclusivement, & sur les Preuves de leurs Prétensions particulieres. Adrien Moetjens. La Haye, 1733 pp. 26, 61 (Parma-Piacenza) and 98 (Tuscany)). However, this decision, by nature, touched upon the European public order. Thus, Charles had to consult his colleagues, derived the legitimacy of his decision from them and was de facto bound by the general rules of the system. If Charles were to act without broader consent, his decision would be all but a paper one. (Steiger, Heinhard: Völkerrecht versus Lehnsrecht ? Vertragliche Regelungen über reichs-italienische Lehen in der Frühen Neuzeit. In: Steiger, Heinhard: Von der Staatengesell-schaft zur Weltrepublik? Nomos Verlag. Baden-Baden, 2009, pp. 233-266). As a result, the power to grant the investiture in Italy, although it ought to be less restrained than within the Empire, where the Peace of Osnabruck applied, fell into the same category of formal and ritual respect, but material decline. See Stollberg-Rillinger, Barbara: Le rituel de l'investiture dans le Saint-Empire de l'époque moderne : histoire institutionnelle et pratiques symboliques. In : Revue d'histoire moderne et contemporaine LVI (2009), pp. 7-29.

[43] McKay, Derek : Bolingbroke, Oxford and the defense of the Utrecht settlement in Southern Europe. In: *English Historical Review* LXXXVI (apr. 1971) pp. 264-284. Promise by treaty in art. XIV, Treaty of Peace & Alliance between Queen Anne of Great Britain and Philip V of Spain, 13 July 1713, Ibid., p. 396.

cession act by Philip V dating 10 June 1713. This document contained a right of reversion to the Spanish crown for the kingdom, which had been in the hands of the house of Aragon since 1282[44].

Philip V manifested his discontent by bluntly invading Sardinia in 1717[45], and Sicily the subsequent year. James Stanhope (1673-1721)[46], principal minister of George I, and archbishop Guillaume Dubois (1656-1723)[47], French envoy in London, mustered a coalition with the attacked powers Habsburg and Savoy. The Treaty of the Quadruple Alliance, dating 2 August 1718 (N.S.) and signed in London, foresaw an exchange between Savoy and Austria, the former changing the rich island of Sicily for the less interesting Sardinia[48].

---

[44] Art. II, Instrumento de la Cession del Reyno de Sicilia, hecho por el Serenissimo Duque de Anjou como Rey de España a Victor Amadeo Duque de Saboya por el y sus Descendientes masculinos per perpetuamente, 10 June 1713, published in Du Mont : Corps universel, VIII/1, nr. CLXII, pp. 389-392.

[45] More in particular for this question, see Mongiano, Elisa : "Universae Europae Securitas" I trattati di cessione della Sardegna a Vittorio Amedeo II di Savoia. G. Giappichelli Editore. Torino, 1995. Philip launched the invasion while the Austrian army was occupied fighting the Ottomans on the Balkans, see Parvev, Ivan: Habsburgs and Ottomans between Vienna and Belgrade (1683-1739). Columbia University Press. New York, 1995 pp. 168-176.

[46] James 1st Viscount Stanhope, see Williams, Basil: Stanhope. A Study in Eighteenth-Century War and Diplomacy. Clarendon Press. Oxford, 1932.

[47] Guillaume Cardinal Dubois, rose from humble origins to de facto prime minister during the Regency, see Aujol, Jean-Louis: Le Cardinal Dubois, ministre de la paix. Éditions du bâteau ivre. Paris, 1948; Chaussinand-Nogaret, Guy. Le Cardinal Dubois, 1656-1723 ou une certain idée de l'Europe. Perrin. Paris, 2000; Thomas, Jean Pierre : Le Régent et le cardinal Dubois ou l'art de l'ambiguïté. Payot. Paris, 2004.

[48] Treaty & Alliance between Charles VI, Louis XV and George I, 22 July O.S./2 August N.S., London, Du Mont : Corps universel diplomatique, VIII/1, nr. CCII, pp. 531-541. The legal construction of the treaty is trilateral, putting forward the conditions under which the Duke of Savoy and Charles VI should proceed to the exchange of Sardinia for Sicily and with a possibility for the States-General to adhere to it (which did not happen). Although the mechanism was analogous to that of the 1697 and 1700 partition treaties for the Spanish succession, which were elaborated between Louis XIV and William III, to be subsequently opened within a limited delay to the Emperor, the accession of Charles VI was to be expected. Victor Amadeus II of Savoy, although a victim of the Spanish invasion, did not spontaneously join the coalition. The reason is geopolitical: situated between France and Austria, Victor Amadeus did not see a reason to oppose the sole invasion of Sardinia in 1717. He started negotiations with Spain in order to divide the map of Italy to his advantage. Turin chose sides only when Sicily, attributed to in 1713 to raise its court to the status of a royal one, was invaded in July 1718. The de facto loss of control of Sicily made Sardinia the second best choice.

Philip V had no choice but to accede to the Treaty and to delegate his ministers to Northern France[49]. His fleet being destroyed by the British and both the Basque country and Catalunya invaded by the French, he sacked his principal minister Giulio Alberoni[50]. The Peace Congress of Cambrai[51], which was called together in 1722, but had to delay its opening until 1724, served as a forum for the execution of the Quadruple Alliance.

2.2. The slow and potentially painful Congress of Cambrai

Legally, Philip's point of view was much firmer than one could expect. He still had to agree to the non-application of the reversion right concerning Sicily demanded by the Quadruple Alliance treaty, to which he was not a party[52]. Moreover, he still had not signed a peace treaty with Charles VI.

The unilateral renunciations called for by the Treaty of the Quadruple Alliance, whereby both monarchs gave up their claims to each other's territory[53], did not constitute a binding international norm. In practice, they continued to carry the titles referring to the territories lost (Milan,

---

[49] Philippi V. Regis hispaniarum accessio iterata, & per plenipotentiarum suum, ad Tractatum sive Concordatum Londini 2. Augusti cujusdem anni initum extensa, Den Haag, 17 February 1720, Du Mont: Corps universel diplomatique, VIII/2, nr. XI, p. 26.

[50] 1664-1752. Giulio Alberoni made his career as a diplomat for the Dukes of Parma, came to Spain with the French general Vendôme during the War of the Spanish Succession and arranged Philip's wedding with Elisabeth Farnese (1715). In 1717, he is created a Cardinal, just before the invasion of Sardinia. See Moore, George: Lives of Cardinal Giulio Alberoni and the Duke of Ripperda and Marquis of Pombal, three distinguished political Adventurers of the last Century exhibiting a View of the Kingdoms of Spain and Portugal during a considerable Time of that Period. J. Rodwell. London, 1814[2].

[51] We refer to Lingens, Karl-Heinz : Kongresse im Spektrum der Friedenswahrenden Instrumente des Völkerrecht. In: Duchhardt (Hrsg.): Zwischenstaatliche Friedenswahrung in Mittelalter und früher Neuzeit. Böhlau. Köln, 1991 pp. 205-226. Lingens bases his research on the archival records kept at the Quai d'Orsay (presently La Courneuve, Archives Diplomatiques), Alfred Braudrillart's Philippe V et la Cour de France Didot. Paris, 1890, t. 2-3 and Ottocar Weber's Die Quadrupel-Allianz vom Jahre 1718. Ein Beitrag zur Geschichte der Diplomatie im 18. Jahrhundert. Wien, 1887. The present intervention studies adds British diplomatic sources to this.

[52] Art. VI, Treaty of the Quadruple Alliance, Du Mont : Corps universel diplomatique VIII/1, nr. CCII, pp. 531-533. Philip acceded to the Quadruple Alliance, which served as a Preliminary Peace, by the Treaty of The Hague, 17 February 1720, Ibid., VIII/2, pp. 26-27.

[53] Renunciation by Charles VI, Vienna, 16 September 1718 (in execution of the Treaty of the Quadruple Alliance of 2 August 1718, cf. supra); Renunciation by Philip V (at the occasion of his accession to the Quadruple Alliance, San Lorenzo, 22 June 1720).

Naples, Sicily, Sardinia, the Southern Netherlands in the case of Philip V; Catalunya for Charles) or never even controlled (Castille, Leon, in the case of Charles VI).

When the congress opened, the expectations were such that the Anglo-French mediators would be the enforcers of the general European order, which would be reflected in a "Treaty of Cambrai". No union between the crowns of France and Spain, peaceful settlement of the succession questions in Parma-Piacenza and Tuscany, legal remedies for a swift exchange of Sicily and Savoy and respect for the British trade privileges in Spanish America[54]. In addition to this, British and Dutch anger over the setting up of the Ostend Company, which traded with the Eastern Indies at the expense of other powers' merchants, would probably lead the Emperor to suppress it[55].

At Cambrai, the Austrian plenipotentiaries Windischgrätz and Penterriedter[56] asked the European sovereigns to recognize the

---

[54] Treaty of Navigation & Commerce between Queen Anne of Great Britain and Philip V, Utrecht, 28 November O.S./9 December N.S. 1713, Du Mont: Corps universel diplomatique, VIII/1, nr. CLXIX, pp. 409-422; Hatton, Ragnhild: George I. Yale University Press. New Haven, 2001² p. 273.

[55] Starting 1714 an extended in 1722, the Company (mainly run by foreigners) was destined to develop economic activity in the Austrian Netherlands. See Hertz, Gerald B., England and the Ostend Company. In: English Historical Review XXII (April 1907), pp. 255-279; Huisman, Michel: La Belgique commerciale sous l'empereur Charles VI: la Compagnie d'Ostende: étude historique de politique commerciale et coloniale. Lamertin. Bruxelles, 1902 XII + 555 p. The opening of the Spanish market in America went against the British commercial dominance agreed at Utrecht (e.g. Asiento or privilege for the introduction & sale of black slaves in Spanish America, Madrid, 26 March 1713, Du Mont : Corps universel diplomatique VIII/1, nr. CXXXIX, pp. 330-337). From a legal point of view, the Dutch Republic denied the Emperor the right to start a commerce with the Indies from the Southern Netherlands, on the basis of art. V of the Spanish/Dutch Peace Treaty of Münster (30 January 1648), which forbade commercial undertakings in the Spanish Netherlands. These dispositions were confirmed by the Barrier Treaty of 15 November 1715 between Charles VI, George I and the States-General (Du Mont, VIII/1, nr. CLXXX, pp. 458-468). However, Charles' jurists claimed the natural law principle of *mare liberum* –nota bene developed by Hugo Grotius against the Spanish and British opinions of *mare clausum*- overruled private treaties between nations (e.g. Jean Du Mont de Carels-Kroon : La vérité du fait, du droit et de l'intérêt de tout ce qui concerne le commerce des Indes, établi aux Païs-Bas Autrichiens par octroi de Sa Majesté Impériale et Catholique. Mathieu Roguet. La Haye, 1723). On the subject and the role of the Flemish jurist Patijn and the continuous stream of pamphlets regarding the matter, see De Pauw, Frans : Het Mare Liberum van Grotius en Pattijn. Die Keure. Brugge, 1960.

[56] Ernst Friedrich Graf von Windischgrätz (1670-1727), president of the *Reichshofrat* since 1714; Christoph Freiherr von Penterriedter (+ 1728), experienced Imperial diplomat,

Emperor's Pragmatic Sanction[57]. By this document dating 19 April 1713[58], Charles wanted to avoid a foreign succession in the Habsburg hereditary lands. Having succeeded to his older brother Joseph, who – like himself – only had a female offspring, the risk was real that one of the princesses' spouses would come and seize power in Vienna.

2.3 The return to the "ancien sistéme" and the rupture of the Balance

Both Philip and Charles only stood to lose from a Franco-British mediated deal at Cambrai: Philip would have to accept another humiliation by France and British meddling in Italy and would probably not recuperate Gibraltar[59], Charles was about to see the lucrative Ostend

---

secretary to Eugen of Savoy at the Rastatt negociations, also present at Utrecht and Baden, former ambassador in Paris (1719-1722).

[57] E.g. "Demandes de sa sacrée majesté Imperiale et Catholique", N.A., SP 78-174, ff. 48v-49r, 12°. Charles tried to sell the recognition of his Pragmatic Sanction as a necessary complement of his guaranty of the French, Spanish, British and Savoyard successions through the Quadruple Alliance and Philip's accession to that instrument.

[58] Turba, Gustav : Die Pragmatische Sanktion. Authentische Texte samt Erläuterungen und Übersetzungen. Wien, 1913.

[59] "le Roy de la Grande Bretagne, embarassé par l'affaire de Gibraltar et de Port Mahon, bien loin de faciliter nôtre Paix avec l'Espagne, la traversoit, ainsi il nous étoit convenable de finir sans lui" (Eugen of Savoy to the Savoyard envoy Breille, N.A., SP, 80-55, Lettre Secrète, Vienna, 11 May 1725, s.n.) James Stanhope (1673-1721), principal minister of George I, agreed to the restitution of the rock and city of Gibraltar (conquered during the War of the Spanish Succession). This was confirmed by a handwritten letter from his king to Philip V, dated 12 June 1720. The promise was needed to get Philip V to agree to the framework of the Quadruple Alliance (Treaty of London, 2 August 1718), which he subsequently did (17 February 1720, Treaty of The Hague). Internal British political circumstances (notably the absence of a parliamentary majority), however, did not permit the execution of this promise. The possession of the rock was too important for commercial and naval control over the Mediterranean. This interference in what the Spanish saw as their mare nostrum caused considerable tensions with Madrid, leading to the siege of Gibraltar in 1727. Elisabeth Farnese repeatedly confronted British ambassador William Stanhope (the later Lord Harrington) with the original letter, symbol of British betrayal (Kamen, Henry : Philip V of Spain: the King who reigned twice. Yale University Press. New Haven, 2001, p. 160).
Writing 44 years later, Réal de Curban pointed to George's letter as a proof that unilateral declarations by a monarch do not create any obligations on his side: "Les Plénipotentiaires doivent bien se garder de croire qu'on puisse assurer des conditions importantes, sur la foi de quelques lettres que les Princes, qui accordent ces conditions, & qui ne voudroient pas qu'elles parussent, offrent quelquefois d'écrire au Souverain en faveur duquel ces

Company, instrument of an ambitious policy to turn Austria from an exclusively territorial to a maritime power, sink to the bottom of the sea[60]. However, concluding a treaty with the "King of Spain and the Indies" could open the gates of America to his subjects[61].

This happened, when dynastic coincidence blocked the workings of the diplomats. On 10 January 1724, Philip V suddenly abdicated in favor of his son, don Luis (°1707 out of the king's first wedding)[62]. However, on 31 August of the same year, Luis succumbed to the pocks. His father returned to government, after papal consultation. But the influence of Elisabeth Farnese grew: she pushed her husband to accept the crown.

The following year 1725 brought a grave abdominal colic to the young Louis XV (1710-1774), putting his life in danger. The Spanish Infanta María Ana Victoria (1718-1781) had been promised to the 14 year-old king in a double Franco-Spanish arrangement, involving don Luis and Mademoiselle de Beaujolais, the Duke of Orléans' daughter. Nevertheless, at the age of six, it was very unlikely the Infanta would be able to produce an heir in the short term. The Duke of Bourbon, prime minister, decided to send her back to Spain in February, for the sake of the dynasty. Subsequently, the enraged Spanish court[63] decided to bypass

---

conditions sont stipulées. Ce n'est point par des lettres que la foi des conventions peut être assurée, c'est par des Traités autentiques, surtout lorsque les conditions ne sont pas personnelles, ou qu'on traite avec un Prince dont l'Etat n'est pas purement monarchique" (Réal de Curban : La Science du Gouvernement – t. V, Ch. III, Sect. I, Art.VIII/V p. 562).

[60] Charles VI could engage in competition with Britain in two commercial arena's, by granting privileges to the Imperial Company at Ostend, which could replace the once flourishing port of Antwerp for the Atlantic, and at Trieste, in the Adriatic. Commerce was at the forefront of Imperial diplomacy and was only second to the recognition of the Pragmatic Sanction. At the Peace of Passarowitz with the Ottomans, Charles insisted on commercial advantages as well, which he effectively obtained (Treaty between Charles VI and Sultan Ahmed, 21 July 1718, Passarowitz, Du Mont, VIII/1, nr. CXIX, pp. 520-523; Commerce Treaty, 27 July 1718: 528-530). Already during the Congress of Cambrai, Charles insisted on the necessity of opening the Spanish colonies for his merchants, as a concession for the Italian investitures (N.A., SP, 78-174, f. 49r, 13°).

[61] Subsequently, when news of the Ripperda Treaty leaked, the Imperial Company's stock jumped by 18 pct (Pirenne, Henri: Histoire de Belgique. Des origines à nos jours. T.3: de la fin du régime espagnol à la Révolution belge. La renaissance du livre. Bruxelles, 1950 p. 110).

[62] The abdication episode is a symptom of Philip V's recurring mental disorder. The King vacillated between dark depression (during which he pretended to be dead, or to be a frog) and moments of frenetic hyperactivity (coinciding with periods of martial tension). See Kamen, Henry : Philip V of Spain, pp. 139-150.

[63] "La reine d'Espagne a pressé avec tant de soin ces epousailles dans l'esperance de lier

the Congress. Since both Britain[64] and France had proven to be unreliable when it came to direct Spanish interests, Elisabeth Farnese turned to the Emperor, her erstwhile direct opponent in Italy. At the Congress of Cambrai, "From apparent contempt and animosity, [the Imperial and Spanish ministers] were come at once to the greatest complaisance and intimate correspondence[65]".

The relations of the Viennese court intrigues have come to us by the relations of British ambassador St-Saphorin[66] and du Bourg[67], Louis XV's emissary. The mere fact that the two diplomats composed their insights together, points to the intimate relationship between both powers' targets and visions. Ripperda negotiated in secret with Prince Eugene of Savoy-Carignan[68] and Court Chancelor Ludwig Philip Graf Sinzendorf[69], but most of his transactions were leaked in court gossip[70].

---

tellement par là le Roy Trés Chrétien, que [...] le Mariage de l'Infante ne pût pas [...] être rompu." (Common relation of St-Saphorin and du Bourg to Charles Townshend, N.A., SP 80-55, Vienna, 11 May 1725, s.n.).

[64] Elisabeth Farnese offered the mediation to Britain alone after the sending back of the Infanta, but George I declined this offer (Coxe, William: Memoirs of Horatio, Lord Walpole: Selected from his Correspondence and Papers, and connected with the History of the Times, from 1678 to 1757. I: 1678-1740. Longman. London, 1820, p. 178).

[65] Marchmonth and Whitworth to the Duke of Newcastle, Cambrai, 31 January O.S./11 February N.S. 1725, N.A., SP 78-176, f. 17r.

[66] François Louis de Pesme, seigneur de St-Saphorin (1669-1737). Protestant Swiss diplomat (Geneva). In Austrian military service during the Turkish War (1683-1699), confident of Eugen of Savoy. Left Vienna, angry with the intolerant catholic policy of Bishop Friedrich Karl von Schönborn, Imperial Vice-Chancelor. Served from 1716 as a diplomat for George I of Great Britain-Hannover (see Thompson, A.C. : Pesme de Saint-Saphorin, François Louis de. In: Oxford Dictionary of National Biography. Oxford University Press, 2005; online edition, Jan 2008 [http://www.oxforddnb.com/view/article/73886, last accessed 13 March 2010].

[67] Jean Baptiste du Bourg (1690-1728), French ambassador in Vienna, 1717-1725. See Ulbert, Jörg: Frankreichs Deutschlandpolitik im zweiten und dritten Jahrzehnt des 18. Jahrhunderts. Duncker & Humblot. Berlin, 2004 p. 441.

[68] 1663-1736, Eugen of Savoy negotiated parts of the agreement at night in his Viennese Belvédère gardens. Braubach, Max : Prinz Eugen von Savoyen: eine Biographie. 4: der Staatsmann. Oldenbourg. München 1964 p. 227; Most recent biography: Paoletti, Ciro : Il Principe Eugenio di Savoia. Stato Maggiore dell'Esercito. Roma, 2001.

[69] 1671-1742. Since 1715, Sinzendorf supervised foreign relations and domestic legal affairs as *Hofkanzler*. See Linda and Marsha Frey: The Treaties of the War of the Spanish Succession p. 411.

[70] "Nous nous sommes prévalus de l'esprit singulier qui régne parmi les ministres italiens,

In his separate very private letter, relating amongst others a vivid discussion with the Viennese minister Count Palm, St-Saphorin stressed the importance of the union between the crowns of France and Britain for the safeguarding of the system. Doing otherwise, would give lead to Austro-Spanish hegemony, which would be detrimental to the general tranquillity and –of course – to Britain in particular.

These two letters explains us in particular why the balance did matter in the eighteenth century, contrary to what has been suggested in our introduction. The reference to the balance in art. III as "duraturum in Europa aequilibrium [...] ut pro regula statuatur, nè Regna Galliae & Hispaniae [...] unirique possent[71]", is not exactly one of observance of Utrecht's rules. Who could tell this better than Sinzendorf? When asked by Saint Saphorin whether his manoeuvre would not bring "de l'ombrage à l'Europe, the Court Chancellor replied "il seroit bon que nous fussions réunis avec l'Espagne; car par là les choses seroient remises dans l'ancien sistéme[72]". In other words, Sinzendorf was satisfied to have constructed an entangling alliance, possibly restored a dynastic encirclement of France[73]. "Ils veulent chercher à exciter de tous côtés

---

pour les mettre tous en mouvement ; ces messieurs, dont le principal but est de ramasser des nouvelles pour écrire à leurs cours, et parmi lesquels nous n'en connoissons aucun qui soit assés prudent pour distinguer ce qu'ils doivent taire d'avec ce qu'ils doivent dire…" (N.A., SP 80-55, Vienna, 11 May 1725, Common Relation, ibid.).

[71] Du Mont: Corps universel diplomatique, VIII/2, nr. XXXVI, p. 106. Philip V formally abandoned his rights of succession to the French throne by a unilateral declaration on 5 November 1712 (Du Mont, VIII/1, nr. CXXXVI, pp. 310-312). Throughout his reign, there was discussion about their validity, since it was publicly known the monarch eyed the French throne, occupied by a monarch without heir until 1729 and the birth of a Dauphin. During the 1719 invasion of Spain by a French army (as a collective reprisal for the invasion of Sicily the past year), Philip V inundated the French armies with leaflets asserting his rights to the French throne (Kamen, Henry: Philip V of Spain p. 126). Already during the negotiations ending the War of the Spanish Succession, Jean-Baptiste Colbert de Torcy (1665-1746), Louis XIV's Secretary for Foreign Affairs, held the declaration, drafted by jurists from the University of Oxford, to be contrary to the French *lois fondamentales* (see Baudrillart, Alfred : Examen des droits de Philippe V et de ses descendants au trône de France, en dehors des renonciations d'Utrecht. In : Revue d'histoire diplomatique III (1899), pp. 161-191, 354-384).

[72] N.A, SP 80-55, Common Relation, ibid.

[73] Confirmed by count Palm in his conversation with St Saphorin (N.A., SP 80-55, St Saphorin to Townshend, Vienna, 11 May 1725, private letter, s.n.): "[…] nous avons rétabli l'ancien sistéme, et nous avons séparé l'Espagne de la France, tellement que nous sommes en état de prendre a present avec Sa Majesté des mesures solides et efficaces contre cette derniere Puissance."

des differens, afin de tenir, comme le dit fort plaisamment le marquis de Breille[74], boutique ouverte de mediations."

However, the necessity of the balance metaphor underlines its cardinal place in the *Société des princes*[75] of the moment. Consisting the most recurrent pretext for going to war in the 17th Century, the diplomat who violated the principle, exposed himself to the wrath of all other European monarchies. St-Saphorin confirmed the centrality of the balance in his conversation with the Habsburg minister count Palm, explaining why a counterbalance of Austria an France made sense to him:

"J'avoüe que la France est une Puissance formidable, et qu'il n'y a aucune comparaison entre les forces de l'Empereur, et celles d'aucune autre Puissance de l'Europe, prises separement comparativement avec celles de cette Couronne mais les extrémités où Elle a été reduite pour avoir voulû donner sous le Regne de Louis XIV l'essort à son ambition, et ce qu'Elle en souffre encore à present, luy ont appris, et apprendront à tous ceux qui voudront s'ériger en Dictateurs de l'Europe, les perils auxquels une pareille entreprise expose. Et tandis que cette couronne suivra des maximes aussi modérées et aussi saines que celles qu'Elle a observées depuis la mort de Louis XIV, il est bon qu'Elle soit dans un degré de puissance capable de retenir tous ceux qui voudroient troubler la tranquilité publique.[76]"

By plotting with the Emperor and writing a universalist plan to dominate Europe, the Spanish diplomacy actively undermined the transactions at Cambrai[77]. The Congress, as the expression of balance

---

[74] Envoy of the duke of Savoy.

[75] Bély, Lucien: La société des Princes, p. 18.

[76] N.A., SP 80-55, St Saphorin to Townshend, Vienna, 11 May 1725, Private Letter, s.n., Ibid.

[77] Cf. letter from the Earl of Marchmont and baron Withworth, having sounded out Spanish Extraordinary Ambassador and Plenipotentiary Santistevan on his knowledge of Ripperda's entertakings *"nay he went so far as to suppose that the Queen of Spain herself was ignorant of it, but there are so many solid reasons to persuade us of the contrary, and these have been strengthened by so many circumstances which we have observed here, from the very beginning of this intrigue, that we cannot give any credit to what he has asserted"*, Cambrai, 16th May 1725 N.S., N.A., SP 78-176, f. 160v-161r. Cf. also Count Morville, French Secretary of State for Foreign Affairs on the Imperial diplomat Fonseca: *"pretty much out of countenance, when it was likewise observed to him, how little the dates agreed with the turn he endeavour'd to give this transaction in his harangues."* (Ibid., f. 164r)

diplomacy, counted representatives from the lesser Italian princes. Among those, count Maffei, representing the king of Sardinia, who had his territory invaded by Spain in July 1718. Quoting British representatives Marchmont and Withworth[78],

"[he] looks upon the Balance of Italy to be render'd very precarious by this new agreement, and the abandoning entirely the interests of all the lesser Princes there; and consequently his Master's security to be pretty much weaken'd by it [...] The mortification will scarce be personal.[79]"

When the Congress broke apart, the Spanish diplomats Santistevan[80] and Beretti Landi[81] did not invite the French representatives. Doing this, they prolonged the exclusion strategy, aiming at a division in the mediating couple. To no avail, since the British ambassadors extraordinary Marchmont and Withworth withheld their agreement[82].

And what better mark of the importance of representations and symbols to our Balance-phenomenon, than the downgrading of the festivities at the Imperial representative Penterridter's residence, to a

"handsome entertainment as usual, instead of a solemn feast [...], with their families in their plain liveries; no mask of distinction as to the occasion, not so much as a health drunk on the good conclusion of the treaty and not the least mention made of it in all their discourse[83]."

---

[78] Alexander Hume Campbell, 2nd earl of Marchmont (1675-1740) and Charles Baron Withworth (1675-1725) were both experienced diplomats, but not first rank.

[79] Ibid., ff. 163v.-164r.

[80] Manuel Domingo de Benavides y Aragón, count of Santisteban del Puerto (1682-1748) (Ozanam, Didier; Ozanam, Denise: *Les diplomates espagnols au XVIIIe siècle*. Casa de Velázquez – Maison des Pays Ibériques. Madrid – Bordeaux, 1998 p. 182).

[81] Lorenzo Verzuso, Marquis de Beretti Landi (1654-1725). In Philip V's service since 1702, retired to Brussels in March 1725 after the break-up of the Congress (Ozanam: Les diplomates espagnols. p. 465).

[82] "Great Britain and France continue firmly united for preserving the Peace of Europe" (Ibid., f. 168v) [...] it was to be feared the signing [...] of such a guaranty [...] would extremely lessen the Reputation of Great Britain & France in the eyes of the World, since they had appeared at the Congress at first in the quality of mediators; and were now only suffered to come in as accessories, a favour usually reserved for petty princes, or such at least as had no minister on the Place." (Ibid., ff. 168v-169r).

[83] Ibid., f. 162r.

The British representatives concluded their description of the final symposia at Cambrai by pointing to the necessity of informing the Duke of Newcastle of these *"Trifles"*. "Everything is material in such a crisis, when the eyes of the Publick are on each step[84]". Few days later, the Congress was no more[85]. Europe prepared itself for the building-up of two power blocks, threatening to set the continent ablaze from the Baltic to the Mediterranean[86].

3. Conclusion: the image of the balance in legal doctrine

The Balance of Power did matter to the community of contemporary diplomats. Citing the Ripperda Treaty as an example of its *discursive power*[87], is relevant. Not as regards its application, since the treaty without any doubt tried to undermine the European system, but with respect to the *opinion iuris* between the monarchs on its vigour.

Much more than the Peace Instruments of Westphalia, the Treaties of Utrecht can be considered to be the true *"naissance"* of this political concept, consequence of the legal liberty and equality of states[88]. If the

---

[84] Ibid, f. 162v.
[85] Polwarth (created Lord Marchmont in the meanwhile) and Withworth to the Duke of Newcastle, Secretary of State for the South, Cambrai, 23 May 1725, N.A., SP 78-176, s.n.
[86] Alliance between Louis XV, George I and Frederick William I of Prussia, Hannover, 3 September 1725 (later joined by Denmark, Sweden and the Dutch Republic). Charles VI and Philip V made an alliance with Czarina Catharina I and detached Frederick William from the former treaty in 1726. Since none of the promises made by Charles VI regarding don Carlos (installation of in Parma/Piacenza and Tuscany, marriage to the Archduchess Maria Theresia) were honored, Elisabeth Farnese deserted the Austrian alliance and made a separate Treaty with France and Britain (Treaty of Seville, 9 November 1729). A new congress was called together at the Preliminaries of Paris (31 May 1727), where Charles VI had to acquiesce to a seven year suspension of the Ostend Company's Imperial patent. See: Höfler, C. : Der Congress von Soissons. Nach den Instructionen des Kaiserlichen Cabinetes und den Berichten des Kaiserlichen Botschafters Stefan Grafen Kinsky. Kaiserlich-Königlicher Hof- und Staatsdruckerei. Wien, 1871-1876 (2 v.).
[87] An association supporting a possible application of Bourdieu's group analysis (cf. supra), also made by Rill, Bernd : Karl VI.: Habsburg als barocke Grossmacht. Verlag Styria. Graz, 1992 p. 138.
[88] Jouannet, Emmanuel : Emer de Vattel et l'émergence doctrinale du droit international classique. Pédone. Paris, 1998 pp. 238-248 ; Osiander, Andreas : The States System of Europe, 1640-1990 : Peacemaking and the Conditions of International Stability. Clarendon Press. Oxford, 1994 p. 133 ; Steiger, Heinhard : Rechtliche Strukturen p. 613.

mainstream 19th century doctrine is to be labelled "*Positivist*[89]", since it adhered to the balance as a way of coordinating formal legal state acts, it derived this framework from the predecessor's treatises in the 18th century[90].

Starting with Christian Wolff (1679-1750)[91], the balance came in the perimeter of legal doctrine. The Swiss scholar Emer de Vattel (1714-1767), considered the continent to be bound by the common rules of international society, although he was writing in the middle of the wars initiated by Frederick the Great of Prussia. The balance was classified in Book III, within the "*causes justes de la guerre*". One could thus see it as an argument easy to twist and turn one side or another. However, this rule should be interpreted in the light of the events that preceded Vattel's work.

"L'Europe fait un système politique, un Corps, où tout est lié par les relations & les divers intérêts des Nations, qui habitent cette partie du Monde. Ce n'est plus, comme autrefois, un amas confus de pièces isolées, dont chacune se croyait peu intéressée au sort des autres, et se mettait rarement en peine de ce qui ne la touchait pas immédiatement. L'attention continuelle des souverains à tout ce qui se passe, les ministres toujours résidents, les négociations perpétuelles, font de l'Europe moderne une espèce de république, dont les membres indépendants, mais liés par l'intérêt commun, se réunissent pour y maintenir l'ordre et la liberté [...] On entend par là une disposition des choses, au moyen de laquelle aucune puissance ne se trouve en état de prédominer absolument, et de faire la loi aux autres[92]. [...] Il est plus simple, aisé, et

---

[89] Koskenniemi, Martti : The Gentle Civilizer of Nations: the rise and the fall of international law, 1870-1960. Cambridge University Press. Cambridge, 2001 p. 17.

[90] Abbé de Burlé Réal de Curban: La science du gouvernement, t. 5: contenant le droit des gens. Les libraires associés. Paris, 1764; Moser, Johann Jakob: Grund-Sätze des jetzt-üblichen europäischen Völcker-Rechts in Fridens-Zeiten. Hanau, 1750.

[91] Wolff, Christian: Ius gentium methodo scientifica pertractatum. Clarendon Press. Oxford, 1934 [1764], IX, Ch. VIII, V, pp. 298-299.

[92] De Vattel, Emer : Le droit des gens. London, 1758, Livre III (de la Guerre) ch. III (Des justes causes de la guerre), § 47, edited in: The Classics of International Law. Carnegie Institute. Washington, 1916, v. 2. (cf. also Steiger, Heinhard. Ius bändigt Mars. Das klassische Völkerrecht und seine Wissenschaft als frühneuzeitliche Kulturerscheinung. Reprinted in: Steiger, Heinhard : Von der Staatengesellschaft zur Weltrepublik p. 127).

plus juste [...] de former des confédérations, pour faire tête au plus puissant et de l'empêcher de donner la loi."

Vattel saw the balance as an integrated, perpetually managed system of negotiation and amendment, just as the episode described above indicates. In order to obtain the realisation of their wishes, Europe's monarchs had to conform to common expectations and to a common discourse. These patterns resided in formal treaties (*pacta sunt servanda*[93]), but they were but one of the many instruments to express the *droit public de l'Europe*, which needed to influence behaviour outside of solemn, but incidental moments of reconciliation after a major crisis.

I would like to conclude on this third representation of the balance: first in diplomacy as a political-practical system, secondly in public opinion as a legitimate title, and finally in international doctrine as the framework of norm-creation. Far from being a "*chimère*", the Balance of Power was so strong a norm on the international stage, that even those who violate her, like the Spanish and Viennese courts, advocated her and needed to conform their ambitions to this commonly accepted discourse. In this sense, it was as normative as many concepts of contemporary international law[94].

---

[93] On the doctrinal "sacred" character of treaties and the seriousness of their perpetration, see Lesaffer, Randall: The Classical Law of Nations (1500-1800). In: Working Paper Series - SSRN http://ssrn.com/abstract=1594444, 22 April 2010, p. 14 [Last Accessed 30 April 2010].

[94] In response to Goldsmith and Posner's skeptical approach of international law's effectiveness, Howse and Teitel argue that such discursive convergences indicate the true scope of its normative force: "The language of [international] law communicates a level of "seriousness" to a commitment that may have consequences for how other actors respond in their own behavior and the reputational consequences of reneging these commitments. States tend to want to justify their actions in universalist terms, and the language of law is particularly amenable to it, given its formal character. States need to water down their rhetoric appeal to more and more audiences and "law" that does not have such a content tied to particular religious, moral or civilizational outlook serves well this purpose." Howse, Robert; Teitel, Ruti: Beyond Compliance: Rethinking Why International Law Matters. In: New York University School of Law Public Law & Legal Theory Research Paper Series. Working Papers X (Feb. 2010), p. 23.

Annex 1: Simplified Genealogy of the Farneses in the Duchy of Parma/Piacenza

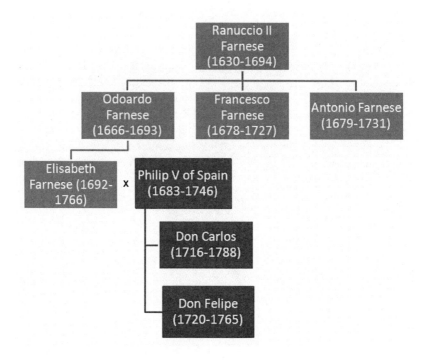

Annex 2: Simplified Genealogy of the de'Medici in the Grand Duchy of Tuscany

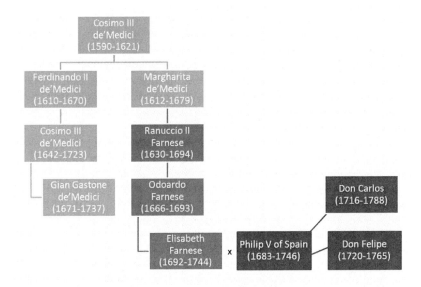

Autorenverzeichnis

Sarah Bachmann, Research Assistent at the University of Hamburg, Instute for German and Nordic Legal History. Currently writing on a doctoral thesis on the acceptability of notarial documentary evidence through the Hamburgian town council and the imperial chamber court.

Johanna Bergann, Dipl. Jur., M. A., research assistant at the faculty of media at the Bauhaus Universität Weimar, an assotiate member of the graduate research group „Medial Historiographies". Currently working on a doctoral thesis on arbitration and mediation in law and literature.

Ninfa Contigiani, Ph.D. in History of Law. She teaches history of social legislation for the faculties of jurisprudence at the University of Macerata. Currently working on the repression of blood crimes within families between the 19th and the 20th century.

Bart Coppein, postdoctoral researcher at Leuven University, Belgium. Current working on: "The Brussels' Bar. Two centuries of history (1811-2011)"

Wim Decock, Fellow of the Flemish Research Foundation (Aspirant FWO), K. U. Leuven, Research Unit of Roman Law and Legal History, Leuven.

Frederik Dhondt, Ph.D. Candidate at Ghent University, Belgium. Ph.D.-thesis: "Balance of Power and International Law. European Diplomacy and the Elaboration of International Order, 18th Century and post-1945", funded by a Ph.D. – Fellowship from the Research Foundation Flanders (FWO).

Sebastian Felz, research assistant at the Chair of Modern and Recent History II (Prof. Dr. Hans-Ulrich Thamer). Currenty working on a doctoral thesis „Law Faculty of the Westfälische Wilhelms-Universität 1925-1955".

Dóra Frey, LL. M (Universität Bukarest), Doktorandin an der Eötvös Loránt Universität (Prof. Dr. Barna Mezey), wissenschafliche Mitarbeiterin an der Andrássy Universität sowie wissenschaftliche

Assistentin bei der Rechtshistorischen Forschungsgruppe an der Akademie der Wissenschaften.

Lea Heimbeck, Ph.D. student at the Max Planck Institute for European Legal History, Frankfurt/ Main, Germany. Current work: "100 Years of State Bankruptcies. Debt Settlement through Public International Law, 1824-1924", funded by a grant from the Excellence Cluster "The formation of normative orders", Frankfurt University, Frankfurt/ Main, Germany.

Egbert Koops, postdoctoral researcher at Leiden University, The Netherlands. Currently working on: "Risk, finance and enterprise: the 'peculium' as an instrument for capital investment under the Roman Empire", funded by a grant from the Netherlands Organisation for Scientific Research (NWO).

Alexander Krey, research assistant at the Institute for Legal History at Goethe University in Frankfurt/Main. A Ph.D. thesis on the law, which is recognizable in the decisions of the jurymen.

Ivan Milotić, Ph.D. candidate, assistant at University of Zagreb Faculty of Law, Croatia. Currently working on a doctoral theis: Arbitration in Roman Law. Current work: "Types and Functions of Arbitration in Roman Law".

Adam Moniuszko, Dr. jur., a researcher (adiunkt) at the Faculty of Law and Administration of the University of Warsaw.

Birgit Näther, Doktorandin im DFG-Projekt "Herrschaftsvermittlung in der Frühen Neuzeit" (Universität Duisburg-Essen), Teilprojekt "Verwaltung und Herrschaft: Eine Studie zur landesherrlichen Visitation im vormodernen Bayern" (Arbeitstitel)

Tamás Nótári, Dr. iur. Dr. phil., Associate Professor at Károli Gáspár University Budapest (H-1042 Budapest, Viola u. 2-4.), Research Fellow at Institute for Legal Studies if the Hungarian Academy of Sciences (H-1014 Budapest, Országház u. 30.). Currently working on forensic strategies in Cicero's speeches of defence (Roman Law), law and society in Lex Baiuvariorum (medieval legal history).

Regina Schäfer, born 1967; Ph.D. 1997; research associate since 1998, Department of Medieval History and Comparative Regional Studies, Johannes Gutenberg Universität Mainz; Main research areas: nobility in the middle Rhine valley, town houses of the nobility, social mobility, castles in villages, rural jurisdiction in the late middle ages.

Jukka Siro, Assistant Judge in the Helsinki Appeal Court, Finland. He has written his doctoral dissertation about the revolutionary judiciary in the Finnish Civil War of 1918.

Die Herausgeber

Viktoria Draganova, Dipl.-Jur., from 2006 till 2009 Ph.D. student at the Max Planck Institute for European Legal History in Frankfurt/ Main. Currently working on a doctoral thesis on the formation of a legal system in Principality of Bulgaria (1878-1915).

Stefan Kroll, Dipl.-Sowi., from 2008 until 2011 Ph.D. student at the Max Planck Institute for European Legal History, Frankfurt/Main, Germany. His thesis was about "The Emergence of Norms through Reinterpretation: China and European International Law in the 19th and 20th Century", funded by a grant from the Excellence Cluster "The formation of normative orders", Frankfurt University, Frankfurt/Main, Germany.

Helmut Landerer M. A., Ph.D. student at the Max Planck Institute for European Legal History in Frankfurt/Main, Germany. Currently working on a doctoral thesis: "Living in the Automobile Society. Life Course, Age-specific Law and Road Traffic."

Ulrike Meyer, Dipl.-Pol., from 2008 till 2011 Ph.D. student at the Max Planck Institute for European Legal History, Frankfurt/Main, Germany. Her thesis is about "The normative Balance of the Rule of Law-Concept. Actuality of and Update on an Ideal of political Order", funded by a grant from the Excellence Cluster "The formation of normative orders", Frankfurt University, Frankfurt/Main, Germany.

Rechtstransfer in der Geschichte/Legal Transfer in History

(Jahrbuch junge Rechtsgeschichte/Yearbook of Young Legal History 1)
Hg. von Christina Börner et al.

2006, 542 Seiten, Paperback, Euro 29,90/CHF 51,00, ISBN 978-3-89975-046-1

Das Wort „Rechtstransfer", resp. „legal transfer" ist in aller Munde. Es spielt im internationalen Handels- und Wirtschaftsrecht und in der Rechtsvergleichung eine Rolle, tritt aber beispielsweise auch auf im Zusammenhang mit der EU-Osterweiterung und den sich dadurch stellenden Rechtsproblemen.

Dieser Band widmet sich dem Thema in seiner historischen Dimension. „Recht" kann dabei in Form von Gesetzen, Rechtskonstrukten, -theorien oder -ideen, aber auch von Rechtspraktiken Gegenstand der Betrachtung sein. Zur Frage seiner Übertragung von einem Ort an einen anderen als Gegenstand der Geschichte äußern sich in diesem Band 28 europäische Nachwuchswissenschaftlerinnen und -wissenschaftler. Rechtstransfer in der Geschichte bietet einen aktuellen Überblick über den Stand der rechtshistorischen Forschung auf diesem Gebiet.

Erinnern und Vergessen/Remembering and Forgetting

(Jahrbuch junge Rechtsgeschichte/Yearbook of Young Legal History 2)
Hg. von Oliver Brupbacher et al.

2007, 562 Seiten, Paperback, Euro 29,90/CHF 51,00, ISBN 978-3-89975-595-4

Während in der Geschichtswissenschaft schon seit Jahren über Aspekte des sozialen, kulturellen oder kollektiven Gedächtnisses diskutiert wird, haben diese Konzepte in der Rechtsgeschichte bisher nicht die gleiche Aufmerksamkeit gefunden.

28 junge Rechtshistorikerinnen und Rechtshistoriker, Philologen, Politologen und allgemeine Historiker unternehmen daher in diesem Band den Versuch, über die Facetten des Erinnerns und Vergessens im Recht nachzudenken. Dabei zeigt sich, wie zeitlich und kulturell differenziert die Lösungen sind, die das Recht hinsichtlich seiner Funktion der Stabilisierung von Verhaltenserwartungen und der Lösung von Konflikten im Umgang mit der beschränkten menschlichen Gedächtnisleistung gefunden hat.

Ihr Wissenschaftsverlag. Kompetent und unabhängig.

Martin Meidenbauer »

Verlagsbuchhandlung GmbH & Co. KG
Schwanthalerstr. 81 • 80336 München
Tel. (089) 20 23 86 -03 • Fax -04
info@m-verlag.net • www.m-verlag.net

Crossing Legal Cultures
(Jahrbuch junge Rechtsgeschichte/Yearbook of Young Legal History 3)
Hg. von Laura Beck Valera et al.

2009, 552 Seiten, Paperback, Euro 29,90/CHF 53,50, ISBN 978-3-89975-154-3

Mit ihren 34 gesammelten Beiträgen zielt diese Publikation darauf ab, die Reihe *European Yearbook of Young Legal History* mit einem anspruchsvollen wissenschaftlichen Grenzbereich zusammenzuführen. Sie nähert sich der Disziplin der Rechtsgeschichte in einem komplexen Ansatz, indem sie sich ganz bewusst über die ungeschriebenen roten Grenzlinien allgemein anerkannter Rechtsgeschichte hinaus begibt, welche bisher von der vorherrschenden Geschichtsschreibung geprägt ist. Dabei gelingt es dem Band, Disziplinen benachbarter sozialwissenschaftlicher Richtungen, wie beispielsweise die der Linguistik, der Theorie Internationaler Beziehungen, der Geschichte des Altertums und sogar der Römischen Gesetzgebung aufzugreifen und einzubeziehen.

Insofern strebt dieses Projekt danach, zu einem besseren, nicht notgedrungen konfliktgeladenen Verständnis der interkulturellen Erzeugung gesetzlicher Praktiken, Mechanismen und Normen in Europa beizutragen.

Turning Points and Breaklines
(Jahrbuch junge Rechtsgeschichte/Yearbook of Young Legal History 4)
Hg. von Szabolcs Hornyák et al.

2009, 504 Seiten, Paperback, Euro 29,90/CHF 53,50, ISBN 978-3-89975-159-8

Dieser vierte Band in der Reihe „Yearbook of Young Legal History" enthält Texte der Präsentationen, die beim 14. jährlichen „Forum of Young Legal Historians" im Jahr 2008 in Pécs vorgetragen wurden. Die Konferenz konzentrierte sich auf die wichtigen Wendepunkte, die im letzten Jahrhundert in der Geschichte beinahe aller europäischen Länder beobachtet und als mögliche Auslöser immenser und radikaler politischer, rechtlicher, kultureller und wirtschaftlicher Veränderungen betrachtet werden konnten.

Die Teilnehmer der Konferenz stimmten überein, dass die wichtigsten Faktoren, welche die Regeln menschlicher Koexistenz bestimmen, Recht, Kultur, gesellschaftliche Traditionen und Religion sind.

Ihr Wissenschaftsverlag. Kompetent und unabhängig.

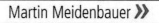

Martin Meidenbauer »

Verlagsbuchhandlung GmbH & Co. KG
Schwanthalerstr. 81 • 80336 München
Tel. (089) 20 23 86 -03 • Fax -04
info@m-verlag.net • www.m-verlag.net